THE CONFUCIUS CHRONICLES

The Confucius Chronicles

TRANSLATED AND EDITED BY

Wai-yee Li

Columbia University Press

New York

Columbia University Press wishes to express its appreciation for assistance given by the Wm.
Theodore de Bary Fund in the publication of this book.

Columbia University Press
Publishers Since 1893
New York   Chichester, West Sussex
cup.columbia.edu
Copyright © 2026 Columbia University Press
All rights reserved

Library of Congress Cataloging-in-Publication Data

Names: Li, Wai-yee translator editor
Title: The Confucius chronicles / translated and edited by Wai-yee Li.
Description: New York : Columbia University Press, [2026] |
Includes bibliographical references and index.
Identifiers: LCCN 2025028678 (print) | LCCN 2025028679 (ebook) |
ISBN 9780231214827 hardback | ISBN 9780231214834 trade paperback |
ISBN 9780231560481 epub | ISBN 9780231560481 pdf
Subjects: LCSH: Confucius
Classification: LCC B128.C8 C585 2026 (print) | LCC B128.C8 (ebook)
LC record available at https://lccn.loc.gov/2025028678
LC ebook record available at https://lccn.loc.gov/2025028679

Cover design: Milenda Nan Ok Lee

Cover image: Rank Badge with Qilin, 1662-1722, artist/maker unknown.
Silk plain weave with silk and gilt thread embroidery in couching, satin, outline,
and padded satin stitches. Philadelphia Museum of Art. Purchased with the
John T. Morris Fund from the Carl Schuster Collection, 1940-4-731.

GPSR Authorized Representative: Easy Access System Europe, Mustamäe tee 50,
10621 Tallinn, Estonia, gpsr.requests@easproject.com

Contents

Acknowledgments

Most of the research, writing, and translations for this book were done during a year of sabbatical leave supported by the National Endowment for the Humanities and Harvard University. I gratefully acknowledge their generous support. I thank Zhou Yiqun, Emily Sun, Antje Richter, and Matthias Richter, who read earlier drafts, for their comments and encouragement. The book benefitted greatly from the insights of Michael Nylan, who offered excellent suggestions. I am grateful to the readers of the book proposal and the manuscript for their helpful comments and advice. I gave talks based on the first chapter of this book at Harvard University, the University of Colorado, and the University of Science and Technology in Hong Kong, and students and colleagues provided forums for stimulating intellectual exchange on those occasions. The cover image shows a rank badge with a qilin from the Kangxi reign. (On the connection between Confucius and this mythical animal, see chapter 1, 1.64.) I thank the Philadephia Museum of Art for permitting its use. The editors and the staff at Columbia University Press were helpful and dedicated as they saw this book through production. Eileen Chow and Christine Dunbar helped me come up with the title. My family remains the pillar of support that makes all my endeavors possible.

Abbreviations and Brief Explanations
of Frequently Mentioned Texts

Analects   *Lunyu* 論語. Sayings attributed to Confucius and his followers (ca. fifth–second century BCE). Cited by chapter and entry number. For commentaries on the *Analects*, see *LY*.

Annals   *Spring and Autumn Annals* (*Chunqiu* 春秋). A year-by-year chronicle from the state of Lu spanning 242 (722–481 BCE) or 244 (722–479 BCE) years, depending on the exegetical tradition to which it is attached. Its concise entries were probably compiled when the events took place or shortly thereafter.

CDB   Cui Shu 崔述 (1740–1816). *Cui Dongbi yishu* 崔東壁遺書 (*Writings of Cui Shu*). Ed. Gu Jiegang 顧頡剛 (1893–1980). 2 vols. Shanghai guji chubanshe, 2013.

DDLJ   *Da Dai Liji huijiao jizhu* 大戴禮記彙校集注 (*The Elder Dai's Record of Rituals: With Annotations and Commentaries*). Ann. and comm. Huang Huaixin 黃懷信. 2 vols. San Qin chubanshe, 2005. A collection of anecdotes, prescriptions, and arguments about rituals (comp. ca. second–first century BCE, earlier layers dated to ca. fourth–third century BCE).

Documents *Shu* 書. A compilation of pronouncements on governance attributed to rulers and ministers of antiquity (dated to ca. eleventh–third century BCE). One of the Five Classics.

Gongyang   *Gongyang zhuan* 公羊傳 (*Gongyang Tradition*). *Chunqiu Gong-yang zhuan zhushu* 春秋公羊傳注疏 (*The Gongyang Commentary on the Spring and Autumn Annals*). Comm. He Xiu 何休 (129–182) and Xu Yan 徐彥 (late eighth–early ninth century). Ed. Diao Xiaolong 刁小龍. Shanghai guji chubanshe, 2014. An exegetical tradition of the *Annals* (comp. ca. third–second century BCE).

Guliang   *Guliang zhuan* 穀梁傳 (*Guliang Tradition*). Comm. Fan Ning 范甯 (fourth century) and Yang Shixun 楊士勛 (seventh century). In *Chongkan Songben Shisan jing zhushu fu jiaokan ji* 重刊宋本十三經注疏附校勘記 (*Reprint of the Song Edition of the Thirteen Classics, With Commentaries and Collation*), ed. Ruan Yuan 阮元 et al. Yiwen yinshuguan, 1993. An exegetical tradition of the *Annals* (comp. ca. third–second century BCE).

GY   *Guoyu* 國語 (*Discourses of the States*). Ed. Shanghai shifan daxue guji zhengli yanjiusuo 上海師範大學古籍整理研究所. 2 vols. Shanghai guji chubanshe, 1995. Anecdotes and arguments organized by states (comp. ca. fourth century BCE).

HFZ   *Han Feizi xin jiaozhu* 韓非子新校注 (*Master Han Fei: Edition with Revised Annotations and Commentary*). Ann. and comm. Chen Qiyou 陳奇猷. Shanghai guji chubanshe, 2000. Writings linked to Han Fei 韓非 (ca. 280–233 BCE) and concerned with expanding state power based on enforcement of laws and judgment of expediency.

HHS   *Hou Hanshu* 後漢書 (*History of the Later Han*). Fan Ye 范曄 (398–446). Zhonghua shuju, 1973.

HNZ   *Huainanzi* 淮南子 (*Master of Huainan*). Ann. Liu Wendian 劉文典 (1889–1958). Zhonghua shuju, 1989. A collection of essays drawing from divergent intellectual trends and compiled by scholars at the Huainan court, submitted by Liu An 劉安 (d. 122 BCE), King of Huainan, to Emperor Wu of Han in 139 BCE.

HS   *Hanshu* 漢書 (*History of the Han*). Ban Ku 班固 (32–92). Ann. Yan Shigu 顏師古 (581–645). Zhonghua shuju, 1980.

HSWZ   *Han shi waizhuan jianshu* 韓詩外傳箋疏 (*Han's Exegesis: With Annotations and Commentaries*, abbr. *Han's Exegesis*). Comp.

Han Ying 韓嬰 (second century BCE). Ann. Qu Shouyuan 屈守元. Ba Shu shushe, 2011. A collection of anecdotes and arguments that use lines from the *Odes* as illustrative quotations.

KCZ   *Kongcong zi jiaoshi* 孔叢子校釋 (*The Kong Family Masters' Anthology: With Annotations and Commentaries*, abbr. as *Kong Anthology*). Ann. Fu Yashu 傅亞庶. Zhonghua shuju, 2011. Sayings of and anecdotes about Confucius and his descendants (comp. ca. third–fourth century, with materials dated to earlier periods).

KJY   *Kongzi jiyu jiaozhu* 孔子集語校注 (*Sayings of Confucius: With Annotations and Commentaries*). 3 vols. Ann. Sun Xingyan 孫星衍. Ed. Guo Yi 郭沂. Zhonghua shuju, 2018. Sayings attributed to Confucius (in texts other than those familiar to traditional scholars) compiled by Sun Xingyan (1753–1818). The modern edition edited by Guo Yi includes the sayings of Confucius in the canonical classics as well as excavated texts.

KZJY   *Kongzi jiayu jiaozhu* 孔子家語校注 (*Sayings from the House of Confucius: With Annotations and Commentaries*; abbr. as *Sayings*). Ann. Gao Shangju 張尚舉, Zhang Binzheng 張濱鄭, and Zhang Yan 張燕. Zhonghua shuju, 2021. A collection of lore about Confucius and his disciples, overlapping significantly with pre-Han and Han sources, possibly compiled or edited by Wang Su 王肅 (195–256).

LH   *Lunheng jiaoshi* 論衡校釋 (*Balanced Discourses: With Annotations*). Wang Chong 王充 (27–100). Ann. Huang Hui 黃暉. Zhonghua shuju, 1990.

LJ   *Liji jijie* 禮記集解 (*Record of Rituals: With Collated Commentaries*). Ann. and comm. Sun Xidan 孫希旦 (1736–1784). Ed. Shen Xiaohuan 沈嘯寰 and Wang Xingxian 王星賢. 3 vols. Zhonghua shuju, 1998. A collection of anecdotes, prescriptions, and arguments about rituals (comp. ca. second–first century BCE; earlier layers dated to ca. fourth–third century BCE).

LSCQ   *Lüshi chunqiu jiaoshi* 呂氏春秋校釋 (*Mr. Lü's Annals: With Annotations and Commentaries*, abbr. *Mr. Lü's Annals*). Ann. Chen Qiyou 陳奇猷. Shanghai guji chubanshe, 2002. An eclectic and comprehensive text compiled by scholars patronized by Lü Buwei 呂不韋 (d. 235 BCE), a powerful minister in Qin, ca. 239 BCE.

LY   *Lunyu jishi* 論語集釋 (*Analects: with Collated Commentaries*). Comp. Cheng Shude 程樹德 (1877–1944). Ed. Cheng Junying 程俊英 and Jiang Jianyuan 蔣見元. 4 vols. Zhonghua shuju, 2014.

LZ   *Liezi jishi* 列子集釋 (*Master Lie: With Collated Commentaries*). Ann. Yang Bojun 楊伯峻. Zhonghua shuju, 1979. Writings attributed to a figure mentioned in Warring States texts (comp. ca. third century).

Mencius   Writings associated with Mengzi 孟子 or Master Meng (ca. fourth century BCE), who developed the legacy of Confucius. Cited by chapter and entry number.

MZ   *Mozi jiangu* 墨子閒詁 (*Master Mo: With Collated Commentaries*). Ann. and comm. Sun Yirang 孫詒讓 (1848–1908). Ed. Sun Yikai 孫以楷. Huazheng shuju, 1987. Comp. ca. fifth–third century BCE by the followers of Mo Di, ca. fifth century BCE.

Odes   *Shi* 詩. A collection of 305 odes, hymns, and songs (dated to ca. 11th–5th century BCE).

SJ   *Shiji huizhu kaozheng* (*Shiki kaichū kōshō*) 史記會注考證 (*Historical Records: With Annotations and Commentaries*). Sima Qian 司馬遷 (145–ca. 86 BCE). Comp. Takigawa Kametarō 瀧川資言 (1865–1946). Wenxue guji kanxing she, 1955.

SY   *Shuoyuan shuzheng* 說苑疏證 (*The Garden of Eloquence: With Annotations and Parallel Accounts*). Comp. Zhao Shanyi 趙善詒. Huadong shifan daxue chubanshe, 1985. A collection of anecdotes and disquisitions compiled by Liu Xiang 劉向 (79–8 BCE). Cited by chapter and entry number.

XZ   *Xunzi jianshi* 荀子柬釋 (*Master Xun: with Commentaries*). Comp. Liang Qixiong 梁啟雄 (1900–1965). Shangwu yinshuguan, 1993. Writings associated with Xunzi 荀子 or Master Xun (ca. fourth–third century BCE), who developed the legacy of Confucius.

YM   Yuan Mei 袁枚 (1716–1797). *Yuan Mei quanji xinbian* 袁枚全集新編 (*Collected Works of Yuan Mei: New Edition*). Ed. Wang Yingzhi 王英志. 20 vols. Zhejiang guji chubanshe, 2015.

YZCQ   *Yanzi chunqiu jishi* 晏子春秋集釋 (*Mr. Yan's Annals: With Commentaries*). Ann. Wu Zeyu 吳則虞. Zhonghua shuju, 1962. Lore and arguments associated with the Qi minister Yan Ying 晏嬰 (ca. sixth–fifth century BCE), collated by Liu Xiang based on materials in circulation in earlier centuries.

Zuo   *Zuo Tradition / Zuozhuan: Commentary on the "Spring and Autumn Annals."* Trans. with intro. by Stephen Durrant, Wai-yee Li, and David Schaberg. University of Washington Press, 2016. Historical narratives and arguments dated to the period spanning 722–468 BCE (comp. ca. fourth century BCE), traditionally understood as a commentary on the *Annals*.

ZY   *Ziyue quanji* 子曰全集 (*Comprehensive Compendium of the Master's Sayings*). Comm. Guo Yi 郭沂. Zhonghua shuju, 2018.

ZZ   *Zhuangzi jishi* 莊子集釋 (*Master Zhuang: With Collated Commentaries*). Ann. Guo Qingfan 郭慶藩. Ed. Wang Xiaoyu 王孝魚. 4 vols. Zhonghua shuju, 1995. Writings associated with Zhuangzi 莊子 or Master Zhuang (ca. fourth century BCE). Comp. ca. fourth–third century BCE.

THE CONFUCIUS CHRONICLES

Introduction

This is a book of stories about Confucius, the Latinized name of Kong fuzi or Kongzi (Master Kong, ca. 551–479 BCE). The word "chronicles," derived from the Greek word for time (*khronos*), encompasses both history and fiction. It implies unembellished information about the past, since the chronicler is supposedly less prone to offer analytic or interpretive interventions, although it is not hard to divine the chronicler's design and agenda in famous examples such as *Froissart's Chronicles* (fourteenth century) or *Holinshed's Chronicles of England, Scotland, and Ireland* (1577). Yet the word has the Proteus-like quality of also evoking fictional or even fantastic elaborations, given that fiction spanning the spectrum from the realistic to the fantastic has used chronological order as the bedrock of world-making: think of works such as the *Barchester Chronicles* by Anthony Trollope (1815–1882) and *The Narnia Chronicles* by C. S. Lewis (1898–1963). For my purpose, its range of associations mean reprieve from the quest to recover "the authentic Confucius," the stated or implicit mission of numerous studies.[1] While I still weigh in on questions of veracity to the extent permitted by evidence, my primary focus is on the power of storytelling in turning Confucius into the symbol of cultural ideals and the engine of intellectual arguments and ideological debates. Confucius has become many different things to different people over the last twenty-five centuries. To focus on how his stories are told is to understand the history of ideas and sociocultural history through his transformations.[2]

[1]

How do we get our ideas about Confucius? The answer obviously hinges on time, place, and historical context. If memory serves, my first-grade calligraphy classes in Hong Kong began with copybooks featuring Chinese characters printed in red that we traced with brush and ink. The main challenge was how to avoid making a mess when fiddling with the ink-soaked cotton pads in little containers, but the first graphs had very few strokes and were easy enough: 上大人，孔乙己。化三千，七十士 "The supremely great man, Kong the second son (*yi*), transformed seventy among three thousand men into worthy scholars."[3] We may say that these simple lines already encapsulate the kernel of a story to be impressed upon the mind of a seven-year-old: Confucius was a great sage with numerous followers, among whom seventy—those who love learning and apply themselves—became distinguished. Did it also convey to our juvenile minds a hint of the daunting success rate with the unforgiving pyramidal examination system in that era? (A snapshot: 100,000 students took the secondary school entrance examination in 1972, of whom 10,000 metriculated in the advanced level examination in 1979 to compete for 1,000 slots in the University of Hong Kong.) That the Confucian copybook was in use at all testified to the Hong Kong / China divide at that time. It was 1967, the year of violent antigovernment and pro-Communist riots in Hong Kong. At that point, China was in the throes of the Cultural Revolution; its "Smashing the Four Olds Campaign" (geared to attacking old modes of thinking, old culture, old customs, old habits) targeted among other things the reviled figure of Confucius.

The elementary school curriculum at the time no longer included traditional primers such as *Three-Character Classic* (*Sanzi jing* 三字經) or *Rules for Students* (*Dizi gui* 弟子規), which were then still in use in Taiwan. The only Confucius temple in Hong Kong is tucked inside Wong Tai Sin Temple, a Daoist temple that honors all three teachings (Confucianism, Daoism, and Buddhism). Many of the better schools were (and still are) linked to various Christian denominations. All the same, our textbooks duly rehearsed the rudiments of the life and teachings of Confucius for our edification: his humble beginnings; his interest in ritual, history, and textual traditions; his emergence as a teacher of ethical principles and classical learning; his peregrinations during a failed quest to seek recognition from rulers who could implement his ideals; his stint as an official in his natal state, Lu (in present-day Shandong); and his final years as a teacher and transmitter of canonical texts. The emphasis was on Confucius as "the exemplary teacher for all ages" (*wanshi shibiao* 萬世師表) who "made no categorical distinctions" in his pedagogical fervor (*Analects* 15.39), transmitted knowledge of textual traditions, and laid down moral precepts for his disciples and posterity. The fact that classical virtue words—such as benevolence or humaneness (*ren* 仁, also translated in this book as "the highest good"), proper duty (*yi* 義, also translated as "righteousness"), ritual propriety (*li* 禮), wisdom (*zhi* 智), reverence (*jing* 敬), filial piety (*xiao* 孝), or good faith (*xin* 信)—continue to be used in modern Chinese fosters a sense of their perennial applicability and translatability to modern contexts. What better way to impose discipline in the classroom, for example, than by harping on the themes of reverence and ritual propriety?

The primacy of Confucius as the model teacher setting forth moral precepts may explain the choice of *Analects* 4 and *Analects* 11 for our secondary school curriculum: the former gives various definitions of key virtue words that can be conveniently linked to important passages in other chapters, and the latter showcases his judgment of and interactions with his students. The *Analects* purports to be a record of the sayings and teachings of Confucius transmitted by his disciples and their followers. Although the received text might have taken shape only about a century to four centuries after the death of Confucius, its format of the Master's utterance or exchange between the Master and his interlocutors (either his disciples or men seeking his advice or commenting on his choices) can hint at complex interactions and generate a sense of immediacy.[4] Some of the sayings in the *Analects* seem to be nuggets of insights or information crying out for contexts; other passages contain kernels of stories that become more fully fledged in other texts. But it was taught as a wisdom text, and not much attention was paid to its possible contexts or the stories that could have given rise to, or could have been elaborated from, its entries.

We studied Chinese history from the Paleolithic "Peking Man" to "Chinese victory in the War of Resistance against Japan" in 1945 in the first three years of secondary school (the equivalent of seventh to ninth grade), but Confucius the Sage seemed to hover above history despite the temporal anchoring points from those history lessons. There were lessons about the foundational order of the Zhou dynasty (ca. 1046–256 BCE) which preceded Confucius by five centuries and to which he harked back as ideal. The declining Zhou became an evolving multistate system (ca. eighth century–221 BCE). The latter part of that period of division, from about fifth century to third century BCE, saw the flowering of different ideas about sociopolitical order and personal well-being, starting with those of Confucius. We were taught that rulers of the Han dynasty elevated Confucius about three and a half centuries after his death.[5] Confucianism, along with its history and reinterpretation, received much greater emphasis than Daoism and Buddhism. At the same time, sagehood is absolute, and Confucius was sometimes associated with lofty political ideals that seemed to lie beyond history. To focus on narratives is one way to return Confucius to history—not in the sense of authenticating details of his life but by way of showing how stories of Confucius, be they sacralizing, polemical, irreverent, or adversarial, mark how and why he matters in Chinese history.

What Counts as a Story and How to Read It

The sage as "exemplary teacher for all ages" is a more complex proposition than it appears. For one thing, the epithet itself was made ubiquitous because the Kangxi emperor (r. 1661–1722) wrote it in his calligraphy and had it carved on stone, and rubbings of it were distributed to temples of government schools all over the empire.[6] Is Confucius totally identified with or coopted by the functioning or justification of imperial rule? How are his ideas related to state power? Being an "exemplary teacher" also means complex interactions with students that take us to the motives, circumstances, and processes of mutual appraisal—in other words, the stuff of storytelling. *Analects* 11.26, the longest entry in the text, is one such example of psychological drama.

> Zilu, Zeng Dian, Ran Qiu, and Gongxi Chi were seated in attendance upon the Master.[7] The Master said, "Just because I am somewhat older than you, do not let that deter you. Staying in your place from one day to the next, you say, 'I'm not recognized.' Suppose you're recognized—how would you use your talents then?"
> Zilu responded right away, without the least hesitation: "For a state commanding a thousand chariots, pincered between powerful states, facing troops bearing on it, and then being afflicted by famines—if I were to govern it, I could, in three years, instill valor in its people and they would, what's more, know what's right." The Master smiled at him quizzically.

"Qiu! What about you?" Ran Qiu responded: "A state of sixty or seventy square *li*, or perhaps fifty or sixty—if I were to govern it, I could, in three years, satisfy the people's needs. As for ritual and music, we would have to wait for the noble man."

"Chi! What about you?" Gongxi Chi responded: "It's not that I could do it, but I would be willing to learn. When it comes to sacrifices at the ancestral temple or diplomatic meetings, I would don ritual cap and gown and wish to serve as a minor officiant."

"Dian! What about you?" Zeng Dian was strumming fading strains on his zither. With a final twang he pushed it aside, stood up, and responded: "My idea is different from what the three of them have come up with."

The Master said, "What harm is there in that? You are just each articulating your ambition." Zeng Dian said, "Let's say it's the end of spring, when spring garments have been made. I should like, with five or six grown men, and six or seven boys, to bathe at River Yi, enjoy the breeze at the Altar of Rain Dance, and chant odes as we return." Heaving a sigh, the Master said, "I am with Dian!"

Three of the disciples left, and Zeng Dian stayed behind. He said, "What are we to make of what the three of them said?"

The Master said, "Each was just articulating his ambition, and that was all."

"Why did you, Master, smile quizzically at Yóu [Zilu]?"

"A state should be governed through ritual propriety. His words showed he would not yield to others. That was why I smiled quizzically at him."

"But wasn't Qiu talking about the polity?"

"How can we say that a state of sixty or seventy *li* square, or indeed fifty or sixty, would not count as a polity?"

"But wasn't Chi talking about the polity?"

"Sacrifices at ancestral temples or diplomatic meetings—what are these if not affairs of the lords? If even Chi could only perform such a minor task, who would be capable of the great ones?" (*Analects* 11.26)

Zilu, nine years younger than Confucius, is depicted as fearless, decisive, forthright, and somewhat rash or uncouth in various early sources. In the

Analects, he appears as the interlocutor who sometimes challenges the Master and is by turns praised and criticized by the latter. He served in government in the states of Lu and Wei. Ran Qiu, twenty-nine years younger than Confucius, is praised for his administrative prowess but also rebuked for his political compromises and missteps in the *Analects*. Gongxi Chi, forty-two years younger than Confucius, is commended for his mastery of court and diplomatic rituals. Zeng Dian is not mentioned elsewhere in the *Analects* and there is no reference to his age in other early texts. He was the father of Zeng Shen, also a disciple of Confucius and forty-six years his junior. According to Mencius (fourth–third century BCE)—the Latinized version of Mengzi or Master Meng, and traditionally honored as the "Second Sage" who developed the legacy of Confucius—Confucius considers Zeng Dian "untamed and overreaching" (*kuang* 狂) (*Mencius* 7B.36).[8]

The first three speakers follow the sequence of seniority. As the oldest among the four disciples, it is fitting that Zilu should speak first. But Zilu's manner is too eager and over-confident, and his ambitious vision of social and moral transformation of a state facing multiple crises earns a quizzical smile from Confucius. The others, sensing Confucius's criticism, scale back their aspirations accordingly and sound more and more humble. Zeng Dian is strumming the lute softly while this exchange is going on but stops and rises to his feet when Confucius poses the question to him. He announces his difference and proceeds to articulate a vision of a convivial late spring excursion that involves bathing in the river and chanting odes on the way home. Confucius expresses his approval despite his consistent concern with political engagement elsewhere in the *Analects* and in other early sources. The subsequent exchange between Confucius and Zeng Dian on the evaluation of the other three disciples seems to confirm their affinities.

What do we make of the four disciples' aspirations and Confucius's attitudes? How should we parse and contextualize the above story? We may begin with horizontal associations by recalling related and analogous passages in early Chinese texts. In one passage, a Lu minister asks Confucius whether Zilu, Ran Qiu, and Gongxi Chi have attained the highest good (*ren*). Echoing the passage cited above, Confucius credits them with, respectively, competent levying of military taxes in a great state, administrative expertise in a smaller polity, and mastery of court rituals, but demurs on the question of "the highest good" (*Analects* 5.8). In another entry in the *Analects*, Confucius asks Zilu and his favorite disciple, the virtuous Yan Hui, about their aspirations. Zilu speaks of his desire to generously share his possessions, and Yan Hui wants to avoid the pitfalls of boastfulness and self-aggrandizement. Zilu poses the same question to Confucius, who replies: "Care for the aged, earn the trust of friends, and cherish the young" (*Analects* 5.26). In other iterations of the theme of "articulating intent" found in various early texts, Confucius asks Zilu, Zigong (a disciple famous for his rhetorical prowess), and Yan Hui about their ambitions. Zilu articulates the martial ambition of a valiant man; Zigong, the diplomatic ambition of a rhetorician; Yan Hui, the moral ambition of a virtuous man, and Confucius appraises them accordingly.[9] The lines about Zeng Dian's aspiration and Confucius's endorsement of it appear as an isolated exchange in the chapter on Confucius's disciples in the Han historian Sima Qian's (145–ca. 85 BCE) *Historical Records*. In these instances, Confucius's judgment is declarative and authoritative. Articulating intent, ambition or aspiration (*yanzhi* 言志) defines the speakers and facilitates their appraisal. If *Analects* 11.26 seems less straightforward and "more of a story" than the above examples, it may be because articulation is embedded in intriguing psychological contexts and judgment emerges as mutual and interactive. Both trajectories introduce potential polyvalence.

Suspense and uncertainty over intention, expression, and communication drive narrative momentum and open up the space for interpretation. In that sense, story interest—the question of how and why a story unfolds—takes us to its "vertical associations," the history of its interpretation. In the case of *Analects* 11.26, its divergent readings through the ages constitute a veritable mini history of Confucianism, especially how it responds to the promise of transcendence in Daoism and Buddhism.[10] This passage with 315 characters has generated twenty-four pages of commentary in the standard modern edition of the *Analects* (*LY* 3: 1029–53), a mere sampling of what is available. What does Dian's vision mean? Why does Confucius approve of it? To the modern reader this looks like a vision of personal happiness and contentment, a simple celebration of the beauty of nature and the pleasure of a spring outing. Over the centuries, however, commentators try to explain this pleasure and ground it in worldviews.

The Han scholar Bao Xian (6 BCE–65 CE) describes Dian's wish to "sing and chant about the Way of the early sage kings as he returns to the gates of the Master" (*LY* 3: 1042). Dian's pleasure then is specifically joy in affirming an ideal political order or "joy in the Way" (*le Dao* 樂道). Another Han scholar, Wang Chong (27–97), ties the excursion to the rain sacrifice, ignoring pleasure altogether or implying that it lies in the correct practice of ritual: "The grown men and the boys are musicians of the rain sacrifice. 'To bathe at River Yi' is to wade into River Yi: this is to mimic how a dragon comes out of the water. . . . Confucius approves of Dian's words because he wants to use the rain sacrifice to harmonize yin and yang" (*LY* 3: 1043). Wang Chong raises a concrete objection to the idea of bathing in River Yi: the water is simply too cold in late spring in North China.[11] In a collection of sayings attributed to Confucius and his disciples (ca. third century), Dian becomes the ritualist correcting contemporary lapses; that is why Confucius approves of him (*KZJY* 38.505).

"The joy of the Way" and the rain sacrifice (or, in some other commentaries, purification rites) keep Dian within ritual and political boundaries, but there is something vaguely Daoist in his speech that implies rejection of such boundaries. The Qing scholar Cui Shu (1740–1816) suspects that this passage expresses Daoist views and belongs to a later stratum in the *Analects*, which he views as an amalgam of different sources and viewpoints.[12] Perhaps an implicit dialogue with Daoist perspectives is endemic to the formation of the *Analects*. The scholar and poet Zhongchang Tong (180– 220) uses this passage to affirm a Daoist vision: "Sing beneath the Rain Altar, and chant odes on the way back to the grand hall. Calm my spirit in the inner chamber, and think of the dark mysteries in *Laozi*. Breathe the essence of harmony, and seek the evanescence of the supreme being. . . . In this way, I can scale the high heavens and come out of the universe. Why would I be envious of those who enter the gates of emperors!"[13] If Dian proposes an alternative to the political realm, it may be because disengagement is timely. In the words of Zhou Shenglie (third century): "Confucius approves of Dian because he alone understands timeliness (*zhishi* 知時)" (*LY* 3: 1047). The scholar Huang Kan (488–545), possibly influenced by contemporary Daoist discourse, believes that Confucius agrees with Dian "because the Way was in abeyance and the age was in chaos. There were many who raced and jostled, and so the various disciples all set their heart on serving in government. Dian alone understood that the times had changed. That was why Confucius agreed with him" (*LY* 3: 1047).

The Daoist overtones can be ameliorated if withdrawal from politics is but the necessary condition for moral self-cultivation, as the exegete Xing Bing (932–1010) implies: "The three disciples failed to understand the times, and set their ambition on government. Zeng Dian alone could understand timeliness, and set his ambition on purifying himself and being immersed in virtue, chanting his thoughts and finding joy in the Way. That was why

Confucius agreed with him."[14] "Purifying himself and being immersed in virtue" is literally "washing his body and bathing in virtue" (*zao shen yu de* 澡身浴德):[15] bathing in the river becomes the metaphor for cleansing and self-transformation.

"Joy in the Way" gains new dimensions of interiority and transcendence in the discourse of Song Neo-Confucian scholars and thinkers. It becomes synonymous with self-containment, a supreme sense of ease and equanimity (*congrong* 從容), and intuitive understanding of cosmic principles. For Cheng Hao (1032–1085), "Confucius and Dian share the same aspiration as sages, for theirs is already the aura of the sage kings Yao and Shun." His younger brother Cheng Yi (1033–1107) tones down the elevation of Dian but still upholds his perfect empathy with Confucius: "Zeng Dian is an untamed spirit. He may not be able to perform the sage's actions, but he is able to understand the aspirations of Confucius. . . . Confucius's aspiration is to 'care for the aged, earn the trust of friends, and cherish the young,' so that the myriad things and beings without exception fulfill their nature. Zeng Dian understands this. That is why Confucius, heaving a sigh, said, 'I am with Dian.'"[16] Dian's excursion expresses his joy in cosmic oneness and how all things and beings find their proper place. The moral vision of Confucius as enunciated in *Analects* 5.26 (cited earlier) and quoted by Cheng Yi becomes a metaphysical vision, which Zeng Dian understands and thereby earns Confucius's approval. The Cheng brothers' comments are quoted in the commentary on the *Analects* compiled by Zhu Xi (1130–1200), who adds the notion of "heavenly principle" (*tianli* 天理): "From Zeng Dian's learning, we see how heavenly principle flows forth where private human desires have come to an end, so much so that it fills all corners and nothing is wanting. That is why between his movement and repose there is such supreme ease. . . . Truly he flows with heaven and earth and the myriad things. Such is the wonder as everyone and everything find their proper place."[17] Zhu Xi reportedly later regretted the transcendental flights of his comment on Dian, but it remained dominant for the next five centuries, not least because an imperial decree in 1313 made Zhu Xi's commentary on the Four Books de rigueur for the civil service examination, which lasted until 1905.[18]

Song Neo-Confucians like to talk about "supreme ease," the joyous equanimity springing from the intuitive understanding of heavenly principle that is most often associated with Confucius and Yan Hui in their writings. The "untamed" or "wild" Zeng Dian does not fit this model perfectly, hence Cheng Yi's attempt to take him down a peg, as quoted above. Four centuries later, when Confucianism took a further inward turn in Wang Yangming's (1472–1529) teachings that identify the human mind with heavenly principle, he and his followers embraced Zeng Dian's sensibility as a venue of subjective illumination and spiritual transcendence. Wang Yangming prided himself on attaining "the vision of an untamed spirit" 狂者的胸次. In 1524, when Wang celebrated the Mid-Autumn Festival with his disciples in a grand feast, he wrote two poems. The second one ends with these lines: "With a twang he pushes aside the zither in the spring breeze. / Untamed Dian may be, but he captures my sentiments." 鏗然舍瑟春風裡, 點也雖狂得我情."[19] One of his disciples recorded Wang's praise of the untamed spirit on that occasion: "it is like the aura of the phoenix soaring to the cerulean heights."[20] Commentators elevating Dian as the embodiment of transcendent freedom or harmony with cosmic order are often implicitly trying to meet the metaphysical challenge of Daoism and Buddhism. They sometimes have to do so at the expense of the first three disciples, interpreting Confucius's reaction to them as simple dismissal. The concluding exchange between Confucius and Zeng Dian, however, reaffirms Confucius's political engagement.

Some commentators rejected Dian's transcendental elevation as too speculative, almost bordering on "Zen talk." From the mid-seventeenth century onward, intellectual trends took a philological and ritual turn. Scholars revisited earlier arguments on the ritual significance of the spring excursion, drawing on the importance of ritual and music in the Confucian vision of social, moral, political, and cosmic order. This perspective in effect rehabilitates the other three disciples, in contrast to their negative judgment by those who emphasize Dian's transcendence. Zhang Lüxiang (1611–1674) sees a pattern of progression in the visions of the four disciples: Facing hostile armies and famines, Zilu focuses on instilling valor and moral purpose in the people. Having quelled disorder, there is room for economic well-being and self-sufficiency, hence Ran Qiu's goals. The achievement of such goals facilitate moral transformation through correct rituals as envisioned by Gongxi Chi. Finally, there is peace and harmony recalling the ideal political order of antiquity, of which Zeng Dian's joyous excursion is the tangible emblem (LY 3: 1053).

The logic of progression reclaims Dian's pleasure as political expression. Song Xiangfeng (1779–1860) opines: the first three disciples use ritual propriety to regulate people's minds, whereas Dian, whether playing the zither or chanting, is using music to bring harmony to the people. "Music comes from within, while rituals are applied from without. That is why Confucius has a unique affinity with Dian" (*LY* 3: 1044). Music is also tied to a deep and spontaneous joy, a constant refrain in traditions of Confucian thought that prize subjective illumination. According to a canonical work on music and ritual, "the greatest music harmonizes with heaven and earth" (*LJ* 3: 988)—it claims transcendence through moral and cosmological significance.[21] The modern discourse on "Confucian aesthetics" often invokes Zeng Dian as an example.[22] In some ways, this discourse follows not only the valorization of music through its fusion with ritual but also its ties with transcendent experience as "Confucian aesthetics" charts the fusion of ethics, aesthetics, and metaphysics.

Unlike declarative statements, such as Confucius's pithy definition and explanation of various virtue words in the *Analects*, stories steer us to interstices of the unspoken. In this case, different interpretations hinge on the hidden and inferred intentions and the psychological states of Confucius and the disciples. When Confucius smiles quizzically (*shen* 哂) at Zilu, is criticism of Zilu's manner combined with general approval of his ambition? When Ran Qiu aims to satisfy the material needs of the people, is he too timid or too eager to comply with his Master's expectations? Elsewhere in the *Analects*, Ran Qiu is said to impose limits on himself (*tui* 退) and, as steward of the Ji lineage, considered too ready to collect excessive taxes on behalf of his aristocratic patrons (*Analects* 11.22, 11.17). When Confucius says that a small state still counts as a polity, does he imply approval of Ran Qiu or critique of his self-censorship? Gongxi Chi aims no higher than the role of minor officiant in sacrificial and diplomatic ritual; Confucius seems to chide him for being too modest but maintains that ritual ambition *is* political ambition. Does Dian embody ease, self-containment, and unself-conscious naturalness? If that is the case, why does he need to ask about Confucius's views of the other three disciples? Do his questions convey uncertainty about the interpretation of the four disciples' choices? Are the four in implicit competition? Is Confucius wholeheartedly "with Dian"? Perhaps he simply approves of Dian's naturalness and self-knowledge (Dian knows he is not cut out for seeking office). After all, Confucius is not "breaking into a smile" (*wan'er* 莞爾) but "heaving a sigh."[23] Perhaps he is simply disappointed with his times and is momentarily drawn to a vision of withdrawal, as when he says that he would "board a raft and drift away on the seas" because the Way does not prevail (*Analects* 5.7).[24] Confucius's reaction may be incidental, hinging on his humor at that moment.[25] Can there be a gap between Zeng's expression and Confucius's implied inter- pretation? In other words, does Confucius "get it?" Is Confucius simply nostalgic for the ideal world of peace and unity, which he chooses to equate with Dian's joyous outing irrespective of Dian's intention?[26] These ques- tions, which inform divergent interpretations (including those mentioned above), show how the meanings of political engagement, music, ritual, and inner life shift as we probe the motives, emotional responses, communica- tive processes, and circumstantial constraints that define the momentum of storytelling.

The Organization of This Book

If all the stories about Confucius included in this book were parsed with the same level of details as above, it would have become a much longer book, testing the limits of the reader's patience. I hope, however, that at least some of the stories included here will inspire reflections on their gen- esis, reverberations, and interpretive possibilities even if their discussions are briefer than the one for the story above. One question raised by *Analects* 11.26 is its supposed dating. Whether we place the episode before or after Confucius's political disappointments and the first three disciples' official careers can color our interpretation of their tone or Confucius's sigh. *Ana- lects* 11.26 does not appear in the first chronological account of his life, chapter 47 in the monumental *Historical Records* (*Shiji*), compiled by the Han historian Sima Qian. As we will see, the interpretive implications of chronology can be significant with the stories that Sima Qian does include. There are many overlapping passages in the *Analects* and *Historical Records*. The narrative interest of entries in the former sometimes only fully unfold in the latter. These two texts remain the most frequently cited sources in the retelling of stories about Confucius.

Chapter 1 offers the canonical account of the life of Confucius with an annotated translation of Sima Qian's chapter on Confucius and considers the significance of "chronicling Confucius," or putting Confucius in histori- cal time. Sima Qian is drawing on almost four centuries of diverse lore about Confucius, and his influential account in turn inspires responses and rebuttals. I have divided the chapter into seventy-two segments, with each segment followed by a "translator's note," which explains sources, reverberations, parallel and variant accounts, implicit arguments or dialogues between different positions, commentaries, textual problems, stylistic issues, and questions of historical veracity. Such a mode of "slow reading," extending both vertically in time and horizontally by way of associations, emphasizes intertextuality and highlights how each segment can be read as the product and the generator of narratives and arguments. It alerts us to Sima Qian's possible choices and their reception by later readers. Segmentation of this long chapter will hopefully help the reader recognize patterns of balance and repetition that contribute more to the sense of formal consciousness than sheer narrative momentum. I hope such an arrangement can both serve an introductory purpose and satisfy the interests of readers who want to probe more deeply. In the classroom, the primary focus should be on Sima Qian's account. The translator's notes can be assigned selectively, depending on the parameters of the course.

If the unity and coherence in the account of Confucius's life in chapter 1 is based on negotiating the differences between diverse viewpoints and frames of reference, then the picture of contention and debates in chapter 2, "Arguing with Confucius," magnifies those differences, as the focus shifts to how Confucius becomes the pivot for generating new arguments in early China. The Warring States texts (ca. fourth–third century BCE) discussed in this chapter predate Sima Qian, and excerpts from them are included in chapter 1. The present arrangement of my chapters thus reflects a shift in perspectives rather than chronological sequence. I believe the reader is better equipped to confront the polyphony after perusing a coherent account of Confuicus's life. Chapter 2 offers examples of how Confucius becomes the mouthpiece for thinkers with vastly different ideas about what constitutes or brings about good governance or a happy, fulfilled life. In some cases, Confucius is set up as the voice of apparent wisdom only to be refuted. Arguments supporting or rejecting what Confucius is supposed to represent become the catalyst for articulating a wide range of viewpoints.

Stories featuring Confucius in the context of moral reasoning are especially interesting: potential ambiguities arise in different conceptions of law, justice, and political order. Sometimes this is couched as Confucius's historical judgments, and arguments for or against them, in retrospection on the role of violence, deviance, and power struggles in antiquity or the more recent past. Most of the materials in chapter 2 are derived from texts aligned with the labels "Daoist" and "Legalist" from the Han dynasty onward. The stories featuring Confucius in this chapter help us understand those labels and apprehend the flourishing of the so-called Hundred Schools from the perspective of narrative.

If the Confucius stories in chapter 2 are about worldviews and ideology, their counterparts in chapter 3, "Outsmarting Confucius (or His Followers)," which span narratives from second century BCE to the nineteenth century, are geared toward competitions in wit and knowledge. One of the pieces in this chapter is the Dunhuang ballad, "Confucius and Xiang Tuo Asked Each Other Questions." This ballad, which has antecedents in stories of precocious children who flummox Confucius by their clever questions and answers, features a homicidal Confucius, who murders his youthful interlocutor when he fails to solve the conundrums posed by the boy and is worsted in the competition of "broad knowledge" with him. Stories about women and children outsmarting Confucius are usually not tied to alternative worldviews, although the persecution of Buddhists in the mid-ninth century and Xiang Tuo's assimilation into the Buddhist pantheon suggest that the ballad may be explained in part by the competition between Confucianism and Buddhism.

Even more blatantly propagandistic is the flogging of Confucius in the quasi-Christian Heaven in *The Taiping Heavenly Chronicle* (*Taiping tianri*), the tract (published in 1862) chronicling the rise of Hong Xiuquan (1814–1864), the self-proclaimed brother of Jesus and leader of a millenarian movement that led to the cataclysmic Taiping Wars (1850–1864). Here there is no battle of wit or competition of knowledge, but one cannot help but connect the vindictive fury of the Taiping chronicle to Hong Xiuquan's frustration as a failed examination candidate. In other words, it has that element of "getting even with Confucius" common to all accounts of Confucius's confrontation with unlikely opponents. But the Xiang Tuo ballad and *The Taiping Heavenly Chronicle* are limit cases. There are relatively few examples of outright condemnation of Confucius, as we can glean from the slim and repetitive anthologies produced during the anti-Confucius campaign (1974) at the height of the Cultural Revolution. They bore titles such as *Brief Compilation of Historical Sources on the Anti-Confucian Struggles of the Toiling Masses Through the Ages* (*Lidai laodong renmin fan Kong douzheng shiliao jianbian*, 1975). Even such determined efforts yielded but a smattering of examples and had to be shored up by more general critiques of the ruling classes. More often than not, critical voices expressing discontent with the Confucian tradition direct their barb not at Confucius but at his misguided followers who miss the point of the sage's teachings. I have selected the supposedly "anti-Confucian" writings of the iconoclastic late Ming thinker Li Zhi (1527–1602), two jokes collected in an eighteenth-century anthology, and a story by Yuan Mei (1716–1798), as examples of this predilection.

A more radical reappraisal emerges in early twentieth-century writings. Chapter 4, "Settling Scores with Confucius," presents famous modern Chinese writers' portrayal of Confucius from the 1910s to the 1930s: "Kong Yiji" (1919) and "Confucius in Modern China" (1935) by Lu Xun (1881–1936); "Marx Enters the Temple of Confucius" (1925) by Guo Moruo (1892–1978); and a one-act play, *Confucius Meets Nan Zi* (1928), by Lin Yutang (1895–1976). By turns parodic and despairing, savagely sarcastic and oddly apologetic, these works are not really concerned with the search for the authentic Confucius or the serious engagement with his intellectual legacy. Instead, their critique of Confucius turns into shadowboxing with China's problematic transition to modernity. Confucius is amorphously identified with all the reactionary forces in early Republican China and blamed for its social ills and political problems. Even under this pall, however, we see glimpses of hopes for accommodation. Thus, Guo Moruo postulates a hypothetical meeting point between Marxism and Confucianism in "Marx Enters the Temple of Confucius," while Lin Yutang imagines Confucius's secret attraction to the ethos of a free and independent woman in *Confucius Meets Nan Zi*.

These early twentieth-century works still have cultural currency in contemporary China. Lu Xun's "Kong Yiji," whose eponymous protagonist emblematizes the pathetic fate of a supposedly Confucian scholar, remains a staple in PRC textbooks. But his latest iteration in a rap song from 2023, "The Sunny and Cheerful Kong Yiji," the final piece translated in this book, turns him into the voice of protest against inequities and the repression of dissent in contemporary China. "Marx Enters the Temple of Confucius" by Guo Moruo appeared as an essay question in the "Political Thought" section in the 2015 national entrance examination for masters programs, reflecting a new emphasis on Confucian teachings as cultural nationalism and the bedrock of social order. Following the footsteps of earlier emperors—as well as Yuan Shikai (1859–1916) and Chiang Kai-shek (1887–1975)—Xi Jinping paid his respects at the temple of Confucius on November 26, 2013; on September 24, 2014, Xi attended a conference commemorating Confucius's 2,565th birthday, the first time a top Chinese

Communist Party leader did so. In fall 2023, Hunan Television put out a widely and justly derided five-episode miniseries, *When Marx Meets Confucius* (*Dang Makesi yujian Kong fuzi*). It rehashes the notion of "the great common good" (*datong* 大同) as the meeting point of Confucius and Marx in Guo's 1925 piece but is more inane, simplistic, nationalist, celebratory, and blatantly propagandistic. In it, Marx declares "he has long become Chinese" after a hundred years in China and expresses satisfaction with an image of himself in Confucian robes, even as Confucius is pleased with his representation in a Western suit. The real reference point is Xi Jinping's speech (June 2, 2023) on "the second synthesis" of Chinese civilization and Marxism.

The protean transformations of Confucius in this book may suggest ruptures and discontinuities, yet there are also secret affinities and unexpected connections. Consider, for example, "The Sunny and Cheerful Kong Yiji," the 2023 song that reinvents Lu Xun's Kong Yiji to articulate the frustration of contemporary Chinese youths as they lament unemployment, diminishing opportunities, and the futility of protest. We may see here a mundane or deliberately trivialized iteration of the theme of the quest for recognition in Sima Qian's account of Confucius. Indeed, the refrain of Confucius "not being employed" (*buyong* 不用) and his ideas "not being implemented" in *Historical Records* signals the gap between self and world that underwrites some of the most important works in the Chinese tradition.

Another thread is the notion of adaptability and judicious weighing of alternatives. In Lin Yutang's *Confucius Meets Nan Zi*, Confucius repeats the line "there is no inevitable affirmation or inevitable rejection of alternatives" (*Analects* 18.8), or the idea behind it, like a mantra. It signals both mockery of Confucius's evasiveness and vague hopes for the renewal and transformation of the Confucian tradition by accommodating new ideas. The notion of expediency is more pointedly critical when Lu Xun describes Confucius as "the modern sage," whereby Confucius remains relevant only by being assimilated into evolving power structures. It recalls Zhang Taiyan's (1869–1936) mocking appellation of Confucius as "the national goody two shoes" (*guoyuan* 國愿) in an essay dated 1906; the term echoes "the village goody two shoes" (*xiangyuan* 鄉愿), whom Confucius decries as "the plunderer of virtue" (*de zhi zei* 德之賊) because of their conformism and readiness to compromise (*Analects* 17.13).[27] This addresses a longstanding issue in the tradition. The necessity of and problems with expediency and adaptability is a persistent theme in Sima Qian's account of Confucius. It also informs the reinvention and critique of Confucius in writings with wildly divergent agendas and orientations during the Warring States, when Confucius is sometimes criticized for failing to respond to changing historical circumstances or attacked for opportunistically evolving with the times and falling short of his avowed principles. Whether eulogized, dismissed, parodied, attacked, or cloaked in new guises, the representation of Confucius at any historical moment is better understood if we can connect his stories from different periods.

I have numbered the stories by chapter and their sequence of appearance in order to facilitate easy cross reference. To minimize confusion, Confucius's disciples are referred to by their most commonly used names (for example, Zilu, Zigong, Yan Hui) or by their clan names plus given names (*ming* 名), even though the stories typically refer to them both by their given names and their style names (*zi* 字). Confucius addresses his disciples and refers to them by their given names. I refer to the Yellow River and the Yangzi River by their modern names, although in early Chinese texts they are just called "the River" (He 河, Jiang 江).

CHAPTER I

Chronicling Confucius

S ima Qian, one of China's greatest historians, gives us the first chronological account of the life of Confucius in his monumental *Historical Records* (*Shiji*). What follows is an annotated translation of chapter 47 of *Historical Records*, "The Hereditary House of Confucius" (Kongzi shijia 孔子世家). But first a few words about *Historical Records*. Drawing on archival materials, earlier chronicles and canons, anecdotes and arguments from diverse discourses, oral traditions, contemporary witnesses, and possibly work done by his father Sima Tan, Sima Qian presents a comprehensive history of the known world from its origins (ca. 3000 BCE) down to his own time, the reign of Emperor Wu (r. 141–87 BCE). As court archivist, he defended the general Li Ling (150–74 BCE), who had surrendered to the Xiongnu in one of the many battles that the Han Empire fought with its nomadic neighbor in the north. For this supposed effrontery, he suffered the humiliating punishment of castration, which he chose over suicide because his great work had not yet been completed. In 130 chapters, *Historical Records* presents history from different perspectives: the enactment of royal power and the fortunes of dynasties in a chronological framework; tables with genealogical information; treatises on subjects such as calendars, court rituals, music, water management, and government finance; accounts of ruling houses and noble lineages; and biographies of notable individuals, including ministers, generals, rebels, thinkers, poets, merchants, jesters, and assassins, among others.

"Hereditary Houses" or "lineages that last for generations" (*shijia* 世家) is one of the five sections in *Historical Records*. It comprises mostly histories of the lineages of rulers, princes, and enfeoffed ministers. The inclusion of Confucius's biography in this section instead of in the "Biographies" section has sparked questions and debates (*SJ* 47.1–3). Those who object to this apparent attempt to exalt Confucius argue that self-evident sagehood does not require the trappings of power and privileges associated with this section. Defenders of the placement point out that Sima Qian intends to redefine "lineage" in terms of moral teachings, lasting influence, and historical significance. The very category of "Hereditary Houses" is after all his invention.

I have divided Sima Qian's biography of Confucius into seventy-two segments (1.1–1.72). I follow each segment with a "translator's note" that brings it into dialogue with relevant passages (for example, subsections 1.1a, 1.1b, and so on) and incorporates additional comments to highlight possible sources, reverberations, and embedded arguments. The goal is to demonstrate the complex, ambiguous, and polyvalent construction of narrative in a textual universe where texts are composite and sedimented and textual units often have fluid boundaries. Many scholars, including Cui Shu (1740–1816), Liang Yusheng (1745–1819), Gu Jiegang (1893–1980), and Qian Mu (1895–1990), have questioned the historical accuracy of Sima Qian's account, noting its discrepancies with other chapters in *Historical Records* and extant early Chinese sources. While bringing in observations by them and other skeptics in my explanatory notes, I focus on the power and functions of stories.

1.1 Confucius was born in the settlement of Zou in the region of Changping in Lu. His ancestor, a man of Song, was called Kong Fangshu. Fangshu sired Boxia, Boxia sired Shuliang He. Shuliang sired Confucius as a result of his union with a woman of the Yan lineage in the wilds. They prayed at Ni Hill and got Confucius. Confucius was born in the twenty-second year of Lord Xiang of Lu [551 BCE].[1] It is said that the top of his head was concave, and that was why he was given the name Qiu [Hill]. His style name was Zhongni, and his lineage name was Kong.

[translator's note]
Sima Qian begins with the obvious questions: What is Confucius's ancestry? Are there signs of his destiny from the beginning? The name of

Confucius's great grandfather, Kong Fangshu, does not appear in extant texts predating *Historical Records*. The fact that he had a lineage name (Kong) suggests a measure of distinction. *Zuo Tradition* credits Confucius's father Shuliang He with Herculean feats of physical prowess. ("Shuliang" is his style name and "He" is his given name.) When Jin and its allies (including Lu) besiege the small state of Biyang (563 BCE), the men of Biyang release the portcullis of the inner gate, but Shuliang He holds up the gate to allow the officers storming the gate to go in (*Zuo* Xiang 10.2, 2: 966–67). Seven years later (556 BCE), he is one of three brave Lu officers who lead three hundred armored soldiers to raid the Qi army at night and break the Qi siege of Fang (in Lu) (*Zuo* Xiang 17.3, 2: 1044–45). Perhaps inspired by such accounts of Shuliang He's strength and valor, some early stories refer to Confucius's great physical strength. *Mozi* (the writings associated with Master Mo or Mo Di) claims that Confucius removes the wooden bar locking a gate so the Ji lineage head can escape, an act that seems to reprise his father's feat (*MZ* 274). *Mr. Lü's Annals* also implicitly invokes his father's image: "Confucius was so strong that he held up the gates of the capital, but he refused to be known for his strength" (*LSCQ* 1: 845, see also *HNZ* 12.385, *LH* 37.588, *LZ* 8.252). On the whole, this beginning is understated. Later in this narrative, the Lu minister Meng Xizi lists Song nobles among Confucius's ancestors (1.4). Some accounts trace Confucius's ancestry to a Shang king, Di Yi, and give him a longer and more distinguished list of forbears that include Song ministers.[2]

"Union in the wilds" (*yehe* 野合) can mean a clandestine rendezvous, sexual relations outside marriage, or some less serious infraction of ritual propriety. "The wilds" (*ye* 野) refers to the area beyond a settlement and its outskirts. Some commentators argue that impropriety in this case refers merely to the age difference between Confucius's parents,[3] citing this account from *Sayings from the House of Confucius* (hereafter *Sayings*, ca. third century CE):

> 1.1a Shuliang He said, "Although I have nine daughters, I have no son." His concubine gave birth to Mengpi, who had the style name Boni and was lame. He thus sought to form marriage ties with the Yan lineage. The Yan lineage head had three daughters; the youngest of them was named Zhengzai.[4] The father asked his three daughters: "Although the father and grandfather of the officer of Zou were

but officers, his ancestors were descendants of sage kings. Now this man is ten *chi* in stature and his martial prowess has no equal.[5] I very much want him for our family. Even though he is older and stern, it should not make you doubt his eligibility. Who among the three of you is willing to become his wife?" Two of his daughters did not respond. Zhengzai stepped forward and said, "We should follow what our father arranges. Why ask us?" The father said, "It is you who can do this." He thus made her Shuliang He's wife. Having gone to Shuliang He, she presented herself at the ancestral temple. Because her husband was old, she was afraid that she would not be able to bear a son in time, so she privately offered prayers at Ni Qiu [Ni Hill] in supplication. She gave birth to Confucius. That was why he was named Qiu and had the cognomen Zhongni. (*KZJY* 39.527–28)

"Zhongni" combines the name of the hill (Ni) with his sequence of birth as the second son (*zhong*). Other commentators focus on the prayers and the implied construction of a sacrificial altar at Ni Hill as the crux of ritual impropriety.[6] The open-air prayer echoes stories of impregnation by cosmic forces, which Confucius affirms in a passage from an excavated text (*KJY* 3: 923–24). Thus Jiang Yuan steps on a giant toe print and becomes pregnant with Lord Millet (Houji), the Zhou ancestor, and Jian Di swallows the egg of a black bird and becomes pregnant with Qi, the Shang ancestor.[7] A more explicit iteration of this idea of "cosmic impregnation" regarding Confucius is found in a Han text belonging to the tradition of apocrypha and omenology (ca. first–second century CE):

1.1b Confucius's mother Zhengzai wandered at the edge of a great marsh. She fell asleep and dreamed of the Black God's messenger summoning her. She went and dreamed of intercourse with the Black God, who said to her, "You will nurse inside a hollow mulberry tree for certain." When she woke up, she felt as if she had been touched by the god. She gave birth to Qiu in a hollow mulberry tree. (*ZY* 962)[8]

In the system of "five phases" (*wuxing* 五行), the color black is associated with law and order, as is Confucius in the Han imagination (1.13, 1.16).[9] "Mulberry grove" is where lovers have their rendezvous in the canonical *Odes* (*Shijing*).[10] Mulberry Grove is also supposedly where Tang, the founder of the Shang dynasty, prayed for rain, and it comes to be identified as the place for Shang ancestral sacrifices. Legend has it that Yi Yin, wise minister of Tang, was born in a hollow mulberry tree. His mother was told by a god to flee an impending flood without looking back. She looked back and was turned into a hollow mulberry tree, and her infant was later found by a girl picking mulberry (*LSCQ* 1: 739). Possibly alluding to the connection between Confucius and Yi Yin or the story cited above (1.1b), Gan Bao (286–336) claims that Confucius was born at a place called Kongsang (meaning "hollow mulberry"), whose spring flows only with sacrificial offerings (*SJ* 47.8).[11]

To read "union in the wilds" as clandestine sexual union would align Confucius with other stories about sages with unworthy parents. Zhang Hua (232–300) wrote in *Record of Broad Knowledge of Things* (*Bowu zhi*): "The Blind Old Man and his wife were murderous and stubborn, but the sage king Shun was born to them. Shuliang He was a licentious man and Zheng-zai was guilty of misconduct. Furthermore, they had their union in the wilds, but Confucius was born. How can there be such a thing as nurturing moral cultivation in the womb?"[12] In some ways, the literal reading of "union in the wilds" answers the same purpose as the defensive explanations of that idea: it serves to emphasize extraordinary destiny by going beyond normal marriage and procreation.

On a mirror screen from the tomb of Lord Haihun (Liu He, d. 59 BCE) excavated in 2011, we find images of Confucius and five of his disciples. Next to Confucius's image is an account of his life that overlaps significantly with passages from *Historical Records*. That account has *ju* 居 (settle) instead of *he* 合 (union): "Shuliang He sired Confucius as a result of settling in the wilds with a woman of the Yan lineage."[13] It is possible that the two graphs are confused because of orthographic similarity, but "settling in the wilds" would obviate speculations about sexual impropriety.

According to an early dictionary, Confucius's name, Qiu, means hill or "elevation on four sides with depression in the middle."[14] The concave image is more obvious in early orthography: *qiu* 丘 is 𝕄 in oracle bones, 𝕪 in bronze inscriptions, and 𝕸 in seal script. In explaining Confucius's name, Sima Qian uses the word "it is said" (*yun* 云) to convey his sense of uncertainty. Ni Hill (Ni Qiu) is supposed to be a lower hill surrounded by higher ones.[15] His name and cognomen thus reflects both the place of his parents' prayer and the unusual shape of his head. Confucius's physical peculiarity is often mentioned in tandem with the anomalous features of other sages in late Warring States and Han texts. His unusual height is mentioned in 1.5 and his appearance is described in 1.22.

1.2 After Qiu was born, Shuliang He died and was buried at Mount Fang.[16] Mount Fang was in the eastern part of Lu. So it happened that Confucius was in doubt about his father's burial place, for his mother avoided mentioning it. When Confucius was playing games as a child, he often set forth wooden sacrificial vessels and assumed the mien of proper ritual.[17] Upon his mother's death, he thus performed funerary rituals for her at the Crossroads of the Five Fathers.[18] This was on account of his caution. The mother of Wanfu, a Zou man, told Confucius about his father's grave, and that was why he went ahead to have his parents buried together at Fang.

[translator's note]
The first thing we are told about Confucius is his response to his parents' death. Why does his mother avoid reference to his father's burial place? This detail again implies a taboo surrounding his parents' union or his mother's problematic status in relation to the Kong lineage.[19] Confucius's precocious interest in ritual is echoed in a similar story about Mencius, whose childish games come to incorporate sacrificial vessels after his mother moves their residence next to a "house of learning."[20] Confucius's concern with proper ritual paradoxically prompts him to commit a ritual infraction. He performs funerary rites for his mother at a thoroughfare (instead of at home) in order to provoke an outcry, apparently trying to force people to confirm rumors of his paternity and find out where his father was buried. This account in *Historical Records* is often discussed in tandem with a related passage in *Record of Rituals* (*Liji*, compiled ca. second–first century BCE, with earlier layers dated to ca. fourth–third century BCE).

1.2a Confucius was orphaned when he was young and did not know where the grave of his father was. When his mother died, he performed funerary rituals for her at the Crossroad of the Five Fathers. People who saw this all thought that it was the actual burial. This was due to his caution:[21] for this was just the funerary rituals. He asked questions of the mother of Manfu, a man of Zou, and it was thus that his parents could be buried together at Fang (*LJ* 1: 171).

Zheng Xuan's (127–200) explanation of this elliptical (and possibly corrupt) passage draws from details in *Historical Records*: Confucius's mother does not tell him about his father's burial place because she is ashamed of their "union in the wilds." Confucius flouts ritual rules in order to provoke questions and get answers. "Manfu" and "Wanfu" are variants of the same name.

In *The Kong Family Masters' Anthology* (hereafter *Kong Anthology*, compiled ca. third–fourth century, with some materials dated to earlier periods), a man born of a clandestine union cites Confucius as a precedent, only to be attacked for spreading rumors (*KCZ* 15.330). Chen Hao (1260–1341) finds it unlikely that Confucius should have failed to ascertain his father's burial place before his mother's death. The ritual infraction of performing funeral rites at a thoroughfare is likewise unthinkable to him and some other scholars, who thus express skepticism about these accounts in *Historical Records* and *Record of Rituals* (*SJ* 47.9–10, *LJ* 1: 171). Those who maintain that the ritual impropriety of his parents' union lies only in age difference find the secrecy even harder to justify.

At stake in the above passages (1.2, 1.2a) is the balance and tension between emotions and propriety, a concern evident in another passage on the funerary rituals for Confucius's parents in *Record of Rituals*:

> 1.2b Having managed to have his parents buried together at Fang, Confucius said, "I have heard that the ancient practice is to have the grave but not the grave mound. Now I am a person who is wandering east, west, south, and north. I have no choice but to mark out this place." He thus built a grave mound that was about four *chi* in height. Confucius was the first to return, while his disciples stayed behind. It rained heavily, and then they came. Confucius asked them, "How did it happen that you're so late in coming?" They said, "The grave mound at Fang collapsed."[22] Confucius did not respond. Only after they asked three times did Confucius speak, with tears streaming down: "I have heard that it was not the ancient practice to build a grave mound." (*LJ* 1: 168–69)[23]

According to Zheng Xuan, "ancient practice" refers to Shang customs while the four-*chi* grave mound signifies a Zhou tradition (*LJ* 1: 168–69). This would imply that Confucius is torn between Shang and Zhou practice. *Record of Rituals* and *Sayings* repeatedly refer to Confucius deciding between funeral customs traced to Shang and Zhou (see also this chapter,

1.52, 1.68).²⁴ A more straightforward interpretation would hinge on the balance between the ritual prescriptions to restrain grief and the emotional need to mark grief.

1.3 Confucius wore a hempen mourning sash. When the Ji lineage head offered a feast for officers, Confucius took part by going. Yang Hu dismissed him with these words: "The Ji lineage head is offering a feast for officers. We do not presume to offer a feast for you, sir." On account of this, Confucius withdrew.

[translator's note]
What was Confucius's status? Did he begin with a recognized place in society? Yang Hu's statement implies that only someone already serving a lord or a minster can be considered a *shi* 士, translated here as "officer." *Shi* has also been rendered as "gentleman," "scholar," "scholar-official," "knight," "men of service": these are men sandwiched between the aristocracy and commoners, distinguished less by pedigree than by their abilities in serving men of a higher social position. Their role is a pervasive concern in Warring States writings. The term is defined several times in the *Analects*, notably in the following example:

1.3a Zigong, "What should one be like in order to be considered a *shi*?" The Master said, "He who conducts himself with the highest standards, being ashamed to fall short, and does not disgrace the ruler's command no matter where he is sent as envoy can be called a *shi*." "May I ask, what is the next level?" "To be commended for filial piety in one's lineage and for deference to elders in one's kinship community." "May I ask, what is the next level?" "He who always keeps his words and sees his actions through—a humble man with flinty resoluteness. That too can be considered the next level." "What about those in charge of government these days?" The Master said, "Those are but paltry men, how can they be worth considering!" (*Analects* 13.20)²⁵

In the *Analects* (13.20), the gradation of commendation goes from the honorable fulfillment of public duty to virtuous conduct in the context of family and kinship, and from thence to personal resolution and integrity. The gradient implying the greater importance of public life as compared to private life may not prepare us for the concluding dismissal of men "in charge of government": "paltry men" is literally "men like mere pecks and baskets," men who, like meager vessels, do not amount to much. Herein lies a paradox: a *shi* needs the power and authority of office to fulfill his destiny, but this means dealing with unworthy men wielding power and authority.

Why begin the account of Confucius's public life with his undignified dismissal? He wants to join the feast presumably because of his eagerness for political engagement. According to *Mencius*, Confucius is passionate about serving in government: "When Confucius did not serve a lord for three months, he became anxious. When he left a state, he was certain to carry with him the introductory gifts to be presented to another ruler" (*Mencius* 3B.3). But when asked, perhaps later in life, why he does not participate in politics, Confucius claims that to be truly filial and fraternal is to already "engage in government" (*Analects* 2.21); the passage implies that the realization of virtues in family relationships can become the cornerstone of moral, social, and political order and render political participation unnecessary.

Here Confucius seems eager to serve. Yang Hu (aka Yang Huo), a tall man said to look like Confucius in some accounts (see 1.19), was the steward of the powerful Ji lineage and an ambitious retainer who later fomented disorder in Lu (1.11, 1.12). Why would Confucius want to have an audience with him, especially when other accounts record Confucius's reluctance to meet him? In the *Analects* (17.1), the balance of power is reversed, and Yang Huo (as Yang Hu is called in the passage)[26] is the one trying to entice Confucius to serve in government:

1.3b Yang Huo wanted to meet Confucius. Confucius was not there to meet him. He sent Confucius a piglet. Confucius waited for the time when Yang Huo was away to go to offer thanks but met Yang Huo on the way. Yang Huo said to Confucius, "Come! I will speak with you." He said, "To have a treasure in your embrace and let the domain sink in confusion—can that be called the highest good? It cannot. To desire to serve and yet to repeatedly miss the moment— can that be called wisdom? It cannot. The days and months are passing. The years are not on our side."[27] Confucius said, "I agree. I will serve then!" (*Analects* 17.1)

Mencius (3B.7) tells a slightly different story: Yang Huo sends Confucius a steamed piglet when he knows that Confucius is not at home, presumably to force Confucius to visit him to offer thanks, thereby implicitly reasserting his superior status even as he is seeking Confucius's service. Gifts create and reproduce social relations, as Marcel Mauss (1872–1950) observes, but gift-giving can be competitive and antagonistic. Different accounts of Confucius's relationship with those wielding power in Lu were probably available to Sima Qian, who chose an account that emphasizes Confucius's eagerness rather than his scruples.

Why would Confucius want to participate in a feast while still in mourning (unless we presume a temporal break between the first and second lines)? Many commentators find this scandalous and unbelievable. Sima Zhen (679–732) calls this "slander" and advances the improbable variant, "attached to his waist canonical classics" (*yaojing* 要經) instead of "wore a hempen mourning sash" (*yaodie* 要絰). The version of this story in *Sayings*, cited below, seems designed to address the ritual impropriety of the account in *Historical Records*. It also tries to reconcile the account in *Historical Records* with the *Analects* and *Mencius* by implying that Yang Hu wants to invite Confucius despite the intention of his master, the Ji lineage head, to exclude Confucius:

> 1.3c Confucius was in mourning for his mother. After the completion of the sacrifice for the first anniversary of her death, Yang Hu came to offer condolence and said privately to Confucius, "Now the Ji lineage head is going to offer a great feast for officers in the realm. Have you, sir, heard about it?" Confucius replied, "I have not heard about it. Had I heard about it, I would have wished to attend even though I would be wearing hempen mourning clothes." Yang Hu said, "Don't you think that it's improper? The Ji lineage head offered a feast for officers but did not include you." After Yang Hu left, Zeng Dian asked: "What did you mean by your reply?" Confucius said, "As for me, I am in mourning clothes. Even so, I responded in that way to his words to show that I did not disapprove of him." (*KZJY* 43.649)

Confucius's concluding remark suggests that his initial response uses his hypothetical attendance to hide his disapproval of Yang Hu. But this does not excuse the impropriety of his hypothetical willingness to attend a feast while in mourning. Cui Shu criticizes this account as being as problematic as its analogue in *Historical Records*, if not more so: "Furthermore, if indeed Yang Hu violated ritual propriety, it would suffice to refrain from criticizing him. Why make the violation even more extreme by expressing the wish to go? That would be flattery. If he was not going and falsely spoke of wanting to go, that would be deception. The sage would certainly not act like this" (*CDB* 268, *SJ* 47.10). Fang Bao (1668–1749) argues that the Ji lineage holds a feast in preparation for military action, and that is why Confucius feels the call of duty and the imperative to go (*SJ* 47.11). Dispensing with apologia may take us closer to Sima Qian's point on Confucius's eagerness to claim a place denied by the status quo and his willingness to bear the potential indignity of service in government. The price of political engagement and the compromise it may exact will reverberate later in this chapter (1.12, 1.20, 1.29).

1.4 Confucius was seventeen. The Lu high officer Meng Xizi became very ill and was on the verge of death when he admonished his heir, "Confucius is a descendant of sages whose line was extinguished in Song. His ancestor Fufu He started out with the expectation of ruling Song but yielded to Duke Li, who became the heir. When it came to Zheng Kaofu, he assisted Dukes Dai, Wu, and Xuan, and with each of his three commissions he became more reverent. Thus, the cauldron inscription says,

> With the first commission I bent,
> With the second I stooped,
> And with the third I bowed low,
> Hurrying along beside the wall.
> And indeed no one dared insult me.
> Make porridge in this vessel,
> Make gruel in this vessel,
> And with it fill my mouth.

This is how reverent he was. I have heard when it comes to the progeny of a sage, even if he does not rule in his own time, there will certainly be an accomplished man among his descendants. Now Confucius is young and loves ritual propriety. He could be the accomplished one! After I die, you should certainly take him as your teacher." When Meng Xizi died, Yizi and the Lu man Nangong Jingshu went to Confucius to learn about ritual propriety. Ji Wuzi died that year [535 BCE], and Pingzi succeeded him in his position.[28]

[translator's note]
With two noble, though self-effacing, ancestors, Confucius's lineage here seems more august than in 1.1. Fufu He, a son of Duke Min of Song (r. 691–682 BCE), was in line for the succession after Duke Min's assassination, but declined in favor of his younger brother, Duke Li (*Zuo* 3: 1430, n396). Zheng Kaofu, the great grandson of Fufu He, is said to have consulted a Zhou music master and regularized twelve Shang hymns that came to be included in the received text of the *Odes*.[29] The successive commissions may indicate positions of increasing importance and honor. Zheng Kaofu's ritual propriety and humility stand in sharp contrast to the image of Shuliang He's ostentatious martial prowess (see 1.1, translator's note). The inscription on the cauldron in Kaofu's mortuary temple is also included in *Zhuangzi* as an example of laudable self-effacement (*ZZ* 32.1056). Echoes of *Zhuangzi* and *Laozi* in such an attitude may explain why this episode from *Historical Records* is embedded in an account of Confucius's visit to Zhou to seek ritual instruction from Laozi in *Sayings* (*KZJY* 11.152–53). Note that this is the first of three references to the "sage" (*shengren* 聖人) in Sima Qian's account. Here it refers to Confucius's ancestors and implies potential claims to sovereignty as well as exemplary virtue, especially reverence.

In an entry dated to 535 BCE in *Zuo Tradition* (compiled ca. fourth century BCE), the Lu minister Meng Xizi, chagrined by his ignorance of rituals, decides to practice them and include ritual experts in his entourage. The passage looks ahead to what happens seventeen years later (518 BCE) when, on the verge of death, he praises Confucius as "an accomplished man" (*dazhe* 達者) and enjoins his two sons, Yue (Nangong Jingshu) and Heji (Meng Yizi), to study ritual with Confucius. His speech (*Zuo* Zhao 7.12, 3: 1430–31) largely overlaps with 1.4 above. Why did Sima Qian conflate two events dated to 535 BCE (when Confucius would have been seventeen) and to 518 BCE (when he would have been thirty-four)? Either he misread the *Zuo Tradition* passage or saw a version of the story that effaces the temporal distinction. Sima Qian also seems to have misidentified Nangong Jingshu as "a Lu man" rather than Meng Xizi's son. Nangong

Jingshu has his name in this form because he became the head of the Nan-gong ("southern palace") branch lineage of the Meng lineage.

1.5 Confucius was impoverished and had a lowly position. When he grew up, he served as an overseer for the Ji lineage, and his handling of measurements was just. He once served as a manager of grounds keeping cattle, and the animals flourished. He then became the overseer of works. Not long after, he left Lu, was dismissed at Qi, was driven away from Song, and was in great distress between Chen and Cai. At that point, he returned to Lu. Confucius's stature was nine *chi* and six *cun*, everyone called him "the tall one" and marveled at him. Lu again treated him favorably, and he thus returned to Lu.

[translator's note]
In the *Analects* (9.6), Confucius says of himself, "Being of a lowly station in my youth, I thus became adept at many plebian tasks" (see also 1.63). According to *Mencius*, Confucius fulfills the duties of his humble posts without articulating grand ambitions: "Confucius once served as overseer of storehouses and said, 'The accounts should be in order and that is all.' He once served as manager of the fields and said, 'The bovines and sheep should grow robustly and that is all.' It is an offense to talk about grand issues while holding humble posts" (*Mencius* 5B.5). The context concerns broader arguments about the balance and tension between political ideals and pragmatic compromise, the ethics of renumeration, and the proper mode of conduct for gentlemen serving in lowly positions. The logic of accommodation and the eagerness to serve (1.3) may explain Confucius's position as overseer for the Ji lineage, even though Confucius criticizes its ritual transgressions and greed in the *Analects* (3.1, 3.6, 11.17). The Ji lineage eventually drove the Lu ruler into exile in 517 BCE (see 1.8). According to Sima Zhen, "overseer for the Ji lineage" 季氏史 appears as "overseer of storehouses" 委吏 in some recensions of the text, as it does in *Mencius* (5B.5) (*SJ* 47.13). What seems to be acceptable in Han and pre-Han sources—Confucius serving the Ji lineage—becomes more of a travesty that needs to be explained away in later commentaries (*CDB* 268). Irrespective of connections to the Ji lineage, Sima Qian presents a picture of Confucius's rise in bureaucratic ranks due to his merits.

Confucius's impressive height (ranging from about six to seven feet in various modern estimates) is noted in the chapter "Against Physiognomy" (*feixiang* 非相) in *Xunzi*, where he is also said to have a crab-like face (*XZ* 5.46–57).[30] Xunzi disparages physiognomy and enumerates examples whereby inner attributes have no outward manifestations. Confucius's appearance is discussed again in 1.22. The summary of Confucius's peregrinations, travails, and return to Lu overlaps with their elaboration later on in the narrative and might have been inserted here by mistake, unless it is meant as a kind of prefatory summation.

1.6 Nangong Jingshu of Lu said to the Lu ruler, "I beg leave to go to Zhou in the company of Confucius." The Lu ruler gave them one carriage, two horses, and a young servant to accompany them. They went to Zhou and asked questions about rituals. It is said that Confucius might have met with Laozi. As he was taking his leave, Laozi sent him off with these words: "I have heard that men of wealth and position send people off with monetary gifts, and benevolent men send people off with words.[31] I lay no claim to wealth and position but have undeservedly gained the reputation of being a good man. I will send you off with words: Those keen of sight and hearing become deeply discerning and thus come close to death; they are the ones given to discussing and judging others. Those who are eloquent and expansive on many subjects thus endanger themselves; they are the ones given to exposing the ills and faults of others. To be a true son, have no thought of yourself. To be a true subject, have no thought of yourself." Upon Confucius's return to Lu from Zhou, his disciples made some improvements.

[translator's note]
Does the meeting of Laozi and Confucius imply Laozi's superiority, Confucius's eagerness to learn, or the affinities between their respective teachings? Sima Qian keeps the possibilities open and signals his uncertainty about the supposed meeting, a popular topic in Han iconography appearing in about seventy extant stone carvings,[32] with the words *gai* 蓋 ("might have") and *yun* 云 ("it is said"). Nangong Jingshu, a Lu noble's son, honors Confucius as a teacher (see 1.4). Laozi also appears as a ritual expert whom Confucius quotes with respect in "Master Zeng's Questions" (Zengzi wen 曾子問) in *Record of Rituals* (*LJ* 2: 524, 546, 547, 549). Sima Qian offers a different account of this meeting in "The Biographies of Laozi and Han Fei" (*SJ* 63), where the markers of uncertainty are absent; Laozi conveys a similar message but is more explicitly critical of Confucius; and Confucius concludes with an encomium of Laozi:

1.6a Confucius went to Zhou with a view to asking Laozi questions about rituals. Laozi said, "As for whom you are speaking about, those people and their bones have all rotted.[33] Only their words remain. Furthermore, a noble man who meets with the right times would ride in his carriage; if he does not, he would go forward wearily like a tumbleweed. I have heard, a good merchant keeps his resources deeply hidden as if he had nothing; a noble man of great virtue has the appearance of folly. Divest yourself of arrogant airs and multifarious desires; of an imposing mien and excessive ambitions: all these are of no benefit to your person. What I have to tell you is this and nothing else." Confucius left and said to his disciples: "As for birds, I know they can fly. As for fish, I know they can swim. As for beasts, I know they can run. For the running ones, one can make traps; for the swimming ones, fishing lines; for the flying ones, arrows. But when it comes to the dragon, I cannot know it, for it rides winds and clouds and soars to heaven. I saw Laozi today: Isn't he like a dragon?!" (SJ 63.4–5).

Exchanges between Confucius and Laozi are found in five chapters in *Zhuangzi* (ca. fourth–third century BCE).[34] The one that mentions Laozi's connection with Zhou appears in the chapter titled "Way of Heaven" (Tiandao 天道), where Confucius wants "to store his texts in the west at the house of Zhou" and requests Laozi's assistance, as Zhou archivist, in doing so. Laozi asks about the main points of these texts and, when Confucius in response expatiates on the meanings of the highest good (*ren* 仁) and proper duty (*yi* 義), dismisses him as one who "causes confusion in human nature" (*luan ren zhi xing* 亂人之性). In "The Circuit of Heaven" (Tianyun 天運), Confucius at fifty-one "has not heard of the Way" and Laozi disabuses him of the illusion that the Way can be sought through "principles and regulations" (*dushu* 度數), "yin and yang," "the highest good and proper duty." Confucius expresses his total admiration of Laozi by comparing him to the dragon that defies limits of conception (as in 1.6a). In another passage in "The Circuit of Heaven," Confucius asks Laozi why, with all his command of the Six Classics and the way of sage kings, no ruler would heed him. Laozi replies, "The Six Classics are but the old traces of former kings, how can they be the means whereby they leave their traces! Now your words are like traces. For traces are made by shoes, yet how can traces be shoes!" In "Tian Zifang," Confucius declares himself no better than "a midge floating in a wine jar" when it comes to understanding the

Way after listening to Laozi's exposition of Daoist transcendence. Although Sima Qian takes up the story of the meeting of Confucius and Laozi from *Zhuangzi*, he does not follow its presentation of Confucius's befuddlement and self-abnegation or its denigration of Confucian virtues.

Laozi's recommendation of "having no thought of oneself" echoes Confucius's abjuration of arbitrary willfulness, dogmatism, intransigence, and egoism (*Analects* 9.4, 1.57) and can even be interpreted as selfless devotion to one's parents and ruler. The ethical imperative of transcending egoism is concurrently the practical imperative of survival, a recurrent theme in Warring States and Han writings, and will be brought up in 1.57. In *The Garden of Eloquence (Shuoyuan)*, compiled by Liu Xiang (79–78 BCE), and *Sayings*, Confucius encounters during his visit to Zhou a bronze statue whose mouth is sealed three ways. On its back is an inscription urging caution and self-preservation reminiscent of Laozi's speech (*SY* 10.25, *KZJY* 11.158–59). Laozi's advice also reminds us of this story about Confucius from *Xunzi* (see also *HSWZ* 3.165, *HNZ* 12.417, *SY* 10.4, *KZJY* 9.121):

1.6b Confucius looked over the temple of Lord Huan of Lu and saw that there was a leaning vessel. Confucius asked the temple guardian: "What vessel is this?" The temple guardian said, "This is the vessel to be kept on the right of the ruler's seat." Confucius said, "I have heard that for the vessel kept on the right of the ruler's seat, it leans on one side when empty, rights itself when half filled, and overturns when it is full." Confucius looked at his disciples and said, "Fill it with water." The disciples ladled water and filled the vessel. When the vessel was half filled, it righted itself; when it was full, it overturned; when emptied, it leaned on one side. Confucius heaved a sigh, "Alas, how is it possible that what is full would not overturn!" Zilu said, "May I ask whether there is a way to hold on to fullness?" Confucius said, "For the acuity of sagely wisdom, guard it with foolishness. For achievement that overspread all under heaven, guard it with pliancy. For valorous strength that touches the whole world, guard it with timidity. For wealth encompassing the four seas, guard it with humility. This is called the way of diminishing what is being filled up." (*XZ* 28.389)

In a similar vein, in *Huainanzi* (submitted to the throne in 139 BCE) Confucius describes himself as being "benevolent yet ruthless, eloquent yet inarticulate, brave yet timid" when asked why his disciples Yan Hui,

Zigong, and Zilu submit to him if, according to Confucius, they are superior in benevolence, eloquence, and bravery (*HNZ* 18.616).[35] In *Record of
Ritual*, Confucius discusses "music without sounds," "ritual without forms,"
and "funerals without mourning clothes" (*LJ* 3: 1276; see also *KJY* 3: 920-
21; *SY* 19.31; *KZJY* 15.223, 27.379). In other words, common concerns with
overcoming egoism and transcending opposites crop up over a wide range
of texts later classified as belonging to different "schools."

1.7 At that time, Lord Ping of Jin was licentious, and the six ministers of
Jin who had full control of the government launched an eastward expedition against other lords. King Ling of Chu, with his military strength, tyran-
nized over the central states. Qi, with extensive territories, was powerful
and close to Lu. Lu was small and weak. If it attached itself to Chu, it
would anger Jin. If it attached itself to Jin, Chu would attack it. It did not
prepare for Qi aggression, and the Qi army invaded Lu.

  In the twentieth year of the reign of Lord Zhao of Lu [522 BCE], Confucius was thirty.[36] Lord Jing of Qi and Yan Ying came to visit Lu. Lord
Jing asked Confucius, "Formerly Lord Mu of Qin ruled over a small state
tucked away in a remote place. How did he come to attain hegemony?"
Confucius responded, "Although the state of Qin was small, its ambitions
were great. Situated in a remote place, its conduct was yet correct and
proper. Lord Mu personally promoted the High Officer of Five Sheep Pelts
[Baili Xi], conferred on him the title of high officer, raised him from the
coils of incarceration, talked to him for three days, and gave him the reins of
government. Judging from this, he could even have become a king, for him
to have become a hegemon was but a minor matter." Lord Jing was pleased.

[translator's note]
Recognizing worth is the key to political power. A minister in the small
state of Yu, Baili Xi (seventh century BCE) becomes a captive in Jin when
Jin annexes Yu. Sent to Qin as part of the retinue of the Jin bride marrying
Lord Mu of Qin (r. 659–621 BCE), he flees to Chu, where he is captured.
Lord Mu redeems Baili Xi, by then seventy, with five black sheep pelts,
talks to him for three days, and gives him the reins of government, honoring him as the High Officer of Five Sheep Pelts (*SJ* 5.21–22). In variations
of this story, Baili Xi sells himself for five black sheep pelts and/or becomes
a cattle breeder to attract Lord Mu's attention.[37] The Yu ruler fails to use
Baili Xi and Yu perishes; Lord Mu recognizes his talents and becomes a

hegemon. The discussion of the moral and political expectations of king-ship (*wang* 王) as distinct from hegemony (*ba* 霸) recurs in Warring States texts, notably the *Analects, Mencius, Xunzi*, and *Han Feizi*. Baili Xi is featured in many Warring States and Han anecdotes and speeches about the imperative for a ruler to recognize a man's worth even in unlikely scenarios (see *SJ* 83, 87, 92). The theme of recognition and its political implications reverberates in early Chinese writings[38] and also underlies Sima Qian's account of Confucius.

The summary of interstate relations and balance of power here seems almost a non sequitur.[39] Nagai Rikan (1732–1817) suspected that misplaced bamboo strips were responsible for interrupting the narrative sequence (*SJ* 47.15). There are also factual errors. According to *Zuo Tradition*, after the negotiations for the cessation of conflicts in 546 BCE (Xiang 27), Jin and Chu maintained an uneasy truce and there was no record of Chu or Qi aggression against Lu. Lord Ping of Jin (r. 558–532 BCE) and King Ling of Chu (r. 541–529 BCE) died about a decade before the next date mentioned (Zhao 520 or 522 BCE) (see Liang Yusheng's comment, *SJ* 47.15).

According to *Zuo Tradition*, Lord Jing of Qi (r. 547–490 BCE) hunted at Pei (in Lu) in 522 BCE (*Zuo* Zhao 20.7, 3: 1584–85). This record might have given rise to stories about the Qi ruler and Yan Ying using the opportunity of the hunt to visit the Lu court and ask questions about rituals (*SJ* 14.136, 32.47, 33.44). It is not clear why Confucius is now prominent enough to have an audience with the visiting Qi ruler.

1.8 When Confucius was thirty-five, Ji Pingzi and Hou Zhaobo, on account of a cockfight, was found guilty by Lord Zhao of Lu. Lord Zhao led troops to strike Pingzi. Pingzi combined his forces with those of the Meng and Shusun lineages, and the three lineages together attacked Lord Zhao. Lord Zhao's troops were defeated, and he fled to Qi. Qi placed Lord Zhao in Ganhou. Not long after, Lu was plunged into chaos. Confucius went to Qi and became Gao Zhaozi's retainer, hoping thereby to gain access to Lord Jing of Qi. He spoke with the Qi grand music master about music, heard the notes of Shao, studied it, and for three months no longer knew the taste of meat. The men of Qi praised him.

[translator's note]
Confucius's sublime musical experience in Qi follows a political crisis in Lu that results in its ruler's expulsion. The cockfight incident, dated to 517

BCE, exemplifies the minor incident stoking deeper conflicts. According to *Zuo Tradition*, "the Ji and Hou lineages held cockfights. When the Ji lineage put armor on their cocks, the Hou lineage made spurs for theirs. Angered by this, Ji Pingzi increased the number of his palaces at the expense of the Hou lineage and further rebuked them. Hou Zhaobo therefore bore a grudge against Ji Pingzi" (*Zuo* Zhao 25.6, 3: 1642–43).[40] Hou Zhaobo, instead of being blamed by Lord Zhao as noted above (1.8), sides with the latter in attacking Ji Pingzi. After some initial hesitation, the Meng and Shusun lineages join the Ji lineage to fight Lord Zhao, who is defeated and leaves Lu with his supporters from the Hou, Zang, and Zijia lineages. From 517 BCE till his death in 510 BCE (*Zuo* Zhao 32.4, 3: 1722–25), Lord Zhao lives in exile, seeking to secure Qi and Jin assistance for his reinstatement without success. In 516 BCE, Qi takes Yun from Lu and puts Lord Zhao there—not in Ganhou, as told above.[41] Two years later, Lord Zhao moves to Ganhou (in Jin) and eventually dies there.

The de facto expulsion of the Lu ruler, Lord Zhao, was a major crisis in Lu history. How did Confucius view these developments? Did he go to Qi because Lord Zhao fled to Qi? Should Confucius have commented on the crisis? In any case, he is silent here. As mentioned earlier, Confucius condemns the Ji lineage for its ritual transgressions and greed (*Analects* 3.1, 3.2, 3.6, 11.17). He also criticizes Lord Zhao of Lu for his ritual violation in marrying a woman with the same clan name (*Analects* 7.31). In *Zuo Tradition*, Confucius is less strident in his disparagement of the Ji lineage, and implicit criticism is sometimes linked to evasiveness and gestures of ritual accommodation (*Zuo* Ai 11.7, 12.2, 3: 1904–07).

Whereas the earlier exchange between Confucius and Lord Jing of Qi implies the latter's deference (1.7), in this passage (1.8) Confucius gains access to Lord Jing only through intermediaries. The contradiction is one of the reasons why Cui Shu and Liang Yusheng find the account questionable. Gao Zhaozi is a morally dubious character who will later humiliate Lord Zhao of Lu (*Zuo* Zhao 29.1, 3: 1694–95, *SJ* 47.48) and invade Lu (*Zuo* Ding 8.6, 3: 1780–81). In line with other passages signaling the necessity of accommodation (see 1.3, 1.20), Sima Qian gives credence to the idea of Confucius seeking to become Gao Zhaozi's retainer, although he paints an unflattering picture of Gao Zhaozi elsewhere (*SJ* 32.51–53, 46.7–8).

The parallel passage in the *Analects* (7.14) about Confucius's enjoyment of music does not date it or connect it to the process of studying music: "The Master was in Qi and heard Shao music. For three months he did not know the taste of meat, saying, 'I did not know that music could be like this!' " The Neo-Confucian thinker Cheng Yi views such obsession with music as aesthetic excess (*LY* 2: 589). Here enthusiasm for musical education takes the place of aesthetic absorption and perhaps tones down the excess. The juxtaposition of Confucius's sublime absorption in studying music with his ambiguous political choices (his silence on the expulsion of Lord Zhao of Lu and his maneuvers in Qi) can seem incongruous. At the same time, a deliberate musical education or transcendent musical experience can be seen as a response to the pressure of the historical moment.

The complex implications of supplying a historical context for the *Analects* passage (7.14) become apparent when we contrast Sima Qian's account with the explicit moralization in *The Garden of Eloquence*:

> 1.8a Confucius reached the area outside the outer city wall of Qi, encountered a child carrying a jug, and walked with him. The child's gaze was acute, his mind was upright, and his conduct was proper. Confucius said to his driver, "Let's drive faster! Let's drive faster! Shao music is about to begin." Confucius arrived and listened to Shao music, and for three months he did not know the taste of meat. Hence, not only does music bring joy to oneself; it brings joy to others. Not only does it rectify oneself; it rectifies others. He found joy in this music, not expecting that music could be like this. (*SY* 19.35)

The child distills history and politics out of the anecdote and focuses attention on music's power of moral transformation.

Commentators often fuse Confucius's aesthetic appreciation with moral approbation of the music as the embodiment of political ideals (for example, Zhu Xi's comment, *LY* 2: 592). Shao music is associated with the sage king Shun and is pronounced to be "like heaven, which leaves nothing uncovered; like earth, which leaves nothing uncradled" (*Zuo* Xiang 29.13, 2: 1246–47), "the fullest realization of beauty and of goodness" (*Analects* 3.25).[42] The theme of music will come up again (see 1.19a, 1.30, 1.31, 1.32, 1.41, 1.45d, 1.45e, 1.53, 1.54, 1.61).

1.9 Lord Jing of Qi asked Confucius about government. Confucius said, "Let the ruler be the ruler; the subject, the subject; the father, the father; the son, the son." Lord Jing said, "Well said! Indeed, if the ruler is no ruler; the subject, no subject; the father, no father; the son, no son, then even if there are grains, how can I get to eat them!" On another day, he again asked Confucius about government. Confucius said, "Government depends on regulating the uses of wealth." Lord Jing was pleased and wanted to turn the fields of Nixi[43] into a fief for Confucius.

Yan Ying came forward and said: "Experts in traditional rites and music confound categories with their glib rhetoric and cannot be held to account by rules and laws. Arrogant, conceited, and self-satisfied, they cannot manage those in inferior positions. Elevating funeral rites as the way to fully express grief, they exhaust everything they own for lavish burials: this cannot be encouraged as a custom. As wandering persuaders, they beg for financial gains: this cannot be the way to govern. Ever since the abeyance of great sages, the Zhou house has been in decline, and there are gaps and flaws in ritual and music. Now Confucius magnifies the importance of deportment and regalia, complicates the ritual of going up and down steps as well as the regulations for rapid and slow movements, so much so that even generations cannot fully grasp the extent of his learning and people in this era cannot plumb the depths of his rituals.[44] If you, my lord, want to use him to change the mores of Qi, it is not the way to advance the well-being of ordinary people."

Later, Lord Jing respectfully received Confucius but did not ask about his idea of ritual. On another day, Lord Jing stopped Confucius with these words: "I am not capable of serving you, sir, as if you were the Ji lineage head." He treated him as someone between the position of the Ji and that of the Meng lineage heads. The high officers of Qi wanted to harm Confucius, and Confucius heard about it. Lord Jing said, "I am already old, I am not capable of putting your ideas into practice." Confucius thus left and returned to Lu.

[translator's note]
The debate between the Confucian and the Mohist positions on government is dramatized through the power struggle between Confucius and the Qi minister Yan Ying as they compete to gain sway over the Qi ruler. Confucius's affirmation of the normative fulfillment of roles as the foundation of good government, found also in the *Analects* (12.11), is often cited as an example of "the rectification of names" (*zhengming* 正名), which will be brought up in 1.49.[45] Lord Jing's ready acquiescence is belied by his political failings: the Qi ruling house is losing ground to the Chen lineage and Lord Jing is often criticized for his extravagance and malfeasance in

anecdotes in *Zuo Tradition* and *Master Yan's Annals* (*Yanzi chunqiu*, collated by Liu Xiang based on materials dated ca. fourth–third century BCE).

In the *Analects* (1.5), Confucius links "regulating the uses of resources" (*jieyong* 節用) to "cherishing others" (*airen* 愛人) and "putting the people to work at proper times." Elsewhere Confucius credits the legendary rulers of high antiquity with such regulation (*DDLJ* 2: 690, 709; *KZJY* 23.333). He also praises frugality (*jian* 儉) (*Analects* 3.4, 7.36, 9.3). In *Han Feizi*, Confucius explains that Lord Jing of Qi's extravagance prompts him to advise frugality (see also *SY* 7.20, *KZJY* 14.202), but there Confucius is criticized for advocating improper restraints on rulers (*HFZ* 38.904–07). By placing Confucius's counsel on frugality *before* Yan Ying's accusation of wastefulness, Sima Qian preemptively neutralizes the latter as unjust.

Yan Ying's disparagement of Confucius echoes the Mohist critique of complex and expensive Confucian rituals. Versions of this passage are found in *Mozi* (*MZ* 39.271–74) and *Master Yan's Annals* (*YZCQ* 8.491–92). In *The Garden of Eloquence*, Mozi sees Yan Ying as a kindred spirit (*SY* 20.5). Since Yan Ying is the hero in *Master Yan's Annals*, it is not surprising that Confucius should be cast either as his appreciative admirer (as in the eight examples in the Inner Chapters) or obtuse critic (as in the three examples in the Outer Chapters, where Confucius suspects Yan Ying of moral compromise in his long career of serving three problematic Qi rulers). The passage above represents the most severe castigation of Confucius in *Master Yan's Annals*. Compared to the analogous accounts in *Mozi* and *Master Yan's Annals*, 1.9 adds the charge of "glib rhetoric" (*huaji* or *guji* 滑稽), a term also used for jesters, referring to rhetorical prowess that defies rules and categorical distinctions. This, together with the related accusation that experts in traditional rites and music are like "wandering persuaders begging for financial gains," seem to belong to a late Warring States discourse on the power and pitfalls of rhetoric and come across as anachronistic (*CDB* 274–75).

Note that in *Zuo Tradition* (Zhao 26.11, 3: 1670–71), Yan Ying speaks grandly about the power of rituals and the fulfillment of social roles in a tone similar to Confucius in 1.9. Instead of implicit rivalry, Confucius and Yan Ying express mutual admiration and approbation in other Confucian texts despite intermittent criticism of Yan Ying's excessive frugality (*LJ* 3: 1113, *KZJY* 42.595). In the *Analects* (5.17), Confucius praises Yan Ying as one "excelling in social interactions with people, who maintained their respect for him with the passage of time." In Sima Qian's chapter on the disciples of

Confucius, Confucius is said to honor Yan Ying as a teacher (*SJ* 67.3). In *Sayings*, Confucius commends Yan Ying's loyalty, judgment, and reverence (*KZJY* 14.209, 15.237). In *Kong Anthology*, Yan Ying seeks Confucius's help and advice on how to deal with the treacherous political situation in Qi (*KCZ* 1.3). By contrast, Yan Ying is cast as antagonist in 1.9 to dramatize the Confucian-Mohist divide on the conception of government.

The final exchange between Lord Jing and Confucius in 1.9 also appears in the *Analects* (18.3). Although the Meng lineage was not as powerful as the Ji lineage, it was also highly honored in Lu. Confucius is thus promised a position of honor, but Lord Jing's conclusion that he is "already old" and cannot put Confucius's ideas into practice (literally, "cannot use him") prompts him to leave Qi for Lu.[46] Sima Qian thus juxtaposes two exchanges of Confucius with Lord Jing of Qi, with the latter moving from apparent acquiescence to suspicion and distance, by bringing in Yan Ying's critique as the explanation for Lord Jing's change of heart. Jealous rivals blocking Confucius's advancement is a recurrent trope (see 1.36, 1.41, 1.46).

Confucius's sojourn in Qi is the beginning of prolonged peregrinations. In his preface to the "Chronological Table of the Twelve Lords' Reigns," Sima Qian claims that Confucius "sought audience with more than seventy rulers" but failed to see his ideas implemented (*SJ* 14.6). *Zhuangzi* and *Mr. Lü's Annals* give the number as seventy-two and eighty respectively (*ZZ* 14.531; *LSCQ* 2: 822). Stories of Confucius's extensive travels must have developed in tandem with Warring States traditions of the peripatetic persuader seeking patronage and implementation of his ideas.

1.10 When Confucius was forty-two years old, Lord Zhao of Lu died at Ganhou [510 BCE]. Lord Ding was instated as ruler. In the summer of the fifth year of Lord Ding's reign [505 BCE], Ji Pingzi died, and Huanzi succeeded him.[47] Ji Huanzi was drilling a well when he found an earthen basin, with something like a sheep inside. He asked Confucius about this, saying that he "got a dog." Confucius said, "From what I heard, it was a sheep. I have heard: the anomalies of vegetation and rocks are the one-legged *kui* and the mountain spirit *wangliang*, the anomalies of waters are dragons and the water spirit *wangxiang*, the anomaly of earth is the entombed sheep."[48]

Wu attacked Yue. When Kuaiji fell [494 BCE], Wu obtained a section of a bone that filled a carriage. Wu sent its envoy to ask Confucius: "Which among bones are the largest?" Confucius said, "When Yu brought the myriad spirits to Kuaiji Mountain,[49] the head of the Fangfeng lineage was late in arriving. Yu killed him and exposed his corpse. A section of one of his bones filled a carriage. This was big indeed." The Wu envoy asked, "Who were the spirits?" Confucius said, "The spirits of mountains and rivers have enough sway to establish principles of order for all under heaven; their guardians are these spirits. Altars of earth and grain are the province of lords and princes. All of them belong to the rulers." The envoy said, "What was guarded by the Fangfeng lineage?" Confucius said, "The rulers of the Wangwang lineage guarded the Feng and Yu mountains; their clan name was Xi. During the Yu, Xia, and Shang dynasties, the guardians were the Wangwang. During the Zhou, they were the Chang Di.[50] Now we call them giants." The envoy asked, "What is the range of human stature?" Confucius replied, "The Jiaojiao lineage measures three *chi*, they are the shortest. The tallest ones cannot be more than ten times that height. That is as far as the numbers would go." At that point the envoy said, "Excellent indeed is the sage!"[51]

[translator's note]
Sima Qian disregards chronological sequence here in order to group together two instances (dated 510 BCE and 494 BCE) of Confucius's knowledge of anomalous things. They are found, with small variations, in *Discourses of the States* (*Guoyu*, ca. fourth century BCE) (GY "Luyu" 2.9, 201; 2.18, 213), where they are followed by an anecdote on an ancient arrow (dated 494 BCE) that will appear in 1.24. They explicitly violate the observation that the Master does not speak about "anomalies, mere feats of strength, violation of norms, and the spirits" (*Analects* 7.21),[52] a line quoted later in this chapter (1.62). These anecdotes suggest that the disclaimer in the *Analects* may be a rebuttal of traditions exalting Confucius as the sage mastering esoteric knowledge.

Here esoteric knowledge plays a role in the implicit negotiation of power balance between Confucius and his interlocutor. Thus, the newly ascendant minister Ji Huanzi, whose father drove out the Lu ruler Lord Zhao (1.8), misleads Confucius about his find to test the latter's knowledge. In the second anecdote, Wu, freshly ascendant because of its victory over Yue, is exerting pressure on Lu for concessions. Twenty years later, it will make extravagant demands on Lu (1.48). Perhaps Confucius's display of his knowledge is also a way to assert Lu cultural superiority.

Commanding "broad knowledge of things" (*bowu* 博物) means the ability to categorize and historicize. It is thus not enough that Confucius should know that an "entombed sheep" could be found in the process of digging a well, he would have to list different kinds of anomalies aligned with different elements in nature. Likewise, he does not simply identify the gigantic bone as that of a leader from the Fangfeng lineage, he offers information on the lore of the Fangfeng lineage since high antiquity: the sage king Yu's punishment of the Fangfeng lineage head, its connection with various geographical markers, and its changing names in different periods. The Wu envoy's concluding exclamation (not found in *Discourses of the States*) implies that one way of understanding sagehood in the Warring States and the Han involves comprehensive knowledge of what we would call the supernatural. Apocryphal and omenological texts (*chen wei* 讖緯, *weishu* 緯書) support this understanding of sagehood. Later traditions of fantastic stories, such as Zhang Hua's *Record of Broad Knowledge of Things* and Ren Fang's (460–508) *Telling of the Strange* (*Shuyi ji* 述異記), repeat the story of the Fangfeng lineage, while the story about the sheep in the well also finds its way into Gan Bao's *In Search of the Supernatural* (*Soushen ji* 搜神記).

Credulity and skepticism are often intertwined. We recall that Zichan (d. 522 BCE), a Zheng minister remembered among other things for his stern refusal to sacrifice to battling dragons in the river (*Zuo* Zhao 19.10, 3:1566–67) and his stout declaration that "the way of heaven is far away; the way of humans is near at hand" (*Zuo* Zhao 18.3, 3: 1552–53), also authoritatively explains the political and moral meanings of a Jin ruler's dream of a tawny bear, and is praised as "a noble man with broad knowledge of things" on the basis of his dream interpretation (*Zuo* Zhao 7.7, 3: 1422–23). The line between what may be classified as rational (or even scientific) knowledge and mastery of esoteric lore is fluid. In *Zuo Tradition*, the Lu minister Ji Kangzi asks Confucius about locusts in 483 BCE. Confucius replied, "I have heard that only after the Fire Star has set are all the dormant insects in place. Now the Fire Star is still moving to the west: the supervisor of the calendar has made a mistake" (*Zuo* Ai 12.5, 3: 1910–11). That insects are still active and the Fire Star (Antares) can still be seen above the western horizon at evening signifies to Confucius that it cannot yet truly be the twelfth lunar month of the year (which often falls in January in the Gregorian calendar; Antares is visible above the Western horizon at dusk only through late November); he believes that the supervisor of the calendar should have added an intercalary month in the previous year, so that the month in which there are locusts should be reckoned the eleventh month rather than the twelfth.

Perhaps such stories about Confucius's entomological and calendrical knowledge can easily branch into accounts of his esoteric and prophetic knowledge. In *Sayings*, the story about locusts is found in the chapter "Discerning Things" (Bianwu 辨物), which also includes the stories about the sheep in the well and the gigantic bone, as well as stories about Confucius's ritual assessment, moral judgment, and political prescience (see 1.35a), thus implying a continuum between these categories of knowledge that seem distinct and separate to the modern reader (*KZJY* 16.242–60). When Xunzi observes that "the great men of learning" (*daru* 大儒) bring up the appropriate categories and respond without doubts and confusion" to "strange things and aberrant transformations, hitherto unheard of and unseen, suddenly arising in one corner" (*XZ* 8.91), he can be referring to human situations or what we classify as anomalies. Confucius's "broad learning" (*boxue* 博學) can encompass different kinds of knowledge (see 1.35, 1.42, 1.62).

The principle behind such a continuum is articulated in the chapter "Discerning Things" in *The Garden of Eloquence*:

> 1.10a Yan Hui asked Confucius, "What are the actions of a fully developed person like?" The Master said, "The actions of a fully developed person realize to the greatest extent his essential nature and plumb the depths of the transformations of categories of things. He understands the workings of the realms of darkness and light and observes the source of the moving breaths of vital energy. If he is like this, he can be called a fully developed person. Having understood the Way of Heaven, he realizes the highest good and proper duty in his actions and adorns his person with ritual and music. The highest good and proper duty, ritual and music: these constitute the actions of a fully developed person. To completely grasp the workings of spirits and understand the processes of transformation: that is the flourishing of virtue."[53] (*SY* 18.1; see also *KZJY* 18.276)

Following this logic, that chapter contains the story about the sheep from the well (*SY* 18.20), Confucius's correct interpretation of a juvenile ditty, omens and portents (*SY* 18.21), and his explanation of the moral and ritual implications of speculating on the sentience of the dead (*SY* 18.31). Confucius justifies prognostication by stalks and turtle shells in *Balanced Discourses*

(*LH* 24.998–99) and his prophetic power is elaborated in many stories (*LH* 45.666; *KZJY* 38.510; *ZY* 920, 921). In one sixth century story, the First Emperor of Qin wants to dig up Confucius's grave, only to encounter a ditty left behind by Confucius foretelling the emperor's doom (*ZY* 920). An early Qing anecdote tells of Confucius stepping down from his pedestal in a Confucius temple in 1641, bewailing the impending fall of the Ming dynasty with tears of blood.[54]

1.11 Ji Huanzi had a favored retainer named Zhongliang Huai who was at loggerheads with Yang Hu. Yang Hu wanted to drive Huai away. Gongshan Buniu stopped him. That autumn [505 BCE], Huai became even more arrogant, and Yang Hu seized Huai. Ji Huanzi was furious. Yang Hu thus held Huanzi captive and released him only after swearing a covenant with him. Yang Hu, on account of this, became even more disdainful toward the Ji lineage. The Ji lineage for its part encroached on the prerogatives of the ruling house. Retainers of high officers held the reins of government. Thus it was that Lu, from high officers all the way down, transgressed and departed from the correct way. That was why Confucius did not serve in government, withdrew, and rectified the traditions of the *Odes*, *Documents*, *Ritual*, and *Music*. His disciples became ever more numerous. They came from afar, and without exception studied with him and learned from him.

[translator's note]
In the power struggles between lineage heads and their retainers, the lord's ruling house (*gongshi* 公室) is often brought in as the triangulating factor— that is, a rebellious retainer may claim to be restoring the ruler's power by weakening the ministerial lineage. Such is the rationale espoused by the retainer Nan Kuai when he rebels against the Ji lineage in *Zuo Tradition* (530–529 BCE) (*Zuo* Zhao 12.10, 13.1, 3: 1 476–81, 1486–87). In *Historical Records*, Zhongliang Huai is Ji Huanzi's favorite and the cause of the latter's conflict with Yang Hu and Gongshan Buniu. In *Zuo Tradition*, Zhongliang Huai opposes the Ji lineage's transgressive ambitions by claiming to be defending the prerogatives of the Lu ruling house (505 BCE) (*Zuo* Ding 5.4, 3: 1762–63). Sima Qian does not explicitly address this triangulation in *Historical Records*, neither through Confucius nor through other characters, but the broader question of whether rebellion or rejection of one's

designated role can serve a higher moral imperative does come up later in the text (1.12, 1.29), as it does in the *Analects* (17.5, 17.7).

The devolution of power described in 1.11 echoes the *Analects* (16.2):

> 1.11a When the Way prevails under heaven, decisions on ritual, music, punitive expeditions, and military attacks come from the Son of Heaven; when the Way does not prevail under heaven, decisions on ritual, music, punitive expeditions, and military attacks come from the lords. When they come from the lords, rare it would be that their authority is not lost over ten generations. When they come from the high officers, rare it would be that their authority is not lost over five generations. When the ministers' retainers control state affairs, rare it would be that their authority is not lost over three generations. When the Way prevails under heaven, high officers do not control the government. When the Way prevails under heaven, commoners do not debate policies.

According to this model, the lower power devolves, the less firm and legitimate its foundation. Confronted with political disorder, Confucius turns to education and the preservation and transmission of textual traditions, which will be described in greater detail toward the end of this chapter (1.52–1.56).

1.12 In the eighth year of Lord Ding's reign [502 BCE], Gongshan Buniu, failing to achieve his aims under the Ji lineage, went along with Yang Hu to foment rebellion. He wanted to oust the legitimate heirs of the three Huan lineages and replace them with the sons born to the lineage heads' concubines—men who had always been on good terms with Yang Hu.[55] He thus seized Ji Huanzi, who managed to escape through subterfuge. In the ninth year of Lord Ding's reign [501 BCE], Yang Hu was defeated and fled to Qi. At that time Confucius was fifty years old. Gongshan Buniu used Bi as a base to rebel against the Ji lineage and sent someone to summon Confucius. Confucius, evermore following the Way, was filled with ideas and aspirations,[56] but had no wherewithal to put his talents to the test and was not able to find one who could use him. He said, "King Wen and King Wu started their enterprises at Feng and Hao and became kings. Now although Bi is small, perhaps it can come close to that?" He wished to go. Zilu was not pleased and stopped Confucius. Confucius said, "Could he have summoned me in vain? If he could make use of me, it would be possible to create another Zhou in the east!"[57] However, even so, in the end he did not go.

[translator's note]
Does the goal of achieving ideal governance justify rebellion? In the above passage as well as in 1.29, Confucius is tempted to join the causes of rebels. *Zuo Tradition* names Gongshan Buniu as one of the disaffected retainers who join Yang Hu in an attempted coup in 500 BCE (*Zuo Ding* 10.8, 3: 1784–85), but there is no mention of Gongshan summoning Confucius. Sima Qian's dating of the rebellion to 502 BCE may be a deliberate attempt to dissociate it from the revolt provoked by the decision, championed by Confucius, to reduce the ministerial lineages' city walls in 497 BCE (1.15).[58] The analogue for the above passage is found in the *Analects* (17.4), where Gongshan Buniu is called Gongshan Furao:

> 1.12a Gongshan Furao used Bi as a base to rebel. Confucius was summoned. The Master wanted to go. Zilu was not pleased and said, "If there is no place where we can go, so be it. Why must we go to the Gongshan lineage?" The Master said, "Could he who summoned me have done so in vain? If there is one who can use me, I may be able to create another Zhou in the east!"

This episode has sparked heated controversy (*LY* 4: 1533–44), especially among late imperial commentators. Some reject its historicity, citing the impossibility that Confucius should support a rebel, others maintain that the unmarked subject of "summon" is Ji Huanzi, who is asking Confucius to help him quell Gongshan's rebellion. Some read the subject of "use" as indefinite ("if someone can use me"). Perhaps Confucius wishes to side with the rebellious retainer against the Ji lineage in order to restore power to the Lu ruling house, reprising the triangulation mentioned earlier.[59] Zhai Hao (1736–1788) exemplifies the imperial insistence on aligning Confucius with legitimate political authority: "When the Master said, 'how could it be *in vain* (tu 徒)," he is saying: *not merely* (tu 徒) would I suppress Furao—if someone could use me, then I would help the Zhou house extend and illuminate the great principle behind the hierarchy of ruler and subject, those above and those below. Even the likes of the Ji lineage would be brought to book" (*LY* 4: 1540).

Not only does Sima Qian disambiguate the subject of "summon" and "use," but he also lets Confucius explicitly articulate the logic that Bi, the power base of local rebels, could, with the right moral guidance, become the next Zhou dynasty. Zhu Xi, without acknowledging the option of Bi becoming the "new Zhou," implies the justification of expediency in an authoritative interpretation of the analogous *Analects* passage (17.5), quoting Cheng Yi: "From the sage's perspective, there is no one under heaven who is incapable of achieving good, and there is also no one who is incapable of correcting his errors, that is why he wants to go. However, he ultimately does not go because he realizes that Gongshan would certainly not be capable of correcting his errors." In other words, at fifty, when Confucius is supposed to "know the will of heaven" (*Analects* 2.4), frustrations drive him to consider even the rebel Gongshan as a viable vehicle for achieving laudable political goals.[60] Wang Fuzhi (1619–1692) also justifies the defiance of norms in supporting a rebel, "What Zilu knows and is familiar with are the distinctions between lords and high officers and how each has separate duties, but what Confucius is intent on is the glorious governance when ritual and music, punitive expeditions and military attacks can be unified."[61]

The following passage, included in the chapter "Supreme Public Good" (Zhigong 至公) in *The Garden of Eloquence* (*SY* 14.10), dispenses with the question of implementing ideals through compromise by dissolving the supposed historical context of Confucius's statement.

1.12b Confucius lived during an age of disorder which could not accommodate him. . . . The land within the seas did not receive the mantle of his transformative power, and myriad living creatures could not be covered by his beneficence. That was why Confucius sighed deeply and said, "If there is one who can use me, then perhaps I can create Zhou in the east?" Thus, when Confucius tried to implement his teachings, it was not because he wanted to, through his own person, move the spirit of virtue in one city; instead, he intended to unfurl it all under heaven and establish it among myriad creatures.

1.13 Later, Lord Ding appointed Confucius as the steward of Zhongdu. In one year, people from four directions all upheld him as exemplary.

From being the steward of Zhongdu, he became the supervisor of works. From being the supervisor of works, he became the great supervisor of corrections.

[translator's note]
How did Confucius govern? Scholars debate the nature, dating, and plausibility of Confucius's appointments listed here. *Record of Rituals* credits Confucius with institutionalizing the "four-inch-thick inner coffin" and the "five-inch-thick outer coffin" as steward of Zhongdu (*LJ* 1: 217), although steward is a relatively humble position and Zhongdu (central capital) in Lu is not mentioned elsewhere. (Alternatively, *zhongdu* can be understood as "middle-sized city.")[62] No extant sources mention Confucius's stint as supervisor of works. Xunzi claims that the mere expectation that Confucius would become the supervisor of corrections is enough to rectify mores: dishonest merchants no longer dare to cheat, an adulterous wife is sent away, a notoriously extravagant man leaves the domain (*XZ* 8.77).

According to *Zuo Tradition*, Confucius as supervisor of corrections tacitly defends the rights of the Lu ruling house. As mentioned earlier, Lord Zhao of Lu dies in exile as a result of the power struggle between him and the Ji lineage (1.10). Ji Pingzi demeans Lord Zhao by creating a partial separation of his tomb from those of his ancestors by interring him south of the tomb road, although tombs of rulers should be located to the north of the road. Confucius "had a ditch dug to join Lord Zhao's tomb with the other tombs" (*Zuo* Ding 1.4, 3: 1736–37). Note that the gesture is more about amelioration of the situation than active opposition. This episode turns into Confucius's direct admonition of Ji Huanzi and is assimilated, along with the reference to coffins in *Record of Rituals*, into a triumphalist and hagiographic account of Confucius's official career in *Sayings*:

1.13a When Confucius first served in government, he was the steward of Zhongdu. He instituted the regulations for nourishing the living and sending off the dead. As a result, the old and the young ate different food; the strong and the weak bore different responsibilities; men and women went on separate paths; none picked up lost items left on the road; vessels presented no false appearance through decorations. He set rules for four-inch-thick inner coffins and five-inch-thick outer coffins, had graves made alongside low hills and mounds, and did not have earth piled or trees grown to mark the graves. After all these had been done for a year, the lords of the west upheld these practices as examples to be followed.[63] Lord Ding said to Confucius, "How about it if we are to follow you, sir, in using this method to govern Lu?" Confucius responded, "Even governing the whole world would become possible, how can this merely pertain to Lu!" Then in the second year, Lord Ding appointed him as supervisor of works, and he thus made distinctions between the nature of five earthen elements.[64] Each category of things obtained what was optimal for its flourishing, and everything gained its rightful place. Sometime earlier, the Ji lineage buried Lord Zhao south of the tomb road. Confucius dug a ditch to join Lord Zhao's grave with those of the other Lu lords. He said to Ji Huanzi: "To demean the ruler and thereby manifest one's offense contravenes ritual propriety. I have now joined the graves to cover up your violation of duty as a subject, sir." From being supervisor of works, he became the great supervisor of corrections. He set up laws but did not need to use them. There were no miscreants among the people. (*KZJY* 1.1–4)

1.14 In the spring of the tenth year of Lord Ding of Lu (500 BCE), Lu and Qi reached an accord. In the summer, the Qi high officer Liju said to Lord Jing of Qi, "Lu has employed Confucius. Lu's momentum will threaten Qi." Qi thus sent an envoy notifying Lu of the arrangement for a meeting of concord that would take place at Jiagu. Lord Ding of Lu intended to attend the meeting in carriages in the spirit of amity.[65] Confucius, acting as the lord's assistant, said to him, "I have heard that civil affairs must involve military preparation, and that military affairs must involve civil preparation. In ancient times, when lords leave their states, they were certain to include officials in their retinue. I request that the left and right supervisors of the military be included." Lord Ding said, "Agreed," and included the left and right supervisors of the military in his retinue.

The Lu delegation met the Qi lord at Jiagu. They set up an altar with three levels of earthen steps. The two rulers met according to the ritual proper for such meetings, bowing and yielding to each other as they ascended. When the ritual of ceremonial toasts had been completed, the presiding Qi functionary hastened forward with small steps[66] and said, "I beg leave to have the music from four directions performed." Lord Jing said, "Agreed." At that point, banners and standards, feathered staffs and dancers' poles, spears and lances, swords and shields descended on the scene in great clamor with the drums rolling. Confucius hastened forward. Having ascended the steps one after another, he stopped at the penultimate level of the altar, raised his sleeves and said, "Our two rulers are meeting in amity, what use is there for the music of Yi and Di barbarians here! I request the functionary to issue his command!" The functionary dismissed them, but they did not leave. Confucius then turned right and left to look steadily at Yan Ying and Lord Jing. Lord Jing was ashamed and waved them away.

A few moments elapsed. The Qi functionary hastened forward and said, "I beg leave to strike up the kind of music played in the palace." Lord Jing said, "Agreed." Jesters, entertainers, and dwarves advanced while playing and clowning. Confucius hastened forward. Having ascended the steps one after another and reached the penultimate level of the altar, he said, "Commoners who confuse and delude lords are guilty of crimes that deserve execution. I request the functionary to issue his command!" The Lu functionary imposed punishments according to the law, and the performers ended up with their hands and feet in different places. Lord Jing was terrified and shaken. He knew that righteousness on his side did not match up to that of Lu. Upon his return, he became very fearful and told all his officials: "Those in Lu use the way of the noble man to assist their ruler, but you, sirs, only use the way of the Yi and Di barbarians to teach me and have made me guilty of offense against the Lu ruler. What is to be done?" A functionary came forward and responded, "Noble men who err apologize with something substantive; petty men who err apologize with fine phrases. If you, my lord, regret this, then you should apologize with something substantive." As a result, the Qi lord, to apologize for his error, returned the lands of Yun, which lay north of the Wen River, and Guiyin, which Qi had annexed through invasion.

[translator's note]
Confucius's diplomatic success at the Jiagu meeting is the high point of his political career in this narrative. Many find his reliance on force incompatible with their image of the sage.[67] In the analogous and somewhat more credible passage in *Zuo Tradition* (*Zuo* 3: 1766–97), Confucius shows resolve, rhetorical prowess, and ritual expertise in forestalling Qi aggression, but stops short of resorting to violence:

1.14a In summer, our lord [Lord Ding of Lu] met with the Prince of Qi [Lord Jing of Qi] at Zhuqi, properly Jiagu. As Confucius was assisting, Limi said to the Prince of Qi, "Confucius understands ritual but lacks valor. If we have Lai men threaten the Prince of Lu, we are certain to achieve our aims."[68] The Prince of Qi followed the plan. Retreating with our lord, Confucius said, "Men, use your weapons! The two rulers have come together in amity, yet captive Yi from the margins are using their weapons to disrupt the meeting. This is not how the Qi ruler should command the lords. Those from the margins should not plot against the central domains; Yi barbarians should not cause havoc among the civilized Hua; captives should not interfere with covenants; and weapons should not strain amity. These things are inauspicious with regard to the spirits, transgression against duty with regard to virtue, and violation of ritual propriety with regard to the human realm. You, my lord, should certainly not act this way." When the Prince of Qi heard this, he immediately sent the Lai men away.

As they were about to swear the covenant, the Qi leaders added language to the document: "If the Qi army should leave its borders and Lu does not follow us with three hundred chariots, then let this covenant be our pledge!" Confucius had Zi Wuxuan bow and respond in these words, "And should you not return our lands north of the Wen River, whereby we should respect your commands, then also let this covenant be our pledge!"

The Prince of Qi was going to offer our lord ceremonial toasts. Confucius said to Liangqiu Ju, "How is it that you, sir, have not heard of the wonted practice of Qi and Lu? To offer our ruler ceremonial toasts when the meeting had been concluded is to overtax the functionaries. Furthermore, wine vessels in the shapes of sacrificial bulls and elephants should not leave the gates, nor should fine music be played in the wilds. To offer ceremonial toasts with all the vessels included would be to discard ritual propriety; and if they are not included, it would mean using the most meagre implements. Using meagre implements would bring shame to the rulers; discarding ritual propriety would mean infamy. Why not reconsider? Ceremonial toasts are for displaying virtue, and if there is no such display, then it would be better to desist." Therefore, they did not end up having ceremonial toasts.

According to Du Yu (222–284), Confucius surmises that the Qi ruler plans some deception and therefore refuses toasts, citing ritual requirements as the excuse.

The account in *Historical Records* shows obvious affinities with the parallel episode in the *Guliang Tradition*, which also depicts a severe and punitive Confucius:

> 1.14b At the meeting at Jiagu, Confucius was the assistant. The two rulers came to the altar; the two assistants bowed to each other. The men of Qi rose up with the clamor of drumroll and was about to seize the Lu ruler. Confucius ascended the steps one after another, stopped at the penultimate level of the altar, turned to look steadily at the Prince of Qi and said, "The two rulers are meeting in amity. Why have Yi and Di barbarians come?" He gave order for the supervisor of the military to stop them. The Prince of Qi yielded and apologized, "This was my error." He withdrew and admonished some of his high officers: "That man leads his ruler to fulfill the way of the ancients. You, sirs, only lead me to enter into the mores of Yi and Di barbarians. Why is that?" When the meeting was concluded, the men of Qi had entertainer Shi dance beneath the tent of the Lu ruler. Confucius said, "He who mocks the ruler should die for his crime." He had the supervisor of the military execute the law, and the entertainer's head and feet came out by different doors. It was because of this that the men of Qi returned the lands of Yun, Huan, and Guiyin. This shows that even for civil affairs, there must be military preparation. Confucius at the Jiagu meeting shows how this is so. (*Guliang* Ding 10, 19.12b–13b)

The *Guliang* exegetes Fan Ning (fourth century) and Yang Shixun (seventh century) are conspicuously silent on Confucius's order to execute the entertainer Shi. The parallel account in the early Han text *New Discourses* (*Xinyu*) by Lu Jia (d. 170 BCE) includes lines that also appear in *Zuo Tradition* but by and large follows the *Guliang Tradition*. The Qi performer in this account is more deliberately offensive and dangerous.

> 1.14c The men of Qi rose up with the clamor of drumroll and were about to seize the Lu ruler. Confucius ascended the steps one after another, stopped at the penultimate level of the altar, and said, "When

two rulers meet in amity, they use rituals to persuade each other and music to move each other. I have heard, fine music should not be played in the wilds, nor should wine vessels in the shapes of sacrificial bulls and elephants leave the gates. What are these Yi and Di people trying to do?" Lord Ding said, "Agreed." The Prince of Qi yielded and stood up, saying, "This was my error." He withdrew and reprimanded his officers. After the meeting was over, the men of Qi sent the entertainer Zhan to dance beneath the tent of the Lord of Lu. He performed in an insolent fashion, trying to seize Lord Ding as he waited for the moment when the latter could be caught off guard. Confucius sighed and said, "When the ruler suffers humiliation, it is his subject's duty to die [defending him]." He had the supervisor of the military execute the law and cut down the entertainer, whose head and feet came out of different doors. (*Xinyu jiaozhu* 5.78–79)

All four accounts above invoke "barbarians" as agents of disorder. The role of Lai men as "barbarians" is most clearly articulated in *Zuo Tradition*. Lai's geographical proximity to Qi and Lu notwithstanding, Confucius relegates it metaphorically to the distant margins.[69] The Lai men are likely captives taken upon the Qi conquest and annexation of Lai (567 BCE, *Zuo* Xiang 6.7, 2: 930–31). They constitute the visible emblem of Qi military strength and successful expansion. Why use Lai men to threaten the Lu ruler? Perhaps Qi men bearing arms would provoke Lu delegates to do the same, while the Lai men as a marginal group would not invite similar vigilance; perhaps Lai men as "barbarians" are supposed to inhabit a ritual gray zone where the rules are not spelled out and would thus give Qi the opening for maneuvers.

In the *Guliang Tradition* and *New Discourses*, "Yi and Di barbarians" seem to refer to Qi men who are about to seize the Lu ruler, although Qi is one of the central states. This is in line with the definition of "cultural otherness" in purely moral and ritual terms in the *Gongyang* and *Guliang* traditions. Thus, the commentator Fan Ning explains that Qi men are called barbarians because their scheme to seize the Lu ruler violates ritual propriety. The reference to "barbarians" is also implied in *Historical Records*: "music from four directions" signals the threat of violence from marginal groups, the connection between music and military action being well attested in ritual and historical sources. In "The Hereditary House of Qi" in *Historical Records*, the episode at Jiagu, following *Zuo Tradition*, involves the plan to unleash the Lai musicians' surprise attack on the Lu ruler (*SJ* 32.50). In "The Hereditary House of Lu," however, the account seems to summarize the *Guliang Tradition* and states that Confucius "cut down the licentious musicians" of Qi (*SJ* 33.50). The analogous account in *Sayings* describes Lai men attempting to abduct Lord Ding of Lu and places Confucius's speech against barbarians in *Zuo Tradition* right before the execution of Qi dwarves and performers, implying a causal connection between the two (*KZJY* 1.5–6).

Qi and Lu are sometimes juxtaposed in Warring States and Han texts as examples of pragmatic, even opportunistic adaptability versus strict, sometimes outmoded adherence to ritual norms.[70] Qi representatives also mock Lu ritual specialists for their insistence on protocol in one of the last recorded covenants in *Zuo Tradition*, dated 474 BCE (*Zuo* Ai 21.3, 3: 1968–71). The image of Confucius in all four accounts cited above might have been meant to respond to the assumptions behind such arguments: he advocates ritual propriety that is also diplomatic aplomb and effective political action. The difference is that ritual correctness veers toward violence in *Guliang*, *New Discourses*, and *Historical Records*, with the offenders—the entertainer Shi in *Guliang*, the entertainer Zhan in *New Discourses*, the group of clowns and dwarves in *Historical Records*, who seem to have become symbols of ritual transgression—summarily executed. It is as if ritual prescriptions can be truly effective only when they are harshly imposed as legal interdiction and preemptive violence. In *Historical Records* and the *Guliang Tradition*, Qi territorial concessions are directly linked to the fear and shame inspired by Confucius's decisive action.

Although Sima Qian criticizes the punitive excesses of Qin laws (*SJ* 5) and castigates harsh Han officials (*SJ* 122), he does not rule out the importance of punishment: "The whip of instruction cannot be discarded at home, punishment cannot be forsworn in the state, punitive expeditions cannot be stopped in the entire realm under heaven. The issue is whether their employment is skillful or inept and whether their execution violates or follows the proper way" (*SJ* 25.6).[71] Here too punishment and violence seem integral to Confucius's effective political action. This idea will come up again with reference to his execution of Shaozheng Mao (1.16).

1.15 In the summer of the thirteenth year of Lord Ding's reign [497 BCE], Confucius said to Lord Ding, "Lineage retainers should not have a stash of weapons; high officers should not have city walls of a hundred *zhi*."[72] Zilu was made the steward of the Ji lineage, and he prepared to raze the walls of the three main cities. As a result, the Shusun lineage took the lead to raze Hou. When the Ji lineage was preparing to raze Bi, Gongshan Buniu and Shusun Zhe led the men of Bi in a surprise attack on Lu. Lord Ding and the heads of the three Huan lineages entered the palace of the Ji lineage and ascended Ji Wuzi's terrace. The men of Bi set upon them but did not prevail. When they entered the palace and were closing in on the lord, Confucius ordered Shen Quxu and Yue Qi to go down and charge at them. The men of Bi were routed, and the lord's forces pursued them, defeating them at Gumie. The two of them, Gongshan Buniu and Shusun Zhe, fled to Qi. Bi's walls were then razed. As they were preparing to raze Cheng, Gonglian Chufu said to Meng Yizi, "If you raze the walls of Cheng, Qi forces are sure to arrive at Lu's northern gate. Furthermore, Cheng is the bulwark protecting the Meng lineage. Without Cheng, there is no Meng lineage. I will not raze the walls." In the twelfth month, Lord Ding laid siege to Cheng but did not overcome it.

[translator's note]
The plan to reduce the city walls of ministerial strongholds (Bi, Hou, Cheng) is a key factor in the triangulation of the ruling house, the dominant lineages, and their retainers (see 1.11, translator's note). It can be the lineage heads' attempt to rein in rebellious retainers taking over those strongholds, but it can also be presented as the ministerial lineages' willingness to cede authority to the ruling house. The *Gongyang* account suggests the latter interpretation and names Confucius as the agent bringing it about after gaining sway over Ji Kangzi (head of the Ji lineage), so much so that "for three months Ji Kangzi did not deviate from his advice" (*Gongyang* 2: 1107). *Historical Records* follows *Gongyang* (see 1.16) and further implies that Lord Ding, persuaded by Confucius, appoints Zilu steward of the Ji lineage. (In the original, the subject of the verb *shi* 使 [to appoint, to make] is not given, and I have rendered the sentence in passive voice: "Zilu was made the steward of the Ji lineage.") In all three commentaries of the *Annals*, this event is dated to the previous year (498 BCE).

Other details in 1.15 tally with *Zuo Tradition*, which is reticent and ambiguous on the fault lines of the above-mentioned triangulation. It starts with this line: "As steward of the Ji lineage, Zilu was about to raze the walls of the three main cities" (*Zuo* Ding 12.2, 3: 1806–07). Without the word *shi*, Zilu's agency comes more to the fore. Who directs him to do this?

What is his purpose? Without Confucius's statement as preamble, the alliance of the Lu ruler with the lineage heads against the lineage retainers seems merely contingent and expedient. Gonglian Chufu's speech to Meng Yizi (who studied with Confucius; see 1.4) in *Zuo Tradition* contains a line omitted in *Historical Records*: "You pretend not to know," suggesting more pointedly collusion between the two. So long as the retainer is not turning against the lineage head, there is no reason for the latter to raze the city walls, and the two can be allies against any attempt to expand the ruler's power. In other words, although the accounts from *Zuo Tradition* and *Historical Records* significantly overlap, the implications are different. Confucius in 1.15 seems to advocate expanding and centralizing the ruler's power, while his disciple Zilu in *Zuo Tradition* seems most concerned with defending the Ji lineage. The stance in favor of the ruler becomes quasi-imperial and much more unequivocal and triumphalist in *Sayings*:

> 1.15a Confucius said to Lord Ding, "Lineages should not have a stash of weapons, settlements should not have city walls of a hundred *zhi*. Such were the regulations of old. Now the three lineages have exceeded those regulations, I request that they should all be diminished." Lord Ding thus made Zilu, the steward of the Ji lineage, raze the walls of the three main cities. . . . The men of Bi were defeated, and as a result the walls of the three main cities were reduced. Confucius strengthened the lord's house, weakened the ministerial lineages, exalted the ruler and brought low the subject, and the transformative power of good governance prevailed. (*KZJY* 1: 10)

1.16 In the fourteenth year of Lord Ding's reign [496 BCE], Confucius was fifty-six. From his position as great supervisor of corrections, he took up the duties of a chief minister and showed joy in his countenance. His disciples said, "We have heard that a noble man is not fearful when calamity overtakes him, nor is he joyful when good fortune comes to him." Confucius said, "There is such a saying, but isn't it said that 'there is pleasure in using one's exalted position to humble oneself vis-à-vis others?'" It was at this point that he executed the Lu high officer Shaozheng Mao, the one who fomented disorder in politics. For three months Confucius was consulted on policies of the state: vendors of sheep and pigs no longer inflated prices,[73] men and women on the move walked on different sides of the roads, and none picked up lost items left on the road. Travelers from four directions arriving at settlements did not need to seek the help of functionaries, and they were all provided for before they went home.[74]

[translator's note]
How much power did Confucius wield? How did he govern? According to Mencius, Confucius served in Lu under Ji Huanzi, "hoping to see what could be done" (*Mencius* 5B.4). Here Confucius holds high office and imposes order through judicious punishment and stringent application of the law. Commentators question whether Confucius was ever chief minister (*xiang* 相); in any case it would be anachronistic to use the word *xiang* in that sense in the fifth century BCE. When he is said to take up the duties of *xiang* at the Jiagu meeting, it is as assistant in ritual matters (*xiangli* 相 禮). Confucius's reply (not found in any extant sources) also smacks of sophistry: he claims to be glad only because of the opportunity to use humbled dignity to honor worthy men in low station. Sophistry, linked to "disputation and litigation" (*biansong* 辯訟) (*XZ* 22.312), is one of the crimes Shaozheng Mao is accused of in *Xunzi*:

1.16a Confucius took up the role of chief minister in Lu and put Shaozheng Mao to death after holding audience at court for seven days. His disciples came forward and asked, "Shaozheng Mao was a famous person in Lu. You, Master, have taken charge of government and began by putting him to death. Could you not have been mistaken?" Confucius said, "Alas! Let me give you the reason. There are five kinds of human iniquity, and we are not even counting banditry and larceny: first, a mind with capacious understanding that yet plots evil; second, actions that are perverse yet persevering; third, words that are false yet eloquent; fourth, the power to recall the ugly and the bizarre that yet passes for broad knowledge; fifth, going along with what is wrong and yet giving it luster.[75] If a person is guilty of even one of these five things, he cannot escape being put to death by noble men. Yet Shaozheng Mao encompassed all of them. That was why staying in one place was enough for him to gather disciples by droves; his words and discourses were enough to dress up deviations from the right path and stir up the crowds; his strength was enough to overturn what was right even when he stood alone. He was the bold and vicious representative of the small-minded. It would have been unacceptable not to put him to death." (*XZ* 28.389–90)

The above passage, which goes on to enumerate examples of "just execution" decreed by moral exemplars in earlier eras, also appears in *Master Yin-wen* (ca. fourth–third century BCE, cited in *SY* 423), *New Discourses* (*XY* 3.55), *The Garden of Eloquence* (*SY* 15.26), and *Sayings* (*KZJY* 2: 13–14). Shaozheng Mao is not named but his crimes are listed among those punishable by death in *Record of Rituals* (*LJ* 1: 373–74, see also *KZJY* 31.410–11). Wang Chong (27–100?) in *Balanced Discourses* (*Lunheng*) describes Shaozheng Mao as Confucius's rival:

> 1.16b Shaozheng Mao was on a par with Confucius. Thrice were Confucius's gates thronged with disciples and thrice did they empty out. Yan Hui was the only one who never left, for Yan Hui alone understood that Confucius was a sage. For the disciples who left Confucius and turned to Shaozheng Mao, not only did they not understand the sageliness of Confucius, but they also failed to understand Shaozheng Mao. The disciples were all deluded. (*LH* 50.724)

Starting with Zhu Xi and Ye Shi (1150–1223) in the Song dynasty, many have expressed skepticism about the Shaozheng Mao episode.[76] His crimes are all described as attributes that could be mistaken for virtues. Several lines here echo Xunzi's attacks on contemporary proponents of pernicious views and dangerous rhetoric (*XZ* 5.55–56, 6.63) and a list of offenses deemed heinous in *Record of Rituals* (*LJ* 1: 374). The idea of penalizing incipient evil recalls the need to punish even minor infractions when there is "deliberate intention to break the law" in "Proclamation to King Kang" (Kang gao 康誥) in *Documents*. But what passes for sagacious judgment can also seem like harsh law imposed by proponents of state power. The latter also prosecute hidden transgressions on the basis of suspicion. Indeed, the accusations of pernicious rhetoric and misapplied learning are reminiscent of the attacks against scholars and classicists in *Han Feizi* (*HFZ* 41.950–51, 49.1104, 1122).

The decisive action against Shaozheng Mao contrasts with Confucius's forbearance and critique of punitive severity in another account from *Xunzi* (see chapter 2, 2.21). In the *Analects*, Confucius lauds the efficacy of moral suasion:[77]

> 1.16c Ji Kangzi asked Confucius about government, "How about killing those who violate the Way in order to come close to those who

master the Way?" Confucius responded, "You, sir, are in charge of government. What need is there to resort to killing? If you desire goodness, the people will become good. The noble man's virtue is like wind, that of the common man is like grass. The wind above the grass will certainly bend it." (*Analects* 12.19)

Another passage expatiates on forbearance toward deceivers and one's political enemies:

1.16d Gongbo Liao slandered Zilu to Ji Huanzi. Zifu Jingbo told Confucius about this and said: "Our master has indeed been deceived by Gongbo Liao, but I still have the power to have his corpse exposed at the market and at court." The Master said, "Is the Way going to prevail? That is a matter of fate. Is the Way going to be abandoned? That is a matter of fate. What can Gongbo Liao do about fate!" (*Analects* 14.36)

In *Zuo Tradition*, however, we find Confucius defending the necessity of harsh policies. The context is the political situation in Zheng. The Zheng minister Zichan (d. 522 BCE) on his deathbed advises his successor You Ji to be harsh when he takes charge of government because "only one who has great virtue is capable of controlling the people by means of leniency." You Ji fails to follow Zichan's advice and changes course only after excessive leniency breeds banditry. Confucius comments,

1.16e "When government is overly lenient, the people are presumptuous, and when they are presumptuous, one corrects them with harshness. When government is harsh, the people get wounded, and when they are wounded, one indulges them with leniency. Leniency seasons harshness, harshness seasons leniency, and in this way the policies are harmoniously adjusted." . . . When Zichan died and Confucius heard of it, he shed tears and said, "His was a way of cherishing people that was passed down from ancient times." (*Zuo* Zhao 20.9, 2: 1590–91)

According to this reasoning, a judicious use of harsh policies was a way of "cherishing people." Elsewhere in *Zuo Tradition*, Confucius is anything but harsh when he praises Zichan for refusing to suppress dissent and criticism of his policies: "Judging from this, when people say that Zichan was not humane, I do not believe it" (*Zuo* Xiang 31.11, 2: 1286–87). In sum, from the accounts ascribing different political and legal attitudes to Confucius that could have been available to Sima Qian, he chose the ones emphasizing Confucius's political efficacy and legal strictures.

1.17 When the men of Qi heard about this, they were fearful and said, "With Confucius in charge of government, Lu will certainly become the hegemon. If it becomes the hegemon, then our territories, being so close, would be the first to be annexed. Why don't we just offer our territories?" Liju said, "I beg leave to first try to demoralize them. If demoralization fails, then we can offer territories. How can that be deemed tardy!" They thus chose eighty beauties among the women of Qi, had them all dressed in embroidered clothes and dancing to "Salubrious Music," added thirty foursome teams of horses draped with beautiful decorations, and sent them to the Lu ruler. The female musicians and decorated horses were arrayed outside the tall gate on the south side of the Lu city. Ji Huanzi, dressed in inconspicuous clothes, went twice or thrice to look at them. He was about to receive them and thus spoke to the Lu ruler about making a circuit of the roads around the city. They went, spent whole days looking at the musicians and the horses, and slackened attention to government affairs.

Zilu said, "Master, you would be justified in leaving." Confucius said, "Now Lu is about to offer sacrifices to heaven and earth at the outskirts of the city. If sacrificial meat is sent to the high officers, then I would still have reason to stay." Ji Huanzi finally received the women musicians from Qi and for three days did not attend to government affairs. Also, after the sacrifice at the outskirts, he did not send the sacrificial meat in the vessels to the high officers. Confucius thus left, spending the night at Tun. And then Music Master Ji saw him off, saying, "Master, you were not at fault." Confucius said, "Should I sing?" This was his song: "The mouths of those women / can drive away fine men, / Those women with their entreaties / can bring death and defeat. / It is only by wandering in leisure / that I can while away the years."[78] When Music Master Ji returned, Huanzi said, "What did Confucius say?" Music Master Ji told him the truth. Huanzi heaved a sigh and said, "Could it be that the Master blamed me on account of those serving women!"

[translator's note]
If Confucius were so successful, why did he have to leave Lu? Blame falls on the ritual infractions of Ji Huanzi, chief minister of Lu. According to

the *Analects* (18.4): "The men of Qi sent female musicians to Lu and Ji Huanzi received them. For three days he did not attend court. Confucius set off." Beautiful women and sensuous music, as emblems of excess and decadence, are regularly featured in Warring States anecdotes about political decline. In *Han Feizi*, the gift of women and music is used to undermine the political will of adversarial states. The most famous example of this is the story of Youyu, the "barbarian" Rong envoy to Qin. Youyu's vigorous defense of barbarian simplicity so alarms Qin ministers that they plot to send female musicians to Rong (that is, to use "civilized pleasures" to corrupt the barbarians) and to detain Youyu in Qin.[79] This account in 1.17 seems to be a variation of the same theme, especially as told in *Han Feizi*:

> 1.17a Confucius was in charge of government in Lu, and none picked up lost items left on the road. Lord Jing of Qi was worried about this. Liju said to Lord Jing: "To remove Confucius is as easy as blowing a hair. Why don't you, my lord, welcome him with a high position and generous emolument and send female musicians to Lord Ai to flatter his pride and confuse his will? Lord Ai, newly taking pleasure in them, will certainly slacken his attention to government. Confucius will remonstrate for certain, and remonstrance will certainly lead to his easy dismissal at Lu." Lord Jing said, "Excellent." He thus had Liju send sixteen female musicians to Lord Ai. Lord Ai took pleasure in them and indeed slackened his attention to government. Confucius remonstrated with him, was not heeded, and left for Chu.[80] (*HFZ* 31.649)

The story about sacrificial meat appears in *Mencius* in the context of an exchange on how and when a man of principle should leave office, and how his decision should be understood:

> 1.17b Confucius was the supervisor of corrections in Lu and his counsel was not heeded. He followed the lord and participated in a sacrifice, but no portion of the sacrificial meat arrived for him. He left without even waiting to take off his headgear. Those who did not understand surmised it was because of the meat; those who understood surmised it was because of the violation of ritual propriety. (*Mencius* 6B.6)

To serve in a state requires constant deliberation on the level of acceptable compromise. As an official in Lu, Confucius participates in the Lu custom of competing for the sacrificial animal in a hunt (*liejiao* 獵較), although the hunting competition, of dubious ritual propriety, is irrelevant for Confucius's goal of "serving the Way" (*shidao* 事道, *Mencius* 5B.5). At the same time, he corrects the use of ritual vessels in sacrifice to discourage the use of animals from hunting competitions and to test whether his ideas will be accepted:

> 1.17c Mencius said, "He was setting up a test. When the test showed that there was enough basis to put his ideas into practice and yet they were not, he left. That is why he never stayed for more than three years. Confucius served when he hoped to see what could be done, when the circumstances were acceptable, and when he was supported by the court. With Ji Huanzi, it was when he hoped to see what could be done. With Lord Ling of Wei, it was when the circumstances were acceptable. With Lord Xiao of Wei, it was when he was supported by the court."[81] (*Mencius* 5B.4)

The departure of Confucius in 1.17 is dated to 496 BCE, although elsewhere in *Historical Records* the date is given as 498 or 497 BCE (*SJ* 14.147–48, 33.50, 37.20). Ji Huanzi's errors explain Confucius's departure, yet there are some inconsistencies. Instead of offering remonstrance, he simply leaves, when Ji Huanzi's final comment suggests that he is aware of his error and might have been capable of correction. Confucius's song professing equanimity also seems somewhat incongruous, scarcely in keeping with the description of his frustrations later in the narrative. In addition, the women accused of slander have said nothing in the narrative.

1.18 Confucius thus went to Wei, where he was hosted at the home of Yan Zhuozou, the brother of Zilu's wife. Lord Ling of Wei asked Confucius, "How much did you receive as emolument when you stayed in Lu?" He responded, "The salary was sixty thousand measures of grain."[82] The men of Wei also gave him sixty thousand measures of grain. After staying there a while, someone slandered Confucius to Lord Ling of Wei. Lord Ling sent Gongsun Yujia to go in and out of Confucius's abode.[83] Confucius feared being accused of an offense. After staying for ten months, he departed from Wei.

★ ★ ★

[translator's note]

Who hosts Confucius during his wanderings? (See 1.20, 1.23.) This is a central question for evaluating Confucius and is discussed in *Mencius*, where Yan Zhuozou 顏濁鄒 is called Yan Chouyou 顏讎由:[84]

1.18a Wanzhang asked: "Some people say that Confucius is hosted by Yongju in Wei and by the eunuch Jihuan in Qi. Did this happen?"

Mencius said, "No, it did not. This was made up by those who liked to fabricate stories. At Wei, Yan Chouyou hosted him. Mi Zi's wife and Zilu's wife were sisters. Mi Zi said to Zilu, 'If Confucius would let me host him, he could get to be a minister in Wei." Zilu reported this to Confucius, who said, 'There is the higher command.' Confucius advanced according to ritual propriety and withdrew according to principles of proper duty. Even when he could receive office, he chose not to do so, saying, 'There is the higher command.' To let himself be hosted by Yongju and the eunuch Jihuan is to go against principles of proper duty and the higher command. . . . I have heard that one can judge a subject at court by whom he hosts, and one can judge a subject from afar by whom he chooses as host. If Confucius was hosted by Yongju and the eunuch Jihuan, how could he still be Confucius?" (*Mencius* 5A.8)

Yongju, who does not appear in other extant texts, means "ulcer," and some commentators have glossed his name as "a doctor of ulcers." Yongju may be a variant of Yongdan (*dan* means jaundice), named as a disreputable favorite of Lord Ling of Wei in *Stratagems of the Warring States* (*Zhanguo ce*). Later we learn of a Wei eunuch named Yongqu: Can that figure be somehow linked to Yongju? Mi Zi (aka Mi Zixia) is said to be Lord Ling's lover. In some accounts, Mi Zixia is the intermediary who brings Confucius to the attention of Lord Ling of Wei (*HNZ* 20.683, *LSCQ* 2: 927). Mencius pointedly refutes stories about Confucius stooping to accept the hospitality of unworthy hosts for the sake of advancement. Such refutations might also be meant to defend Confucius against Mohist writings attacking Confucius and his followers for fomenting disorder in Wei.

Some commentators claim that Yan Zhuozou is a worthy high officer in Wei. *Zuo Tradition* refers to one Yan Zhuoju 顏涿聚 (also called Yan Jun) as a Qi high officer. Yan Zhuozou is identified later in Sima Qian's account (1.56) as one of Confucius's disciples. According to *Mr. Lü's Annals* (*LSCQ*

4.205), Yan Zhuoju is a brigand who studied with Confucius. In *Han Feizi* (*HFZ* 10.226–27), Yan Zhuoju offers good advice to the leader of the Chen (also called Tian) lineage, which eventually seizes power in Qi. Thus, in some stories Yan is a morally dubious character (or starts out as a miscreant) and belongs to a cluster of anecdotes that emphasize Confucius's suasive and transformative power as a teacher. If he is not yet reformed when he hosts Confucius, we may speculate that he belongs to stories that use Confucius's choice of hosts (or lack of choice) during his wanderings to debate means and ends and to consider questions of expediency and compromise.

1.19 Confucius prepared to go to Chen and passed by Kuang. Yan Ke, his attendant, pointed at Kuang with his whip and said, "Formerly I entered this place from that opening." When the men of Kuang heard this, they thought it was Yang Hu of Lu, who had once terrorized the people of Kuang. They thus detained Confucius. Confucius resembled Yang Hu in his appearance, and he was kept in custody for five days. Yan Hui came afterward. The Master said, "I thought you had died!" Yan Hui said, "You, Master, are still here. How dare I perish!" The men of Kuang kept Confucius in custody under even direr circumstances, and his disciples were terrified. Confucius said, "King Wen having passed on, is not culture right here in me? If heaven intends to destroy this culture, then I, the latecomer, should not get to have anything to do with this culture. If heaven is not yet set to destroy this culture, then what can the men of Kuang do to me?" Only when Confucius sent his followers to become Ning Wuzi's retainers in Wei was he allowed to leave.[85]

[translator's note]
Confucius's travails at Kuang highlights his equanimity in face of adversities (see also 1.21, 1.40–45). Kuang has been variously identified as a place in Wei, Zheng, or Song. According to *Zuo Tradition*, Lu invaded Zheng and took Kuang in 504 BCE (*Zuo* Ding 6.2, 3: 1768–69). Yang Hu was the de facto commander of Lu forces and presumably "terrorized Kuang." Yan Ke could have been part of that military campaign.

Passage 1.19 incorporates the two entries in the *Analects* (9.5, 11.23) that mention Kuang. The analogous story in *Zhuangzi* emphasizes timing (*shi* 時) and fate (*ming* 命):

1.19a Confucius was traveling in Kuang. The men of Song encircled him and his followers in several rounds, but Confucius did not cease playing the zither and singing. Zilu entered to see him and said, "How can you, Master, be so joyous?" Confucius said, "Come! Let me tell you. I have tried to avoid adversity for a long time. That I cannot escape is fate. I have sought success for a long time. That I have not attained it is a matter of timing. During the eras of Yao and Shun, no one under heaven suffered adversity, but that state was not attained through understanding. During the eras of Jie and Zhòu, no one under heaven succeeded, but that did not happen because understanding failed. Timing and the momentum of events happened to make it so. To make a point of not avoiding dragons while traveling on water—that is the fisherman's courage. To make a point of not avoiding rhinoceros and tigers while traveling on land—that is the hunter's courage. To regard death as if it were life when faced with the shining blade—that is the brave man's courage. To understand that adversity is a matter of fate and that success is a matter of timing, and to have no fear when faced with great calamity—that is the sage's courage. Yóu, be at ease! My fate belongs to forces that control it!" Not long afterward, armored men advanced with these words: "We thought you were Yang Hu, that was why we encircled you. Now we know that you are not and beg leave to apologize and withdraw." (ZZ 17.595–97)

Although the idea of equanimity seems to be central in this story as it is told in *Historical Records*, the *Analects*, and *Zhuangzi*, the message is ultimately different. In *Zhuangzi*, equanimity is rooted in acceptance of what is beyond one's control (fate and timing), while in *Historical Records* and the *Analects*, equanimity stems from the conviction of fulfilling higher goals (see also 1.43a). This is in turn connected to the dual meanings of *ming* as cosmic fate or a command from heaven (that is, destiny is the fulfillment of a higher command).[86] The word translated as culture (*wen* 文) also means civility, civilization, writing, literature, pattern, ritual refinement, textual traditions. In this context, *wen* suggests Confucius's mission of transmitting ritual and textual traditions. In the *Analects* (5.15), *wen* is specifically identified with the striving for knowledge: "How is it that Kong Wenzi is called 'Wen' [in his posthumous honorific]?" The Master said, "He had a nimble mind and loved learning, and was not ashamed of asking questions even of those inferior to him. Thus, he was called 'Wen.'"

The detail of Confucius playing music and singing appears later in another moment of distress for Confucius and his disciples (see 1.41, 1.45e) and works its way into the retellings of the above story in *Han's Exegesis* (*HSWZ* 6.296), *The Garden of Eloquence* (*SY* 17.18), and *Sayings* (*KZJY* 22.321). In those three almost identical accounts, Zilu starts by waving his halberd, eager to fight, and is moved to play the zither and sing after Confucius's speech about accepting fate with equanimity based on his certainty of a higher purpose (it combines the messages of the *Analects* and *Zhuangzi* and bears similarities with 1.45d). Confucius then joins in the singing, and after three rounds of songs, the assailants remove their armor and leave. *Han's Exegesis* matches the story with this line from the *Odes*: "They come roaming, they come singing," and concludes: "This is to show how abundant virtue is all about harmony and nonaction" (*HSWZ* 6.296). The power of music becomes cosmological and literal when this story is told in *Zither Music* (*Qin cao*, ca. third century): "Confucius then sang along to the accompaniment of zither music. The notes of the music were extremely doleful. A furious wind struck up, and the soldiers froze and stumbled. The men of Kuang thus understood that Confucius was a sage and left of their own accord" (*ZY* 744).

1.20 Having left, Confucius then passed through Pu. A month or so later, he returned to Wei, where he was hosted in the home of Qu Boyu. Lord Ling's wife, Nan Zi, sent someone to tell Confucius: "Noble men from four directions who condescend to wish for fraternal amity with our humble ruler never fail to have an audience with our ruler's humble consort. Our ruler's humble consort would like to receive you." Confucius declined, but, having no alternatives, had an audience with her. The lady stayed behind finely woven hempen curtains. Confucius entered through the door and, facing north, bowed with his forehead touching the ground. The lady bowed twice from behind the curtains, and her girdle jade and pendants tinkled melodiously. Confucius said later, "Formerly I declined to have an audience with her, but having done so, I responded with the proper ritual." Zilu was not pleased. Confucius swore: "If I went against what was right, may heaven abandon me! May heaven abandon me!" He had been staying for about a month in Wei, when Lord Ling, sharing the carriage with his wife and making the eunuch Yongqu take the third place on its right side, came out of the palace. Lord Ling had Confucius take a second, inferior carriage. Lord Ling and his entourage made a spectacle of themselves as they passed through the marketplace. Confucius said, "I have not yet seen one who loves virtue as much as he loves sensuous beauty." Being thus ashamed of the whole thing, he left Wei and passed through Cao. That year [495 BCE], Lord Ding of Lu died.

[translator's note]
Why would Confucius meet a licentious woman of ill repute? Presumably his goal is to gain access to the Wei ruler in order to realize his political ideals. The scandalous history of Nan Zi is well-known. She is rumored to have an affair with Zizhao, a lord's son from her natal state of Song, and Lord Ling of Wei summons Zizhao to the Wei court at the behest of Nan Zi. When Lord Ling's heir apparent Kuaikui "passed through the Song countryside, a local sang to him, 'She's satisfied now, your sow in heat— / Why not give us back our fine stud boar?'" (*Zuo* Ding 14.8, 3: 1818–19). Ashamed of this, Kuaikui plans Nan Zi's assassination but fails (496 BCE). Kuaikui goes into exile; what ensues after Lord Ling's death is a bloody decades-long succession struggle between Kuaikui and his own son Zhe, known posthumously as the Ousted Lord of Wei. Zilu will die as a result of being embroiled in these power struggles. Nan Zi is relegated to the chapter on "Destructive Favorites" (Niebi 孽嬖) in *The Biographies of Notable Women* (*Lienü zhuan*) compiled by Liu Xiang (77–6 BCE).[87]

The corresponding entry on this episode in the *Analects* (6.28) is laconic: "Confucius had an audience with Nan Zi. Zilu was not pleased. The Master said, 'If I went against what was right, may heaven abandon me! May heaven abandon me!'" The notion of Confucius swearing an oath, possibly in a state of emotional distress, and the impropriety of the meeting, lead commentators to propose other readings: "What I go against [i.e., the likes of Lord Ling and Nan Zi]—may heaven abandon them! May heaven abandon them!" "That all go against me [i.e., being reduced to meeting Nan Zi] is because heaven has abandoned me! Heaven has abandoned me!" "The misfortune that I suffer—heaven is tired of it! Heaven is tired of it!" Xing Bing (quoting Luan Zhao) compares the necessity of meeting Nan Zi with King Wen being imprisoned at Youli, and he explains Confucius's exclamation thus: "it means 'the way I had to go against myself and suffer this indignity is what heaven abhors'" (*LY* 2: 540–41). Some reject the idea of swearing an oath altogether and take *shi* (translated above as "swore") to mean "set forth." Some even go as far as identifying Nan Zi with male historical characters to absolve Confucius of impropriety (*LY* 2: 542), but Sima Qian's account rules out that conjecture.

Sima Qian supplies a context: a date (495 BCE, one year after Kuaikui's abortive assassination attempt), Nan Zi's invitation, Confucius's hesitation, the setting of the meeting (down to Nan Zi's tinkling pendants), and Confucius's self-justification. Nan Zi claims mediatory authority: visiting dignitary can gain access to the Wei ruler only through her. The struggle with weighing alternatives and necessary compromise runs through other passages in this chapter (1.3, 1.12, 1.28). Confucius's final statement ("I have not yet seen one who loves virtue as much as he loves sensuous beauty") is found in the *Analects* (9.18, 15.13; see also *KZJY* 38.508–09). The latter entry, in the chapter titled "Lord Ling of Wei" (Wei Ling gong 衛靈公), has these additional words, "It is all over!" It is the kind of statement that begs for a context. It can be attached, for example, to the episode about Ji Huanzi's fascination with female musicians (1.17). Indeed, the logic of pitting the attraction of virtue (embodied by Confucius) against the seductive wiles of women defines both 1.17 and 1.20. The difference is that in the Nan Zi episode Confucius's failure is more poignant—his choice of expediency yields no result and the challenge to his dignity is more flagrant.

Confucius is said to serve Lord Ling of Wei because "the circumstances were acceptable" (see 1.17c). In contrast to Confucius's commitment to serve, his host Qu Boyu exemplifies timely withdrawal: "A noble man indeed is Qu Boyu! When the Way prevails in the realm, he serves in government. When the Way does not prevail in the realm, he gathers up his convictions and keeps them in his breast" (*Analects* 15.7). In some other accounts, he serves ably as a minister of Lord Ling of Wei; more often than not he is described as a man of integrity who withdraws from the court (or leaves the state) because of political disorder. He embodies Daoist self-transformations in *Zhuangzi* and *Huainanzi* (*ZZ* 4.165; *HNZ* 1: 25). In *Zuo Tradition*, Qu Boyu twice leaves via a nearby pass when disorder threatens to engulf Wei in 559 and 547 BCE (*Zuo* Xiang 14.4, 2: 1016–17, Xiang 26.2, 2: 1160–61), more than half a century before the event described here. The chronological discrepancy is one of the reasons why Cui Shu questions the authenticity of the Nan Zi story, joining a chorus of skeptics that include Kong Anguo (ca. second–first century BCE), He Yan (ca. 195–249), and the compiler of *Kong Anthology*, among others (*LY* 2: 541, 544; *KCZ*

13.297–98; *CDB* 290–91). The Nan Zi episode was at the center of one of the culture wars in Republican China (see chapter 4, 4.2).

1.21 Confucius left Cao and went to Song. He practiced ritual with his disciples under a big tree. The Song supervisor of the military, Huan Tui, wanted to kill Confucius and pulled up that tree. As Confucius was leaving, his disciples said, "We should hurry!" Confucius said, "Heaven has given birth to the virtue in me. What can Huan Tui do to me!"

[translator's note]
Confucius's declaration above appears in the *Analects* (7.23) without context. In spirit and mode of reasoning, it is similar to 1.19, and some commentators suggest that the two incidents are variants of the same story. But the context of a ritual practice and Confucius's implied lack of alacrity even when physically threatened may make Confucius seem almost pedantic, as Cui Shu opines (*CDB* 296–97). Pulling up a tree is a feat of superhuman strength that may remind the reader of Lu Zhishen in *Water Margin* (*Shuihu zhuan*). The back story of Huan Tui's enmity is not told in any extant texts, though his persecution of Confucius is mentioned in a passage in *Mencius* (5A.8) on Confucius's choice of hosts during his wandering and in a disparaging account of Confucius's travails in *Zhuangzi*:

> 1.21a Confucius traveled westward to Wei. Yan Hui asked Music Master Jin: "How would you consider the Master's actions?" Music Master Jin said, "What a pity! That the Master is in such dire straits!" Yan Hui said, "How so?" Music Master Jin said, "For straw dogs, before they are presented for sacrifice, are carefully placed in a bamboo basket, swathed in patterned embroidery, and handled by the shaman upon self-purification through fasting and abstinence.[88] After they have been presented for sacrifice, passersby trample on their heads and backs, grass-cutters take them for lighting fires, and that is all. If at that point someone again takes them and places them carefully in a bamboo basket and swathes them with patterned embroidery, and, under their auspices, moves, stays, sleeps, and reclines, then even if one does not get bad dreams, one must surely be blinded again and again! Now the Master is also taking the straw dogs that had been set forth by the former kings, and gathers his disciples to move, stay, sleep, and recline under their auspices. That is why he

met with foes who axed the tree next to him in Song, had to remove his traces in Wei, and was in dire straits in Shang and Zhou. Was that not his bad dream? To have been besieged at the area between Chen and Cai and to have been deprived of cooked food for seven days, so much so that he was hovering on the border between life and death, was that not being blinded? (*ZZ* 14.511–12)

Confucius's trials and tribulations, cited as evidence that his teachings are irrelevant in *Zhuangzi*, become the opportunity for Confucius to reaffirm his sense of mission in 1.19, 1.21, 1.41–45.

1.22 Confucius went to Zheng. He and his disciples lost sight of each other, and Confucius stood alone at the eastern gate of the outer city wall. A certain Zheng man said to Zigong, "There is this person at the eastern gate: his forehead resembles Yao's, his neck is similar to Gao Yao's, his shoulders are similar to Zichan's, but from the waist down he is three inches shorter than Yu. He is cast down and worn out, just like a homeless dog." Zigong related this factually to Confucius, who smiled in delight and said, "His words about my form and appearance are of no consequence. But when he said that I look like a homeless dog—how true that is! How true that is!"

[translator's note]
The physiognomy of Confucius belongs to stories about the extraordinary appearance of sage kings and worthy ministers. In *Balanced Discourses*, Wang Chong summarizes some prevalent assertions found also in traditions of apocrypha (*LH* 11.108–12):

> 1.22a Legend has it that the Yellow Emperor had a dragon's countenance; Zhuanxu bore spears on his head; Di Ku had double rows of teeth; Yao's eyebrows had eight colors; Shun's eyes had double pupils; Yu's ears had three openings; Tang's arms had two elbows; King Wen had four breasts; King Wu had his eyes turned upward; the Duke of Zhou was hunchbacked; Gao Yao had a horse's mouth; Confucius's head was concave.

Each strange trait is explained—for example, King Wen's four breasts symbolize nourishment for the realm, and the Duke of Zhou's hunchback signifies the burden he carries as regent. Physiognomy is tied to broader questions of judging character and recognizing worth. Confucius is credited with this saying in *Elder Dai's Record of Rituals* (*DDLJ* 1: 127): "Formerly, Yao chose men according to their shape; Shun chose men according to their countenance; Yu chose men according to their words; Tang chose men according to their voice; King Wen chose men according to their deportment." Judging Confucius's physiognomy thus addresses the issue of whether his inner power has tangible manifestation or can be recognized for its political significance.

Kong Anthology asserts the unqualified resemblance of Confucius to ancient sages: "He has elongated [literally, "river like"] eyes and high cheekbones, the form and appearance of the Yellow Emperor, long legs, a turtlelike back, a stature of nine *chi* six *cun*, and the deportment and body of Cheng Tang, the first king of Shang" (*KCZ* 1.1). In 1.22, Confucius is said to resemble sage kings of antiquity like Yao and Yu, the legendary minister of justice Gao Yao, and the famous Zheng minister Zichan. At the same time, he is said to have fallen short and is compared to "a homeless dog." Confucius's appearance already came up in 1.1 and 1.5. The account in *Historical Records* also appears (with small variations) in *Discussions in White Tiger Hall* (*Baihu tong, juan* 3), *Balanced Discourse* (*LH* 11.122–23), and *Sayings*, which also mentions Confucius's unusual height (see 1.5) and credits him with "elongated eyes and high cheekbones" (*KZJY* 12.323–24). The analogous account in *Han's Exegesis* is more detailed and staged as a deliberate encounter between Confucius and the physiognomist Gubu Ziqing.

1.22b As Confucius was leaving Wei, he went to the east gate to meet Gubu Ziqing and said, "You gentlemen should move the carriage aside to make room. There is a person coming; he will judge my physiognomy for sure. Make note of it." Gubu Ziqing also said, "You gentlemen should move the carriage aside to make room. There is a sage coming." Confucius started walking. Gubu Ziqing, facing him, gazed at him making fifty steps and then, following him, gazed at him making fifty steps. He turned around to look at Zigong and said, "Who is this?" Zigong said, "This is my teacher, whom they call Confucius of Lu." Gubu Ziqing said, "Is this Confucius of Lu then? I have already heard of him." Zigong said, "To whom should my teacher be compared?" Gubu Ziqing said, "He has Yao's forehead, Shun's eyes, Yu's neck, Gao Yao's mouth. Beheld from the front, he has a rich fullness like a master of the land. Beheld from behind, he has hunched shoulders and a weak spine. He follows along, having obtained the right way, but turning, he is at a distance of one *chi* and four *cun* away. This is where he does not measure up to the four sage kings." Zigong sighed. Gubu Ziqing said, "Why should you be troubled? A clouded face that yet is not ignoble; a pig snout that yet is not debased. Gazing at him from afar, he is weak and worn out like a dog from a house of mourning. Why should you be troubled?" Zigong told Confucius about this. Confucius did not disclaim anything except the comparison to a dog from a house of mourning, saying, "How dare I accept that?" Zigong said, "'A clouded face that yet is not ignoble; a pig snout that yet is not debased.' I have already understood the implied compliment. I do not understand the comparison to a dog from a house of mourning: Why is that a compliment worth disclaiming?" Confucius said, "Have you never seen a dog from a house of mourning? When the funerary ritual has been completed and the deceased has been put in the coffin, when the vessels have been set forth for sacrifice, it looks around but sees no one. My intention is to carry out the Way, but above there is no enlightened ruler and below there are no worthy lords. The way of the kings is in decline; the teachings of governance are lost; the powerful oppress the weak; the multitude tyrannizes over the few; the myriad clans let their hearts defy all constraints; and there is no way to impose order and discipline. That person insists on regarding me as the dog's close match. How dare I accept the compliment?" (*HSWZ* 9.414)

In *Historical Records*, Confucius is said to resemble ancient worthies, but he falls short (being three inches shorter than the sage king Yu). His comparison to a homeless dog develops this notion of failure, yet Confucius is delighted by the analogy, presumably because the image captures the spirit of his itinerant quest for the realization of political ideals. The term I translated as "homeless dog" has also been glossed as "dog from a house of mourning," which is explicitly marked as such in the account in *Han's Exegesis*. A dog from a house of mourning "looks around and sees no one" after the completion of rituals for burial. In other words, its cast-down and worn-out state marks its ritual propriety when it is surrounded by the violation of and disregard for ritual. While the moment in *Historical Records* conveys a sense of irony or perhaps even self-mockery, the episode in *Han's*

Exegesis frames "a dog from a house of mourning" as a positive image in a more straightforward affirmation of ritual correctness in a world oblivious to ritual. In 2004, the scholar Li Ling published *Homeless Dog: My Reading of the Analects* (*Sangjia gou: wo du Lunyu*), presenting Confucius as the lonely and unaccommodated intellectual: "Any person who holds on to ideals without finding a spiritual home in the mundane world is a homeless dog."[89]

1.23 Confucius then went to Chen and was hosted in the home of the supervisor of the city, Zhenzi. A little over a year later, the Wu king Fuchai attacked Chen, gained control over three settlements, and withdrew. Zhao Jianzi attacked Zhaoge. Chu laid siege to Cai, and Cai moved to Wu. Wu defeated the Yue king Goujian at Kuaiji.

[translator's note]
Confucius being hosted by Zhenzi is mentioned in *Mencius* 5A.8, a passage debating the character of Confucius's hosts and by implication the nature of his choices (see 1.18, 1.20). Almost as a kind of time marker, Sima Qian refers to events dated to 494 and 493 BCE: Wu invades Chen (*Zuo* Ai 1.4, 3: 1835–36);[90] the Jin minister Zhao Jianzi attacks Zhaoge in a move against rival Fan and Zhonghang lineages in Jin (*SJ* 14.150, *Zuo* Ai 1.7, 3: 1837–38); Cai, caught in the conflict between Chu and Wu, moves into Wu territory (*SJ* 14.150, *Zuo* Ai 1.1, 3: 1832–33); Wu defeats Yue (*SJ* 14.150, *Zuo* Ai 1.2, 3: 1832–33). Wu's victory over Yue is also mentioned in 1.10, where Confucius's excursus on a gigantic bone and the following passage (1.24) appear in sequence in *Discourses of the States* as instances of his esoteric knowledge (*GY* "Luyu" 2.19, 213–15).

1.24 There was an eagle that landed at the Chen court and died. It was pierced through by a wooden arrow with a stone arrowhead. The arrow was one *chi* eight *cun*. Lord Min of Chen sent a messenger to ask Confucius about this. Confucius said, "The eagle has traversed a great distance. This is the arrow of Sushen. In the old days, when King Wu overcame Shang, he created passages reaching the nine Yi and the hundred Man groups at the margins and beyond. He had them all offer their own regional goods as tributes so that they would not forget their fealty and proper duties. As a result, Sushen sent as tributes wooden arrows with stone arrowheads, and they measure one *chi* eight *cun*. King Wu wanted to make manifest the exemplary virtue of ancestors and apportioned the Sushen arrows to his daughter Daji, who was matched with Lord Hu, descendant of the sage king Shun, and was put in power at Chen. For those with the same clan name, King Wu apportioned gems and jade to confirm ties of kinship; for those with different clan names, he apportioned tokens of fealty from far-away places, so that they would not forget their submission. That was why Chen was apportioned the arrows of Sushen." Lord Min tried to have this investigated in the old archives and actually obtained the same information.

[translator's note]
Confucius's journey to Chen is dated to 495 BCE in *Historical Records* (*SJ* 14.149, 36.16). His excursus on the Sushen arrows is grouped with his discussion of the entombed sheep and the gigantic bone (1.10) in *Discourses of the States* (GY "Luyu" 2.9, 201; 2.18, 213; 2.19, 214–15) and in the chapters titled "Discerning Things" in *The Garden of Eloquence* (SY 18.18–20) and *Sayings* (KZJY 16.247). Unlike Confucius's earlier remarks in 1.10, here his knowledge invokes early Zhou political order. More explicitly historical, it is tied to the foundational history of Chen and is verifiable in "the old archives." In other words, although the story bears resemblance to the other passages on anomalies, it is unique in invoking Confucius's historical knowledge and implicit exaltation of the early Zhou order.

1.25 Confucius stayed in Chen for three years. It was at that time that Jin and Chu were fighting for supremacy, and they took turns to attack Chen. By the time Wu invaded Chen, Chen had been suffering frequent raids. Confucius said, "Let us return! Let us return! The young ones in my fold are audaciously ardent and fastidiously scrupulous. They advance and strive for their goals without forgetting the convictions they begin with."

[translator's note]
There is no mention of Jin and Chu attacking Chen in the 490s in extant texts. By then Jin-Chu rivalry has faded into the background as the struggles between Chu, Wu, and Yue take center stage. Confucius's statement here is found in *Mencius* 7B.37. A slightly different version appears in the *Analects* (5.22) and is elaborated later in 1.36. What Sima Qian marks as Confucius's words during two separate sojourns in Chen might well have been two versions of the same anecdote. Mencius explains Confucius's

commendation of the audaciously ardent (*kuang* 狂) and fastidiously scrupulous (*juan* 狷):

> 1.25a Wanzhang asked, "When Confucius was in Chen, he said, 'Why don't we go back! The young ones in my fold are audaciously ardent and fastidiously scrupulous. They advance and strive for their goals without forgetting the convictions they begin with.' Confucius was in Chen: Why did he long for the audaciously ardent ones in Lu?"
>
> Mencius said, "Unable to find those who follow the middle way, he commended these men—he had no choice but to turn to the audaciously ardent and fastidiously scrupulous. The audaciously ardent ones advance and strive for their goals; for the fastidiously scrupulous ones, there are things they would not deign to do." (*Mencius* 7B.37)

Mencius's reply is also framed as Confucius's saying in the *Analects* (13.21). Mencius goes on to explain that the "audaciously ardent" ones brashly invoke the ancients without necessarily being able to live up to their ideals while the "fastidiously scrupulous" ones would at least not deign to sully themselves with unethical acts. What Confucius abhors are "the village goody two-shoes" (*xiangyuan* 鄉愿) who parade their conformism and complacency as self-evident virtue (*Analects* 17.13). What Sima Qian does in the above passage is to frame Mencius's ruminations on the meanings of virtue in the context of Confucius's frustrations in Chen and his implicit wish for effective political engagement.

1.26 They passed through Pu. Just then the Gongshu lineage [of Wei] used Pu as a base for revolt. The men of Pu detained Confucius. Among his disciples was Gongliang Ru, who brought five of his own carriages to follow Confucius. He was tall, worthy, and had the strength of valor. He said, "Back then I followed the master and encountered adversity at Kuang, and now we again encounter adversity here. Destiny would have it so. Now that the Master and I are facing adversity once more, I would rather die fighting." He fought most ferociously. The men of Pu were alarmed and said to Confucius, "So long as you do not go to Wei, we will let you go." They swore a covenant with Confucius and allowed him to leave through the eastern gate. Confucius then went to Wei. Zigong said, "Can we turn against a covenant?" Confucius said, "This was a covenant based on coercion. The spirits would not heed it."

[translator's note]

Pu was a settlement in Wei. When Zilu becomes an administrator in Pu, Confucius cautions him: "Pu had many brave men and is also difficult to govern" (*SJ* 67.12). There is no mention of the Gongshu lineage using Pu as a base for revolt in extant sources, although Lord Ling of Wei did banish the faction of Gongshu Shu (496 BCE), who had opposed the influence of his wife Nan Zi (*Zuo* Ding 14.1, 3: 1814–15). Gongliang Ru is mentioned in passing in Sima Qian's chapter on Confucius's disciples (*SJ* 67.49). *Sayings* retells 1.26 (*KZJY* 22.325) and also identifies Gongliang Ru as a man from Chen (*KZJY* 38.507). His heroic defense of Confucius echoes the consistent emphasis on valor that runs through this chapter. In *Zuo Tradition*, two Zheng ministers argue: "Covenants based on coercion have no substance. The spirits do not oversee them. What they do oversee are covenants sworn in good faith" (*Zuo* Xiang 9.8, 2: 960–63). The context is Zheng's freedom to veer toward Chu against the explicit injunction of their covenant with Jin. Cui Shu finds multiple inconsistencies in 1.26: it is dated to 492 BCE when the banishment of Gongshu Shu is dated to 496 BCE; Confucius should not be passing through Pu if he goes from Wei to Chen (Chen was on Wei's south and Pu on Wei's west); the alacrity with which Confucius turns against a covenant (even a coerced one) seems unworthy of the sage (*CDB* 291). For Sima Qian, the incident in Pu is another example of Confucius's travails and how he responds to them nimbly with sound judgment.

1.27 When Lord Ling of Wei heard that Confucius was coming, he was glad and welcomed him at the outskirts of the city. He asked, "Is it feasible to attack Pu?" Confucius responded, "It is." Lord Ling said, "My high officers consider that untenable. Now Pu is what Wei relies on for dealing with Jin and Chu. To use Wei forces to attack Pu—would that not be unfeasible?" Confucius said, "Its men have the will to die resisting the rebels; its women have the will to defend the Western River against the rebels. What we will be attacking are no more than four or five people." Lord Ling said, "Excellent." But he did not end up attacking Pu.

[translator's note]

Sima Qian charts multiple sojourns in Wei for Confucius, possibly in an attempt to fit in anecdotes featuring Confucius in Wei in various sources.

Lord Ling's welcome of Confucius is consonant with references to the ameliorative effect of wise counselors in Lord Ling's court despite his errant ways (*Analects* 14.19, *XZ* 5.46, *LSCQ* 2: 1659–60, *SY* 7.7, 7.10, 8.18, *KZJY* 13.187–88). Confucius's eager recommendation that Wei should attack Pu stands in sharp contrast to his reluctance to speak about military formations (1.33). The Wei ruler's restraint also deviates from his determination in stamping out domestic unrest and belligerence in confronting Jin as told in *Zuo Tradition.*[91]

1.28 Lord Ling was growing old and slackened his attention to government. He did not make use of Confucius. Confucius heaved a sigh and said, "If there were one who could make use of me, there would be results in no more than a year. There would be fruition in three years." Confucius set off.

[translator's note]
Confucius's saying, with minor variations, is found in the *Analects* (13.10) and in Sima Qian's preface to his chapter on scholars and ritual experts (*ru* 儒, *SJ* 121.3), where the quotation is not tied to disappointment in any specific ruler. The quest for proper employment whereby Confucius could realize his vision is a refrain throughout this account.

1.29 Bi Xi was the steward at Zhongmou. Zhao Jianzi, while striking at the Fan and Zhonghang lineages, attacked Zhongmou. Bi Xi revolted and sent someone to summon Confucius. Confucius wanted to go. Zilu said, "I have heard from you, Master, these words: 'He who personally commits iniquitous acts—the noble man does not enter his camp.' Now Bi Xi personally uses Zhongmou as a base to revolt and you, Master, want to go. How can this be justified?" Confucius said, "Indeed those words were spoken. But do we not say of true resilience that it does not become thin with grinding? Do we not say of true whiteness that it does not become black with sullying? Am I but a gourd? How could I be strung up and not be eaten?"

[translator's note]
In debating means and ends, expediency and compromise, this passage, which also appears in the *Analects* (17.7) with minor variations, recalls Confucius's response to Gongshan Buniu's rebellion in 1.12. In "Questioning

Confucius" (Wen Kong 問孔) in *Balanced Discourses*, Wang Chong cites both episodes as instances of Confucius's "impurity" (*zhuo* 濁), inconsistency, and rhetorical missteps. He suggests that Confucius's response to Zilu should be: "Bi Xi is not all evil. One can still enter his camp" (*LH* 26.426–29). Even with the first two lines that Sima Qian adds by way of historical context, the motive of Bi Xi's revolt and its potential justification are not clear. Some commentators argue that Bi Xi might have been defending the Fan lineage or perhaps the Jin ruling house against the encroaching Zhao lineage (*LY* 3: 1547, 1556–57). Some even claim that Confucius is simply expressing his eagerness to attack the Ji lineage, the Lu counterpart of the Zhao lineage in Jin (*LY* 3: 1553). *Zuo Tradition* dates Zhao Jianzi's siege of Zhongmou to 490 BCE (*Zuo* Ai 5.2, 3: 1860–61), but since 1.35 is dated to 492 BCE, this incident should be dated to 493 BCE or earlier. Cui Shu vociferously attacked the historicity of this incident (*CDB* 291–93).

The last line quoted in 1.29 has invited different interpretations hinging on the implied subject of "eat" and whether Confucius's rhetorical relationship with the gourd is one of contrast or homology. The translation above implies Confucius's identification with the gourd: to find a proper venue for political engagement is to be eaten, even as *yong* in classical Chinese means both "employment" and "sacrifice." Yang Shen believes the gourd refers to the bitter gourd that cannot be eaten (*LY* 4: 1555). Wang Chong takes the comparison to mean that "a person should serve and be supplied with a salary" (*LH* 28.427). Other readings emphasize the implied contrast between the sage and the gourd, thus He Yan opines: "A gourd gets to be tied to one place because it is not eaten. I am naturally the one who eats and has to go east, west, north, and south, and cannot be like the uneaten thing tied to one place." Huang Kan elaborates this contrast: A gourd does not need to eat and grows by being attached to a place, unlike a human being who needs to be on the move to look for food. He also cites an alternative reading: "Gourd" is the name of a constellation; a talented man seeks the opening for action, "How can he be like the gourd, tied to the sky and not be eaten?" (*LY* 3: 1553–54). If the gourd is of the bitter kind that can only be used as a float and not as food, then Confucius is comparing the state of not being properly employed to the gourd that is tied to a person as a float but is not fine enough to be edible (*LY* 3: 1555–56).

The gray zone of expediency becomes fodder for anti-Confucian arguments in *Mozi* ("Against Experts in Ritual and Traditional Learning" [Feiru 非儒]), where Bi Xi is cited as an example of lawlessness associated with

Confucius (*MZ* 39.278). As in 1.12, the issue is whether outward deviance from norms can lead to the realization of ideals. A typical defense of viable expediency is articulated by Zhang Shi (1133–1180), quoted in Zhu Xi's commentary: "What Zilu heard about formerly is the standard rule (*changfa* 常法) for noble men guarding their integrity. What the Master speaks about here is the great power to weigh the odds (*daquan* 大權) in the sage's realization of the Way" (*LY* 3: 1554).

1.30 Confucius was playing the stone chimes. A person who was carrying a straw basket on his back passed by Confucius's gates and said, "He has something on his mind! Is that why he is playing the stone chimes? Such flinty insistence! Could it be that no one understands him? Have done already!"

[translator's note]
Sima Qian places this episode here probably because the corresponding entry in the *Analects* sets the scene in Wei. The *Analects* passage, which has slightly different wording and a heightened sense of drama, ends this way:

> 1.30a And then he said, "Limited indeed are these insistent tones! If no one understands him, then he should only abide in himself and have done already! 'When the water is deep, brave the currents; when the water is shallow, just hitch your skirts and cross.'" The Master said, "How resolute he is! It is hard to argue against that!" (*Analects* 14.39)

The quotation from the *Odes* uses the image of different ways of crossing the river to refer to the choice between political engagement and withdrawal. Either Sima Qian abbreviates the entry from the *Analects* or uses its variant version in sources no longer extant. Four passages in Sima Qian's account (1.30, 1.39, 1.40, 1.47) feature Confucius's encounter with people (laborers, farmers, recluses, madmen) who question his choices and convictions. In all cases, Confucius feels drawn to these characters as the ones who understand his struggles. Note that Confucius is shown as learning important lessons from humble folk (for example, a carpenter, a cicada-catcher) in *Zhuangzi*.

1.31 Confucius was learning how to play the zither from Music Master Xiangzi and did not advance beyond one piece over ten days. Music

Master Xiangzi said, "We can advance." Confucius said, "I am already familiar with its melodies but have not yet grasped its principle." A while later, Xiangzi said, "You are already familiar with its principle; we can advance." Confucius said, "I have not yet grasped the intent behind it." A while later, Xiangzi said, "You are already familiar with the intent behind it; we can advance." Confucius said, "I have not yet grasped the person behind it." A while later, he was deep in reverent contemplation over something, and was complaisantly looking afar at something high up, as if his mind were soaring aloft. He said, "I have grasped what he was like as a person: darkly swarthy, impressively tall, he has eyes that seem to be looking into the distance, as if he were the king over domains on four sides. Who but King Wen could have created this?" Music Master Xiangzi rose from his mat and bowed twice, saying, "My teacher did say that this was called 'King Wen's Music.'"

[translator's note]
King Wen embodies the foundational virtues of Zhou order (see 1.19). An almost identical passage in *Han's Exegesis* (*HSWZ* 5.240) ends thus:

> 1.31a Confucius held on to King Wen's music and knew what he was like as a person. Music Master Xiangzi said, "Dare I ask how you knew that it was 'King Wen's Music?'" Confucius said, "That was it. For the benevolent one likes gentle flow, the harmonious one likes to praise, the wise one likes to judge, the assiduous one likes to make things beautiful. That is why I know that it was 'King Wen's Music.'"

The idea that understanding music is about visualizing its creator echoes Mencius's discussion of how the reader's mind should meet the poet's intent (*yi yi ni zhi* 以意逆志) in ideal interpretation (*Mencius* 5A.4) and the presentation of music as the venue for interpreting history and politics in the concert for the Wu noble Jizha in *Zuo Tradition* (*Zuo* Xiang 29.13, 2: 1242–49). In the chapter "Discerning Music" (Bianyue 辨樂) in *Sayings*, the above account is followed by Confucius's critique of Zilu when the latter plies "the tunes of a failing state" on a zither. "Discerning Music" ends with Confucius's exchange with the musician Binmou Jia (*KZJY* 35.450–65), a passage that also appears in *Record of Rituals*. That exchange shares the same logic of musical hermeneutics as 1.31 but focuses on King Wu instead of King Wen. It makes even finer distinctions by linking specific musical features of "Wu" 武 (meaning "martial") and its dance movements to aspects of King Wu's endeavors:

1.31b Binmou Jia of Zhou sat and attended on Confucius, who talked to him and came to the topic of music: "Why does the preparation for 'Wu' involve a prolonged drumroll of warning?"

Binmou Jia responded, "King Wu was anxious that he had not yet gained the support of the multitudes."

"Why are there drawn out chants and sighs that linger and overflow?"

He responded, "He was fearful that he would not succeed."

"Why are there vigorous movements with waving hands and stamping feet early on?"

He responded, "It was about timely action."

"Why does the dancer kneel on his right knee and raise his left leg for the kneeling parts in 'Wu?'"

He responded, "That is not the kneeling mode in 'Wu.'"

"Why are the musical notes excessive and reach the Shang note?"

He responded, "That is not the tune of 'Wu.'"

The Master said, "If it is not the tune of 'Wu,' what tune is it then?"

He responded, "The functionary in charge made mistakes in the transmission of the music. If that were not the case, then it would mean that King Wu's ambition had run amok."

The Master said, "I agree. I have heard this from Chang Hong, whose words, like yours, made the same point."

Binmou Jia rose from the mat and asked, "As for why the preparation for 'Wu' involves a prolonged drumroll of warning, I have already heard your instructions. May I ask why 'Wu' is so slow and drawn out?"

The Master said, "Stay and sit! Let me tell you. Music is the image of what has been accomplished. For the dancers to hold the shields and stand firm as a mountain: that mirrors King Wu's feat. To move vigorously, with hands waving and feet stamping: that mirrors the Grand Duke Jiang's ambition. All kneel at the end of 'Wu': that mirrors the good governance of the Duke of Zhou and the Duke of Shao. Furthermore, 'Wu' begins by setting forth northward. By the second round, Shang is destroyed. By the third round, they move south. By the fourth round, the southern domains are empowered. By the fifth round, there is a division with the Duke of Zhou on the left and the Duke of Shao on the right. By the sixth round, they have come together to honor the Son of Heaven. . . . Thus do we know that King Wu would no longer have recourse to weapons. . . . In this manner the Way of Zhou reaches all corners, and ritual and music flows unimpeded. So, is it not fitting that 'Wu' should be so slow and drawn out!" (*LJ* 3: 1021–24)

Binmou Jia starts out as the knowledgeable musician explaining to Confucius the meanings of "Wu." He interprets its variations in terms of King Wu's state of mind during the Zhou conquest of Shang and dismisses any forays into "Shang notes" that signify violence and excess as deviations from the real "Wu." But then the table is turned, and Confucius seems to command a broader historical vision as he explains "Wu," the music of martiality, as a celebration not only of the Zhou conquest but also the cessation of conflict and lasting political and ritual order.[92] By this logic, martiality (*wu* 武) is what enables culture and civilization (*wen* 文).

1.32 Confucius, having failed to be properly employed in Wei, prepared to go westward to have an audience with Zhao Jianzi. When he reached the Yellow River, he heard of the death of Dou Mingdu and Shun Hua. Facing the Yellow River, he sighed and said, "How beautiful the water is! How vast and magnificent! That I cannot cross this is fate!" Zigong said, "May I ask what this is about?" Confucius said, "Dou Mingdu and Shun Hua were worthy high officers in Jin. Before Zhao Jianzi attained his ambition, he needed these two persons and only then could he govern. By the time he attained his ambition, he killed them and then he governed. I have heard: slit open a pregnant belly and kill the fetus, and the *qilin* would not come to the outskirts; drain a swamp and let the fish dry up, and the horned dragons would not harmonize yin and yang; overturn a nest and destroy its eggs, and phoenixes would not fly and soar. Why is that so? Noble creatures are chary of the harm inflicted on their kind.[93] If even birds and beasts know how to avoid the unrighteous, how much more so should I!" He thus returned, stopped at Zou village, and composed the "Music of Zou" to lament the two men killed. Then he returned to Wei and was hosted at the home of Qu Boyu.

★ ★ ★

[translator's note]

The "water stories" about Confucius address the understanding of time, agency, virtue, and human nature. In the *Analects*, a river's unceasing flow seems to evoke both inevitable loss and unremitting striving:

> 1.32a The Master, standing by a river, said, "What passes on is just like this! There's no lapse day or night!" (*Analects* 9.17)

Mencius's disciple asks him the reason why Confucius often praised water, and Mencius compares a gushing spring to the natural flow of a noble man's nature:

> 1.32b Mencius said, "The gushing spring flows endlessly; there's no lapse day or night. Only after it fills gaps does it advance, flowing to the four seas. Having a source is like this: that was what Confucius found praiseworthy. If there's no source, then the waterways are all full when rainwater gathers in the seventh or eighth month, but their drying up is also soon to be expected. That's why a noble man is ashamed of a reputation exceeding what the facts warrant." (*Mencius* 4B.18)

While Mencius implicitly compares the ample source and inexhaustible flow of goodness in human nature to a gushing spring, Xunzi offers a list of water's virtues:

> 1.32c Confucius contemplated a river flowing east. Zigong asked Confucius, "Why is it that a noble man never fails to contemplate a great river when he sees one?" Confucius said, "A river gives equally to all living thing without deliberately doing so: that's like virtue. It flows downward, always following in every bend its principle: that's like proper duty. It is vast and inexhaustible: that's like the Way. As if propelled on its course, it speeds along like echoes following sounds, heading toward bottomless ravines with no fear: that's like valor. In filling hollows, it's invariably level: that's like rules and laws. In its fullness, it requires no measuring instruments: that's like rectitude. It is gentle and has subtle reach: that's like discernment. That which comes out of it and enters it moves toward purity: that's like skill at beneficial transformation. Even with ten thousand twists, it always

heads east: that's like steadfast intent. For these reasons, a noble man never fails to contemplate a great river when he sees one." (*XZ* 28.393–94; cf. *CQFL* 73.398, *SY* 17.46, *DDLJ* 2: 782–83; *KZJY* 9.122–23)

Sima Qian links Confucius's exclamation over the river to his sense of insurmountable obstacles, compared to the river that cannot be crossed. Its tone is perhaps closest to the *Analects* (9.17) (1.32a), where the ceaseless flow of the river can evoke, among other things, the relentless passage of time and the limits of human striving.

Passage 1.32 imagines Confucius's choices or lack thereof, given the uncertain fate of talented men engaging in politics. Zhao Jianzi had been active in Jin affairs and interstate relations since 517 BCE. He played a key role in pacifying succession struggles in the Zhou house (519–516 BCE) and emerged as the dominant Jin minister in 493 BCE after quelling the rebellion of a branch lineage and defeating the rival Fan and Zhonghang lineages, a conflict that lasted through the 490s. Qi, Wei, Lu, Zheng, and Song were drawn into this internecine conflict, taking the side of Zhao Jianzi's enemies. Cui Shu, noting Zhao's failings and hostility toward Wei, questions whether Confucius would have sought his patronage (*CDB* 293–94). In fact, Zhao is depicted by and large in positive terms as a decisive political and military leader in *Zuo Tradition*, but Sima Qian is more critical of him. Confucius is said to condemn his ambition in "The Hereditary House of Zhao" (*SJ* 43.26). Parallel accounts of 1.32 appear in *The Garden of Eloquence* (*SY* 13.3), *Sayings* (*KZJY* 22.317–18), and *Kong Anthology* (*KCZ* 5.96). The "Music of Zou" is elaborated as a quadrisyllabic poem on the frustration of Confucius's political ideals in *Kong Anthology* (*KCZ* 5.96).

1.33 On another day, Lord Ling asked about military formations. Confucius said, "As for matters of the sacrificial vessels, I have heard about them; yet of matters of the army, I have learned nothing." The following day, when Lord Ling was speaking with Confucius, he saw wild geese flying by and raised his head to gaze at it. It was plain from his countenance that he was not paying attention to Confucius. Confucius thus set out and again went to Chen.

[translator's note]
The Wei ruler's question and Confucius's answer also appears in the *Analects* (15.1), where it is said that Confucius leaves the next day. A version of

this exchange is also found in an episode dated 484 BCE in *Zuo Tradition*, where the Wei minister Kong Wenzi consults Confucius about attacking Taishu Ji, a Wei nobleman who, having married Kong Wenzi's daughter, secretly sets up another establishment with a woman that he is supposed to have divorced. Confucius tries to dissuade Kong Wenzi from the planned attack (*Zuo* Ai 11.6, 3: 1904–05):

1.33a Confucius said, "As for matters of the sacrificial vessels, I have studied them; yet of matters of armor and weaponry, I have heard nothing." He withdrew and issued the command to drive away. He said, "A bird can choose its tree, but how can a tree choose its bird?" Kong Wenzi hurriedly stopped him and said, "How should I presume to plan private matters? I was trying to forestall troubles in Wei." Confucius was going to stop, but the people of Lu summoned him home with gifts, so he went home.

It is tempting to read Confucius's exchange with Lord Ling in *Historical Records* and the *Analects* (15.1) as an "upgraded version" of the above episode, which will appear below in 1.50. Kong Wenzi's private grudge threatens to stoke a civil war, and it is easy to understand why Confucius advises against it and takes his leave. Divested of an immediate context, Confucius's answer to Lord Ling is potentially more ambiguous: it can mean that military affairs are not important or too important, or simply that he does not deign to become involved or is indeed ignorant about warfare, although Confucius urged Lord Ling to attack Pu earlier (1.27) and is also said to be knowledgeable about military affairs later in this account (1.50). Presented as the final straw that makes him leave Wei (after circling back to it several times) in Sima Qian's account, it highlights the disconnect between Confucius's goals and the concerns of those wielding power.

1.34 In the summer, Lord Ling of Wei died. His grandson Zhe was instated as ruler. He would be known as the Ousted Lord of Wei. In the sixth month, Zhao Jianzi installed Lord Ling's heir apparent Kuaikui at Qī.[94] Yang Hu had Kuaikui wear a mourning cowl and had eight men dressed in mourning pretend to have come from Wei to escort him. Weeping as they entered, they then stayed there. In winter, Cai relocated to Zhoulai. That was the third year of the reign of Lord Ai of Lu [492 BCE], and

Confucius was already sixty. Qi assisted Wei in laying siege to Qī because the Wei heir apparent, Kuaikui, was there.

[translator's note]
Sima Qian gives a snapshot of the Wei succession struggle upon the death of Lord Ling of Wei in 492 BCE. In events dated to 493 BCE (not 492 BCE) in *Zuo Tradition* (*Zuo* Ai 2, 3: 1841–48), Zhao Jianzi, chief minister of Jin, supports Lord Ling's exiled heir Kuaikui's bid for the Wei throne and campaign against his own son Zhe, installing him in the Wei city of Qī. Qi and Zheng are on the side of the newly installed Zhe and also support Jin's Fan and Zhonghang rebels, who oppose Zhao Jianzi. Yang Hu is the Lu strongman who rebels unsuccessfully against the Ji lineage (1.12) and flees to Jin in 501 BCE. When Zhao Jianzi offers refuge to Yang Hu, Confucius predicts: "The Zhao line will have trouble for generations!" (*Zuo* Ding 9.3, 3: 1790–91). Yang Hu comes up with the ruse for smuggling Kuaikui into Qī. In the name of mourning his father Lord Ling, Kuaikui established Qī as his power base to oppose his son Zhe. Sima Qian's snapshot gives us a sense of how the Wei succession struggle deepens divisions in other states and foments an interstate conflict, with the Zhao lineage in Jin and the Lu rebel Yang Hu supporting Kuaikui, and Jin rebels, Qi, and Zheng supporting Zhe.

1.35 In the summer, the temples of Lords Huan and Xi were burnt. Nangong Jingshu fought the fire. Hearing about this in Chen, Confucius said, "The disastrous fire must have taken place in the temples of Lords Huan and Xi!" This later turned out to have been the case indeed.

[translator's note]
Confucius's prescience in 1.35 can be potentially linked to instances of his esoteric knowledge (1.10, 1.24, 1.62), and 1.35 is thus included along with those examples in "Discerning Things" in *Sayings* (*KZJY* 16.242–48, 253). In *Sayings*, Confucius explains his unerring inference, and the Chen ruler calls him a sage because of his predictive powers:

> 1.35a The Chen ruler asked, "How do you know this?" The Master said, "Ritual propriety means that ancestors have merits and progenitors have the power of virtue: that is why their temples are not destroyed. By now the kinship ties with Lords Huan and Xi have come to an end, and their merits and power of virtue do not suffice

to preserve their temples. Yet Lu has not destroyed them. That is why a disaster from heaven has been visited upon it." Three days later, a Lu envoy arrived. When asked about this, it turned out to be the temples of Lords Huan and Xi. The Chen ruler said to Zigong, "Only now do I know that the sage should be valued." Zigong responded, "For you, my lord, to know that is commendable. But that is not as good as focusing on his Way and putting into practice his idea of moral transformation." (*KZJY* 16.253)

The *Zuo Tradition* account of the disastrous fires in the temples of Lords Huan and Xi of Lu in 492 BCE includes Confucius's comment, but the main focus is how Lu nobles distinguish themselves in their fire-fighting measures (*Zuo* Ai 3.2, 3: 1850–51). Later commentators see the fire as retributory. Dong Zhongshu (179–104 BCE) and Liu Xiang (77–6 BCE) believe that the two temples should not have been built because they embodied the transgressions of the Ji lineage, which was descended from Lord Huan and became powerful under Lord Xi (*HS* 27A.1330). This retributory logic is more clearly spelt out when a Zhou temple replaces the Lu temple. In a story in *Garden of Eloquence*, when news of a Zhou temple catching fire comes to Confucius, he quotes from the *Odes* and correctly divines that it is the temple of King Xi, who changed the rules of King Wen and King Wu, indulging in excesses that precipitated dynastic decline (*SY* 13.4, see also *KZJY* 15.220–21).

1.36 In the autumn, Ji Huanzi was ill and rode a palanquin to inspect the Lu city walls. He heaved a sigh and said, "Formerly, this domain almost rose and flourished. It was because I incurred blame in the eyes of Confucius that it has not risen and flourished." He turned around and said to his heir Kangzi: "When I die, you will certainly be chief minister in Lu. When you become chief minister in Lu, you have to summon Confucius." A few days later, Huanzi died, and Kangzi was instated in his position. After Huanzi had been buried, Kangzi wanted to summon Confucius. Gong Zhiyu said, "Back then our former lord sought Confucius's counsel but did not persist to the end, and he was ultimately mocked by the other lords. If now we seek his counsel again without being able to persist to the end, we would once more be mocked by the other lords." Kangzi said, "In that case, whom should we summon?" Gong Zhiyu said, "We have to summon Ran Qiu." They therefore sent a messenger to summon Ran Qiu. Ran Qiu prepared to set out, and Confucius said, "The men of Lu have summoned Qiu: they will not make use of him in small ways; they are prepared to make use of him in great ways." That day, Confucius said, "Let us return! Let us return! The young ones in my fold are audaciously ardent and fastidiously scrupulous. Their manifest brilliance is impressive—they just don't know how to keep them within proper bounds." Zigong knew that Confucius longed to return. When Zigong was seeing Ran Qiu off, it is said that he admonished him with these words: "If you are in a position of power, let Confucius be summoned."

[translator's note]
Sima Qian presents Ji Kangzi's accession to power as another moment of "near miss" for Confucius—a ruler or powerful minister almost turns to Confucius for advice but does not end up doing so. Ji Huanzi's dying injunction here recalls the final words of Meng Xizi (1.4): again, a Lu nobleman asks his heir to honor Confucius. Again, jealous rivals block Confucius's ascendancy (1.9, 1.41, 1.46). According to *Zuo Tradition*, when Ji Huanzi is on his deathbed (492 BCE), he tells his retainer Zhengchang that if his concubine Nan gives birth to a son, that baby should be established as his heir. When Zhengchang presents Nan's infant son at court, Ji Kangzi asks to withdraw. The Lu officer sent to investigate the respective claims of Ji Kangzi and Nan's son is murdered, probably on Ji Kangzi's order. Zhengchang flees to Wei (*Zuo* Ai 3.4, 3: 1852–53). In other words, Jin Huanzi does not intend to establish Ji Kangzi as his heir. Commentators have used that passage to dispute the authenticity of the above account.

Sima Qian puts Confucius's statement on his disciples in 1.36 (based on the *Analects* 5.22) and its variant in 1.25 (based on *Mencius* 7B.37) in the context of Confucius's different sojourns in Chen, a choice criticized by many commentators who see the *Analects* 5.22 and *Mencius* 7B.37 as versions of the same saying. The above passage links Confucius's desire to return and his assessment of his disciples' "manifest brilliance" to Ran Qiu's incipient political career. In the *Analects*, Confucius ranks Ran Qiu as a "qualified minister" (*juchen* 具臣) instead of a "great minister" (*dachen* 大臣), someone who falls short of the highest good (*Analects* 11.24, 5.8; see also *SJ* 67.9, and the introduction, 6). He also criticizes Ran Qiu's failures as Ji Kangzi's steward: Ran Qiu fails to obviate Ji's ritual infractions, helps Ji levy heavy taxes, and tacitly support Ji's unjustified military campaign (*Analects* 3.6, 11.17, 16.1). In *Zuo Tradition*, when Ji Kangzi attempts to consult with

Confucius through Ran Qiu regarding the overhaul of Lu's system of taxation, Confucius refuses to state his views publicly and only privately counsels restraint (*Zuo* Ai 11.7, 3: 1904–05). More generally, Confucius is less strident in his criticism of the Ji lineage in *Zuo Tradition* than he is in the *Analects*. As in *Zuo Tradition*, Sima Qian focuses on Ran Qiu's political efficacy.

1.37 Ran Qiu having left, Confucius moved from Chen and relocated to Cai the following year. Lord Zhao of Cai prepared to go to Wu because Wu summoned him. Earlier, Lord Zhao had deceived his ministers and high officers about the relocation to Zhoulai. Then, when he was preparing to go to Wu, the high officers feared another round of relocation. Gongsun Pian shot an arrow and killed Lord Zhao. Chu invaded Cai. In the autumn, Lord Jing of Qi died.

[translator's note]
Disaffected Cai officers murdered Lord Zhao of Cai (*Zuo* Ai 4.1, 3: 1854–55), who was responsible for shifting Cai's allegiance from Chu to Wu and relocating the Cai capital to Zhoulai (1.34). We are not told how the unrest in Cai affects Confucius. Lord Jing of Qi died in 490 BCE. There is no record of Chu invading Cai at that point, although Chu is said to have tried to expand its influence northward by bringing the men of Cai under its sphere of control in 491 BCE (*Zuo* Ai 4.2, 3: 1856–57). One of the Chu dignitaries involved in that effort is Zhuliang, the Lord of She, who is featured in the following passage.

1.38 The following year, Confucius moved from Cai and went to She. The Lord of She asked about governance. Confucius said, "Governance lies in drawing close those from afar and attaching those who are close by." On another day, the Lord of She asked Zilu about Confucius, and Zilu did not respond. Hearing about this, Confucius said, "Yóu, why didn't you respond by saying, 'As for his character, he is indefatigable in learning about the Way, unflagging in teaching others, forgetting to eat in outbursts of fervor, forgetting his worries in his joy, not realizing that old age is about to come' or words to that effect?"

[translator's note]
The Lord of She, who shows prescient political judgment and plays a key role in quelling a rebellion in Chu in 479 BCE (*Zuo* Ai 16.5, 3: 1946–52),

is mentioned thrice in the *Analects* as someone posing questions to and about Confucius. Two of those exchanges (*Analects* 13.16, 7.19) are presented here. For the first, the analogous passage in the *Analects* implies a causal connection between providing welfare for the people and broadening political influence: "Those close by are pleased, and those from afar draw close." Han Feizi decries this reliance on the people's goodwill as an encouragement for dispensing governmental favors that can potentially undermine the law (*HFZ* 38.906). In the second case, Zilu's failure to answer the Lord of She's question, presumably rooted in his anxiety over doing justice to the Master's momentous significance, gives Confucius the chance to give an account of himself. Confucius's reply here combines three entries from the *Analects* (7.2, 7.19, 7.34), conveying the image of one who disclaims sagely wisdom or the highest virtue, one who delights in learning and teaching, and one who combines fervor and pleasure in the process of striving. According to Sima Qian's chronology, Confucius is at this point sixty-one or sixty-two.

1.39 He left She and was returning to Cai. Chang Ju and Jie Ni were paired up and plowing. Confucius thought they were recluses and sent Zilu to ask them about the ford. Chang Ju said, "Who is that holding the reins in the carriage?" Zilu said, "It is Confucius." "Is it Confucius of Lu?" "Yes." Chang Ju said, "Then he should know about the ford." Jie Ni said to Zilu, "Who are you?" Zilu said, "I am Zhong Yóu." "Are you, sir, a disciple of Confucius?" "Yes." Jie Ni said, "All under heaven, there is the same endless flow. And who can change that? Furthermore, instead of following the one who avoids the wrong people, wouldn't it be better to follow the ones who avoid the entire world!" They sowed seeds without stopping. Zilu reported to Confucius about this, and Confucius said with pensive melancholy, "One cannot belong to the fold of birds and beasts. If the Way prevails under heaven, then I would not be trying to change things."

[translator's note]
Passage 1.39 is one of three (along with 1.40 and 1.47) echoing the *Analects* (18.6, 18.7, 18.5) and featuring recluses or men who renounce politics and society. It also recalls Confucius's critic in 1.30. Chang Ju and Jie Ni criticize Confucius for his futile striving. Their names combine positive attributes (commanding height and duration [*chang* 長], distinction and bravery [*jie* 桀])

with negation (to disappoint and to destroy [*ju* 沮], to drown [*ni* 溺]): one may render their names as Impressively Crushed and Bravely Drowning. They are men who could have achieved great things but, seeing through the futility of trying to change the errant ways of the world given the absence of just rulers, decide to shun it. "Crossing the ford" becomes a metaphor for finding the right way or overcoming obstacles (see 1.30a, 1.32). Chang Ju and Jie Ni imply with sarcasm that Confucius should know about the ford if he is indeed a wise man. Zilu, as Confucius's brashest and most ambitious disciple, seems ideally cut out for a set down. Will following Confucius extricate him from "the endless flow"? Confucius in his response implies his empathy with his critics' perspective but defends the need to persist in his striving precisely because the time is out of joint.

1.40 On another day, Zilu was going on his way when he encountered a hoe-bearing elder. Zilu said, "Did you, sir, see the Master?" The elder said, "Four limbs that don't work hard; five grains that he can't tell apart. Which one is your Master?" He leaned on his hoe to remove weeds. Zilu reported about this to Confucius, who said, "This was a recluse." When they made their way there again, he was gone.

[translator's note]
In the analogous account in the *Analects* (18.7), the exchange between Zilu and the hoe-bearing elder continues after the latter leans on his hoe to remove weeds:

> 1.40a Zilu stood and clasped his raised hands. The old man had Zilu stay overnight, killing a chicken and preparing millet to offer him a meal, and presented his two sons to him. The following day, Zilu went on his way and told the Master about this. The Master said, "This was a recluse." He sent Zilu to go back and see him. But when he arrived, the old man had left. Zilu said, "To refuse to take office serving the state violates duty. The regulations governing the old and the young cannot be abandoned, so how can the bonds of duty between ruler and subject be abandoned? He strives for personal purity and ends up subverting an important normative relationship. When a noble man takes office, he performs its proper duties. As for the Way not prevailing, he already knows it." (*Analects* 18.7)

The longer narrative in the *Analects* augment the mutual respect and mutual critique of Zilu and the hoe-bearing elder. The latter believes in personal exertion in agrarian labor, a position espoused by some Warring States thinkers. He criticizes Zilu, yet he invites him home and presents his sons to him. The elder's hospitality heightens the contrast between his political choice and his affinity with Zilu. In his concluding remarks, possibly addressed to the elder's two sons, Zilu defends his choice but also acknowledges the challenges presented by the abeyance of the Way. The sympathetic recluse here contrasts with his counterpart in the analogous account in *Zhuangzi*, who does not deign to speak to Confucius and his disciples and, in Confucius's imagination, merely disdains Confucius as "a flatterer of the powerful" (*ningren* 佞人) (*ZZ* 25.894–97).

1.41 Three years after Confucius relocated to Cai, Wu attacked Chen. Chu came to Chen's rescue and stationed its troops at Chengfu. Having heard that Confucius was in the area between Chen and Cai, Chu sent someone to offer Confucius an official appointment. Confucius was preparing to go and bow in thanks with proper ritual when the high officers of Chen and Cai conferred among themselves: "Confucius is a worthy man. What he criticizes and censures targets in all cases the lords' errors. By now he has been in the area between Chen and Cai for quite a while, and the policies implemented by the various high officers have in all cases gone against Confucius's wishes. Now Chu, a great state, has come to offer Confucius an official appointment. If they make good use of Confucius, then the high officers in charge of affairs in Chen and Cai will be in danger." They thus colluded and sent their retainers and lackeys to encircle Confucius in the fields. Confucius could not set forth and ran out of food. His followers got sick and could not rise. Confucius continued to lecture, recite texts, play music, and sing without flagging. Zilu, resentful, presented himself and said, "Can noble men also be in dire straits?" Confucius said, "Noble men persevere in dire straits. Petty men, when in dire straits, break all constraints and give way to license."

[translator's note]
The analogous entry in the *Analects* (15.2), corresponding to the last four lines of 1.41 (minus the reference to Confucius's unflagging activities, a detail found in *Zhuangzi*), uses the privations Confucius and his disciples suffer in Chen to emphasize how adversities become the test and

confirmation of virtue. *Mencius* claims that troubles arise for Confucius at the border of Chen and Cai because he "had ties neither with rulers nor with those serving them" (*Mencius* 7B.18). None of the numerous Warring States and Han elaborations of this anecdote supplies a historical context for Confucius's plight. According to the *Annals* and *Zuo Tradition*, Wu attacked Chen in 489 BCE (*Zuo* 3: 1863–64), and one can imagine how warfare leads to privations and food shortage. It is highly implausible, however, that Chen, threatened by Wu and dependent on Chu, and Cai, caught between Wu and Chu, should conspire to besiege a man expected to find favor in Chu.[95] Confucius and his followers could easily have been killed or detained by the forces of Chen and Cai. What would have been the point of depriving them of provisions until the much-feared Chu comes to their rescue? Sima Qian returns to the theme of the unjust persecution of the virtuous and emphasizes Confucius's equanimity and moral convictions in dramatizing this episode. The proper response to "dire straits" (or "distress," "privations," "failure," *qiong* 窮) is discussed in a wide range of texts—should one trust in heaven's ultimate vindication, accept the intractability of timing and fate, find equanimity in inner resources, or regard adversity as the confirmation of virtue?

1.42 Zigong changed color. Confucius said, "Ci, do you take me for one who has broad learning and retains knowledge?" Zigong said, "Yes. Isn't it so?" Confucius said, "It is not so. I follow one principle through all and sundry."

[translator's note]
Confucius repeats his remark on following "one principle" (*yi* 一) to Zeng Shen (*Analects* 4.15), who then proceeds to summarize it to other disciples as "nothing more than integrity (*zhong* 忠) and empathy (*shu* 恕)." Zhu Xi famously glosses *zhong* as "fully realizing one's potential for goodness" and *shu* as "extending one's preferences for oneself to others." Later thinkers define "oneness" as, among other things, "upholding reverence" (*zhujing* 主敬), "investigating things and fully understanding their underlying coherence" (*gewu qiongli* 格物窮理) (Zhu Xi), and "innate understanding of goodness" (*liangzhi* 良知) (Wang Yangming). They also debate the relationship between learning, knowledge, and "one principle." The above passage also appears in the *Analects* (15.3), immediately following the entry on Confucius's plight in Chen. While no context is given in the *Analects*, Sima

Qian frames the passage as a response to events in Chen by adding the line "Zigong changed color," thereby confirming steadfast moral purpose as the response to adversity. That he includes it here may suggest that the version of the *Analects* (or proto-*Analects*) he used could have passages in the same sequence as the received text.

Some commentators have identified the following *Analects* entry as the continuation of the exchange between Confucius and Zilu in 1.41: "The Master said, 'Yóu! Few indeed are those who understand virtue" (*Analects* 15.4). We can imagine Confucius adding this comment, possibly in response to Zilu's objection that perseverance in adversity offers scant consolation. Sima Qian, however, prefers to turn attention to the responses of Confucius's three disciples (1.43, 1.44, 1.45), which encode different arguments about how best to face adversity (cf. *KZJY* 20.297–301). In structure these passages are comparable to other exchanges in which Confucius poses the same question to different disciples, as when he asks them to "each articulate his ambition" (see the introduction) or to define wisdom and the highest good (*XZ* 29.400–01).

1.43 Confucius knew that his disciples were resentful. He thus summoned Zilu and asked him, "As it says in the *Odes*, 'Neither rhinoceroses nor tigers, / We yet roam in the desolate wilds.' Is my Way errant? Why have I come to this?" Zilu said, "I reckon perhaps we have not yet attained the highest good? Others do not trust us. I reckon perhaps we have not yet attained wisdom? Others do not let us carry the day with our Way." Confucius said, "Can this really be true! Yóu, suppose the men embodying the highest good never fail to gain trust, then how could we have Boyi and Shuqi? Suppose the wise ones never fail to carry the day with their way, then how could we have Prince Bigan?"

[translator's note]

The analogous passage in *Xunzi*, which also appears with some variations in *Han's Exegesis* (*HSWZ* 7.314–15), *The Garden of Eloquence* (*SY* 17.16–17), and *Sayings* (*KZJY* 20.298–99), expatiates on the nature of human moral agency when confronting the vicissitudes of existence. Similar concerns appear in "Adversity and Success Determined by Timing" (Qing da yi shi 窮達以時), an excavated manuscript from Guodian. Adversities become the necessary test of virtue in *Xunzi*:

1.43a When Confucius was going south to Chu, he was in distress between Chen and Cai. For seven days, they had no cooked food. Their soup of wild greens included no grains. The disciples all showed signs of suffering from hunger. Zilu came forth and asked, "I have heard, heaven repays those who do good with good fortune and repays those who perpetrates evil with calamity.[96] Now you, Master, have accumulated virtue, heaped up righteousness, and embraced goodness for a long time. Why are we reduced to such dire straits?"

Confucius said, "Yóu! You don't understand. Let me explain to you. Do you think that the wise ones must be heeded? Didn't we see Prince Bigan's heart cut out? Do you think that the loyal ones must be heeded? Didn't we see Guan Longfeng punished? Do you think that the remonstrating ones must be heeded? Wasn't Wu Zixu of Wu dismembered outside the Gate of Gusu? Whether one meets with recognition or not is a matter of timing, while being worthy or worthless comes down to one's qualities. There are many noble men with broad learning and far-reaching plans who do not encounter the right times! Judging from this, numerous are those who do not encounter the right era, how could I have been alone! Furthermore, angelicas and orchids growing in the deep forest do not stop being fragrant because there is no one around. A noble man pursues learning not for the sake of advancement, but so as to remain unfazed in adversity, to maintain his unflagging spirit even in sorrow, and to understand calamity and good fortune, as well as beginnings and endings, with his heart free from confusion. Being worthy or worthless is a question of one's qualities; acting or not acting is a question of human effort; meeting or not meeting with recognition is a question of timing; death and life is a question of fate. Now if a person does not encounter the times right for him, can he act even if he is worthy? If he meets the times right for him, what difficulty is there? That is why the noble man has broad learning, plans far ahead, cultivates his person, and rectifies his conduct to wait for the times right for him."

Confucius said, "Yóu! Stay! Let me explain to you. Formerly, the noble son Chong'er of Jin set his mind on hegemony at Cao; the Yue king Goujian set his mind on hegemony at Kuaiji; Xiaobai, Lord Huan of Qi, set his mind on hegemony at Ju. That is why those not reduced to dire straits do not think far; the ambition of those not eclipsed is not great. How would you know that I did not gain possession of something similar beneath Sangluo?" (*XZ* 28.395–96)

The above exchange implicitly encodes the debate between followers of Confucius and their opponents, who could use the story of his distress to discredit Confucius or to show him championing different ideas, as in some of the examples from *Zhuangzi* discussed below (1.45c, 1.45d).[97] The Mohists could appeal to "heaven's will" (*tianzhi* 天志) to equate circumstantial reversals with moral failure. They could also allege that Confucius and his disciples become unscrupulous when facing hardship (1.45a). Elsewhere Xunzi writes about "controlling the command of heaven and putting it to use" (*XZ* 17.233); here he does not go that far but still insists, through Confucius, on human agency and a steady compass of action in adversity. Confucius argues that one's will and actions, rather than objective situations, determine worth, as shown by ministers serving tyrants and benighted rulers, like Bigan, Guan Longfeng, and Wu Zixu. Sima Qian repeats the example of Bigan and adds Boyi and Shuqi, who starve to death at Mount Shouyang to protest the violence of the Zhou conquest of Shang and are placed at the beginning of the biographical section of *Historical Records*. The second set of examples in *Xunzi* lists rulers whose hegemonic ambitions are first kindled at the nadir of their misfortunes. Sima Qian omits this section and chooses not to present examples of moral worth vindicated by actual power, although elsewhere in this chapter Confucius refers to the discourse of hegemony (1.7, 1.17).

1.44 Zilu came out, and Zigong entered to see Confucius. Confucius said, "Ci, as it says in the *Odes*, 'Neither rhinoceroses nor tigers, / We yet roam in the desolate wilds.' Is my Way errant? Why have I come to this?" Zigong said, "The Master's Way is supremely great, that is why none under heaven can accommodate the Master. Why don't you, Master, scale it back somewhat?" Confucius said, "Ci, good farmers can grow crops and yet cannot be assured of harvest, good craftsmen can have great skills and yet cannot comply with everyone. The noble man can cultivate his Way, structure it through principles, order it through regulation, and yet cannot be accommodated. Now you do not cultivate your Way and instead seek accommodation. Ci, your ambition is not far-reaching enough!"

★   ★   ★

[translator's note]
As Cui Shu points out, both Zilu's skepticism (1.43) and Zigong's readiness to compromise (1.44) are inconsistent with their image in the *Analects* and in the chapter devoted to Confucius's disciples in *Historical Records* (*SJ* 67) (*CDB* 303). Sima Qian may be taking Zilu's brash confidence and occasionally confrontational attitude toward Confucius as well as Zigong's political instincts and rhetorical sleights of hand to their hypothetical conclusion. More to the point, their problematic responses serve as foils to Yan Hui's answer below.

1.45 Zigong came out, and Yan Hui entered to see Confucius. Confucius said, "Hui, as it says in the *Odes*, 'Neither rhinoceroses nor tigers, / We yet roam in the desolate wilds.' Is my Way errant? Why have I come to this?" Yan Hui said, "The Master's Way is supremely great, that is why none under heaven can accommodate it. Even so, you, Master, extend and practice it. What harm is there in being unaccommodated? It is only by being unaccommodated that the noble man reveals himself! If the Way is not cultivated, it is our shame. If the Way, having been assiduously cultivated, is yet not put to use, it is the shame of those who hold power in the domains. What harm is there in being unaccommodated? It is only by being unaccommodated that the noble man reveals himself!" Confucius smiled with delight, "You have it right, son of the Yan lineage! If you had great wealth, I would become your steward!"

It was at that time that Confucius sent Zigong as an envoy to Chu. King Zhao of Chu raised troops to welcome Confucius, and it was only thus that he gained reprieve.

[translator's note]
Yan Hui's answer goes one step further than Confucius's responses to Zilu and Zigong. Instead of simply defending the noble man's principles against suspicions of insufficiency or the challenge to compromise, Yan Hui declares triumphantly that being "unaccommodated" (*burong* 不容) is the proof and validation of Confucius's greatness, perhaps because it will become the impetus for momentous acts of creation. We are only one step away from Sima Qian's assertion that Confucius's suffering between Chen and Cai prompts him to compile the *Spring and Autumn Annals* in the autobiographical final chapter of *Historical Records* (*SJ* 130.28) and his letter to

Ren An (*HS* 62.2735). Note that Yan Hui's argument diverges from the vindication of adversity as the test of virtue or the preparation for power or even kingship (1.43a, *SY* 17.16). If Yan Hui's reasoning is unworldly, then Confucius's humorous rejoinder reminds us how hard it is to forego hopes of being useful or relevant.

As mentioned earlier, the story of Confucius's plight between Chen and Cai becomes a kind of crucible for debating the nature and possibility of moral agency in many Warring States and Han texts. The Mohists use the story to discredit Confucius, derisively referred to as "the Kong fellow":

1.45a The Kong fellow (Confucius) faced extreme privations between Chen and Cai, eating a soup of wild greens without any grains. Ten days later, Zilu cooked a piglet for him. The Kong fellow ate it without asking where the meat had come from. Zilu had forcibly taken someone's clothes and exchanged them to buy wine. The Kong fellow drank the wine without asking where it had come from. When Lord Ai welcomed Confucius back, he would not sit if the mat was not straight and would not eat if the meat was not cut the right way.[98] Zilu came forth and asked, "How come you are acting so differently from the way you did between Chen and Cai?" The Kong fellow said, "Come! Let me explain to you. Back then you and I made do to survive; now we make do to be righteous." When facing hunger and privations, he did not balk at wrongful appropriation; when enjoying abundance and satiated, he acted hypocritically to shore up his dignity. What corruption, deviance, deception, and hypocrisy are greater than this! (*MZ* 39.275–77)

Confucian decorum, tied to ritual and music, is attacked by Mozi as wasteful. Here Confucius's fastidiousness is exposed as hypocritical and circumstantial, no different in principle from his lack of scruples between Chen and Cai. In both cases, he "makes do" (*gou* 苟) to survive and thrive.

The interactions between Confucius and his disciples (1.41–1.45) illustrate how the definition of ethical conduct can be shaped by the social dynamics of mutual judgment. The difficulty of judgment comes to the fore in the following story from *Mr. Lü's Annals*:

1.45b Confucius faced extreme privations between Chen and Cai. They did not even have soup made from wild vegetables and had not tasted grains for seven days. Confucius took a nap in the daytime. Yan Hui went to look for rice. He obtained some and cooked it, and it was almost done. Confucius saw Yan Hui picking up rice from the bowl and eating it. Not long after, the rice was cooked, and Yan Hui came to Confucius to present the food. Confucius pretended he had not seen anything and rose, saying, "Just now I dreamed of my late father. Let us offer it first as sacrifice and then eat."[99] Yan Hui responded, "That will not do. Just now dirt got into the bowl. To discard food is not auspicious. I picked up the dirty rice and ate it." Confucius sighed, "What we can trust are our eyes, and yet even our eyes cannot be trusted. What we can rely on are our minds, and yet we cannot rely even on our minds. Disciples: register this. It is indeed not easy to know people." Thus, knowledge is not difficult to achieve, but the means of knowing people is.[100]

In the *Analects* (12.22), Confucius considers "knowing people" (*zhiren* 知人) the essence of knowing. The above anecdote dramatizes how "knowing people" becomes psychologically more demanding in a situation of distress. Is Confucius testing Yan Hui or indirectly reproaching him? Without purporting to discredit Confucius, it nevertheless makes him seem obtuse, petty, and insincere. Unease with such implications might have prompted the substitution of Zigong for Confucius in the version of this story in *Sayings* (*KZJY* 20.302–03).

Confucius's plight between Chen and Cai, mentioned nine times in *Zhuangzi*, exemplifies the modulated and polyvalent attitude toward Confucius in that text, where he appears alternatively as the sage espousing Zhuangzi's ideas, the sage whose teachings are still recognizably "Confucian" but tinged with a greater emphasis on detachment and equanimity, the benighted pedant, or the misguided seeker of truth enlightened by Laozi or other transcendent figures in *Zhuangzi* (see 1.6, translator's note). Some of these images can be seen in the accounts below:

1.45c Confucius was besieged between Chen and Cai, and for seven days had no cooked food. Taigong Ren went to condole with him, saying, "Are you on the point of death?" Confucius said, "Yes." "Do you abhor death?" "Yes."

Ren said, "I have spoken of the Way of the Undying. There is a bird in the eastern sea named Yitai [meaning "Slackened Will"]. As far as a bird goes, its flight is low and slow, as if it were powerless. Drawing on helpmates, it flies; pressing close to others, it roosts. Advancing, it dares not stay in front; withdrawing, it dares not bring up the rear. Eating, it dares not taste the food first and without exception takes the leftovers. That is why, going among its flock, it is not rejected, and ultimately outsiders cannot harm it, and thus it escapes disaster. Straight trees are the first to be felled; wells with sweet water are the first to dry up. Your intent is to adorn yourself with knowledge to overawe the foolish, and to cultivate your person to show how others are corrupt. Shining brightly, you walk as if you were bearing the sun and the moon. That is why you cannot escape disaster. Formerly, I heard from The Perfected Man, 'He who inflates himself has no merit;[101] he who accomplishes anything will fall, he who makes a name will be diminished.' Who can get rid of his merit and fame and return them to the multitude! The Way flows but does not illumine its resting place; virtue is realized but does not name its whereabouts. Be pure and constant like a mad man. He who removes his traces and gives up power does not act for the sake of merit and fame. That is why he does not ask anything of others, and others also ask nothing of him. The supreme being is not heard of. Why do you delight in making yourself known?"

Confucius said, "Excellent!" He took leave of his associates, dismissed his disciples, and fled to a great marsh. Wearing coarse garments and eating acorns and nuts, he entered throngs of beasts without disturbing them and entered flocks of birds without confusing their ranks. Even birds and beasts did not abhor him, how much less humans! (*ZZ* 20.679–83)

How does the besieged Confucius flee to a great marsh? Historical specificity has all but dissolved in the above account. As Andrew Meyer observes, the Chen-Cai frontier "has lost its status as a particular moment in time and space" and has become the boundary between worlds defined by different values.[102] Although this seems to be a typical "conversion narrative" whereby a misguided Confucius is made to realize his error, he is nevertheless described as shining with the brightness of virtue. In another iteration of the story in the same chapter, Confucius articulates perspectives upheld in *Zhuangzi* as transcendent:

1.45d Confucius faced extreme privations between Chen and Cai, and for seven days had no cooked food. Leaning against a withered tree with his left hand and hitting a withered branch with his right, he sang the airs of Biaoshi. The potential for music was there without the rhythm; the sounds were there without variations in scale. And yet the sounds of drumming wood, in tandem with the human voice, naturally touched the heart of people. Yan Hui, standing respectfully with clasped hands, turned his gaze to Confucius.

Confucius, fearing that Yan Hui would magnify his importance and make much of his greatness, that he would, out of attachment to himself, make much of his grief, said to him, "Hui, it is easy not to be afflicted by heaven, it is difficult not to receive benefits from others. There is no beginning that is not an ending. Heaven and humans are one. Now, who was the one singing?"

Hui said, "May I ask, how is it easy to be unafflicted by heaven?"

Confucius said, "Hunger, thirst, heat, and cold that impose limits on humans belong to the movements of heaven and earth. They are the manifestations of the cycle of things, which is to say that one goes on one's way by their side. He who is a subject does not dare to leave his ruler. If even the way of a subject is like this, how much more so when one is waiting upon heaven!"

"What do you mean by the difficulty of not receiving benefits from others?"

"Suppose once employed one succeeds on all sides, and one is showered with noble titles and emoluments endlessly. These are advantages brought on by things, they have nothing to do with oneself. As for me, my fate lies beyond them. A noble man does not become a bandit, a worthy man does not steal, how can I take these things? Hence it is said: There is no bird wiser than the swallow. Its gaze does not rest where its eyes should not be. Even if it drops its fruit, it abandons it and leaves. It is afraid of people, yet it enters the midst of the human realm just because the altars of soil and grain exist there."

"What do you mean by there being no beginning that is not an ending?"

"That which transforms the myriad things: one does not know how it brings about changes, how can one know its ending? How can one know its beginning? One can only stay the correct course and wait for it!"

"What do you mean by humans and heaven being one?"

"Human exists because of heaven. Heaven exists also because of heaven. That humans cannot cause heaven to exist is the nature of things. The sage comes to an end as he calmly lets his body go." (*ZZ* 20.690–92)

Here Confucius explains away suffering by espousing the need for forgoing one's ego and regarding recognition and advantages as burdens. Privations are manifestations of the cycle of things that can easily be embraced with equanimity. Instead, Confucius warns of the dangers of apparent success, whereby titles and wealth may lure one to fixate on external things. The withered tree that serves as a backdrop highlighting his detachment in this episode brings to mind the wise man compared to "withered wood and dead ashes" in the chapter "Discourse on Making Things Equal" (Qiwu lun 齊物論) in *Zhuangzi*. Confucius shows his equanimity by drumming on a branch. The motif of turning to music in adversity, taken up also in 1.19a and 1.41, is developed more extensively in another version of the anecdote in *Zhuangzi*:

1.45e Confucius faced extreme privations between Chen and Cai, and for seven days had no cooked food. His soup made from wild greens included no grains, and his countenance showed great exhaustion. Yet he played the zither and sang in his chamber. Yan Hui was picking vegetables. Zilu and Zigong said to each other, "The Master was again driven out from Lu, had his traces erased in Wei, was threatened by felled trees in Song, faced privations at Shang and Zhou, and is besieged between Chen and Cai. He who kills the Master will not be deemed guilty of a crime; he who humiliates the Master faces no interdiction. Yet he sings to stringed music and plays the zither without ever stopping. Can a noble man be shameless to this extent?"

Yan Hui could not respond and, coming in, told Confucius. Confucius pushed aside the zither and sighed, "Yóu [Zilu] and Ci [Zigong] are petty men. Summon them and I will explain to them."

Zilu and Zigong entered. Zilu said, "This can be called failure indeed!"

Confucius said, "What are you saying! When the noble man gains success through the Way, it is called 'success.' When he fails in the Way and fails, it is called 'failure.' Now I have encountered troubles in a chaotic world because I embrace the Way of the highest good and proper duty, how can my experience be called failure? Hence, I examine myself inwardly and do not fail in the Way, face troubles and do not lose my virtue. The cold weather having come, frost and snow having fallen, by them I know that the pines and cypresses are flourishing. The troubles at Chen and Cai are my good fortune!"

Confucius quietly returned to his zither and sang to string music. Zilu, in great excitement, seized the shield and danced. Zigong said, "I have not known how high heaven is, nor how low the earth is." Those who gained possession of the Way in antiquity are joyous in failure and in success. The source of their joy is not failure or success. (ZZ 28.981–83)

This passage, which also appears in *Mr. Lü's Annals* (*LSCQ* 1: 803–04), presents a Confucius confidently proclaiming his faith in the highest good and proper duty in similar terms to texts classified as "Confucian."[103] Pines and cypresses withstanding cold as the emblem of steadfast virtue also appears in the *Analects* (9.28). Zilu starts out condemning Confucius's music as shameless, but he is eventually moved by Confucius's speech to participate in the joy of his music through dance.

Sima Qian seems to have drawn from various elements of the Chen-Cai stories in Warring States texts, especially *Zhuangzi*: Confucius expressing his equanimity through music; the different reactions of his disciples; the mutual judgment of Confucius and his disciples; the implicit debate on moral agency and fate; the incident as a pedagogical moment. The main difference, of course, is that he turns the scenario of potential critique into one of resounding affirmation by having Confucius and Yan Hui forcefully responding to negative interpretations of his situation. While this affirmation is premised on a steadfast moral quest defying circumstantial constraints, political considerations still matter: it is Zigong's maneuvers at the Chu court that bring the siege to an end. The account of Confucius's plight takes a fantastic turn in Gan Bao's *In Search of the Supernatural*, where a very tall man threatening Confucius and his disciples turns into a gigantic fish that Zilu cooks for everyone's nourishment (*ZY* 923).[104] In another story (fifth–sixth century), they meet their challenge at Chen with the help of two prescient mulberry-picking girls (see chapter 3, 3.2).

1.46 King Zhao intended to enfeoff Confucius with seven hundred *li* of land with registered hamlets. The Chu chief minister Zixi said, "Are there any envoys sent by Your Majesty to the various lords that can compare to Zigong?" The king said, "There aren't any." "Are there any among Your Majesty's advisors and ministers that can compare to Yan Hui?" The king said, "There aren't any." "Are there any among Your Majesty's generals and commanders that can compare to Zilu?" The king said, "There aren't any." "Are there any among Your Majesty's officials and deputies that can compare to Zai Yu?" The king said, "There aren't any." "There is also this to consider: When the ancestors of Chu were enfeoffed under Zhou, their titles were the lower noble ranks of 'master' and 'head.' Now Confucius transmits the models of the three kings and the five sovereigns and turns the accomplishments of the Duke of Zhou and the Duke of Shao into shining examples. If Your Majesty heeds his counsel, then how can Chu grandly claim control over several thousand *li* for generations? King Wen was in Feng and King Wu in Hao: those rulers of areas of a hundred *li* finally became the sovereign of all under heaven. Now if Confucius gets to be ensconced in the land and has the help of worthy disciples, it is not good fortune for Chu." King Zhao thus stopped. That autumn, King Zhao of Chu died at Chengfu.

[translator's note]
As in earlier passages (1.9, 1.36, 1.41), jealous rivals blocking the employment of Confucius serve to explain why Confucius could not find a chance to fulfill his moral vision and exercise his talents. The above anecdote might have been elaborated on the basis of the following: eulogizing Confucius, Mencius claims that if he could become the ruler of land spanning a hundred *li*, he would gain sway over all under heaven because all the lords would attend his court (*Mencius* 2A.2); Confucius remarks that great enterprises can have modest beginnings, like Kings Wen and Wu at Feng and Hao (1.12); *Record of Rituals* mentions Confucius's visit to Chu; Confucius commends King Zhao of Chu for "understanding the great Way" because he refuses to follow divination results urging him to transfer ill fortune to his ministers by offering sacrifices to the Yellow River (*Zuo* Ai 6.4, 3: 1866–69).

This episode, not told elsewhere in *Historical Records*, is implausible for various reasons. Seven hundred *li* is an improbably large swath of territory to confer on anyone, let alone someone with no sway or prior claims over Chu. King Zhao of Chu was then engaged in a critical battle with Wu at Chengfu (former Chen territory annexed by Chu), scarcely the moment to ponder such an appointment. Zixi refers to Confucius's disciples as worthy and accomplished characters who may challenge the Chu king's rule, but their achievements postdate 491 BCE (the year of King Zhao's death).

1.47 Jieyu, the madman of Chu, sang as he passed by Confucius: "Phoenix! Phoenix! How your virtue is declining! What has gone by cannot be corrected, what is to come is still within reach. Have done! Have done! Those taking part in government now are in peril!" Confucius came down his carriage and wanted to have a word with him. He left with quick steps, and Confucius did not get to talk to him.

[translator's note]
As in 1.39 and 1.40, passage 1.47 features a man outside the sociopolitical realm criticizing Confucius. As noted earlier, the three passages have analogues in three sequential entries in the *Analects* (18.5–18.7). Sima Qian decides to place the account here, perhaps because Jieyu encounters Confucius in Chu in *Zhuangzi*. In that version of the story, Jieyu's admonition is longer, reiterating the dangers of political engagement and self-confident virtue, and extolling "the uses of uselessness":

1.47a Confucius went to Chu. Jieyu, the madman of Chu, wandered by his gate and said, "Phoenix! Phoenix! How your virtue is declining! You cannot wait for the coming generations, nor can you reach generations past. When the Way prevails under heaven, sages bring things to fruition. When the Way does not prevail under heaven, sages just live and let live. At the present moment, the only thing one can hope for is to avoid punishment. Good fortune is as light as feather, but no one knows how to carry it. Calamity is as heavy as earth, but no one knows how to avoid it. Have done! Have done! This act of confronting people with virtue! Perilous! Perilous! This act of marking the ground and hastening toward it! Shroud the light, shroud the light: no harm for my walking! Hide the bends, hide the bends: no harm for my feet! Trees in the mountain bring about their own hacking; the grease feeding a fire burns itself. Cinnamon can be eaten; hence it is felled. Lacquer can be used; hence it is cut up. Everyone knows the uses of the useful, but none knows the uses of the useless." (*ZZ* 4.183)

The peril of political life is a recurrent theme in both *Zhuangzi* and the *Analects*, with the difference that the imperative to escape and avoid punishment in chaotic times is more insistent in *Zhuangzi*. In 1.47 and the *Analects* 18.5, Confucius's eagerness to speak to Jieyu implies potential affinity.

1.48 It was at that time that Confucius returned to Wei from Chu. Confucius was sixty-three that year, and it was the sixth year of the reign of Lord Ai of Lu [489 BCE]. In the following year, Wu and Lu had a meeting at Zeng, and Wu demanded a hundred sets of sacrificial animals. The grand steward Pi of Wu summoned Ji Kangzi. Kangzi sent Zigong to make the case for Lu, and only then was the matter brought to a close.

[translator's note]
The newly ascendant Wu makes egregious demands on smaller states. In "The Hereditary House of Lu," Zigong rebukes Wu for its violation of ritual propriety, and the Wu King replies, "I have tattooed my body; I don't deserve to be reproached on the grounds of ritual propriety" (*SJ* 33.51). In *Historical Records*, Sima Qian implies that Lu repels Wu demands, but in *Zuo Tradition*, Lu apparently submits and merely scores a rhetorical victory by predicting Wu demise (*Zuo* Ai 7.3, 3: 1872–75). In that account, Ji Kangzi, the Lu chief minister, refuses to answer the summons of grand steward Pi of Wu. Zigong, sent to excuse Ji Kangzi's absence, blames Wu's ritual infractions on its barbarian roots: "What does this have to do with ritual propriety? We act out of fear for your great domain. . . . Taibo implemented Zhou rituals in robes and cap, but when Zhongyong succeeded him, he cut his hair and tattooed his body, adorning himself in his nakedness: Was that ritual propriety? There is a reason for the way things are." The Wu founder Taibo was a scion of the Zhou house. Zhongyong was his younger brother. According to legend, they fled south to barbarian Wu so that the future King Wen's father might inherit the throne. Zigong becomes an effective rhetorician who changes the fortunes of states in the chapter devoted to Confucius's disciples in *Historical Records* (*SJ* 67.17–27).

★ ★ ★

1.49 Confucius said, "In their ways of government, Lu and Wei are brothers." At that time Kuaikui, the father of the Wei ruler Zhe, did not succeed in getting instated as ruler and was in exile outside Wei. The various lords again and again took up his cause and reprimanded Wei. And as many of Confucius's disciples were serving in Wei, the Wei ruler wanted Confucius to take charge of its government. Zilu said, "The Wei ruler wants you, Master, to stay and take charge of government. What would be your first priority?" Confucius said, "It would certainly be the rectification of names!" Zilu said, "Is that so! How far-fetched you are, Master! What is there to be rectified!" Confucius said, "Yóu, how uncouth you are! If names are not rectified, words will not follow reason. If words do not follow reason, affairs will not be brought to fruition. If affairs are not brought to fruition, ritual and music will not flourish. If ritual and music do not flourish, punishment will not be just. If punishment is not just, the people will be disoriented, not knowing where their hands and feet should go. For what the noble man undertakes in action can certainly be named, what he speaks about can certainly be put into practice. When it comes to what a noble man speaks about, there is no room for negligence, and that is all."

[translator's note]
The concern with normative roles and the "rectification of names" in 1.49 hark back to 1.9, but the political context here is much more urgent. This passage incorporates two entries from the *Analects* (13.7, 13.3) and links them explicitly to political turmoil in Wei. Lu and Wei were called "brother states" because both had the clan name Ji. Their respective ancestors, the Duke of Zhou and Wei Kangshu, were both younger brothers of King Wu of Zhou. But when Confucius states that their "brotherhood" lies in their "ways of government," the comment seems more pointed. Su Shi (1037–1101) explains, "The time (488 BCE) was the seventh year in the reign of Lord Ai of Lu and the fifth year in the reign of the Ousted Lord of Wei. In the Wei government, the father was no father, the son was no son. In the Lu government, the ruler was no ruler, the minister was no minister" (*LY* 3: 1163). The powerful ministerial lineages in Lu drove Lord Zhao of Lu into exile (1.8). Lord Ai of Lu would later die in exile in Yue. Kuaikui fled Wei after an abortive attempt to assassinate Nan Zi, the wife of his father Lord Ling of Wei (1.20). Lord Ling tried to designate another son, Ying, as heir, but Kuaikui's son Zhe became the next ruler upon Ying's insistence. A protracted power struggle ensued (1.34), and eventually Kuaikui drove out Zhe

(480 BCE), who managed to later reclaim the throne (477 BCE), only to be expelled again (470 BCE). Known posthumously as the Ousted Lord of Wei (although "Ousted" does not sound like an official honorific), he would also die in exile in Yue. Zhu Xi adopts Su Shi's reading, but there are commentators who argue that Lu and Wei share the distinction of having worthy ministers despite political disorder (*LY* 3: 1164).

In his summary of the story of Kuaikui and Zhe, Sima Qian wrote: "Son and father changed places" 子父易位 (*SJ* 130.40). Given this context, Confucius's comment on the "rectification of names" may seem to target specifically Zhe's failure to yield the throne to his father like a dutiful son. Yet the situation is complicated. Even as Zhe defies his father, Kuaikui also defies his own father. Recognized by his grandfather, Kuaikui's father Lord Ling, as the legitimate successor, Zhe could claim the priority of the order of succession over biological lineage, a point developed in the *Gongyang* commentary (*Gongyang* 2: 1141–42, *LY* 2: 594–95). To press his own claim, Kuaikui has also relied on an adversarial state, Jin, to attack Wei. Some commentators believe that Zhe refers to Lord Xiao of Wei, who is said to support Confucius as a worthy man without officially employing him (*Mencius* 5B.4; see 1.17c). *Xiao* means "filial": Could it be that Zhe's supporters consider his repulsion of his father Kuaikui "filial" and give him this posthumous honorific because he defends legitimate succession in the Wei house and resists Jin encroachment? In terms of character, both Kuaikui and Zhe fall far short of a ruler's ideal. Does "rectification of names" mean that father and son should both be made aware of their respective duties and yield to each other? How could that be achieved? Perhaps the impracticability of such a proposition is why Zilu calls Confucius off the mark or "far-fetched."

The virtue of yielding comes up in another entry about the Wei succession struggle in the *Analects*:

1.49a Ran Qiu said, "Will the Master support the Wei ruler [Zhe]?" Zigong said, "I heard you. I will ask him." Entering, he said, "What sort of persons are Boyi and Shuqi?" Confucius said, "They are worthy men of ancient times." "Did they harbor rancor?" "They sought the highest good and obtained it. Why would they harbor rancor?" Zigong came out and said, "The Master will not support him." (*Analects* 7.5)

Why does Zigong have to invoke Boyi and Shuqi in order to ask whether Confucius would support Zhe? Perhaps Confucius and his disciples, as sojourners in Wei, are not supposed to openly criticize the Wei ruler (*LY* 2: 597). Boyi and Shuqi are ancient princes who vie to give up the throne; they embody the virtue of yielding and political disinterestedness. By commending Boyi and Shuqi, Confucius seems to implicitly criticize both Kuaikui and Zhe. Alternatively, he may be referring to his own steadfast adherence to noble principles. If he does not actively support Zhe, however, he also does not condemn him outright.

"Rectification of names" is often understood in terms of normative familial and political relationships. But its application can extend to the proper naming of all things, actions, and events, hence Ma Rong's gloss: "to rectify the name of everything" (*LY* 3: 1148). In *Zuo Tradition*, commenting on how it would be better to grant settlements instead of ritual implements and insignia on a man who deserves reward, Confucius declares, "it is precisely ritual vessels and names that cannot be lent to other people" (*Zuo* Cheng 2.2, 2: 712–13).[105] In 1.49, Confucius elaborates the social and political implications of the "rectification of names." These ideas find reverberations in Xunzi's discussion of the term (*XZ* 22), which broadens it to include disquisitions on the following: naming conventions; the sage king's role in realizing the Way by "instituting names" (*zhiming* 制名); the importance of correct naming for governance and legal order; the goal of "knowing names" (*zhiming* 知名) via the mastery of correspondences and patterning; and the linguistic perversions of errant arguments (*bianshuo* 辯說).

1.50 In the following year, Ran Qiu, as the commander of the Ji lineage's forces, battled Qi at Lang and overcame the latter. Ji Kangzi said to Ran Qiu, "Regarding your expertise in military matters, did you, sir, learn it? Or is this in your nature?" Ran Qiu said, "I learned it from Confucius." Ji Kangzi said, "What sort of person is Confucius?" Ran Qiu responded, "He is to be employed in the name of what is right; he spreads his teachings among the myriad clans; and he asks questions of the spirits with no sense of disquiet. As for this path that I have come to—even if he were plied with a thousand hamlets, he would not consider it rewarding." Kangzi said, "I want to summon him. Can it be done?" Ran Qiu responded, "If you want to summon him, then don't let petty men constrain him, and then it can be done." And then Kong Wenzi of Wei, who was preparing to strike at Taishu, also consulted Confucius about strategy. Confucius, claiming ignorance, declined to intervene. He withdrew and issued the command to drive away, saying, "A bird can choose its tree, but how can a tree choose its bird!" Wenzi persisted in trying to make him stay. Just then Ji Kangzi drove away Gonghua, Gongbin, and Gonglin. He welcomed Confucius back with bolts of silk. Confucius returned to Lu.

[translator's note]
As in 1.38, a nobleman asks one of Confucius's disciples to sum up Confucius. Here Ran Qiu emphasizes how Confucius will not accept the kind of compromises he himself has to make. According to *Zuo Tradition*, Qi invaded Lu in 484 BCE, and the battle took place in the outskirts of the capital (not Lang). Ran Qiu distinguishes himself as a military commander and earns Confucius's praise (*Zuo* Ai 11.1, 3: 1894–97). Here Ran Qiu claims to have learned his prowess in warfare from Confucius. Confucius disclaims knowledge of military strategy, however, when asked to intervene in the internecine struggles in Wei (1.33, *Analects* 15.1).

In *Sayings*, Ran Qiu's exchange with Ji Kangzi is incorporated into a broad affirmation of Confucius's knowledge of military affairs:

> 1.50a After the battle was over, Ji Kangzi asked Ran Qiu, "When it comes to warfare, did you, sir, learn it? Or do you understand it by nature?" He replied, "I learned it." Ji Kangzi said, "You serve Confucius. How could you have learned it?" Ran Qiu said, "It was precisely through Confucius that I learned it. For Confucius is a great sage; there is nothing that he does not encompass. He can deploy both civil and martial skills, having a thorough knowledge of both. As for me, I just happened to hear about his methods in warfare. Even so, I have not grasped them in detail." Ji Kangzi was pleased. Fan Chi told Confucius about this, and Confucius said, "In this way, Ji Kangzi can be said to delight in men showing their competence." (*KZJY* 41.542)

Although *Sayings* is a later text, it is quite possible that the image of Confucius as master of military knowledge has earlier sources. This passage resonates, for example, with his exploits at Jiagu (1.14) and his eagerness to attack Pu (1.27).

The Wei minister Kong Wenzi wants to attack Taishu Ji because the latter, having married Kong's daughter, set up another household with a former concubine, "as if he had two wives" (*Zuo* Ai 11.6, 3: 1902–03). Confucius declines to offer advice when Kong Wenzi consults him: "As for matters of the sacrificial vessels, I have studied them; yet of matters of armory and weaponry, I have heard nothing" (*Zuo* Ai 11.6, 3: 1904–05). These remarks, with slight variations, also appear in the *Analects* (15.1), where the one seeking military counsel is Lord Ling of Wei, as related in 1.33. Kong Wenzi is praised in the *Analects* (5.15) for his love of learning and willingness to seek advice even from those inferior to him. Zilu will die defending Kong Wenzi's son Kong Kui when Kuaikui takes Kong Kui hostage during his bid to return to Wei to seize power (*Zuo* Ai 15.5, 3: 1936–39).

1.51 Confucius left Lu for fourteen years, and then he returned to Lu. Lord Ai of Lu asked about government. Confucius responded, "Government hinges on the choice of ministers." Ji Kangzi asked about government. He said, "Raise the upright and set them above the errant and the errant will become upright." Kangzi was worried about larceny. Confucius said, "If you, sir, have no desire for gain, then even if you were to offer rewards, no one would steal." But ultimately Lu could not make use of Confucius, and Confucius also did not seek office in government.

[translator's note]
Confucius's departure from Lu in 496 BCE is mentioned in 1.16. The scenario of Lord Ai of Lu consulting Confucius on the principles of government recurs in late Warring States, Han, and Wei texts (for example, *XZ* 29.398, 31.406–11; *LJ* 3: 1258–66, 3: 1398–1409; *DDLJ* 1: 42–95; *SY* 1.5, 7.13, 7.20, 8.10, 8.18, 10.24, 15.14; *KZJY* 7.70–87, 13.187–88, 17.260–68). In an analogous passage in "The Mean" (Zhongyong 中庸) in *Record of Rituals*, Confucius explains to Lord Ai that government depends on employing the right people: "The governance of King Wen and King Wu is set forth in tablets and bamboo strips. If the right people are there, then their governance will prevail. If they are gone, then their governance fades away." Confucius's first response to Ji Kangzi echoes two entries in the *Analects*, where the interlocutor is Lord Ai or Fan Chi instead of Ji Kangzi:

> 1.51a Lord Ai asked, "What should we do to gain the people's submission?" Confucius responded, "Raise the upright and set them above the errant, and the people would submit. Raise the errant and

set them above the upright, and the people would not submit." (*Analects* 2.19)

1.51b Fan Chi asked about the highest good. The Master said, "Cherish people." He asked about knowledge. The Master said, "Know people." Fan Chi did not yet grasp the meaning. The Master said, "Raising the upright and setting them above the errant can make the errant ones upright." Fan Chi withdrew and, seeing Zixia, said, "Earlier I had an audience with the Master and asked about knowledge. The Master said, 'Raising the upright and setting them above the errant can make the errant ones upright.' What did he mean?" Zixia said, "Rich in meaning are those words! Shun gained sway over the realm under heaven and chose among the multitudes. He raised Gao Yao, and the ignoble ones stayed away. Tang gained sway over the realm under heaven and chose among the multitude. He raised Yi Yin, and the ignoble ones stayed away." (*Analects* 12.22)

In 1.51, "Raising the upright" follows logically from the beginning exchange on choosing the right ministers. The *Analects* entries indicate that employing the right people is key to political order, which in turn facilitate "knowledge" and "the highest good." Some commentators fault Sima Qian for "misquoting" the *Analects*. How fixed was the text identified as a body of sayings attributed to Confucius and his disciples in Sima Qian's time? For example, a variant version of the *Analects* entry (2.19) appears in *Huainanzi*, only Ji Kangzi is identified as posing the question, as in 1.51 (*LY* 1: 151). Confucius's warning against greed also appears in the *Analects* (12.18). The logic of exemplarity underwrites another of Confucius's remarks to Ji Kangzi: "Governance (*zheng* 政) is about correctness (*zheng* 正). If you lead with correctness, who would dare to violate correctness?" (*Analects* 12.17).

1.52 At the time of Confucius, the Zhou house was in decline. Ritual and music had fallen into disuse, and the *Documents* and the *Odes* had missing portions. Confucius pursued the traces of rituals in the Three Dynasties and organized traditions of the *Documents*, reaching back to sort out accounts of Yao and Shun and proceeding all the way down to Lord Mu of Qin, arranging and ordering the encompassed events. He said, "I can speak about Xia rituals, but there is not enough from Qi to attest to them. I can speak about Yin [Shang] rituals, but there is not enough from Song to attest to them. If there were enough evidence, then I could attest to them." Observing what were cut out or added during the Yin and Xia eras, he said, "What is to come, even a hundred generations hence, can be known: for the era of cultural refinement and that of substance alternate. Zhou, looking back at the two earlier dynasties, has indeed a resplendent culture! I follow Zhou." This is the reason why explanation of the *Documents* and recording of the *Rituals* came from Confucius.

[translator's note]
After recording Confucius's last unsuccessful attempt to advise men in positions of power, Sima Qian turns to his textual labor (1.52–1.67), which he presents as the recompense for Confucius's political failures. In *Zhuangzi*, Confucius tells Laozi that he "sorts out" or "studies" (*zhi* 治) the Six Classics, only to be told that the Six Classics are "faded traces" of ancient sage kings (*ZZ* 14.531). In "The Biographies of Jesters," Sima Qian quotes Confucius as saying, "When it comes to achieving governance, the Six Arts are as one. The ritual texts are used for regulating people; music, for manifesting harmony; the *Documents*, for speaking of important events; the *Odes*, for conveying intent; the *Changes*, for demonstrating the numinous power behind transformations; the *Annals*, for speaking of principles" (*SJ* 126.2). The first detailed account of Confucius's role in transmitting the classics appears in *Historical Records*. According to Sima Qian, in editing or arranging canonical textual traditions (except perhaps in the case of the *Changes*), Confucius is preserving credible accounts of the past and in that sense acting like a historian. In other words, we have here the kernel of the idea that "the Six Classics are all histories" later espoused by, among others, Wang Tong (584–617), Wang Yangming, Li Zhi (1527–1602), Yuan Mei (see chapter 3, 230), and most elaborately, Zhang Xuecheng (1738–1801).

What are the ritual texts that Confucius is said to have "recorded?" These could be texts eventually assimilated into canonical ritual texts. Passage 1.52 offers the earliest extant claim that Confucius compiled the *Documents*. In his preface to "The Table of Generations for the Three Dynasties," Sima Qian contrasts the precise dating in the *Annals* with the silence on chronology in the *Documents*: "But when Confucius organized the *Documents*, the years and months are left out. Perhaps they existed, but there were many gaps and they could not be recorded. That was why he transmitted his doubts in case of doubts, for such was his caution" (*SJ* 13.3). The word translated here as "organized" (*xu* 序) can also mean "wrote prefaces for," hence Ban Gu's assertion that Confucius wrote the prefatory remarks for each chapter in the *Documents* (*HS* 30.1706). Zhu Xi, among others, refuted this idea.

As a text with speeches purportedly by early kings and ministers, the *Documents* can be meaningfully connected to Confucius's comments on the Xia, Shang, and Zhou dynasties; these comments partially overlaps with the *Analects* (2.23, 3.9, 3.14), and "The Mean" and "The Course of Ritual" (Liyun 禮運) in *Record of Rituals*. Qi and Song were small states inhabited by the descendants of the rulers of the Xia and Shang dynasties. But the evidence of Xia and Shang rituals are hard to grapple with because of insufficient documents (*wen* 文) and worthy men (*xian* 獻) (*Analects* 3.9). Sima Qian imagines Confucius turning a purposeful gaze to the past, appraising and comparing traditions, gauging changes, linking the past to the present and the future. In the *Analects,* ideal governance is said to combine elements of Xia, Shang, and Zhou traditions: "Follow the calendar of Xia, ride the carriages of Yin [Shang], and wear the ceremonial caps of Zhou" (*Analects* 15.11). What can the past tell us about the future? Sima Qian's formulation may be compared with the *Analects* (2.23):

> 1.52a Zizhang asked, "Can ten generations hence be known?" The Master said, "Yin followed the rituals of Xia, what it took away and added can be known. Zhou followed the rituals of Yin, what it took away and added can be known. As for what may follow Zhou, even if it is a hundred generations hence, it can be known."

Late Western Han and Eastern Han authors, especially in apocrypha, are prone to concretize what can be known about the future. They claim, for example, that Confucius predicts the rise of the Han dynasty. From the Song dynasty onward, commentators often distinguish between changeable things, such as institutions and ritual specifications, and immutable norms and moral principles, and postulate the latter as what could be known or predicted far into the future (*LY* 1: 165–71). By contrast, Sima Qian seems to be simply asserting that ritual and cultural change is a gradual and incremental process, that Zhou, absorbing what can be learnt from Xia and Shang, is likely to have an enduring legacy that define posterity (that is, one can imagine its legacy "a hundred generations hence," which means that the past and the future will be mutually comprehensible), and that eras of "refinement" (*wen* 文) and "substance" (*zhi* 質) may alternate in a cyclical process. This final point, which Sima Qian reiterates in his concluding comment in the chapter on the first Han emperor Liu Bang (*SJ* 8.87–88), is also developed in writings associated with Dong Zhongshu (179–104 BCE).

1.53 Confucius said to the senior music master of Lu: "The principle of making music can be known. It starts by gathering its force with a bright rhythm; its momentum is released through pure harmony and a continuous flow: in this way it is brought to fruition." "It was only when I returned to Lu from Wei that music was rectified. The odes and hymns each found their proper place."

[translator's note]
Passage 1.53 overlaps with the *Analects* (3.23, 9.15). Confucius's confident pronouncement about music here contrasts with earlier moments of apprenticeship (1.8, 1.31). "Odes" and "hymns" are the names of sections in the received text of the *Odes*. Here "rectification" seems to mean the establishment of their proper place in rituals or their definition and classification as musical categories. "Rectification" may target the transgressive uses of music (for example, a noble using the music reserved for the Zhou king) or improper tempo and rhythm associated with sensual excess. In the "Treatise on Music," Sima Qian claims that sage kings "instituted the sounds of the odes and hymns" to forestall or correct disorder (*SJ* 24.4).

1.54 In antiquity, there were three thousand or more pieces in the *Odes*. When they came to the attention of Confucius, he removed the repetitions and took what could be applicable for illuminating ritual propriety and duty. For the earliest times, he picked works on Xie and Lord Millet; for the middle period, he transmitted the glory of Yin (Shang) and Zhou, and he reached the failings of King You and King Li, which started with their conjugal relations. Hence it is said: The "Airs" section begins with disorder in "Osprey";[106] the "Lesser Odes" section begins with "Deer Cries"; the "Greater Odes" section begins with "King Wen"; the "Hymns" section begins with "Pure Temple." For all the 305 pieces, Confucius put them to zither music and sang them, seeking to match them to the notes of Shao, Wu, Ya (Odes), and Song (Hymns). It was from this endeavor that ritual and music got to be transmitted, amplifying the way of sage kings and bringing the Six Arts to fruition.

[translator's note]
This is the first mention of Confucius establishing the canon of the *Odes* by pruning repetitions and inappropriate works, reducing the number of odes from 3,000 to 305. In Sima Qian's vision, the *Odes* is a microcosm of historical changes. Spanning the fate of dynasties, its topics range from the ancestors of the Xia and Zhou dynasties (Xie and Lord Millet) to the decline and fall of Zhou (King You and King Li). The first poem in the *Odes*, "Osprey," is about desire and marriage, which are interwoven with moral-political foundations and cosmological generation in some early Chinese texts.[107] Contrary to the Mao tradition that interprets "Osprey" and "Deer Cry" as affirmations of Zhou order, Sima Qian claims that the two poems herald Zhou decline in his preface to the "Chronological Table of the Twelve Lords' Reigns": "The Zhou way waned, and the poets traced the waning to defective conjugal relations, that was why 'Osprey' was created. Noble virtue and proper duty were in decline and crumbling, that was what 'Deer Cry' criticized" (*SJ* 14.4). "King Wen" and "Pure Temple," on the other hand, eulogize the Zhou conquest of Shang and the virtue of King Wen. Shao is the music of the sage king Shun (1.8); Wu (meaning "Martial") is the music of King Wu of Zhou (1.31b). Reserving his highest praise for Shao as fully realizing both beauty and goodness, Confucius describes Wu as "fully realizing beauty" but "not yet fully realizing goodness" (*Analects* 3.25). As commensurate categories, Shao, Wu, Ya, and Song are all supposed to glorify the rule of sage kings.

1.55 In his later years Confucius loved the *Changes* and compiled the "Hexagram Judgments," "Appended Commentaries," "Images," "Discourses on the Hexagrams," and "Explanations of the Qian and Kun Hexagrams." The straps for binding the bamboo strips of the *Changes* broke three times. He said, "Give me a few more years, and just like that, I will glory in mastering the wonders of the *Changes*."

[translator's note]
Mr Lü's Annals (*LSCQ* 2: 1505), *The Garden of Eloquence* (*SY* 20.1), and *Sayings* (*KZJY* 9.132) all tell versions of an anecdote in which Confucius engages in divination and, obtaining the hexagram *Bi* (Elegance), declares it

inauspicious because "white should be pure white, and black should be pure black," while *Bi* implies beauty based on mixing colors and obscuring basic essence. But it is in *Historical Records* that we find the first claim among extant texts that Confucius compiled explanations of hexagrams and their underlying principles in the *Changes*. He is so assiduous studying it that the bamboo strips binding the text break three times. Perhaps Sima Qian bases his assertion on the fact that the phrase "the Master says" (*ziyue* 子曰) is attached to various passages in the "Appended Commentaries" (*Xici* 繫辭) and the explanations of the *Qian* and *Kun* hexagrams (*qian wenyan* 乾文言, *kun wenyan* 坤文言). The formula "the Master says" is also ubiquitous in excavated texts related to the *Changes* (*KJY* 3: 761–896).

The corresponding entry in the *Analects* (7.17) offers a different chronology: "Give me a few more years: studying the *Changes* at fifty, I should be able to avoid great errors." Commentators argue whether this means Confucius is only thinking about studying the *Changes* in his forties or, if one accepts both Sima Qian's account and its analogue in the *Analects*, whether there are different stages in his engagement with the text. In another recension of the *Analects*, alternative punctuation and the reading of *Yi* 易 (*Changes*) as *yi* 亦 (also) changes the meaning: "Give me a few more years, and I should also be able to avoid great errors in my studies."

1.56 Confucius used the *Odes*, *Documents*, *Rituals*, and *Music* to teach. He had about three thousand disciples, seventy-two of them were fully conversant with the Six Arts. There were many, like Yan Zhuozou, who learned quite a lot from Confucius without being among his accomplished disciples.

[translator's note]
The *Changes* and *Annals* are conspicuously absent in the first line. The momentous compilation of the *Annals* and its special connection with Confucius sets it apart and will come up later (1.66–67). Several frequently cited passages from the *Analects* discuss the role of the *Odes* in Confucius's program of education:

1.56a Zigong said, "Poor, yet not servile; rich, yet not arrogant: What of that?" The Master said, "That is acceptable. But better still: Poor, yet joyous; rich, yet loving ritual." Zigong said, "As it says in the *Odes*, 'As if cutting it, as if filing it, / As if carving it, as if polishing it.' Isn't that what is meant?" The Master said, "Now we can really talk about the *Odes*! I tell you a settled point and you know what is to come." (*Analects* 1.15)

1.56b The Master said, "The summary judgment of the three hundred pieces in the *Odes* in one line: 'No straying.'" (*Analects* 2.2)

1.56c Zixia asked, "'The dimpled loveliness of her meaning smile! / The liquid brightness of her beautiful eyes! / The white silk sets the colors aglow!' What does that mean?" The Master said, "Paint later, when the white silk background is ready." "So, ritual comes later?" The Master said, "Shang [Zixia] is the one who can bring out my meaning! Henceforth I can discuss the *Odes* with him!" (*Analects* 3.8)

1.56d The Master said, "Be roused by the *Odes*, stand firm through rituals, and reach fulfillment through music." (*Analects* 8.8)

1.56e The Master said, "If, after reciting three hundred of the *Odes*, a person fails to reach his goals upon being given the responsibility to govern, and if, going out as an envoy in the four directions, he fails to respond independently, what is the point even if he has mastered many pieces?" (*Analects* 13.5)

1.56f Chen Kang asked Boyu [Confucius's son], "Have you heard anything different?" Boyu said, "I haven't. Once, as he was standing alone, I hastened across the courtyard in small steps. He said, 'Have you studied the *Odes*?' I responded, 'I haven't.' 'If you don't study the *Odes*, you won't have the wherewithal to speak properly.' I withdrew and studied the *Odes*. On another day, as he was standing alone, I hastened across the courtyard in small steps. He said, 'Have you studied the *Rituals*?' I responded, 'I haven't.' 'If you don't study the *Rituals*, you will have no wherewithal to stand firm.' I withdrew and studied the *Rituals*. These are the two things I have heard." Chen Kang withdrew and said happily, "I asked about one thing and obtained three answers. I heard about the *Odes*; I heard about the *Rituals*, and also heard how the noble man showed no partiality for his son." (*Analects* 16.13)

1.56g The Master said, "Young ones! Why not study the *Odes*? The *Odes* can rouse you, allow you to observe mores, grant you community, and channel your rancor. Close by, it is the basis for serving your father; farther afield, it is the basis for serving your ruler. Through it you can learn much about the names of plants, trees, birds, and beasts." (*Analects* 17.9)

The *Odes* is said to be the channel for self-cultivation, ethical awareness, rhetorical training, social integration, political expression, diplomatic finesse, and botanical and zoological knowledge (*Analects* 8.8, 13.5, 16.13, 17.19). It is a tool for honing sensibility and facilitating communication between Confucius and his disciples: as when Zigong cites lines about moral refinement employing the metaphor of carving and polishing jade and ivory in the *Odes* in response to Confucius's distinctions between levels of praiseworthy conduct (*Analects* 1.15); or when Zixia uses a line about colors being applied to a white background to posit the relationship between ethical foundation and ritual fruition (*Analects* 3.8). Among a trove of bamboo strip manuscripts the Shanghai Museum bought in Hong Kong in the 1990s (dated ca. fourth–third century BCE) are twenty-nine strips commenting on the odes, some of them marked as sayings of Confucius. Scholars have named them "Confucius's Discourse on the Odes" (Kongzi shilun 孔子詩論). Here is one example: "Confucius said, 'The Odes have no hidden intent, its music has no hidden emotions, its writing has no hidden meaning' " (*KJY* 3: 906) (see also n107).

In 1.56 Confucius is said to have seventy-two disciples, and seventy-two seems to be an auspicious number. *Mr. Lü's Annals* claims that Confucius had three thousand followers, and several Warring States texts give seventy as the number of his disciples. In the chapter on Confucius's disciples, Sima Qian states that Confucius had seventy-seven notable disciples, but only twenty-nine are given some sort of description. Twenty-nine disciples are mentioned in the *Analects*. Yan Zhuozou, mentioned in 1.18 as Confucius's host in Wei, is here named as one of the less notable followers who nevertheless benefitted from Confucius's teachings.

1.57 Confucius taught four precepts: cultural refinement, ethical conduct, utmost striving in integrity, good faith. He abjured four things: there was to be no arbitrary willfulness, no dogmatism, no intransigence, no egoism.

Where he exercised caution: ritual abstinence, warfare, sickness. The Master rarely spoke about profit, destiny, and the highest good. He did not open the way of learning for those who had no pent-up frustration from the exertion to understand. If someone could not lift the other three corners when he raised one, then he would no longer return to the point.

[translator's note]
Sima Qian brings up Confucius's teachings only toward the end of the account. The above passage overlaps with five entries in the *Analects*. Two of them (the beginning and concluding lines in 1.57) deal with teaching (*Analects* 7.25, 7.8), a fitting continuation of the section on transmission of the classics and Confucius's disciples. Indeed the word for "cultural refinement" (*wen* 文) encompasses the learning of the classics and mastery of tradition. The other three pertain to his character, preoccupations, and choice of topics of discourse (*Analects* 9.4, 7.13, 9.1). "The Master rarely spoke about profit, destiny, and the highest good" (*Analects* 9.1): the word *ren* 仁 (the highest good, often also translated as "humaneness" and "humanity") is often considered the most important concept in the Confucian tradition, but it comes up only sporadically in Sima Qian's account. (Besides this passage, see also 1.6, where *ren* is translated as "benevolent," and 1.43.) Since there are quite a number of references in the *Analects* to all three topics (profit, destiny, the highest good), especially the latter two, commentators have suggested various emendations: glossing "spoke" (*yan* 言) as "spoke of his own accord" (*ziyan* 自言) (instead of responding to questions), "rarely" (*han* 罕) as the loan word for *gan* 旰 or *xuan* 軒, meaning "openly" or "obviously," reading *yu* 與 as meaning "endorsed" instead of as a conjunction ("and"), thereby breaking the line into two clauses: "the Master rarely spoke about profit, but endorsed notions of destiny and the highest good." Others suggest that "rarely" is relative: Confucius might have spoken rarely about these topics, but the rare utterances have been assiduously recorded by his disciples (*LY* 2: 729–34).

1.58 When Confucius was among his kinsmen in his community, he was mild and respectful, as if he could not hold forth in arguments. When he was at the ancestral temple or at court, he spoke eloquently, albeit with caution. During court audience, when speaking to senior high officers, he was gentle even when remonstrative, and when he spoke with high officers in the lower ranks, he was forthright but congenial. Entering the lord's gates, he bowed low in respect and hastened forward in small steps with reverent decorum. When the lord summoned him to act as assistant to receive guests, his countenance changed in eager expectation. When the summon came as the lord's command, he would set off without waiting for the carriage to be ready.

[translator's note]
Describing Confucius's political conduct and comportment, 1.58 has more detailed analogues in the *Analects* (10.1–10.4), where they could be interpreted as general ritual prescriptions, although traditional commentaries have read them as "descriptive rather than injunctive."[108] The last line capping the references to Confucius's eagerness and reverence when given a chance for public service echoes the affirmation of such eagerness as ritual propriety in *Xunzi* (*XZ* 27.364). Mencius, by contrast, regards the obedience of a lord's summon as conditional, binding only when done in the right way. Indeed, the very use of the word "summon" is an affront to the dignity of a worthy man, who should be the ruler's teacher or his friend, not someone who can be "summoned." Mencius cites Confucius's approval of the game warden who refuses to answer the Qi ruler's summon because he is not summoned properly (*Mencius* 5B.7; see also *Zuo* Zhao 20.7, 3: 1584–85). This provokes Mencius's disciple Wanzhang to ask: Was Confucius in the wrong to go without even waiting for his carriage? Mencius replies, "Confucius was serving and had the duties of his office, and he was summoned because of his office" (*Mencius* 5B.7). Mencius praises Confucius as "the timely among sages" (*Mencius* 5B.1): "He was quick to leave office when it was right to leave quickly, he stayed long when it was right to stay long, he withdrew from politics when it was right to withdraw, he served when it was right to serve" (*Mencius* 5B.1). One of Confucius's disciples describes him as "speaking when it is timely to speak" (*Analects* 14.13). Thus, Confucius is hesitant and deferential when speaking in his own village out of respect to his elders, while he combines eloquence with circumspection when speaking at court or in the ancestral temple of the state because of the momentousness of state affairs and ritual prescriptions.

1.59 If the fish was spoiled, if the meat had gone bad, or if the food was not cut properly, he would not eat. If a mat was not set forth properly, he would not sit. When he was eating next to a mourner, he never ate to his fill. On a day that he had been wailing, he did not sing. When he saw someone in mourning clothes or a blind person, be he but a mere child, he was sure to change his demeanor to show respect.

[translator's note]
Just as Confucius's dignity, restraint, and eagerness are bound up with his fervent political commitment (1.58), the ritual propriety of his general comportment, told also in the *Analects* (10.8–9, 7.9–10, 9.10), is rooted in his sense of decorum and ardent empathy with the emotions of others. While the first two lines about meat and mat, which has analogues in other early texts, can make Confucius seem pedantic and is used in anti-Confucian tirades in *Mozi* (see 1.45a),[109] its juxtaposition with his reactions to his own sadness and that of afflicted persons underline the emotional basis of ritual prescriptions. There is a special emphasis on mourning rituals and music. In *Record of Rituals*, Confucius is said to fail to achieve harmony on the zither five days after the conclusion of funerary rituals, and it is only after ten days that he can play properly on the reed pipe (*LJ* 1: 182). Both the success and failure to attain musical harmony in the wake of mourning speak to its ritual function in regulating emotions (*LJ* 1: 205; *SY* 19.25; *KZJY* 15.221–22).

1.60 "When I walk in a party of three, I am certain to find a teacher in the group." "If I fail to cultivate virtue; if my learning does not involve deeper inquiry; if I do not move toward righteous duty upon hearing of it; if I fail to correct my errors—these are the things I worry about."

[translator's note]
The narrative shifts here to direct quotation (*Analects* 7.3, 7.22), with a vigilant Confucius describing learning and self-cultivation as unremitting effort. In the *Analects* (7.22), the quote about "a party of three" ends with these lines: "What is good among them I choose and follow, what is not good among them I choose and correct." Commentators debate whether the "good" and "not good" refer to the walking companions in their totality as persons or qualities in them. Why three? Perhaps three is the minimal number for thinking about common humanity. Two persons may be trapped in their respective subjectivity; a third person can act as potential arbitrator. The Zheng minister Zichan refuses to disband village meeting places where the people are free to praise or criticize government policies: "I will then carry out what they deem to be good policies and emend

whatever they regard as bad. They are my teachers." Confucius praises Zichan upon hearing this story (*Zuo* Xiang 31.11, 2: 1286–87). Zichan's statement is the public and political version of the notion of "finding a teacher in a group of three." The implied sociality of virtue and its realization through mutual appraisal and critique also underlines the second quote, where "deeper inquiry" in the process of learning can include discussion with like-minded interlocutors and Confucius's disciples (*LY* 2: 568).

1.61 He made others sing. If the singer excelled, he would make him sing again and then he would harmonize with him.

[translator's note]
While the earlier passages on music (1.8, 1.14, 1.17, 1.30–32, 1.41, 1.45d, 1.45e, 1.53) emphasize the political, ritual, and historical meanings and functions of music as well as the way Confucius uses it to express his thoughts and emotions, 1.61 and its analogue in the *Analects* (7.32) emphasize the pleasure and sociality of music as well as Confucius's eagerness to learn, a continuation of 1.60.

1.62 What the Master did not discuss: anomalies, mere feats of strength, violation of norms, the spirits.

[translator's note]
This statement, which also appears in the *Analects* (7.21), would seem to be contradicted by the knowledge of anomalies that Confucius displays in 1.10 and 1.24. Some commentators explain the inconsistency by arguing that *yu* 語 (translated here as "discuss") means "to initiate a discourse" (as distinct from responding to questions) or "to debate with others" (*LY* 2: 620–21).

1.63 Zigong said, "One can get to hear about the Master's cultural achievements, but one cannot get to hear his views regarding the Way of Heaven or human nature and destiny." Heaving a sigh, Yan Hui said, "I look up to his Way, and it seems ever higher; I bore into it, and it seems ever harder. I look ahead, and it seems to be in front of me, and all of a sudden, it is behind me. The Master excels at guiding us step by step. He broadens me with cultural refinement and restrains me with ritual prescriptions. Even had I wanted to stop learning, I couldn't do so. Having pushed my talents to the limits, it is as if I still sense his Way towering over me. Even if I want to follow it, I do not quite know by what path." Someone from Daxiangdang—a child—said, "Great indeed is Confucius! He has broad learning but has not made a name for himself in anything." Hearing of this, Confucius said, "What should I take up? Should I take up charioteering? Should I take up archery? I think I should take up charioteering!" Lao said, "The Master said, 'I have not proved my talents in office, that is why I am skilled in various things.'"

[translator's note]
Here Sima Qian juxtaposes various appraisals of Confucius and concludes with Confucius's own matter-of-fact and modest self-valuation. The corresponding passages, with some variants, are found in the *Analects* (5.13, 9.11, 9.2, 9.7). Sima Qian seems to understand Zigong's comment about Confucius's "cultural achievements" in relation to his role in sorting out and transmitting classical learning (1.52–56). Instead of "the Way of Heaven or human nature and destiny" 天道與性命, the analogous passage in the *Analects* (5.13) has "human nature and the Way of Heaven" 性與天道. Linking human nature to destiny clarifies the former's abstruse nature and explains Confucius's reluctance to discuss the subject. Song dynasty Neo-Confucianism turned "the Way of Heaven" (*tiandao* 天道) into "heavenly principles" (*tianli* 天理), but early references seem to tie "the Way of Heaven" to the movement of heavenly bodies or forces in nature, as in the following passage from the chapter "Lord Ai Asks Questions" (Ai gong wen 哀公問) in *Record of Rituals*:

> 1.63a Lord Ai asked, "May I ask what the noble man values about the Way of Heaven?" Confucius responded, "He values it for its unremitting nature. The way the sun and moon follow each other, eastward and westward, in an unremitting fashion: that is the Way of Heaven. That long process is not foreclosed: that is the Way of Heaven. Things are brought to fruition without purposeful action: that is the Way of Heaven. The bright illumination of what is brought to fruition: that is the Way of Heaven." (*LJ* 3: 1265)

Yan Hui, Confucius's most esteemed disciple, offers a heartfelt account of his engagement with Confucius's teachings. Compelled by Confucius's charisma, Yan Hui describes his process of learning as involuntary and passionate. Awed and inspired by his teacher's apparently ubiquitous presence, Yan Hui offers a vision of self-cultivation implicitly based on imitation of the sage. An analogous passage in *Zhuangzi* describes the moving interaction between a transcendent and ever-transforming Confucius and Yan Hui, his fervent imitator (*ZZ* 21.706–10).

In contrast to the encomia from Zigong and Yan Hui, the third comment may be sarcastic, although traditional commentaries often read it as affirmation of Confucius's broad learning and sincere regret over his failure to make a name for himself. The words "a child" (*tongzi* 童子) do not appear in the corresponding *Analects* entry (9.2). "Someone from Daxiangdang" can also be rendered as "a villager from Daxiang." In *Record of Rituals*, Confucius is said to have assisted Laozi in funeral rites at Xiangdang. In one of his memorials to the throne, Dong Zhongshu cites the person from Daxiangdang as one "who attained knowledge by himself without studying" (*HS* 56.2510). Some commentators identify the child as Xiang Tuo, the prodigy who outsmarts and flummoxes Confucius (see chapter 3, 3.5). Reading this comment as a taunt makes for a more logical transition to Confucius's rueful rejoinder and his final self-deprecating comment. Confucius responds sarcastically by asking whether he should focus on archery or charioteering, the least exalted of the Six Arts, to make his mark. Having various skills is the result of not being able to prove his talent in positions of greater responsibility. He also explains in a related entry in the *Analects* (9.6): "Being of a lowly station in my youth, I thus became adept at many plebian tasks."

1.64 In the fourteenth year of the reign of Lord Ai of Lu [481 BCE], in spring, there was a hunt in the Great Wilds. Zichu Shang, a driver for the Shusun lineage, captured an animal and considered it inauspicious. Confucius inspected it and said, "It is a *lin*." They took it. Confucius said, "The Yellow River has not yielded the Diagram, the Luo Waterway has not yielded the Text. It is all over for me!" When Yan Hui died, Confucius said, "Heaven is destroying me!" By the time when the *lin* was captured at the western hunt, he said, "My way is coming to an end!" He heaved a sigh and said, "There is none who knows me!" Zigong said, "How is it that no one understands you, Master?" The Master said, "I do not blame heaven, nor do I accuse other men. I study mundane affairs below and reach for the higher realms above. That which truly knows me may be heaven and none other!"

[translator's note]
It says in the *Annals*: "In the fourteenth year [of Lord Ai, 481 BCE], in spring, a *lin* was captured during the western hunt." In Han dynasty dictionaries, the *lin* (also called *qilin*), sometimes translated as "unicorn," is said to have "a roe's (or a horse's) body, an ox's tail, and one horn." In one case, the horn is described as "flesh-covered," which commentators regard as the symbol of benevolence and nonviolent power. Later accounts add attributes such as scales, patterns in five colors, and a gentle, calm, benevolent aura. The sober and straightforward account of its capture, misidentification as an inauspicious beast, and Confucius's correct naming, also appears in *Zuo Tradition* (*Zuo* Ai 14.1, 3: 1920–21). This incident could have been presented as just another example of Confucius's broad knowledge (as in 1.10, 1.24), and it is included as such in the chapter "Discerning Things" in *Sayings* (*KZJY* 16.259), but the more prevalent associations come to be Confucius's fate of not being recognized in his lifetime, his destiny as "uncrowned king" (*suwang* 素王, one who wields kingly authority without being a king),[110] his status as the Sage, and his authorship of the *Annals*. This last point has been interpreted in different ways: (1) Confucius is moved to compile the *Annals* because of the *lin*; (2) Confucius brings the *Annals* to an end because of the *lin*; (3) the completion of the *Annals* causes the *lin* to appear.

As we will see, Sima Qian, under the influence of the *Gongyang Tradition*, links the capture of the *lin* to the compilation of the *Annals*, implying a causal connection by the narrative sequence (1.64–1.67). The logic is clearly spelled out in his chapter on scholars and ritual experts: "The *lin* was captured at the western hunt and Confucius said, 'My way is coming to an end!' That was why he followed the historical records and compiled the *Annals* to have it serve as the laws for kings" (*SJ* 121.3). Sima Qian emphasizes the analogy between the misunderstood *lin* and the unrecognized sage. Confucius's failure and lack of recognition are inevitable because the time is out of joint. According to the "Appended Commentary" to the *Changes*, sages of antiquity took the mysterious Diagram from the Yellow River and the Text from the Luo Waterway as models for the creation of the hexagrams. Confucius says in the *Analects* (9.9): "The phoenix has not come, and the Yellow River has not yielded the Diagram. It is all over for me!" Sima Qian draws on this discourse of signs to show how the mismatch between the *lin* and its times reverberates in the absence of omens for ideal governance. As the disciple closest to his heart, Yan Hui is almost part of Confucius. Confucius laments his death as almost his own (*Analects* 11.9), even as the capture of the *lin* heralds the end of his way. Where is understanding to be found then? The exchange between Confucius and Zigong (*Analects* 14.35) offers the hypothetical understanding of heaven as consolation.

A key text in linking the *lin* to the creation of the *Annals* is the *Gong-yang Tradition*:

> 1.64a "In the fourteenth year, in spring, a *lin* was captured during the western hunt." Why was this written down? To record an anomaly. Why was this anomalous? This was not an animal of the central states. But then who hunted it? It was a firewood gatherer. A firewood gatherer was but a humble person, why then was the word "hunt" used? To magnify his significance. Why magnify his significance? It was on account of his capture of the *lin* that his significance is magnified. What does it mean to magnify his significance on account of his capture of the *lin*? The *lin* is a benevolent animal. It comes when there are sage kings; it does not come when there are no sage kings. Someone reported to Confucius, "There is a roe and it has a horn." Confucius said, "For whom has it come! For whom has it come!" He turned his sleeves and wiped his face as tears wetted his robe. When Yan Hui died, the Master said, "Alas! Heaven is destroying me!" When Zilu died, the Master said, "Heaven is cutting me off!" When the *lin* was captured during the western hunt, the Master said, "My way is coming to an end!" . . . Why then did the noble man create the *Annals*? For sweeping away an era of disorder and returning it to rectitude, nothing surpasses the *Annals*. But one cannot yet know whether it was made for that purpose, or whether the noble man simply rejoiced in speaking of the way of Yao and Shun? Did he not in the end rejoice in a latter-day Yao or Shun understanding the noble man? He established the principles of the *Annals* to await later sages. For the noble man also rejoiced in this. (*Gongyang* 2: 1187–1201)

There are no sage kings, and the *lin* should not have come, hence Confucius's question. As Confucius puts it in *Sayings*: "It came at the wrong time and was killed" (*KZJY* 16.259). Its untimely appearance and capture thus provoke lamentation, akin to Confucius's mournful cries over the death of his beloved disciples Yan Hui and Zilu, which immediately follow. The tragic fate of the *lin* is a sign that the corrective principles embodied in his teachings will not prevail against decline and disorder. Its fate of being mis-recognized parallels Confucius's fate, and Confucius's naming of it and his lamentation mark the recognition of his own failure, a point elaborated later in *Kong Anthology*:

1.64b The carriage driver of the Shusun lineage, named Chu Shang, hunted in the wilds and captured an animal. None could recognize it, so they considered it inauspicious and abandoned it at the Cross-road of the Five Fathers. Ran Qiu told the Master, "It has a roe's body and a flesh-covered horn—is this not an anomaly sent by heaven?" The Master said, "Where is it now? I will go and look at it." They thus went, and Confucius said to his driver Gao Chai, "If it is as Qiu said, then it is a *lin* for sure!" They went to see it, and it was as described. Yan Hui asked, "Flying creatures honor the phoenix, run-ning creatures honor the *lin*. May I ask for whom is it a sign, now that it has appeared?" The Master said, "When the Son of Heaven spreads his virtue, he will bring great peace for all under heaven, and the *lin*, the phoenix, the turtle, and the dragon will come first as aus-picious omens. Now the ancestral Zhou is about to be extinguished, and there is no master under heaven. For whom has it come?" He then wept, "I among men is like the *lin* among beasts. The *lin* has now come out and died. My way is coming to an end!" He then sang, "The *lin* and the phoenix roamed in the era of Tang and Yu, / Now is not its time, what did it come for? / Alas for the *lin*, the *lin*! I am heartsick evermore!" (*KCZ* 5.97)

Since the *Annals* transmitted in the *Gongyang* and *Guliang* commentaries end in 481 BCE, the *lin*'s capture also signifies the completion of the *Annals*, whereby Confucius is said to lay down his judgment, his vision of political legitimacy, and his definition of good governance. According to this rea-soning, the *lin* is an auspicious omen, the sign conferring a mandate on Confucius as the "uncrowned king" who will lay down the law for pos-terity. A tradition arose that Confucius predicts the rise of the Han, and these latter-day sage kings (Han rulers) will understand Confucius and follow the precepts of the *Annals*, hence the repeated references to the sage's joy at the end of the passage from the *Gongyang Tradition* cited above (1.64a). In *Luxuriant Dew of the Spring and Autumn Annals (Chunqiu fanlu*, ca. second century BCE), the capture of the *lin* is described as "the auspicious sign of having received the mandate" (*shouming zhi fu* 受命之符), whereby Confucius can "illuminate the principles of changing the rules of governance" (*gaizhi zhi yi* 改制之義) through judgments in the *Annals*. The Gongyang exegete He Xiu (129–182) elaborates the idea that Confucius understands the *lin* as the omen for the rise of the Han dynasty (*Gongyang* 2: 1201). This turns into a full-blown fantastic legitimation of Han rule in Han apocrypha (*ZY* 962, *Gongyang* 2: 1199) and Gan Bao's *In Search of the Supernatural*:

1.64c In the fourteenth year of Lord Ai of Lu, Confucius dreamed one night that a red vapor rose between three locust trees in Feng and Pei.[111] He thus called upon Yan Hui and Zixia to accompany him to observe the phenomenon. They drove their carriage to the Fan Lineage Street in the northwest of Chu, and saw a farm boy hitting a *lin*, wounding its left leg, and covering it with a bunch of firewood. Confucius said, "Child, come here! What is your name?" The child said, "My surname is Red Pine, my given name is Shiqiao, my style name is Shouji."[112] Confucius said, "Did you see anything unusual?" The child said, "I saw an animal that looks like a roe with the head of a sheep. On its head is a horn, whose tip is flesh-covered. It just ran past here westward." Confucius said, "He is already master of the whole world. He is Liu the Red Emperor. Chen and Xiang will assist him. Five stars will enter the Well Asterism, following the Year Star."[113] The child removed the firewood to show Confucius the *lin* under it. Confucius hastened forward to examine it. The *lin* turned to Confucius, flapped down its ears, and spit out three scrolls. They were three inches wide and eight inches long. Each scroll had twenty-four characters. It said, "Liu the Red Emperor will rise. Zhou will soon be destroyed. The red vapor will rise and a fiery brightness will flourish. Confucius, the Black God, will institute the mandate of rule. The emperor's name will have the graphic component *mao* and *jin*." (*ZY* 922)[114]

The yellowish green *lin* symbolizes the element of wood and the Zhou dynasty. The farm boy with his firewood means that the Red Emperor's son (Liu Bang) will rise from the ranks of commoners to replace the Zhou dynasty. The jade texts embody the idea that Confucius will lay down the rules of governance for Han (*wei Han zhifa* 為漢制法). Another Han text states that in the same month of the capture of the *lin*, writings in blood on a Lu city gate predict dynastic succession and Confucius's lasting legacy (*ZY* 963, *Gongyang* 2: 1199).[115] Han apocrypha also states that the *lin* came as the auspicious omen linked to both Confucius's birth and death (*ZY* 978–79), a story retold by Wang Jia (d. 390) in *Collecting Forgotten Stories* (*Shiyi ji*):

> 1.64d Before the Master was born, there was a *lin* that spit out a jade text at a house in Queli. The text said, "The child of the Spirit of Water, he belongs to the era of declining Zhou and will be the uncrowned king." That was why two dragons encircled his mother's room, and the spirits of five stars descended in her courtyard.[116] Confucius's mother, Zhengzai, was good and wise, and she understood that it was a divine sign, so she tied a silk ribbon on the *lin*'s horn, and two days later the *lin* left. A physiognomist said: "The Master belonged to the lineage of King Tang of Yin, he has the virtue of water and will be the uncrowned king." Toward the end of the reign of King Jing of Zhou, in the twenty-fourth year of Lord Ding,[117] Chu Shang, a man of Lu, hunted in the Great Marsh and obtained the *lin*. He showed it to the Master. The ribbon tied to its horn was still there. Knowing that his life was about to end, the Master embraced the *lin* and untied the silk ribbon, his tears streaming down copiously. Almost a hundred years elapsed between the time the *lin* appeared and the year the ribbon was taken off. (*ZY* 731–32)

Note that the capture of the *lin*, which figures so prominently in Han Confucian writings, is relatively neglected in Song and Ming Neo-Confucian traditions, which are more invested in the metaphysics of human nature, self-cultivation, and inward transcendence. The voluminous record of Zhu Xi's conversations with his disciples includes only one dismissive mention of this episode: "Regarding the capture of the *lin* in the *Annals*, I do not dare to insist that it was the completion of the *Annals* that moved the cosmos and caused the *lin* to appear; nor do I dare to insist that Confucius was moved by the *lin* and thus compiled the *Annals*. The general point is that it appeared at the wrong time and was killed. It was inauspicious."[118]

One interesting omission in *Historical Records* is Confucius's final attempt at political intervention in the same year as the *lin*'s capture. According to *Zuo Tradition*, Confucius begs in vain for Lu intervention when the Chen lineage in Qi murders the Qi ruler (*Zuo* Ai 14.5, 3: 1930–31):

> 1.64e In the sixth month, on the *jiawu* day (5), Chen Heng killed his ruler Ren in Shuzhou. Confucius fasted for three days and thrice requested that Qi be attacked. Our lord said, "Lu has been weaker than Qi for a long time. Now you propose to attack them, but how can it be done?" He replied, "Now that Chen Heng has killed his ruler, a full half of the people do not side with him. If we add Lu's multitude to half of Qi, then we can prevail." Our lord said, "Tell it to the Ji lineage." Confucius took his leave, withdrew, and told others, "It was because I took up the rear in the ranks of high officers that I did not dare to fail to speak."

In the analogous passage from the *Analects* (14.21), Lord Ai of Lu tells Confucius to make his request to the three dominant lineages in Lu, and Confucius responds with the words that he tells others in *Zuo Tradition*. If these accounts were available to Sima Qian, then he might have decided to omit it to highlight the capture of the *lin* and the creation of the *Annals* as the summation of Confucius's life.

1.65 "Neither lowering their ideals nor suffering indignity for their persons—is this not true of Boyi and Shuqi?" He said of Liu Xiahui and Shaolian that they "lower their ideals and suffer indignity for their persons." He said of Yuzhong and Yiyi that they "lived in reclusion and spoke freely. Their actions hit the target of purity; their abandonment of society hits the target of expediency." "As for me, I am different from these men. There is no inevitable affirmation or inevitable rejection of alternatives."

[translator's note]
This passage also appears, with some variations, in the *Analects* (18.8). The enumerated characters represent different options at moments of disjunction between troubled times and talented men with high ideals, thus continuing the earlier ruminations on timing and what it means to be unrecognized

and misunderstood. Boyi and Shuqi, already mentioned in 1.43 and 1.49a, are brothers who vie to yield the throne to each other in their natal state and later protest the violence of the Zhou conquest by starving themselves to death (*SJ* 61). Liu Xiahui is a Lu official who does not leave the state despite suffering dismissal thrice (*Analects* 18.2). Mencius says of him: "He was not ashamed of serving a benighted ruler, and he did not refuse a minor office" (*Mencius* 5B.10). Shaolian, Yuzhong, and Yiyi cannot be identified with certainty. It seems logical to regard the third group, Yuzhong and Yiyi, as being situated between the first two, exemplifying both adherence to principles and acceptance of expediency. Confucius declares himself different from these worthy men: abjuring arbitrary will-fulness, dogmatism, intransigence, and egoism (1.57; *Analects* 9.4), he responses to situations in a timely fashion, perhaps adopting the respective attitudes of the earlier worthies depending on how circumstances vary. Mencius concludes: "Boyi is the pure among sages; Yi Yin, the undaunted among sages; Liu Xiahui, the balanced among sages; Confucius, the timely among sages. Confucius can be said to encompass all in a great integra-tion" (*Mencius* 5B.10). Since "Heaven has its timeliness" (*XZ* 17.227), to be timely can mean "resonating with Heaven's will in achieving timely action."[119] Timeliness becomes a more deliberate articulation of adaptabil-ity in *Mr Lü's Annals*, where Confucius responds to criticism of his coop-eration with the usurping Ji lineage: "Dragons eat what's pure and swim in what's pure; ophidians eat what's pure and swim in what's impure; fish eats what's impure and swim in what's impure. Now I do not measure up to dragons above, nor am I comparable to fish below. Perhaps I am an ophidian!" (*LSCQ* 2: 1310; see also *LH* 22.285).

1.66 The Master said, "Isn't it so! Isn't it so! The noble man abhors the idea of leaving the world without making his name known. My way is not going to prevail! How can I reveal myself to posterity?" He followed historical records and compiled the *Spring and Autumn Annals*, going back to Lord Yin, reaching down to the fourteenth year of Lord Ai, and covering the reigns of twelve lords. It uses Lu as the basis, claims ancestral kinship with Zhou, and upholds its former roots in Yin [Shang], moving through the three eras. Confucius condenses its words and phrases, yet its meanings are broad and profound. That is why, even as the rulers of Wu and Chu called themselves "kings," the *Annals* disparagingly gives them the lower rank of "master." At the meeting at Jiantu, Lord Wen of Jin actually summoned the Zhou Son of Heaven, and yet the *Annals* conceals it and says: "The Heaven-appointed king went on the winter hunt at Heyang." Confucius extends this kind of method to judge and evaluate his times. As for the meanings behind critiques and disparagements, there are latter day kings who would uphold and expand them. When the principles of the *Annals* prevail, ministers fomenting disorder and miscreant sons quake in fear.

[translator's note]

In the *Analects*, Confucius both disdains fame and regards it as the way to leave a mark on the world: "The noble man abhors the idea of leaving the world without making his name known" (*Analects* 15.20). Pursuing the theme of recognition, Sima Qian presents the *Annals* as the venue through which Confucius reveals himself to posterity. The idea of self-fulfillment and self-revelation (*zixian* 自見) through writing also appears in Sima Qian's biography of Yu Qing (*SJ* 76.23) and his letter to Ren An (*HS* 62.2735). This retrospective vision of the *Annals* recasting its compilation in the light of Sima Qian's authorship of the *Historical Records* prompts Cui Shu to demur: "With these words Confucius seems to be one eager to seek fame. It certainly misses the mark when it comes to the sage's intention" (*SJ* 47.82). The description of the *Annals*' vision of Lu, Zhou, and Shang echoes interpretations of the *Gongyang Tradition* in views attributed to Dong Zhongshu. The *Annals* is said to express implacable judgment through its concise wording and modes of naming. It also "respectfully conceals" (*hui* 諱) the indignities suffered by Zhou kings and Lu rulers. One example, dated to 632 BCE, is how Lord Wen of Jin confirms his hegemonic status among the lords by treating the Zhou king in a high-handed fashion, having played a key role in defeating the king's challenger. *Zuo Tradition* explains:

> 1.66a At this meeting in Wen, the Prince of Jin summoned the king and presented the princes to him. Moreover, he had the king undertake the winter hunt. Confucius said, "To have a subject summon a ruler is not a salutary example. That is why it is written, 'The Heaven-appointed king went on the winter hunt at Heyang': it is saying that it is not the proper place, and it is also to make a shining example of virtue. (*Zuo* Xi 28.9, 1: 428–29)

The above passage criticizes Lord Wen of Jin for summoning the Zhou king while praising the *Annals* for concealing this undignified fact (see also

SJ 39.61). Such an act of concealment would focus attention on the assistance Lord Wen provides for the Zhou king, making it "a shining example of virtue." Historical judgment has momentous consequences; hence Mencius compares Confucius's compilation of the *Annals* to the most decisive moments in human history as he understood it:

> 1.66b Formerly, Yu quelled the floods, and peace reigned all under heaven; the Duke of Zhou subjugated the Yi and Di barbarians, drove away ferocious wild beasts, and the people enjoyed security; Confucius compiled the *Annals*, and ministers fomenting disorder and miscreant sons quaked in fear. (*Mencius* 3B.9)

While drawing from this formulation in *Mencius*, Sima Qian seems to imply, with a slight rhetorical sleight of hand, that such momentous consequences will unfold only when "the principles of the *Annals* prevail." According to *Mencius* (4B.21), the compilation of the *Annals* results from and responds to the abeyance of sage kings by articulating the principles of ideal kingship: "With the fading of the traces of sage kings, the meaning of the *Odes* was lost. After that loss, the *Annals* was compiled." Sima Qian reiterates this idea: "Jie and Zhòu [the last kings of Xia and Shang] lost the Way, and Tang and Wu [the first kings of Shang and Zhou] rose up; Zhou lost the Way and the *Annals* was compiled" (*SJ* 130.44). The word for both "rise up" and "create" or "compile" is *zuo* 作; textual creation is equated with the creation of a new political order. As Liu Shipei (1884–1919) pointed out, the word *zuo* can imply both a radical beginning (*shi* 始) as well as action (*wei* 為), which can encompass compilation, editorial labor, and interpretation; both sets of meanings seem operative in Sima Qian's presentation of Confucius as "author" of the *Annals*.[120]

In the autobiographical final chapter of *Historical Records*, Sima Qian implicitly compares his historical project to that of Confucius. He describes the *Annals* thus: "Knowing that his words would not be heeded and that his way would not be implemented, Confucius conveyed his judgment on 242 years of history to create a model for all under heaven. He demoted the Son of Heaven, censured the lords, and inveighed against the high officers in order to bring about ideal government, and that was all. The Master said: 'I want to put my ideas in theoretical language, but that is not as profound, urgent, and clear as making them manifest in events.' From on high, the *Annals* illumines the way of the three sage kings; turning to the mundane, it divines the principles of human affairs. It makes distinctions in case of doubts and suspicions, clarifies right and wrong, settles what causes hesitation, approves of good actions and abhors wrongdoings, commends the worthy and degrades the unworthy, preserves destroyed states, continues the generations that had been cut off, repairs the failing and revives the abandoned: it is what is most important about the kingly way" (*SJ* 130.21–22).

1.67 In his position as supervisor of corrections, Confucius heard cases of litigation. The judgments had wording over which he consulted with others; he did not monopolize them. But when it came to the *Annals*, what should be written was written, what should be excised was excised; even learned disciples like Zixia could not modify a word. His disciples received the instruction of the *Annals*. Confucius said, "Posterity will know me through the *Annals*; it will condemn me also through the *Annals*."

[translator's note]
Confucius's historical judgment as embodied in the *Annals* is said to be more implacable than his legal judgment as a judicial official. (One is for the ages; one addresses the situation at hand.) Sima Qian is implicitly critical of contemporary attempts to formulate legal judgment on the basis of the *Annals*, which often results in harsh interpretations of motives and culpability (*SJ* 30.13–14, *SJ* 118.38–39, *SJ* 121.19). More generally, Sima Qian is reticent on the notion of Confucius as the "uncrowned king," linking moral authority to disempowerment rather than hypothetical political authority.[121] In other words, he believes the *Annals* sets forth the principles of ideal political order valid for posterity (including the Han), but not so much that it "formed the laws for the Han dynasty" (*wei Han zhifa*), especially if it just means legitimating the powers that be. Confucius's words on how posterity will know him or blame him through the *Annals* seem to return to the concern with understanding and recognition rather than the supposed presumption of the power to judge, as implied in the original passage from *Mencius* (3B.9):

1.67a When the era was in decline and the way was in abeyance, deviant words and violent acts rose. There were cases of the subject assassinating the ruler or of the son assassinating the father. Confucius was fearful and thus compiled the *Annals*. The *Annals* embodied the concerns of the Son of Heaven. That is why Confucius said, "Those who know me will do so through the *Annals*; those who condemn me will also do so through the *Annals*."

1.68 Zilu died in Wei the following year. Confucius was ill, and Zigong requested an audience with him. Confucius was just then leaning on his staff and wandering outside his gate. He said, "Ci, how late you are in coming!" Confucius then sighed and sang, "Is Mount Tai collapsing? Are the beam and pillar breaking? Is the wise man withering?" His tears streamed down as he sang. He said to Zigong, "The Way has been in abeyance all under heaven for a long time. None is capable of honoring me as master. The men of Xia were coffined and placed on the eastern steps; the men of Zhou did so on the western steps; the men of Yin did so between the two pillars. Yesterday evening I dreamed of my seat being placed between the two pillars. My ancestors were men of Yin." Seven days later, he died.

[translator's note]
Confucius's death is framed by reflections on the future (the fate of his disciples and his legacy) and the past (his ties to the Three Dynasties). The esteemed Yan Hui had died some time earlier. During the internecine conflict in Wei in 480 BCE, Zilu died defending the Wei minister Kong Kui, who was taken hostage by Kuaikui as he reentered Wei and became ruler by ousting his son Zhe (for the succession struggle in Wei, see 1.20, 1.34, 1.49; *SJ* 67.10–14). Knowing Zilu's sense of duty and impetuosity, Confucius predicts his death once he hears of the unrest in Wei (*Zuo* Ai 15.5, 3: 1938–41). Confucius dies two years after the capture of the *lin* and one year after Zilu's death. The overlapping account of his death in *Record of Rituals* shows subtle differences (*LJ* 1: 195–97):

1.68a Confucius rose early. Holding his hands behind him and dragging his staff, he wandered outside his gate and sang, "Is Mount Tai collapsing? Are the beam and pillar breaking? Is the wise man withering?" Having finished his song, he entered and sat facing the door. Zigong heard about this and said, "If Mount Tai collapses, what can I look up to? If the beam and pillar break and the wise man withers, where can I put myself? Surely the Master is going to be very ill!" He thus entered briskly with small steps. The Master said, "Ci! How late you are in coming! Xia rulers were coffined and placed on top of the eastern steps, so they were still taking the host's place. The men of Yin were coffined and placed between the two pillars, flanked by the positions for the host and the guest. The men of Zhou were coffined and placed on top of the western steps, so they were still taking the guest's place. And I am a man of Yin. The other night, I dreamed of my seat being placed between the two pillars. Kings of bright virtue have not arisen. Who under heaven can honor me as Master? Surely I am about to die!" He lay sick for seven days and died.

Critics of these passages in *Historical Records* and *Record of Rituals* note how Confucius "presenting himself as a sage" (*zisheng* 自聖) is inconsistent with his modest self-deprecation in other accounts, and how the reference to dream omens does not accord with his reluctance to predict the future or talk about fate (SJ 47.86, LJ 1: 197). One could argue, however, that Confucius's modesty coexists with his sense of lofty mission as the embodiment of "this culture" (1.19), and that the dream omen is but the expression of Confucius's typical concern with the past, in this case his relationship with the tradition of the Xia, Shang, and Zhou dynasties, a point emphasized earlier (1.52, see also 1.2a).

The passage in *Record of Rituals* seems more "staged" than its analogue in *Historical Records*. Confucius's posture and his song invites attention, "as if he wants others to notice his strangeness" (Zheng Xuan's comment, LJ 1: 196). Explaining the positioning of the coffined body in the Xia, Shang, and Zhou traditions may also imply a kind of self-elevation. Sun Xidan (1736–1784) explains: "For the men of Yin [Shang], the spirits should be placed in a position of honor, so the coffined body was placed between the two pillars, flanked by the positions for host and guest on both sides. . . . When a ruler retired from court and went to his grand chamber to attend to administration, it was precisely between the two pillars that he sat. . . . The Master said that he dreamed of his seat being placed between the two pillars, yet no king of bright virtue had arisen, and there was none under heaven who would honor him as ruler. This meant that the dream image was not about facing south and attending to governance and was certainly the omen for a funeral in the Yin tradition. That was why he used it to divine about his imminent death" (LJ 1: 196–97). It is possible that the notion of the "uncrowned king" is more operative in the account in *Record of Rituals*, and "sitting between the two pillars" is associated with the south-facing position of a ruler. By contrast, the account in *Historical Records* is more affective and private. Confucius does not perform his song to attract attention. He also weeps. The dream is about the weight of mortality as he laments the abeyance of his way.

1.69 Confucius lived to be seventy-three. He died on the *jichou* day (11) of the fourth month in the sixteenth year in the reign of Lord Ai of Lu. Lord Ai eulogized him with these words:

> High heaven, unpitying,
> Would not even leave me one old man,
> Forsaking me, the lone one, in my place.
> Solitary I am in my pain and sorrow.
> Alas! Woe indeed! The venerable Confucius!
> I no longer have the wherewithal of self-regulation.

Zigong said, "The ruler will likely not get to end his days in Lu! Such were the Master's words: 'To lose ritual propriety is to become benighted, to lose the proper name is to commit transgression. To lose one's will is to become benighted, to lose one's place is to commit transgression.' He could not make good use of him when he was alive and eulogized him upon his death: that was violation of ritual propriety. He called himself 'the lone one': that was not the proper name."

[translator's note]
Confucius died in 479 BCE. Passage 1.69 is almost identical with the account in *Zuo Tradition* (*Zuo* Ai 16.3, 3: 1942–45; cf. *LJ* 1: 239; *KZJY* 40.534). Lord Ai's eulogy is a pastiche of slightly modified lines from the *Odes*. In Sima Qian's chapter on Confucius's disciples, Zigong emerges as a master rhetorician charting interstate relations; here he is the judge of another's rhetoric. Zigong criticizes the ritual impropriety of the eulogy: Lord Ai's grief cannot make up for his failure to employ Confucius when he was alive, and "the lone one" is a phrase reserved for use by the Zhou king in referring to himself. Zigong quotes Confucius, who seems to be continuing his critique of those in power even after death. Zigong's prediction is fulfilled, and Lord Ai is driven into exile in 468 BCE. The death of Confucius is the final entry in the *Annals* transmitted along with the *Zuo Tradition*. Zigong is prominently featured in these concluding sections of the

chapter. According to Sima Qian, Zigong was a fabulously successful merchant responsible for spreading Confucius's fame all over the world (*SJ* 129.12).

1.70 Confucius was buried north of the Lu capital by the River Si. His disciples all wore mourning clothes for three years. When three years of heartfelt mourning were completed, they bade each other farewell and left. Then they wailed; again, everyone fully poured out their grief, and some of them came back and stayed behind. Zigong alone built a hut by the grave and left only after six years. His disciples and the men of Lu who built their homes by Confucius's grave made up over a hundred households. The place thus came to be called the Confucius Quarter. Seasonal sacrifices at Confucius's grave were passed on from one generation to the next in Lu, and various scholars of traditional learning also refined upon the practice of rituals, including the ceremonies of drinking in district feasts and of great archery gatherings, at the former abode of Confucius. The area of his grave amounted to one *qing*.[122] His former abode was where his disciples stayed. Later generations thus turned it into a temple storing Confucius's gown, cap, zither, carriage, and books. This tradition did not break off for over two hundred years, lasting all the way to the Han. When the Ancestral Emperor passed by Lu, he offered sacrifices with a set of sacrificial animals. Various lords and ministers came to that place. They often first paid their respects there before they assumed a position in government.

[translator's note]
"Heartfelt mourning" or "inner mourning" (*xinsang* 心喪) refers to a state of grief unmarked by external paraphernalia. According to *Record of Rituals*, "three years of heartfelt mourning" would be the appropriate mourning for a teacher (*LJ* 1: 165). In another entry in that text, Zigong responds when the disciples debate whether they should wear mourning clothes: "Formerly, when the Master lost Yan Hui, he mourned him as if he had lost a son, but he did so without the mourning clothes. It was the same when he lost Zilu. I request that we mourn the Master as if we were mourning our fathers but do so without the mourning clothes" (*LJ* 1: 197; *KZJY* 40.535). Yet another entry claims that, mourning Confucius, the disciples wear hempen mourning clothes when they stay together, but not when they go out (*LJ* 1: 201; *KZJY* 40.535). Sima Qian states that the disciples wear mourning clothes for three years but also claims that they are practicing

"heartfelt mourning." The bond between a teacher and his disciples defines the basis of an intellectual community. Notwithstanding its importance, the ritual prescriptions governing it remain less clear than in the case of kinship.

The disciples' intense mourning is a kind of afterlife of Confucius. Sima Qian also draws from the following passage in *Mencius* (3A.4), where Mencius chides a potential apostate, Chen Xiang, for being bedazzled by the primitive agrarianism of Xu Xing by holding up the mourning of Confucius's disciples as the counter example of steadfast moral compass:

> 1.70a "Formerly, upon the death of Confucius, the disciples were about to pack their bags and return home after three years of mourning. They entered and bowed to Zigong, faced each other and wailed until they lost their voice, and then they returned home. Zigong came back and built a hut on the burial grounds and lived alone for another three years, then he returned home. Sometime later, Zixia, Zizhang, and Ziyou perceived that Youruo looked like the sage, and wanted to serve him in the same way they served Confucius. They forced Master Zeng [Zeng Shen] to join them. Master Zeng said, 'It cannot be done. It is as if the Master had been purified by the waters of the Yangzi River and the Han River and exposed to the bright light of the sun: there is no exceeding the dazzling whiteness.' Now this shrike-tongued southern barbarian has refuted the Way of the former kings. Yet you turn against your teacher to follow him. You are indeed different from Master Zeng!"

Three disciples expose their lack of judgment when, longing for Confucius, they are tempted to elevate Youruo as his substitute. Zeng Shen (son of Zeng Dian, discussed in the introduction) opposes this, because the sage is inimitable. This episode is also told in Sima's chapter on Confucius's disciples, where Youruo is elevated as the disciples' teacher only to be dismissed when he cannot field their questions which credit Confucius with divinatory powers (see 1.10, translator's note) that Youruo apparently lacks (SJ 67.44–45).

In 195 BCE, Liu Bang, the first Han emperor ("the Ancestral Emperor"), used a set of three domestic animals (an ox, a sheep, and a pig) as sacrificial offerings to honor Confucius (SJ 47.89, HS 1B.76). Han lords and ministers followed suit. Sacrifices to Confucius were regularized in 2 CE.[123]

Confucian rituals as moral legitimation came to be intertwined with political authority. No aspirants to political power could fail to ignore Confucius, including rebels like Chen She (d. 208 BCE), who rose up against Qin rule and included a descendant of Confucius in his coterie (see 1.71). Sacrifice at the Temple of Confucius was formalized in different ways throughout Chinese history and reached a new level of elaborateness under the Qing, the last imperial dynasty that ruled China.[124]

1.71 Confucius sired Li, who had the style name Boyu, lived to be fifty, and died before Confucius. Boyu sired Ji (style name Zisi), who lived to be sixty-two and once faced adversity in Song. Zisi composed "The Mean." Zisi sired Bai (style name Zishang), who lived to be forty-seven. Zishang sired Qiu (style name Zijia), who lived to be forty-five. Zijia sired Ji (style name Zijing), who lived to be forty-six. Zijing sired Chuan (style name Zigao), who lived to be fifty-one. Zigao sired Zishen, who lived to be fifty-seven and was once the prime minister of Wei. Zishen sired Fu, who lived to be fifty-seven and was an academician in the coterie of Chen She, king of Chen; Fu died in Chen. Fu's younger brother Zixiang lived to be fifty-seven and once served as an academician in the court of Emperor Xiaohui. He was sent away from the capital and became the governor of Changsha. He was nine *chi* and six *cun* in height. Zixiang sired Zhong, who lived to be fifty-seven. Zhong sired Wu. Wu sired Yannian and Anguo. Anguo was an academician in the court of the present emperor. His position rose to that of governor of Linhuai. He died young. Anguo sired Ang, Ang sired Huan.

[translator's note]
Confucius's grandson Zisi "faced adversity in Song" and composed "The Mean" (a chapter in *Record of Rituals*), echoing the connection between suffering, failure, and creation, a theme adumbrated in the final chapter of *Historical Records* and in Sima Qian's letter to Ren An. Tradition credits Zisi's disciples with the transmission of Confucius's teachings to Mencius. Elsewhere Kong Fu is called Kong Jia and is said to have died with Chen She when Chen's forces were crushed by Qin (*SJ* 121.5). Note that Zixiang had the same impressive height as Confucius. Kong Anguo taught Sima Qian the *Documents* in ancient script and is mentioned in the chapter on scholars and ritual experts in *Historical Records* (*SJ* 121.21–22). Confucius is the only figure in *Historical Records* with an unbroken and clearly enumerated genealogy stretching over four centuries, reaching down to Sima

Qian's generation with descendants personally known to the historian. The Kong clan in Qufu continued to the powerful through much of Chinese history (see chapter 4, 4.2, translator's note).

1.72 The Senior Scribe said, "As it says in the *Odes*, 'To the high hills I look, / On the bright road I proceed.' Even though I am not able to reach his level, my heart is inexorably drawn to it. I study the texts of Confucius and can see in my mind's eye what he was like as a person. When I went to Lu and examined the carriage, gown, and ritual vessels in Confucius's temple, or how various students regularly practiced rituals in his former abode, I lingered and stayed, as if I could not bear to tear myself away. There have been indeed numerous rulers and worthy men under heaven. They attained glory in their time but sank into oblivion when they perished. Confucius was a commoner, but his teachings were transmitted over more than ten generations, and scholars honor him as their ancestral leader. From the Son of Heaven, princes, and lords downward, those in the central domains who speak of the Six Arts seek definitive norms from the Master's teachings. He can be called the supreme sage indeed!"

[translator's note]
Sima Qian weaves numerous accounts of Confucius into an intricate tapestry. Much of his work involves adjudicating, modifying, and reconciling different sources. Yet his sense of a personal connection to Confucius and his belief that he can reach "what he was like as a person" by reading texts by him and about him provides momentum for his account. In that sense, textual mediation facilitates an intuitive and personal encounter, whose palpability Sima Qian seems to experience as he lingers over the physical traces of "the supreme sage" and imagines his aura. Sima Qian uses the word "sage" three times in this chapter, first in connection with Confucius's illustrious ancestors (1.4), second as epithet justified by his broad knowledge (1.10), and here by way of praising his lasting legacy.

Reading Sima Qian's Account of Confucius

In considering Sima Qian's project of "chronicling Confucius," perhaps the most obvious issue is chronology. Commitment to chronology, more strictly observed in the "Annals" and "Hereditary Houses," two of the five sections of *Historical Records*, is itself a marker of public political significance. (The "Annals" is about ruling dynasties, and "Hereditary Houses" deals with lineages of regional rulers and enfeoffed ministers, although there are exceptions in both cases.) In the account of Confucius, it has the effect of linking apparently personal experience to its political context. Consider the example of Confucius's appreciation of music in Qi. Sima Qian dates this event to 517 BCE, the year that Ji Pingzi, head of the dominant ministerial lineage in Lu, drove the Lu ruler, Lord Zhao, into exile. Confucius, then thirty-five, "went to Qi and became a retainer of Gao Zhaozi, hoping thereby to gain access to Lord Jing of Qi. He spoke with the Qi grand music master about music, heard the notes of Shao, studied it, and for three months no longer knew the taste of meat. The men of Qi praised him" (1.8). The parallel passage in the *Analects* (7.14) about Confucius's enjoyment of music does not date it or connect it to the process of studying music: "The Master was in Qi and heard Shao music. For three months he did not know the taste of meat, saying, 'I did not know that music could be like this!'"

Commenting on the above entry from the *Analects*, Song Neo-Confucians are skeptical. Cheng Yi considers such obsessive enthusiasm incommensurate with the image of sagely equanimity (*LY* 2: 589). Zhu Xi fuses Confucius's aesthetic appreciation with moral approbation of the music as the embodiment of political ideals, perhaps implicitly refuting Cheng Yi (*LY* 2: 592). To date this episode to 517 BCE is to frame it as Confucius's reaction to the political crisis in Lu. It raises questions such as the following: Did Confucius go to Qi because Lord Zhao fled to Qi? Why did Confucius choose to become the retainer of a Qi minister of dubious repute upon the de facto expulsion of the Lu ruler? How does music encode or transcend the experience of political disorder? Does the idea of "studying music" in Sima Qian's account ameliorate the anxiety over excessive aesthetic absorption? What is the relationship between transcendent musical experience and the pressure of the historical moment or political expediency?

More generally, chronology grounds the disembodied sayings in the *Analects* in specific historical moments, thereby revisiting the latent tension between their embodiment as immutable ethical principles of universal application and as historically defined utterances. For example, Confucius twice declares in the *Analects* (9.18, 15.13): "I have not yet seen anyone who loves virtue as much as he loves sensuous beauty." In Sima Qian's account, he makes this statement after being publicly humiliated by Lord Ling of Wei and his favored consort Nan Zi (1.20). Lord Ling and Nan Zi make a spectacle of themselves as they pass through the marketplace, yielding a third place in their carriage to a eunuch while putting Confucius in a second, inferior carriage. An apparently categorical distrust of sensuous beauty and sexual desire is here inflected by political disappointment and personal frustration. Imagining a particular historical context can also take the edge off this supposedly misogynistic statement in the *Analects* (17.25): "Women and petty men are the only ones hard to deal with. Draw close to them, and they become insubordinate. Keep your distance, and they become resentful." Nylan suggests that the comment pertains to the notorious Nan Zi and should not be regarded as a universal contempt of women.[125] (Sima Qian does not quote this passage in his biography of Confucius.)

Chronology as well as its flouting highlight organizing principles behind the narrative. We are told in the *Analects* (7.21): "The Master does not speak about anomalies, mere feats of strength, violation of norms, and the spirits." This famous statement about Confucius's recognition of the limits of knowledge and acceptable discourse is quoted (1.62) but contradicted by his display of esoteric knowledge on three occasions (two told in 1.10, one in 1.24) in Sima Qian's account. Confucius answers the Lu minister Ji Huanzi's question about a sheep found inside a well and explains to a Wu visitor the provenance of a gigantic bone discovered in Yue (1.10). The contextual information suggests that apparently arcane knowledge may redress the balance of power between Confucius and his interlocutor. Thus, Ji Huanzi misleads Confucius about his find to test the latter's knowledge. Sima Qian dates this event to 505 BCE. Confucius was forty-seven and Ji Huanzi just succeeded his father Ji Pingzi, who had driven Lord Zhao of Lu into exile.

The anecdote about the gigantic bone that follows is dated to 494 BCE. Why does Sima Qian ignore the temporal gap? Perhaps he perceives a similar agonistic momentum underwriting both anecdotes. The southern state Wu, a hubristic emergent power sometimes characterized as "barbarian," is confronting Lu with new confidence. Twenty years later, it will make extravagant demands on Lu (1.48). Perhaps Confucius demonstrates arcane knowledge to the Wu visitor to implicitly assert Lu superiority. The Wu visitor is so impressed that he declares Confucius a sage. Pushing the boundaries of what is knowable may well be one aspect of sagehood in Sima

Qian's time. In the source text, *Discourses of the States*, the above two stories are separated by a few entries but found in the same chapter, with the story of the entombed sheep appearing first. Sima Qian could simply be following its sequence in incorporating these stories. But if that were the case, why is the story about the ancient arrows, which immediately follows that of the gigantic bone in *Discourses*, moved to a later point in the narrative (1.24)? If chronology is the guiding principle, then the stories about the gigantic bone and the arrows should be grouped together, since both are dated to circa 494 BCE. If the discourse on anomalies is the unifying thread, then all three stories should be grouped together. Sima Qian's arrangement leads us to consider distinctions between stories of Confucius's knowledge driven by contexts of implicit competition or political confrontation (as in the case of the anecdotes about the entombed sheep and the gigantic bone) and those simply showing erudition (as in the case of the anecdote about ancient arrows). Such distinctions may also overlap with the boundaries between truly esoteric knowledge of anomalies and historical knowledge of high antiquity. Of course, one cannot rule out the possibility of Sima Qian was simply guilty of oversight or inconsistency, that the *Discourses* he saw had a different textual arrangement, or that he had other sources lost to us.

Chronicling Confucius draws attention to temporality, contingency, and the need to weigh alternatives (*quan* 權), the last being a mode of reasoning and action tied to our embeddedness in time. In *Mr. Lü's Annals*, this is called "following the situation" or "adaptability" (*yin* 因): Confucius gaining an audience through Mi Zixia is no different from the sage king Yu taking off his clothes in the Land of the Naked (*LSCQ* 1: 937). The Han thinker Yang Xiong (53 BCE–18 CE) describes such constraints imposed on Confucius as the need to "bend (or constrain) oneself" (*qushen* 詘身) in order to "extend the way" (*shendao* 信道)—in other words, apparent compromises can serve higher goals.[126] The first recorded action of the youthful Confucius in Sima Qian's account after the death and burial of his parents is his attempt, while still in hempen mourning clothes, to attend a feast hosted by Ji Wuzi, the most powerful minister in Lu, only to be snubbed by Ji Wuzi's retainer Yang Hu: "The Ji lineage head is offering a feast for officers (*shi*). We do not presume to offer a feast for you, sir" (1.3). Yang Hu (aka Yang Huo) is known in various early Chinese texts as an ambitious retainer fomenting disorder in Lu, and Confucius is said to avoid Yang Hu when the latter seeks his advice or service in the *Analects* and

Mencius. Why would Confucius, still in mourning clothes, flout the protocol of mourning rituals to participate in a feast? To present this encounter as the first public action of Confucius is to emphasize the prize of political engagement for someone without a recognized modus operandi—here his very status as a *shi*, variously translated as "officer," "man of service," "gentleman," "scholar," or "knight," is still in question.

Temporal consciousness heightens the drama of choices and dilemmas. Supposedly role-based morality offers less certainty when roles or social norms are pitted against other, possibly higher but also more elusive, ethical imperatives. In the *Analects* (17.5, 17.7), Confucius is twice tempted to join retainers rebelling against their masters, the heads of noble lineages. Both entries have generated heated debates, with some imperial commentators eager to explain away Confucius's involvement in any action disrupting sociopolitical order.[127] The corresponding passages in *Historical Records* (1.12, 1.29) add details confirming and justifying Confucius's serious consideration of the promise of insurrection. Thus, in the account of Gongshan Buniu's rebellion against the Ji lineage in Lu in 502 BCE, the fifty-year-old Confucius is said to have been motivated by frustrations and failures: "Confucius, evermore following the Way, was filled with ideas and aspirations, but had no wherewithal to put his talents to the test and was not able to find one who could use him. He said, 'King Wen and King Wu started their enterprises at Feng and Hao and became kings. Now although Bi is small, perhaps it can come close to that?' He wished to go. Zilu was not pleased and stopped Confucius. Confucius said, 'Could he have summoned me in vain? If he could use me, it would be possible to create another Zhou in the east!' However, even so, in the end he did not go" (1.12).

Some exegetes of the *Analects* argue that "he" in Confucius's final statement ("if he could use me") does not refer to the rebel Gongshan Buniu. Sima Qian makes the reference incontrovertible and clarifies Confucius's justification of defying social and political norms in the name of a higher political goal. Temporal specificity and historical contextualization thus concretize the logic that a rebel could become a sage king. The rewriting of this anecdote in the Han dynasty collection, *The Garden of Eloquence* (*Shuoyuan*), illustrates the logic of historicization from the opposite angle: it neutralizes the subversive potential of Confucius's statement by detaching it from any historical context, turning it into a general wish to be "of use" to realize his political ideal (1.12b).

The poignancy of compromise also underwrites Confucius's meeting with Nan Zi, the consort of Lord Ling of Wei (1.20). Did he cross boundaries of propriety by meeting a famously unprincipled woman? Did he do so to gain political influence? According to the *Analects* (6.28), "Confucius had an audience with Nan Zi. Zilu was not pleased. The Master swore, 'If I went against what was right, may Heaven abandon me! May Heaven abandon me!'" Sima Qian dates this meeting to 495 BCE, one year after the Wei heir apparent Kuaikui, Lord Ling's son, tried to assassinate Nan Zi because he had been publicly shamed by allegations of her adultery, which means that Nan Zi's notoriety as a licentious woman was widely known when Confucius met her. Sima Qian also supplies a more detailed context: Nan Zi's invitation, Confucius's hesitation, the setting of the meeting, Confucius's self-justification, and his implicit regret and subsequent decision to leave Wei. We see the meeting through Confucius's perspective: "Confucius entered through the door and, facing north, bowed with his forehead touching the ground. The lady bowed twice from behind the curtains with her girdle jade and pendants tinkling melodiously. Confucius said later, 'Formerly I declined to have an audience with her, but having done so, I responded with the proper ritual' " (1.20). Sima Qian juxtaposes the ambiguous allure of Nan Zi's tinkling pendants, which makes us rethink the juxtaposition of "love of sensuous beauty" and "love of virtue" discussed earlier, with Confucius's reiteration of his ritually proper response. The imperative of political engagement and the questions it raises run through the *Analects*, and even more so in *Mencius* and *Xunzi*. In Sima Qian's account, Confucius also confronts contingency and difficult choices as he tries to gain access to rulers.

Despite the uncertainties and frustrations, Sima Qian's account of Confucius follows a broad arc of striving, setbacks, and ultimate vindication in his roles as learner, teacher, and transmitter of classical learning and moral teachings. Studies of chapter 47 of *Historical Records* have tended to emphasize unity and coherence, arguing that Confucius fulfills the destiny of a hero or a sage as he successively embraces various roles.[128] Some even describe the intent of the account as hagiographic. The sage is a "limit concept" and a "God term," "the first cause of things and the last resort of reasoning," as Kai Vogelsang pointed out.[129] But closer inspection reveals how Sima Qian parries divergent perspectives as he weaves together accounts from different sources flourishing between Confucius's lifetime and his own. Fissures can be as illuminating as cohesion. We see an implicit dialogue with various masters, including detractors of Confucius's teachings. For example, the Qi minister Yan Ying's critique of the complexity and extravagance of Confucian rituals during Confucius's sojourn in Qi (1.9), dated to 517 BCE, has analogues in *Master Yan's Annals* and *Mozi* and largely echoes the Mohist critique of Confucian teachings. This Mohist attack is framed as Yan Ying's attempt, possibly motivated by jealousy, to forestall Confucius's influence in the Qi court. Lord Jing is about to turn Nixi into a fief for Confucius when Yan Ying's disparagement successfully dissuades him from further seeking Confucius's counsel. Sima Qian leaves out the libelous accusation that Confucius foments rebellion in Yan Ying's speech in *Mozi* (*MZ* 39.270–71) and focuses instead on the question of expensive ritual. Contextualization preemptively disarms the Mohist critique: Prior to Yan Ying's speech, Confucius says, "Government depends on regulating the uses of wealth." In other words, Confucius advocates regulating resources if not downright frugality, thus implicitly countering the Mohist charge that the elite's extravagant rituals are opposed to the interests of the common people.

Incorporation of stories about Confucius from *Zhuangzi* also shows subtle transformations and sometimes implicit refutations. For example, the meeting of Confucius and Laozi, told five times in *Zhuangzi*, often ends with the denigration of humaneness or the highest good (*ren* 仁) and proper duty (*yi* 義) and Confucius's self-abnegation. In Sima Qian's account, Laozi's advice is more modulated and assimilable into a general admonition on the need to transcend egoistic concerns (1.6). Laozi advises Confucius that one should "have no thought of oneself" as a son and as a subject, and that advice of self-effacement as self-preservation is ambiguous enough to be interpreted as wholehearted devotion to duty. The timing of the meeting is also noteworthy. In Sima Qian's account Confucius is a young man eager to learn; in one of the stories in *Zhuangzi*, Confucius is fifty and has run out of ideas. Structurally, the meeting is comparable to Confucius's encounters with laborers, recluses, or the madman of Chu (1.30, 1.39, 1.40, 1.47), which have analogues in the *Analects* (14.39, 18.5, 18.6, 18.7) and *Zhuangzi* (*ZZ* 4.183). While in *Zhuangzi* Confucius is usually silenced and cowed or expresses abject self-criticism in such encounters, he perseveres in his views in the *Historical Records* and the *Analects* even as he is drawn to his critics as the ones who understand his struggles. Narrative details on the adversities and setbacks that Confucius suffers in Sima Qian's account give those encounters with critics of political engagement added poignancy; the critics' voice is incorporated as the alternative that is understood but ultimately rejected. Confucius gains greater authority as his own critic or at least as one capable of self-criticism.

If the proleptic answer to the Mohist attack is matched by the accommodation of what came to be called Daoist perspectives, then elements associated with the proponents of sovereign power and the enforcement of laws (*fajia* 法家) are employed to affirm Confucius's political efficacy in Sima Qian's account. Here *ren*, variously translated as "humaneness," "benevolence," "goodness," and often rendered in this book as "the highest good," does not emerge as a keyword, although it is often touted as the most important virtue in Confucianism and is repeatedly discussed and defined in the *Analects* and in Sima Qian's chapter on Confucius's disciples. Instead, there is a particular focus on political order and effective governance. Following the account in *Xunzi*, Confucius is said to have used his power as a senior supervisor of corrections to execute Shaozheng Mao for the latter's pernicious influence and dangerous rhetoric (1.16).

The balance between beneficent virtue (*de* 德) and punishment (*xing* 刑) is widely discussed in early Chinese texts; here Confucius seems to sternly champion law and order. In the same spirit, he promptly (and perhaps preemptively) executes Qi entertainers during a diplomatic meeting between Qi and Lu at Jiagu (1.14). It is supposed to be a meeting of concord, but Confucius advises military preparation, and indeed Qi comes to the meeting with designs to intimidate and threaten the Lu delegates. In telling of this episode, Sima Qian eschews the more sober account in *Zuo Tradition* (1.14a, assuming it was available to him), which shows Confucius seeing through Qi stratagems and gaining the upper hand through powerful rhetoric. Instead, he adopts the more sensational account of Confucius making his point by executing Qi performers who violated ritual prescriptions, as told variously in the *Guliang Tradition* (1.14b) and Lu Jia's (d. 170 BCE) *New Discourses* (1.14c).

Sima Qian seems eager to emphasize the political efficacy of Confucius's teachings. There is a brief mention of how he is upheld as example (1.13), but there is no reference to "humane government" (*renzheng* 仁政), a recurrent concern in *Mencius*. Instead, his achievements are couched in terms of efficacy—the people's strict adherence to laws and ritual propriety (1.16)—and the strengthening of the state. Thus, the aforementioned Jiagu meeting ends with Qi returning territories it annexed from Lu. In terms of domestic politics in Lu, the razing of the city walls of the strongholds of ministerial lineages is presented as a move to centralize power for the ruling house (1.15). Many details of this episode overlap with the analogous account in *Zuo Tradition*, but in the latter the razing of the city walls is just the result of an expedient alliance between the Lu ruling house and the Ji lineage against the expanding power of the Ji lineage's retainers. In addition, Confucius's disciple Zilu, as the Ji lineage steward, takes center stage in *Zuo Tradition*, while in Sima Qian's account it is Confucius who persuades the Lu ruler to take action and possibly direct the course of events through Zilu. In other words, Confucius seems more aligned with the vision of centralizing state power at some moments in the narrative.

One of the key sources of tension in Sima Qian's account of Confucius is pitting the need to vindicate the political efficacy of Confucius's ideas against the fact that those in positions of power ultimately did not heed him. Any account of Confucius's success will have to be squared with a trajectory of political failure. The refrain in this account is how Confucius is "not employed" (*buyong* 不用) and that his ideas are not implemented or "put to use" (*yong* 用). If Confucius's ideas translate into such effective governance (1.14, 1.15, 1.16), why does he fail to gain any political foothold in Lu or other states? Slander, jealousy, and the susceptibility of wielders of power to the seduction of sensual pleasures are cited as the usual culprits (1.9, 1.17, 1.20, 1.41).

Sima Qian is ultimately more invested in the notion of failure as affirmation and the genesis of creation than in proofs of political efficacy. Again and again, Confucius is in dire straits, being detained in Kuang (1.19), threatened by Huan Tui in Song (1.21), and reduced to starvation between Chen and Cai (1.41–45). Adversity confirms Confucius's sense of destiny and his conviction of being the embodiment of a wonted tradition of culture and learning. The predicament of Confucius and his disciples between Chen and Cai is spun into an extended narrative wherein the disciples' questions and Confucius's answers develop different perspectives justifying the relationship between virtue and failure. Yan Hui's response is a resounding affirmation of failure as the venue of success: "The Master's Way is supremely great, that is why none under heaven can accommodate it. . . . What harm is there in being unaccommodated? It is only by being unaccommodated that the noble man reveals himself!" (1.45). Note that such accounts of adversities are often meant to undermine Confucius in

Mozi and *Zhuangzi*, either by mocking his powerlessness or criticizing his readiness to alter his principles. In Sima Qian's account, they are reclaimed as evidence of virtue or the chance for understanding and explaining his choices.

The idea of adversity or failure as the genesis of creation is of course bound up with Sima Qian's conception of authorship, as evident in the genealogy of suffering authors he sets forth in the final chapter of *Historical Records* and the letter to Ren An (*SJ* 130.28, *HS* 62.2735).[130] In those passages, Confucius's distress between Chen and Cai is linked to his creation of the *Annals*. In "The Hereditary House of Confucius," however, the decisive event for the genesis or completion of the *Annals* is the capture and killing of the *lin*, a mythical animal whose appearance supposedly augurs the rise of sage kings (1.64). Its misrecognition as an inauspicious animal and untimely appearance become the analogue for the disjunction between Confucius's teachings and his times. As told in the *Gongyang Tradition*, Confucius's grief over the *lin*'s (and by extension, his own) sad fate gives way to his triumphant conviction that the *Annals* "will sweep away an era of disorder and return it to rectitude" and ends with Confucius rejoicing as he anticipates later sage rules (1.64a).[131] Sima Qian leaves out the part about Confucius's joy, perhaps because of its implied confirmation of Han rulers as the "later sage rulers" who would realize the lessons of the *Annals*. Instead, the capture of the *lin* is followed by lines that partially overlap with the *Analects*, whereby Confucius laments the death of his favorite disciple Yan Hui and revisits the key concerns of his life: he ponders what it means to be understood by others or by heaven; deliberates the choice between political engagement and disengagement, expediency and unwavering principles; and reiterates the noble man's anguish if he were to "leave the world without making his name known" (1.65, 1.66). Sima Qian concludes the transition from the capture of the *lin* to the creation of the *Annals* with Confucius speaking lines that have no extant analogues and could have been his invention: "My way is not going to prevail! How can I reveal myself to posterity?" (1.66). In other words, the narrative of failure as the genesis of creation gains an affective, deliberative, and retrospective dimension. Confucius's final acts include the editing and transmitting of the other canonical classics (1.52–1.55). Sima Qian is the first to make such claims in extant sources, and this further cements the link between political failure and the creation of textual traditions.

As noted above, Sima Qian seems intent on showing Confucius's effectiveness as a political agent even while acknowledging a more general narrative of political failure. His reactions to adversities encompass equanimity and despair. He seems to be drawn to considerations of expediency but is nevertheless at times uncompromising. While such inconsistencies are eminently understandable in terms of human reactions to the contingencies and vicissitudes of existence, we can also think of the divergences in terms of Sima Qian's possible sources, which may be making different arguments about Confucius's ideas or his optimal choices. The context is often the price of political power and the concomitant means to make beneficial changes: Is there any necessary connection between virtue and power? How should this power be defined? How should one gain it and use it? What are the choices it imposes? What are the alternative paths to a meaningful existence? Sima Qian offers different answers in chronicling Confucius. But despite fissures, lacunae, and incongruities, he gives Confucius's life a meaningful arc from marginal and uncertain status to lasting importance confirmed through the legacy of his ideas and textual traditions.

CHAPTER II

Arguing with Confucius

A   lthough in the *Analects* (7.34) Confucius disclaims sagehood,
        Sima Qian praises him as "the supreme sage." According to *Han
        Feizi*, Confucius's followers split into eight schools (*HFZ* 50.1124),
and the elevation of Confucius as a sage might well have been part of those
followers' attempt to claim supremacy over rivals. Thus Mencius, quoting
Confucius's disciples, claims that Confucius is "more worthy than Yao and
Shun" and that none could compare to him in the history of humankind.
Mencius coyly refuses to answer the question of his ranking compared to
Confuicus's disciples but elsewhere implies his own sagehood (*Mencius* 2A.4,
2B.12). Xunzi calls Confucius "the sage who did not wield power" and
declares that he "equals the Duke of Zhou in virtue, and his name is on a
par with the three sage kings" (*XZ* 6.61, 21.296). This sounds somewhat
less absolute than Mencius's position but may also serve to justify the claim
that Xunzi is as great a sage as Confucius (*XZ* 32.417).

Arguments for and against what Confucius is supposed to stand for
determine the trajectory of Warring States (453–221 BCE) thought, with
reverberations during the Qin and Han dynasties (221 BCE–220 CE) and
beyond.[1] Sometimes this means presenting Confucius as espousing views
connected with other thinkers and intellectual trends. Sometimes this
involves refuting positions attributed to Confucius. Indeed, it is difficult,
perhaps impossible, to distil or abstract an "ur-Confucius"—the original
and authentic figure—from everything said about him in the centuries after

his death. Unlike the layers of mythologization and sacralization for most of the imperial era, stories about Confucius from the fourth and third century BCE, one of the most vibrant periods in the history of Chinese thought, are characterized by polemical energy and a wide range of perspectives. "Various Masters" (*zhu zi* 諸子) are said to represent "a hundred (that is, many) schools" (*baijia* 百家) in that period. We should remember, however, that classification of these thinkers into "schools" is retrospective and took place during the Han dynasty. The lines between them are often fluid, and intersections and convergences are as common as differences. As rival thinkers competed for the attention of rulers and the elite with blueprints for political success, social order, or personal happiness, they invent, refashion, or denigrate Confucius in the process, attributing ideas to him, borrowing from them, or arguing against them with a plethora of stories.

Inventing Confucius

One of the early critics of Confucius was Mozi (Master Mo), born about a century after Confucius. He advocated frugality, utilitarianism, merit-based advancement, impartial concern for all or "universal love" (*jian'ai* 兼愛), and actively opposed military aggression. The work bearing his name includes outright attacks on Confucius casting aspersions on his character. The chapter "Against Experts in Ritual and Traditional Learning" (Feiru 非儒) in *Mozi*, passages from which are quoted in chapter 1 (1.9, 1.45a), criticizes Confucius for upholding complicated and wasteful rituals, for being hypocritical and opportunistic, and for fomenting disorder in the states of Qi, Chu, Jin, and Lu. On this last point, the tone is ad hominem and flagrantly ahistorical (for example, Confucius is accused of being involved in rebellions that postdated him). The compilers of *Kong Anthology* systematically refute the arguments in that chapter (*KCZ* 18.391–95).

The adherents of Mozi's teachings engaging in vitriolic attacks against scholars and ritual experts, whose ranks include Confucius and his followers, were perhaps responding to their equally vicious critiques. Mencius, for example, laments the prevalence of Mozi's teachings, arguing that the notion of "universal love" erases distinctions and undermines family and political ties, turning humans into "birds and beasts" (*Mencius* 3B.9). Elsewhere in *Mozi*, however, the tone is more measured, and Confucius is referred to by the honorific of Master (Kongzi) instead of dismissively as "the Kong fellow" (*Kong mou* 孔某) or by the bald moniker "Kong Qiu" (see chapter 1, 1.45a). Mozi explains that there is no contradiction in upholding the teachings of Confucius while denigrating *ru* (scholars and ritual experts) (*MZ* 48.422). After all, their teachings share common grounds and become the basis of intellectual traditions that develop through multiple intersections.[2] Followers of Mozi and Confucius are said to both look to ancient sages and canonical classics, and both teach humaneness and duty. There is a tradition that claims that Mozi started out as a follower of Confucius (*HNZ* 21.709).

Comparably vitriolic attacks of Confucius or his followers are found in the later chapters in *Zhuangzi*. As in *Mozi*, the text of *Zhuangzi* encompasses a wide range of materials associated with the thinker Zhuangzi (Master Zhuang), who flourished in late fourth century BCE. According to Sima Qian, Zhuangzi was a follower of Laozi: "He wrote 'The Fisherman,' 'Bandit Zhi,' and 'Rifling Trunk' to slander and disparage the followers of Confucius and to illuminate the techniques of Laozi" (*SJ* 63.10). Diverging from the quietism and mysticism of *Laozi*, however, the Way in *Zhuangzi* is articulated as paths to maneuver existential challenges and transcend mortality and human limitations in an ebullient and sometimes playful tone. Skepticism and relativism in Zhuangzi target convention, tradition, hallowed sages, and consensual ways of approaching reality. The chapters that Sima Qian mentions belong to the so-called Outer Chapters and Miscellaneous Chapters in *Zhuangzi* (as distinct from the Inner Chapters, which some associate with the core teachings of *Zhuangzi*). It is in these "Outer" and "Miscellaneous" chapters, the later layers of *Zhuangzi*, that we find more exaggerated critiques and parodies of Confucius.

In the chapter "Bandit Zhi" (Dao zhi 盗跖), for example, Confucius tries to persuade Bandit Zhi, the brother of his friend, the virtuous Liu Xiaji (aka Liu Xiahui), to change his ways, but he ends up being cowed by Bandit Zhi's superior reasoning and retreats in abjection. Violent and arrogant, Bandit Zhi boasts of nine thousand followers, defies all forms of authority, and terrorizes the people. Yet he is also handsome, brave, and "eloquent enough to justify his errors." At first, he refuses to receive Confucius:

2.1 "Isn't this fellow Kong Qiu, the hypocrite of Lu? Tell him on my behalf: You talk and talk, invoking in vain Kings Wen and Wu. You wear headgear with branches sticking out and belts made from the hide of dead oxen. With your numerous speeches and elaborate rhetoric, you eat without wielding the plough and wear clothes without plying the loom. Moving your lips and waving your tongue, you excel at fostering arguments about right and wrong to confuse the rulers of the world. Because of you, all the scholars under heaven fail to return to fundamentals, making vain shows of filial piety and fraternal duty to angle for noble titles, riches, and honors. Your crime is extreme indeed! Make haste to go back! If not, I will add your liver to my lunch." (*ZZ* 29.991–92)

[Eventually Confucius gains an audience with Bandit Zhi and tries to reform him by urging him to put his impressive appearance, intelligence, and valor to good use in order to become a pillar of sociopolitical order instead of wreaking havoc and destruction. Bandit Zhi mocks him for trying to win him over with flattery.] (translator's summary of the intervening passage, *ZZ* 29.993–94)

2.1 (cont.) Bandit Zhi spoke in great fury: "Qiu, come forward! The ones who can be controlled by the promise of gain or persuaded by remonstrance belong but to the stupid, ignorant, and common herd! Now for me to be tall and handsome and be found pleasing by others is the gift of my parents' lingering power. Even if you don't praise me, don't I know it myself? What's more, I have heard that those who like to praise others to their face also like to defame them behind their back. Now for you to tell me about gaining sway over big walled cities and multitudes is to wish to control me with the promise of gain and to treat me like the common herd. How can these things last long? There is no city greater than the entire world under heaven. Yao and Shun had possession of the entire world under heaven, but their descendants do not even have the space to stick the point of an awl.[3] Tang and Wu were instated as the Sons of Heaven, but their progeny had been cut off and extinguished.[4] Was it not because the promise of gain was great? Moreover, I have heard that in antiquity, birds and beasts were numerous while humans were few, that was why people lived in nests to avoid animals. In the daytime, they picked nuts, and in the evening, they rested on trees, and so they were called the people of the Nesting Lineage. In antiquity, people did not know about clothes. They accumulated firewood in the summer and burnt it in winter, and so they were called the People Knowing Life. In the era of the Divine Farmer, people were carefree when they lay down and were oblivious when they were up and about. Living among animals like the deer and the roe, they knew their mothers but not their fathers. They plowed to grow food and wove to make clothes and had no thought of harming each other. This was when the highest virtue flourished. . . . [Bandit Zhi proceeds to elaborate the violence of the sage kings extolled by Confucius.]

"Now you cultivate the way of Kings Wen and Wu and control the eloquent disquisitions of all under heaven to teach later generations. With your long, flowing gown and broad, loosely tied sash, your contorted words and hypocritical acts, you confound the rulers under heaven and want to seek riches and honors. There is no greater bandit than you, sir! Why does the world not call you Bandit Qiu and instead call me Bandit Zhi? You used honeyed words to convince Zilu to follow you. You made Zilu give up his tall cap, untie his long sword, and receive instructions from you. All under heaven said that Confucius was able to stop violence and forestall wrongdoing. Yet in the end Zilu wanted to kill the Wei ruler and failed, and his pickled corpse was exhibited above the eastern city gate of Wei.[5] This was because your teachings failed. You call yourself a talented officer or a sage? But you were twice driven away from Lu, had to remove your traces in Wei, faced adversity in Qi, and was besieged between Chen and Cai. You found no acceptance in the world, and you taught Zilu and he ended up being pickled. For what matters most, you don't have the means to do anything for yourself; for what comes next, you don't have the means to do anything for others. How can your way be worth anything? . . . [Bandit Zhi enumerates sage kings guilty of violence and unethical contact and virtuous men who suffered misfortunes.] . . .

"Now let me tell you about human nature: the eyes want to see colors, the ears want to hear sounds, the mouth wants to discern flavors, the will and spirit want fulfillment. . . . Heaven and earth have no limit, but humans are mortal. Holding on to a mortal instrument and situating it in infinitude is no different from the sudden flash of a thoroughbred horse speeding through a crack. All those who do not manage to gratify their will and nourish their lifespan fail to fully master the Way. What you spoke about are all things that I have abandoned. Go right away! Run back! Say no more! Your way is wild and eager, it's all deceptive cleverness and empty hypocrisy! This is not the way to preserve one's true being. How can it be worth discussing!" (ZZ 29.994–1000)

[translator's note]

Confucius is completely defeated: "His dazed eyes saw nothing; his countenance had the color of dead ashes. Holding on to the carriage's brow, he could barely breathe." He says to Liu Xiaji, "I can be called the one who cauterized himself without being ill. Running fast, I stroked the tiger's head, plied its whiskers, and narrowly escaped its jaws!"

Bandit Zhi's excoriation of Confucius, however, is by no means representative. Confucius is the figure that appears most frequently in *Zhuangzi*, more than Laozi or Zhuangzi himself.[6] He articulates the inescapability of family and political bonds and expatiates on the difficulty of knowing the human heart with the implied author's apparent approval (*ZZ* 4.155, 32.1054). Even when he is criticized or mocked for his conventionality, ambition, adherence to ritual, or vain striving for political order, it is often with empathy and respect, as in one of the anecdotes about his distress between Chen and Cai (chapter 1, 1.45c). Indeed, in other stories with the same setting in *Zhuangzi*, Confucius can sound like a Daoist sage (chapter 1, 1.45d), or he can be commended for expounding recognizably Confucian ideas (chapter 1, 1.45e). Often, he is described as one eager to learn (as in stories about his encounter with Laozi and other figures representing enlightenment, see chapter 1, 1.6, translator's note, 1.47a). He is referred to as "the worthy man of the north" (*ZZ* 14.516), "the noble man from the central states" (*ZZ* 21.704), and "the noble man of Lu" (*ZZ* 31.1024), credited with noble intentions and deep learning even if he might have been "flawed in his understanding of the human heart" (*ZZ* 21.704).

The most interesting passages are the ones in which Confucius articulates the views associated with Zhuangzi in the "Inner Chapters," as in this famous passage from the chapter "The Human Realm" (Renjian shi 人間世):

2.2 Yan Hui went to see Confucius and begged leave to depart.

"Where are you going?"

"I am about to go to Wei."

"What are you going to do?"

"I have heard that the Wei ruler is in his prime and acts according to none but his own ideas and inclinations. He thinks little of his state and does not see his errors. He makes light of his people's life and death, and those who die because of state policies fill the marshes like so many aquatic weeds. The people have nowhere to turn. I have heard you, Master, put it thus: 'Leave the well-governed state. Go to the state in chaos. There are many sick ones at the doctor's gate.' I wish to use what I have heard from you to think through what should be done. Perhaps there can still be succor for the state!"

Confucius said, "Alas! You are about to go and get yourself executed, that's all. For the Way does not want any admixture: admixture means multifariousness, multifariousness means disturbance, disturbance means anxieties. If you are anxious, there would be no remedy. The supreme beings of antiquity first preserve what is in themselves and only then preserve what is in other people. If what is preserved in yourself is not yet settled, how can you spare the time to confront a tyrant about his actions! Furthermore, do you know how virtue dissipates and how knowledge obtrudes? Virtue dissipates because of the concern over fame; knowledge obtrudes because of contention. Fame is what causes people to injure each other, and knowledge is the instrument of contention. These two things, fame and knowledge, are instruments of misfortune, not the means whereby you can bring your actions to fruition. In addition, great virtue and steadfast good faith are not enough to reach the human spirit; widespread fame and non-contention are not enough to reach the human heart.

"To arbitrarily show off words about the highest good, proper duty, and criteria of judgment in front of a tyrant is to use another's failings to heighten one's own excellence. This is what we call a harbinger of calamity. People will certainly unleash calamity on a harbinger of calamity! Isn't it certain that others will unleash calamity on you! Moreover, if the ruler can appreciate the worthy and abhor the worthless, why would he need you to act any differently? Your only choice is to not argue, for if you do, the Wei lord will certainly rely on his power and position to sharpen his self-justifying rhetoric. Your eyes will be bedazzled, your countenance will lose its agitation and urgency, your mouth will anticipate his reasoning, your demeanor will become compliant, and your mind will bring his ideas to completion. This is just like putting out a fire with fire and stanching a flood with water. It is called 'piling on plenty.' Following a course that has begun, there is no stopping.

"Or perhaps you would speak forcefully without having gained his trust, in which case you would certainly die in front of the tyrant! Furthermore, in the old days Jie killed Guan Longfeng and Zhòu killed Prince Bigan.[7] In both cases, Guan Longfeng and Bigan honed their principles and cherished the people, and from their inferior positions opposed the rulers above them. So, their rulers exploited their scruples to persecute them, for they were the ones who loved fame. Formerly, Yao attacked Cong, Zhi, and Xu'ao, and Yu attacked Youhu. These states ended up as ghostly ruins, with their rulers put to the blade. They engaged in wars without respite and sought gain unremittingly.[8] In all these cases, people were seeking fame and gain. Have you alone not heard about this? Even sages cannot overcome the desire for fame and gain, let alone you! Even so, you must have some ideas in mind. Try to tell me!"

Yan Hui said, "If I embody rectitude and empty my heart of desires and become steadfast and single-minded, would that work?"

"Good heavens! How could that work? The Wei ruler is filled with an assertive energy for all to see. His countenance changes colors with his volatile moods. As a rule, people do not go against him. His heart delights in repressing the arguments made by those trying to move him. What is called 'the daily increment of virtue' would not succeed with him, how much less so the call for great virtue! He is going to hold fast to his views and remains unchanged. Externally he may comply, but inwardly his thoughts cannot be fathomed! How could your plan be feasible?"

"In that case I will stay straight inwardly but bend in compliance outwardly, and in rounding off my arguments I will bring in examples from antiquity. He who stays straight inwardly is the companion of heaven. To be the companion of heaven is to know that both the Son of Heaven and I are what heaven regards as its sons. Then how can I be the only one with hopes for my words, be they approved by others or not approved by others? People call such a person 'the Child.' This is what is meant by being the companion of heaven. To bend in compliance outwardly is to be the companion of human beings. To clasp one's raised hands, to kneel with a straight back, to bow or to bend: these are the proper etiquette for a subject. Everyone does it, how dare I not do it? If I do what others do, others cannot fault me. This is what is meant by being the companion of human beings. To bring in examples from antiquity in rounding off my arguments is to be the companion of the ancients. Although my words comprise in fact instructions and remonstrance, they are also drawn from antiquity, not something I made up. In that sense, although I am forthright, I cannot be blamed. This is called being the companion of the ancients. Would it be feasible to act like this?"

Confucius said, "Good heavens! How could *that* work? You have too many rules—they offer correction without winning him over. Although you would not incur blame, you would also just achieve that and no more. How can you come close to the goal of transforming him? You are still following your heart's dictates."

"I don't know how else to proceed. May I ask about the proper method?"

"Fasting! Let me tell you about it. How can it be easy when you act with such deliberation? To regard that as easy is to flout bright heaven."

"My family is poor, and I have not imbibed wine or tasted meat for several months. Can this be considered fasting?"

"This is the kind of fasting before sacrificial rituals, not the fasting of the heart."

Yan Hui said, "May I ask about the fasting of the heart?"

Confucius said, "Focus your will and make it one. Do not listen with your ears but listen with your heart. No, do not listen with your heart but listen with your spirit. The ears stop at listening. The heart stops at correspondences. The spirit is that which is empty and waits upon things. The Way will gather only when there is emptiness. This emptiness is the fasting of the heart."

"Before I began to grasp this, it was Hui that existed. Now that I have grasped this, there is no longer any Hui. Can this be called emptiness?"

The Master said, "That is all there is to it! Let me tell you. You should be able to enter and wander within the boundaries of the realm without being moved by what is said about it. If there is an entry point, you speak as if involuntarily crying out; if there is not, you stop. With no gates and no signposts, you lodge in oneness and find your abode in the inevitable momentum of things, and you will come close to it!

"To erase your traces is easy, to tread without touching the ground is hard! To carry out a human mission is easy to accomplish; to carry out heaven's mission is hard to accomplish. I have heard of those who fly by having wings; I have not heard of those who fly by not having wings. I have heard of those who know through knowing; I have not heard of those who know by not knowing. Behold that hollowed space: A white light is born in the empty room. Auspicious things come to rest there. Not only that: it is called 'Sitting and Galloping.' To follow the ears and eyes and reach inward and to keep out the mental effort of knowing: even the spirits would come and find their home there, let alone humans! This is the transformation of myriad things, the basis of the making of Yao and Shun, and what Fuxi and

Erqu abide by all their lives, how much more so should this work for lesser things!" (*ZZ* 4.1–50)

[translator's note]
Confucius becomes the proponent of "the fasting of the heart," here understood as a way of attaining inward transcendence by emptying the heart of its preconceived notions and becoming grandly receptive to cosmic processes. The context of political persuasion is noteworthy. Yan Hui articulates different rationales and modi operandi for changing the errant ways of the Wei ruler: his earnest desire to save the people of Wei from their suffering; his plan to be focused, assiduous, ethical, and unselfish; his strategy of outward compliance while keeping his principles; his rhetorical ploy of drawing examples from antiquity; his mental trick of regarding the ruler as his equal; his mental discipline that will allow him to be indifferent to the outcome of his remonstrance. Confucius refutes all of these schemes as futile. The dangers of political life are rampant: the chance of success is small, the lure of fame and gain is fatal, and the trap of being drawn into acquiescence with a forceful ruler's wrongful commands and losing one's bearing is hard to avoid. These are recurrent topics in Warring States writings and also issues that Confucius has to deal with in Sima Qian's account of his life. As the answer to Yan Hui's dilemma, "the fasting of the heart" is thus not only about cultivating mental and emotional responses and reaching a state of ultimate openness and flexibility, but it also a way to negotiate the all too real dangers of political engagement. It is mental and emotional suppleness transcending calculations and allowing true understanding of what is politically possible. A rhetorical sleight of hand links the "transformation" or "reform" (*hua* 化) of the Wei ruler to mastering "the transformation of myriad things" (*wan wu zhi hua* 萬物之化).

Although "The Human Realm" ends with a story about Jieyu and the warning about involvement in politics (chapter 1, 1.47a), it is just as concerned with the possibility of effective political action. In that chapter, Confucius also advises the Lord of She, who is filled with trepidation about acting as the Chu envoy to Qi. Confucius begins by laying down the fundamental premise of filial piety and loyalty: the affective bond between parent and child and the duty to serve the ruler as a political being cannot be evaded. But there is a way to be filial and loyal by "serving one's own mind so that sadness and joy do not bring about any change. To know what cannot be helped, being at ease and accepting that as fate, is the supreme virtue" (ZZ 4.155). Confucius continues with practical advice on the need to avoid exaggeration, mistrust clever rhetoric, and eschew arbitrary intervention, but he concludes with the promise of evading diplomatic snares: "Ride with things and let your mind roam, entrust yourself to what cannot be helped to nourish the centeredness in yourself: that is supreme" (ZZ 4.160). Again, political advice is coextensive with broader ruminations on self-distancing, equanimity, and inner freedom, all qualities with political relevance. In another chapter, "The Sign of Virtue's Fulfillment" (De chong fu 德充符), Confucius explains to Lord Ai of Lu the virtue of a deformed man. Lord Ai is convinced and commends Confucius as "the perfect being" (zhiren 至人) and describes their relationship as "friends in virtue" (de zhi you 德之友). The ideal ruler-subject relationship is paradoxically fulfilled through a discourse on virtue beyond its usual social and political boundaries.

"To erase your traces is easy, to tread without touching the ground is hard": the desire for political engagement that sidesteps its conundrums and compromises and avoids its dangers comes to be associated with Confucius in Zhuangzi. Stories about Confucius's encounters with recluses often hint at their mutual sympathy and affinities (see chapter 1, 1.39, 1.40, 1.47). The sentiment echoes Confucius's approval of Zeng Dian's vision discussed in the introduction.[9] For Zhuangzi to speak through Confucius is thus not necessarily a matter of deliberate distortion or simple appropriation of Confucius as a figure of cultural authority: Zhuangzi can be expressing his understanding of what Confucius's teachings are about. Alternatively, we can consider the assimilation of the perspectives associated with Zhuangzi into the Confucian tradition. Indeed, there have been poets, authors, scholars, and commentators who implicitly or explicitly argue for this common ground since the Han dynasty.[10] In Han's Exegesis, for example, Confucius strives to save the world by "lingering in the realm of the Way and its power; wandering in the arena beyond form" (HSWZ 5.230). Yang Xiong's (53 BCE–18 CE) Supreme Mystery (Taixuan) contains numerous references to Laozi and Zhuangzi, yet he also says it was written "for the sake of humaneness and a sense of duty."[11] The fact that Tian Zifang, the disciple of Confucius's disciple Zigong, is praised in the chapter titled "Tian Zifang" in Zhuangzi led the Tang master of poetry and prose Han Yu (768–824) to suggest connections between Confucius and Zhuangzi. The famous Song dynasty poet and scholar-official Su Shi maintains that Zhuangzi "on the rhetorical level disapproves of Confucius but in truth approves of him."[12]

Those who uncover secret affinities between Confucius and Zhuangzi sometimes identify Yan Hui as the crucial link.[13] In the *Analects* (5.9, 6.3, 6.7, 6.11, 7.11, 11.9, 11.10), we are told that Yan Hui's joy and commitment to learning are not diminished despite his poverty, also that Confucius has a special regard for him as a paragon of virtue and as a kindred spirit, praises his understanding as superior to his own, and bitterly laments his early death (see chapter 1, 1.45, 1.64). Unlike other notable disciples of Confucius, Yan Hui was not involved in politics and was not linked to traditions of learning and textual transmission. Instead, his moral stature and bond with Confucius suggests a more intuitive and affective self-sufficiency, upheld as transcendent joyousness by Song and Ming Neo-Confucians. In the following two passages from "The Great Venerable Teacher" (Da zongshi 大宗師) from *Zhuangzi*, Yan Hui is again featured with Confucius, first as interlocutor in a discussion on the attitude toward death and then as the realization of self-forgetfulness that wins Confucius's admiration.

2.3 Yan Hui asked Confucius, "When Mengsun Cai's mother died, he wailed without tears, his heart was not stricken, and he showed no signs of grief while in mourning. He fell short on all three accounts and yet was known for being adept at mourning throughout Lu. Are there indeed those who gained a good name with no basis in reality? I find this very strange!"

Confucius said, "Mengsun has fully understood it! He has advanced to wisdom! It is just that people wish to reduce mourning but cannot, but something has already been reduced. Mengsun does not know the reason for life or the reason for death; he does not know what comes first or what comes later. If one turns into something else, is it in order to wait for the transformation that is as yet unknown? Moreover, having just been transformed, how does one know there are no further transformations? Having just been left untransformed, how does one know whether one is already transformed? Are you and I the dreaming ones who have not awakened? What's more, his form is altered but his heart is not diminished; as temporary abode, his body changes, but the truth of his being does not die. Mengsun alone is awakened. He wails when others wail: that is what is naturally fitting. Further, we each use this 'I' as we consort with each other. How do we know whether this 'I' is what we call 'I'? You can dream of becoming a bird and soar to the heavens; you can dream of becoming a fish and sink into the deeps. I do not know whether the present words belong to the awakened state or to dreams. We reach a state of comfort, and our smiles cannot catch up. We reveal our smiles, and there is no time for maneuverings. Be at ease and go along with the maneuvers, banish the fear of transformations, and enter the oneness of the vast heavens." (*ZZ* 4.274–75)

2.4 Yan Hui said, "I have improved!"

Confucius said, "What do you mean?"

"I have forgotten about the highest good and proper duty."

"Good! But you are not there yet."

Some days later, Yan Hui presented himself again and said, "I have improved!"

Confucius said, "What do you mean?"

"I have forgotten about rituals and music."

"Good! But you are not there yet."

Some days later, Yan Hui presented himself again and said, "I have improved!"

Confucius said, "What do you mean?"

"I just sit and forget."

Confucius changed color and said, "What do you mean by sitting and forgetting?"

Yan Hui said, "Let go of the limbs, banish sensory perception. Be detached from the body and remove knowledge, attain union with the Great Way. This is called 'sitting and forgetting.'"

Confucius said, "If all things can be regarded in the same way, then there is no such thing as inclination. If all things transform, then there is no constancy. You are indeed resolute and worthy! I beg to become *your* follower." (*ZZ* 6.282–85)

[translator's note]

Prescriptions for rituals of mourning are precise and elaborate in the Confucian tradition. *Zhuangzi* presents transcendent beings who accept life and death as phases of an endless process of transformation. In an exchange between Confucius and Zigong in "Great Venerable Teacher," Confucius refers to men who disdain mourning rituals and laugh at death as "wandering beyond the realm" (*you fang zhi wai* 遊方之外)—and thus distinct from himself who "wanders within the realm" (*you fang zhi nei* 遊方之內), because he belongs to those "marked by heaven for punishment" (*tian zhi lumin* 天之戮民). He tells Zigong that there is still hope for people like them because they can be absorbed in their striving like "fish that help each other forget in the rivers and lakes." In discussing Mengsun Cai's mourning with Yan Hui, Confucius seems to have gone further: he does not position himself as having chosen another path; he is simply the empathetic interpreter. Yan Hui's progressive forgetting suggests that the way of becoming transcendent beings who "wander beyond the realm" may yet be learned. Instead of the forgetfulness based on absorption and sincerity, the forgetfulness in Yan Hui's case is active self-transformation, although paradoxically it is nondeliberate and ultimately not directed toward an object.

Han Feizi is another text in which Confucius is featured prominently. Confucius is honored as "the sage of the entire realm under heaven," but as the only perfect embodiment of the highest good and righteousness, he is the exception that proves the rule that such ideals cannot be widely implemented. The limitations of his historical situation—Confucius had only seventy followers; he had to submit to an inferior ruler like Lord Ai of Lu—are said to prove implacable historical changes and the momentum of power that render the pursuance of the highest good in government impossible in any period except high antiquity (*HFZ* 49.1096–97). The key is to create a strong and stable state through just laws properly enforced, for "there is no Confucius on a helter-skelter chariot" (*HFZ* 25.526). The historical Han Fei (d. 233 BCE) was a prince from the beleaguered state of Han. He studied under the great Confucian thinker Xunzi, but from the Han dynasty on, he is classified as a proponent of state power enforced through impartial laws (*fajia* 法家).[14] The teachings associated with his name are concerned with political order, efficacious governance, empowering the state and the ruler, judicious use of reward and punishment, and strict application of laws. In some anecdotes in *Han Feizi*, Confucius embodies these values.

2.5 Lord Ai of Lu asked Confucius, "The *Annals* said, 'In the twelfth month, in winter, frost descended but did not kill the beans.' Why was this recorded?" Confucius responded, "This is to say that the frost could kill but did not kill. It should have killed them but did not, and plum and pear trees bore fruit in winter. When heaven loses its way, even plants defy it. How much more so when rulers lose their way!" (*HFZ* 30.584)

[translator's note]
The *Annals* recorded anomalous weather in 627 BCE (Xi 33.12, *Zuo* 1: 445–46): frost descended but did not kill the grass, and plum and pear trees bore

fruit out of season. What is the lesson? *Zuo Tradition* does not comment on this line. The *Gongyang Tradition* explains that the purpose of the entry is to record an untimely anomaly (*Gongyang* 1: 504). A later comment on the *Gongyang Tradition* interprets this as the ascendancy of yin over yang, whose correspondence in Lu politics is the dimunition of the Lu ruling house (*Gongyang* 1: 504). The *Guliang Tradition* argues that killing when it is not appropriate to kill is a weighty matter, while the reverse (as in the case here) is less important (*Guliang* 9.18a). The *Han Feizi* anecdote preserves the exegetical format of classicists, but its rather startling message is that leniency (refraining from inflicting proper punishment) undermines the ruler's authority, tantamount to heaven losing its way. Other anecdotes present Confucius justifying harsh punishment:

2.6 According to the laws of Yin, a person who discarded ashes on roads would be subjected to mutilating punishment. Zigong considered this too severe and asked Confucius. Confucius said, "This shows understanding of the way to achieve good governance. To discard ashes on the road will certainly result in the ashes covering another person. When that happens, the person covered with ashes will certainly get angry. If he gets angry, there will be combat, and combat will result in their kinsmen fighting and injuring each other. This opens the way leading to injury for many people— even mutilating punishment would be acceptable. Moreover, severe punishment is what people abhor; not discarding ashes is what people consider easy. To have people do what they consider easy so that they will not encounter what they abhor: this is the way of governance." (*HFZ* 30.584)

[translator's note]
The Shang dynasty (ca. 1600–1046 BCE) is also called Yin or Yin Shang after its capital moved to Anyang (ca. 1300 BCE). What is translated as "ashes" can also mean "embers" that could start a fire, in which case the draconian punishment may seem somewhat less arbitrary. The minister Shang Yang (d. 338 BCE), who used legal reforms to buttress state power in Qin, is said to have made the crime of discarding ashes on the road punishable by mutilation (*SJ* 87.30).[15] *The Book of Lord Shang* (*Shangjun shu*), attributed to him and his followers, as well as *Han Feizi*, come to be considered key texts advocating the use of laws, rewards, and punishments to enhance state power. In the following anecdote, Confucius argues that

punishment is more efficacious than rewards as a motivating factor, when a fire supposed to smoke out animals for a hunt gets out of control:

2.7 The men of Lu set fire to Jize. A wind blew from the north, the fire spread southward, and there was fear that the Lu capital would burn. Horrified, Lord Ai personally led the crowd and urged them to put out the fire. There was no one by his side, for the men were all chasing the animals, and the fire was not put out. He thus summoned Confucius to consult him. Confucius said, "Those chasing the animals are enjoying themselves and not being punished; those who put out the fire are suffering and not being rewarded. This is why the fire was not put out." Lord Ai said, "Right." Confucius said, "The situation is urgent. There is not enough leeway to offer rewards. If everyone who puts out the fire is rewarded, then the resources of the state would not suffice for rewarding these people. I request that we use only punishment." Lord Ai said, "Right." Confucius thus issued the command: "Those who do not put out the fire are deemed as guilty as those who surrender or run away in battle. Those who chase the animals are deemed as guilty as those who entered the inner palace without permission." Before the command was circulated everywhere, the fire had been put out. (HFZ 30.589)

Reinvented as proponents of Han Feizi's views, Confucius and his disciples nevertheless sometimes combine those views with attributes associated with the Confucian tradition, as in the following examples (2.8–21.11):

2.8 When Confucius was the chief minister of Wei, his disciple Zigao served as a prison official there.[16] Zigao had a person's leg cut off as punishment, and the maimed man became the gatekeeper. Someone slandered Confucius to the Wei ruler: "Confucius wants to foment a rebellion." The Wei ruler wanted to arrest Confucius. Confucius fled and his disciples all escaped. Zigao got to the gate after it was closed for the night. The maimed man led Zigao and let him escape to a chamber under the gate, and the officers pursued him without success. In the middle of the night, Zigao asked the maimed man, "I could not fail the ruler's law and command and had to personally cause your leg to be cut off. This is the moment when you can wreak vengeance. Why did you help me escape? How did I earn this from you?" The maimed man said, "For me to have my leg cut off was in truth a fitting punishment for my crime. It could not have been helped! But when you, sir, was judging my case, you carefully considered the law from all sides. You explained the case to me and helped me with the confession. You really wanted to exonerate me, and I understood it. When the case was settled and the punishment decided, you were dismayed and unhappy, and your dejection was obvious. I saw and also understood it. You were like that not because you were partial to me but because of your inborn nature of humaneness. That was why I was pleased and was grateful to you." Confucius said, "He who is good at being an official built gratitude in others; he who failed as an official built resentment. A weighing beam is the thing that makes measurements fair. An official is the one who applies the law in fairness. He who governs a state cannot fail in this fairness." (*HFZ* 33.722, 727)[17]

[translator's note]
Harsh laws are implemented with compassion and fairness, so much so that the person punished holds no grudges against the official inflicting the punishment. In the following story, Confucius demythologizes Kui by parsing the word *zu* 足, which can mean both "leg" and "enough." This seems to conform with the notion that Confucius does not discuss anomalies (chapter 1, 1.62, *Analects* 7.21). The emphasis here, however, is on how a ruler should choose his ministers:

2.9 Lord Ai of Lu asked Confucius: "I have heard that in ancient times there was Kui with one leg. Did he indeed have one leg?" Confucius responded, "No, Kui did not have one leg. Kui was hot-tempered, violent, and resentful, and most people did not like him. Nevertheless, he could escape harm because of his good faith. Everyone said that this alone was enough. It was not that Kui had one leg, but that having that one quality was enough." Lord Ai said, "If it was indeed so, then actually it was enough."

Another version: Lord Ai asked Confucius, "I heard that Kui had one leg. Was that true?" Confucius said, "Kui was human, why would he have one leg? He had no other special attribute but had this one talent of understanding music. Yao said: 'For Kui to have this one talent is enough.' He thus appointed him the music master. That is why the noble man said, 'For Kui to have one talent was enough.' It was not that he had one leg." (*HFZ* 33.730–31)

[translator's note]
In the *Documents*, the ancient sage king Yao puts Kui in charge of music, but *kui* is also the name of an anomalous creature said to have one leg. The

possibility of a "one-legged Kui" belongs to the kind of esoteric knowledge that Confucius is sometimes credited with (chapter 1, 1.10, 1.24), but here Confucius's broad knowledge is expressed as "syntactical rationalization," which serves to support the definition of "a useful minister." *Yi zu* 一足 can mean either "one is enough" or "one leg." The second version of the "one is enough" story appears with some variations in *Mr. Lü's Annals* (*LSCQ* 2: 1526–27, see also *KCZ* 2.16). The first version, however, more aptly serves the pragmatic vision of government in *Han Feizi*: an able ruler knows how to ignore his minister's moral flaws and focuses on what can render him a reliable servant of the state. Confucius is also used to deliberate the relationship between a ruler and his minister in the following story from *Han Feizi*:

2.10 Confucius was sitting in attendance of Lord Ai of Lu. Lord Ai bestowed on him peaches and millet and invited him to eat. Confucius first ate the millet and then bit into a peach. The attendants on both sides all covered their mouths and snickered. Lord Ai said, "The millet is not for eating. It is for wiping the fuzz off the peach." Confucius responded, "I already know that. Millet is the first of five grains and the most exalted item in the sacrifices to former kings. There are six main kinds of fruit. Peaches rank the lowest and cannot be brought into the temple for the sacrifices to former kings. I have heard that the noble man uses the lowly to wipe the exalted, I have not heard that the exalted should be used to wipe the lowly. Now to use the first of five grains to wipe a lowly fruit is to use what ranks above to wipe what ranks below. I considered this a violation of proper duty, that was why I did not dare to supersede what should be honored in the ancestral temple." (*HFZ* 33.734–35, see also *KZJY* 19.291)

[translator's note]
Here an apparently typical Confucian concern with ancestral ritual turns into a focus on political hierarchy, specifically the balance of power between the ruler and the minister. The abiding concern with the ruler's dignity and authority comes out in two ways: first, its justification in terms of effective government; second, its implication for the minister who wants to gain sway over the ruler. In *Han Feizi*, Confucius becomes a staunch defender of a ruler's prerogatives and articulates artful calculation on how to allay a ruler's suspicion. He criticizes the Qi minister Guan Zhong for gaining excessive wealth and privileges that threaten the ruler (*HFZ* 33.749).

He also attacks Zilu for providing relief for the people in such a way that can potentially upset the balance of power between the ruler and the minister:

2.11 Jisun [Ji Kangzi, head of the Ji lineage] was the chief minister in Lu, and Zilu served as the prefect of Hou. From the fifth month on, Lu mobilized its multitudes to dig a long waterway. During this operation, Zilu used his personal salary to buy grain and make gruel and invited the diggers to a meal at the Crossroad of the Five Fathers. When Confucius heard this, he sent Zigong to overturn the gruel and break the vessels, saying, "The Lu ruler lays claim to his people, what are you doing, so much so that you should be feeding them?" Furious, Zilu marched in waving his arms and asked, "How could you, Master, blame me for putting into practice humaneness and proper duty? What I have learned from you are humaneness and proper duty, which are about sharing with the world what you own and reaping the benefit together. Now I am using my own salary to feed the people. Why would it be unacceptable?"

Confucius said, "Yóu! Such is your uncouthness! I thought you understood this, but you have not reached the requisite level. How could you have been ignorant of ritual propriety to this extent! You fed them because you cherished them. According to ritual propriety, the Son of Heaven cherishes all under heaven; the lords cherish what lies within their territories; the high officers cherish what is within the jurisdiction of their office; the officers cherish their families. To exceed what one should cherish is called encroachment. Now the Lu ruler lays claim to his people, and you cherish them without permission. It is you who have been encroaching. Is this not vain swagger!"

Before Confucius had finished speaking, a messenger from Jisun arrived with a reprimand: "I mobilized the people and set them a task. You, sir, made your disciple issue orders to the workmen and fed them. Are you about to wrest from me control over the people?" Confucius set off on his carriage and left Lu. Even in this case—considering Confucius's worthiness and the fact that Jisun was not the Lu ruler—for a subject to use his resources to appropriate the exertion of a ruler's authority is something that has to be forestalled before it takes shape. In that way, Zilu cannot get to exercise his private acts of charity and harm cannot arise. How much more so when the ruler is involved? If Lord Jing of Qi, with power and momentum on his side, had forestalled Tian Chang's transgression, then the disaster of his line's oppression and assassination would certainly have been averted. (*HFZ* 34.767–68)

[translator's note]
Confucius chides Zilu for being "uncouth" (*ye* 野) when the latter questions his insistence on "rectification of names" as "far-fetched" (*yu* 迂) and impractical (chapter 1, 1.49, *Analects* 13.3). Here Confucius uses the same word to reproach Zilu when the latter tries to realize his teachings on "humaneness and proper duty" by implementing policies that benefit conscripted Lu laborers. While Mencius places the welfare of the people above the state and the ruler, here the people become just a factor in defining the spheres of influence of power holders. Private or personal (*si* 私) acts of charity can thus challenge the power of the state; a functionary advertises his own virtue at the expense of his superior. Confucius becomes a prescient figure who fully understands this logic. In versions of this story in *Garden of Eloquence* (SY 2.25) and *Sayings* (*KZJY* 8.99), Confucius offers the same advice but couches it in terms of procedural irregularity (Zilu should have first notified the Lu ruler) and a gentler caution against failure "to illuminate the ruler's beneficence." Those stories omit the dire consequence that immediately follows.

In the passage from *Han Feizi* (2.11), the narrative shifts its focus from the peril of officials who incautiously arouse their superior's suspicion to the threat for the ruler who allows his authority to be eroded by ministers dispensing favors to the people. The last line refers to how the Jiang lineage of the Qi ruling house was eventually displaced by leaders of the Tian (Chen) lineage. The latter started out as ministers in Qi but became increasingly dominant by taking credit for policies that benefit the people (*Zuo Zhao* 3.3, 3: 1348–49). Chen Heng assassinated the Qi ruler in 481 BCE. In some sources, Confucius is said to urge Lord Ai of Lu to attack Qi on account of this usurpation, although this episode is left out in Sima Qian's account of Confucius (see chapter 1, 1.64e).

Justice, Law, Order

The hierarchical virtues upheld in the ethical system in Confucian teachings, such as filial piety or loyalty to the ruler, may raise potential moral dilemmas, since the imperatives of deference and submission, added to the inherent power differentials, can run up against other notions of justice and proper conduct. Xunzi is unequivocal on how choices should be made in the following anecdote featuring Confucius:

2.12 To fulfill filial and fraternal duty inside and outside the home is a minor achievement. To follow orders from above and sincerely care for those below is a medium achievement. To obey the Way instead of one's ruler and to obey proper duty instead of one's father is a great achievement. . . . That is why to disobey when it is acceptable to obey is to fail as a son; to obey when it is not acceptable to obey is to violate one's integrity; to understand the principles behind obeying and disobeying and meticulously act by fulfilling precepts of reverence, loyalty, good faith, and sincerity—that can be called great filial piety. . . . (XZ 29.397)

Lord Ai of Lu asked Confucius: "For a son to obey his father: Is that filial piety? For a subject to obey his ruler: Is that probity?" He asked thrice, but Confucius did not answer. Confucius withdrew with quick steps and said to Zigong, "Just now the Lu ruler asked me, 'For a son to obey his father: Is that filial piety? For a subject to obey his ruler: Is that probity?' He asked thrice and I did not answer. What do you think was the reason?" Zigong said, "For a son to obey his father is filial piety; for a subject to obey his ruler is probity. Why would you, Master, have to respond to that?"[18] Confucius said, "What a limited fellow! You have not understood! Formerly, if a state of ten thousand chariots had four remonstrating subjects, then its territories would not suffer encroachments. If a state of a thousand chariots had three remonstrating subjects, then its altars of state would not be imperiled. If a clan of a hundred chariots had two remonstrating subjects, then its ancestral temple would not be destroyed. A father with a remonstrating son would not act against ritual propriety; an officer with a remonstrating friend would not undertake undutiful actions. For a son to just obey his father, how can that make him a filial son? For a subject to just follow his ruler, how can that make him a subject of probity? To carefully consider the reasons for obeying: that is called filial piety and probity." (XZ 29.398)

[translator's note]
What is translated as "remonstrating" (zheng 爭) can also mean "contending" or "fighting." This oppositional element is heightened when legal infractions lead to a conflict of loyalties. In Zuo Tradition, in a passage on

events dated 528 BCE, Confucius praises the Jin minister Shuxiang as one who can boast of "the kind of rectitude passed down from ancient times" for his impartiality when he condemns his younger brother and has his corpse exposed in the marketplace after the latter had been murdered on account of his corruption: "In governing the domain and administering punishments, he concealed nothing for the sake of his kin. . . . By killing his kinsman he added to his own glory. How true to his duty he was!" (*Zuo* Zhao 14.7, 3: 1518–21).[19] This contrasts with the gentler view Confucius expresses in this famous passage from the *Analects*:

2.13 The Lord of She said to Confucius, "Among my people there is Just Gong: his father stole a sheep, and he as a son bore witness against him." Confucius said, "The just ones among my people are different from that. When a father conceals the truth on behalf of his son, and when a son conceals the truth on behalf of his father, there is justice in it" (*Analects* 13.18).

[translator's note]
Instead of translating "Just Gong" as a proper name, it is also possible to render it as "a just man" or "an upright man." In another example of a conflict of loyalties, Mencius advocates impartiality but in effect equivocates when his disciple Taoying asks him about the sage king Shun's options if his father, the benighted Blind Old Man, commits murder (*Mencius* 7A.35):

2.14 Taoying asked: "Shun was the Son of Heaven and Gaoyao the Minister of Justice. What should they do if the Blind Old Man commits murder?"
   Mencius said, "Gaoyao would arrest him—that's all."
   "So would Shun not forbid it?"
   "On what basis could Shun forbid it? For Gaoyao would be acting according to rightfully received rules."
   "But then what would Shun do?"
   "Shun regards abandoning the entire realm under heaven as being no different from abandoning a worn-out shoe. He would secretly carry his father on his back and flee, go along the seashore, and stay there. Joyous to the end of his days, he would forget about the entire realm under heaven in his bliss."

[translator's note]
In this conflict between private ties and public justice or political duty, Gaoyao's decision to implement the law is unequivocal. Shun's choice,

however, is more ambiguous. As a ruler, he would not contravene his father's arrest, but as a son he would later secretly flee with him to the seashore. Mencius changes the focus to Shun's laudable indifference to power ("Shun regards abandoning the entire realm under heaven as being no different from abandoning a worn-out shoe"), but he sidesteps the question as to whether sacrificing his position earns Shun the right to break the law.

Self-sacrifice is often presented as an honorable solution for a person caught between kinship ties and the law, between conflicting loyalties toward the family and the state. One example is the following story told in *Han's Exegesis* (*HSWZ* 2.85), which reprises Confucius's punch line in the stolen sheep anecdote (see 2.13):

2.15 King Zhao of Chu had an officer named Shi She. He was just, fair-minded, and upright. The king put him in charge of administration. At that time, someone committed murder on the road. Shi She pursued the murderer and it turned out to be his father. He returned to court and said, "The murderer was your servant's father. To sacrifice one's father to achieve the goals of governance is not filial piety. To fail to carry out the ruler's law is not loyalty. Submission to the punishment for having let the guilty one escape and abusing the law is what your servant should abide by." He then prostrated himself on the executioner's block, saying, "It is as you command, my lord." The ruler said, "You pursued him but did not catch up with him. How can you be deemed guilty? You, sir, should attend to your duty." Shi She said, "Not so. To fail to be partial to one's father is not filial piety. To fail to carry out the ruler's law is not loyalty. To live while having committed a crime punishable by death is not honesty. For you, my lord, to want to pardon me is your beneficence as the ruler, but it is my proper duty as the subject to not accept any travesty of the law." He then stayed at the executioner's block, slit his throat with his sword, and died at court. When the noble man heard this, he said, "This is integrity indeed! Such adherence to the law! Such was His Honor Shi!" Confucius said, "When a father conceals the truth on behalf of his son, and when a son conceals the truth on behalf of his father, there is justice in it." It says in the *Odes*: "That fine man / is the supervisor of justice in the realm." That refers to His Honor Shi.

[translator's note]
Confucius is cited to affirm the justice of a son defending his father at all costs. Such "justice" depends on the logic of substitution in Shi She's

self-sacrifice: he offers himself to the king as his father's substitute; his crime of perverting justice takes center stage and deflects from his father's crime of murder. One can easily object to this "solution": his suicide is if anything a loss for the king, and his death cannot atone for his father's crime. All the same, Shi She is upheld as an exemplary character in Han and later sources.[20] The question of whether self-sacrifice (or the putative intention of self-sacrifice) makes any difference for the scales of justice (whether in the eyes of the law or in terms of the standards of moral rectitude) is also taken up in a version of the stolen sheep anecdote in *Mr. Lü's Annals*, where Confucius is unforgiving and unmasks the supposed intention of self-sacrifice as self-serving:

2.16 There was this Just Gong in Chu. His father stole a sheep, and he reported it to the authorities. The authorities arrested the father and were about to execute him. Just Gong requested to take his father's place. When he was about to be executed, he said to the officer, "To report on one's father who stole a sheep, isn't that good faith? To take the place of one's father and submit to execution, isn't that filial piety? If even a person of good faith and filial piety is to be executed, would there be anyone in the state who can escape that fate?" When the Chu king heard about this, he did not execute him. Hearing of this, Confucius said, "Strange indeed is the good faith of Just Gong! Using his one father, he twice obtained a good name." That is why Just Gong's good faith is worse than faithlessness (*LSCQ* 1: 596).

[translator's note]
Confucius's comment implies that Just Gong cares more about the reputation of being a just man than actual justice. With his clever rhetoric of self-exoneration, he absolves both himself and his father. Both indicting and absolving his father redounds to his credit, hence the line "he twice obtained a good name." In some other texts (*ZZ* 29.1007, *HNZ* 13.442), Just Gong is juxtaposed with Wei Sheng, a man who refuses to break his promise of waiting for a woman under a bridge and ends up being drowned. Both are cited as lamentable examples of apparent good faith (*xin* 信) applied in an overly rigid fashion. In fact, the two cases are quite different: Wei Sheng is just blindly following the precept of not breaking a promise, while Just Gong's choice presumes a real weighing of alternatives in an ethical dilemma.

The conflict between filial piety and legal justice broadens into an ineluctable conflict of interests between rival loci of authority (the father and the state), between the ruler and the ruled, and becomes a more general attack against scholars and followers of Confucius who "use rhetorical embellishments to confound the law" (*yi wen luan fa* 以文亂法) in the chapter "The Five Vermins" (Wudu 五蠹) in *Han Feizi*:

2.17 There was this Just Gong in Chu: his father stole a sheep, and he reported it to the authorities. The chief minister said, "Put him to death." He considered Just Gong to be just vis-à-vis his ruler but in the wrong vis-à-vis his father, and so he punished him according to his crime. Judging from this, the ruler's just subject is the father's ruthless son.

A Lu man followed his ruler into war and thrice ran away in three rounds of battle. Confucius asked him how this happened, and he responded, "I have an aged father, and if I die, none will take care of him."[21] Confucius considered him filial and recommended him for office and raised him up. Judging from this, the father's filial son is the ruler's treasonous subject. Thus, as a result of the chief minister's execution of Just Gong, crimes are not reported to those above, and because of Confucius's act of rewarding the filial son, the people of Lu are prone to surrender and run away in battle. Such is the gap between the interests of those above and of those below.

For a ruler to broadly promote the virtuous acts of commoners and through this seek good fortune for the altars of the state is certainly hopeless. In antiquity, when Cang Jie created writing, drawing a circle around oneself is called "private," and turning against "private" is called "public good." Public good and private interests go against each other—this is something that Cang Jie understood already. Now to consider that they share the same interests is to invite troubles through the lack of discernment. (*HFZ* 49.1104–05)

[translator's note]
Han Feizi goes on to argue: A commoner who cultivates and advertises his virtue and expertise in traditional learning can gain glory by becoming a "brilliant teacher" (*mingshi* 明師), but honor independent of state service and state ranks threatens to sow political disorder (*HFZ* 49.1105). The argument on conflict of loyalties and rival loci of authority thus develops into a broader distrust of scholars identified with the Confucian tradition.

Cang Jie is the legendary creator of the Chinese script. The graph for "private" or "personal" is *si* 私. Its earlier form is *si* 厶, which appears as a half closed or fully closed circle or triangle in seal script 𠫔, bronze inscription ▽, and excavated manuscripts ◁. The word *gong*, translated here as "public good," also means "lord," "elder," "fair, just": it is associated with the ruler's interests, state interests, or the greater good. By the late Warring States and early Han, the meaning of *gong* as "just" and "shared realm" is common, as in "The Course of Ritual" (Liyun 禮運) in *Record of Rituals*: "All under heaven was justly and commonly shared" 天下為公 (*LJ* 2: 582; see also chapter 4, 4.1). The upright official Zhang Shizhi (second century) declares in *Historical Records*: "The law is what the Son of Heaven justly shared with all under heaven" (*SJ* 102.8). According to a Han dictionary, *gong* means "to divide evenly." The graph for *gong* 公 (seal script 公, bronze inscription 公, oracle bones 公, excavated manuscripts 公) combines *si* with *ba* 八, which means the number eight but has an earlier meaning of "turning against each other," a meaning more self-evident in its earliest forms (seal script ㇀, oracle bone ㇆). The conflict between family interests and state interests is resolved or glossed over in Confucian texts like *Record of Rituals* or *Classic of Filial Piety* (*Xiaojing*, ca. second century BCE), when filial piety is said to faciliate loyalty to the ruler, a logic that Sima Qian reiterates in the autobiographical final chapter of *Historical Records* (*SJ* 130.18).

In *Han Feizi*, public good, often identified with the interests of the state or of the ruler, is based on the promulgation and strict application of codified laws. Abiding by the law is also linked to superior judgment in the following story from *Mr Lü's Annals*:

2.18 According to the law of Lu, anyone who could redeem a Lu person enslaved in another lord's domain could claim gold at the treasury. Zigong redeemed a Lu person at another lord's domain. He came and declined to take the gold. Confucius said, "You erred! From now on, the men of Lu will not redeem anyone! Taking the gold would not detract from your virtuous conduct, not taking the gold means that none would redeem anyone again." Zilu rescued a drowning man, and that person bowed in thanks, giving a bull as a gift. Zilu accepted it. Confucius said, "The men of Lu are sure to rescue drowning people!" Confucius discerned things by small clues and envisioned their far-reaching transformations (*LSCQ* 2: 1003; see also *HNZ* 12.388, *SY* 7.46, *KZJY* 2.114).

[translator's note]
In *Mr. Lü's Annals*, Confucius disparages Zigong's virtuous disinterestedness for its potentially deleterious consequence. *Huainanzi* tells the same

story and commends Confuicus for "understanding ritual propriety" and underscores the point by quoting *Laozi*: "To discern small things is called illuminating insight." In both cases, efficacy takes precedence over virtuous intention, and adamantly adhering to the law is linked to social order, although the point is more the value of perspicacity rather than the functioning of the law per se.

In *Zuo Tradition*, Confucius speaks out against the introduction of penal codes inscribed on cauldrons in Jin in 513 BCE (see 2.19). That passage may reflect the views of thinkers like Mencius and other self-identified successors to Confucius, who favored an emphasis on unwritten ethical norms in the management of behavior.

2.19 Confucius said, "Jin will perish, for it has lost its standards. Jin should maintain the legal standards received by its ancestor Tang Shu from the Zhou king so as to provide guidelines for the governance of the people, while ministers and high officers maintain these standards, each according to his rank. By this means the people are able to esteem the nobles, and the nobles are able to maintain their hereditary duties. When nobles and commoners do not deviate from the rules, that is what we call 'standards.' . . .

"Now that Jin has abandoned these standards and made a penal cauldron, the people attend only to the cauldron! How are they to respect the exalted, and how will the exalted maintain their hereditary duties? When there is no proper order for the exalted and the lowly, how will they manage the domain? What is more, Fan Gai's penal code is derived from the muster at Yi, a period of disorder in Jin.[22] How can it be used as a legal norm?" (*Zuo* Zhao 29.5, 3: 1702–03)

[translator's note]
Here Confucius claims that publicized penal codes encourage people to pay attention to the letter of the law, but they will not cultivate virtues such as reverence, ritual propriety, or a sense of shame that will strengthen social and political bonds. In texts in the Confucian tradition, Confucius often speaks about avoiding litigation and achieving political goals through moral suasion rather than laws, as in the following examples from the *Analects* and *Xunzi*.

2.20 The Master said, "Guide them with laws and regulations, restrain them with punishments, and the people will shirk their duties and become shameless; guide them with virtue, restrain them with ritual propriety, and they will have a sense of shame and correct themselves." (*Analects* 2.3)

The Master said, "In listening to cases of litigation, I am just like other people. The hope is to make litigation unnecessary" (*Analects* 12.13; see also *DDLJ* 1: 127).

2.21 Confucius was the supervisor of corrections in Lu, where there was a case of litigation with a father and a son charging each other with wrongdoing. Confucius detained them for three months without reaching a verdict. The father asked to bring the case to a close, and Confucius dropped it. The Ji lineage head heard about it and was displeased, saying, "The Elder deceived me! He said to me, 'We must rule the domain by upholding filial piety.' Now by putting one man to death we can penalize the unfilial, and yet he dropped the case." Ran Qiu told Confucius about this. Confucius heaved a sigh and said, "Alas! Those above who have lost the right way kill the errant ones below—can that be acceptable? To fail to instruct the people and let litigation run its course is to kill the innocent. If the three armies suffer total defeat, they cannot be summarily executed. If the laws are not properly carried out, punishment cannot be inflicted, for the crimes do not lie with the people. To be lax about issuing proper orders and stern about execution is cruel misrule; now production has its seasons but taxation is unremitting, that is brutality; to fail to instruct and yet demand successful results is ruthlessness. Stop these three things and then one can apply punishment. The *Documents* says, 'Punishment and killing should proceed by the principles of proper duty, do not use them for your own goals. I would only say: events do not yet follow the right course.' It is speaking of the need to first instruct" (*XZ* 28.391; see also *HSWZ* 3.153, *SY* 7.12, *KZJY* 2.18–19).

[translator's note]
The balance or tension between *xing* 刑 (punishment) and *de* 德 (beneficent virtue, implying greater forbearance, leniency, the use of rewards, or the focus on ethical cultivation) is a recurrent concern in Warring States and Qin-Han writings. In the following exchange between Confucius and the Lu ruler—a passage from the Chu bamboo strips in the Shanghai museum (ca. fourth–third century BCE) given the title "The Domain of

Lu Suffered a Great Drought" 魯邦大旱—punishment and virtue are pitted against the importance of sacrifice:

2.22 There was a great drought in the domain of Lu. Lord Ai said to Confucius, "Why don't you, sir, make plans to deal with this on my behalf?" Confucius answered, "The domain of Lu has suffered a great drought: Is that not because of lapses in the implementation of punishment and beneficent virtue? . . ." "What is to be done?" Confucius said, "The common people know about serving the spirits through the Yue rain sacrifice; they do not know anything about punishment and beneficent virtue. If the ruler does not begrudge jade discs and silk as offerings to be made to the spirits of mountains and rivers, then rectifying the uses of punishment and . . ." Confucius came out and encountered Zigong: "Ci, from what you have heard of the talk in lanes and alleys, wouldn't it be said of my response that it missed the mark?" Zigong said, "Not so. Yet how you, Master, set store by supplication to the spirits! If this is about rectifying punishment and beneficent virtue to serve heaven, then it is right! But if one does not begrudge jade discs and silks as offerings to the mountains and rivers, wouldn't it be unacceptable? As for the mountains, the rocks are their skin and the trees their people. If heaven does not let rain come down, then the rocks will be scorched, and the trees will die. The mountains' desire for rain is greater than ours. Why would they wait for our supplication? As for the rivers, the water is their skin and the fish their people. If heaven does not let rain come down, then the water will dry up and the fish will die. The rivers' desire for rain is greater than ours. Again, why would they wait for our supplication?" Confucius said, "Alas! . . . Does the lord not reach satiety with fine grains and meat? But what is to be done about the common people?" (KJY 3: 927).[23]

[translator's note]
Despite gaps in the text (indicated by ellipses), its main concerns are obvious. Confucius identifies the misuse of punishment and lapses of virtue as the cause for the drought but proposes the rain sacrifice as remedy because that is what the common people expect, although the incomplete textual fragment that follows suggests policies addressing "punishment and virtue" would accompany the sacrifice. Zigong implicitly criticizes Confucius for conceding to popular desire for the sacrifices. Confucius's response, partially missing, implies that the ruler's response to the drought should include

renunciation of luxuries and concern for the people. Perhaps the sacrfices introduce a sense of urgency that would make the ruler more amenable to arguments for abstinence, but the crucial issue remains the proper use of punishment through its balance with virtuous leniency. One may speculate that Confucius also acknowledges Zigong's objection as justified in his reply even as he defends his approach. Whatever the case, the balance, tension, or synthesis of punishment and moral suasion or ritual propriety continues to be an important theme in the Confucian tradition.

In *Sayings*, Confucius articulates well-tempered perspectives aligning governance with ritualized law and punishment in exchanges with his disciples in the chapters "Five Punishments" (Wuxing 五刑) and "Punishment and Governance" (Xingzheng 刑政); in both chapters, passages on law and punishment in antiquity that also appear in *Elder Dai's Record of Rituals* (DDLJ 2: 828–52) and *Record of Rituals* (LJ 1: 370–73) become part of Confucius's speeches. The following excerpt is from "Punishment and Governance" in *Sayings* (KZJY 31.406–08):

2.23 Zhonggong asked Confucius: "I have heard that the extreme use of punishment leaves no room for governance and that ideal governance leaves no room for punishment. The extreme use of punishment leaving no room for governance: such were the eras of the tyrants Jie and Zhòu. Ideal governance leaving no room for punishment: such were the eras of Kings Cheng and Kang. Is that true?"

Confucius said, "The government of sage kings transforms the people, and to achieve that, punishment certainly works in tandem with governance. The highest of all is to use virtue to instruct the people and to restrain them with ritual propriety. Next to that is to use governance to guide the people and to use punishment to stop them from committing crimes, for transgressors would be punished. When moral suasion fails to transform and guidance is not followed, people flout proper duties and corrupt the mores, and that is when one uses punishment. Properly applying the five punishments requires proximity to the judgment of heaven. Putting punishment into practice, even minor offenses are not forgiven. Punishment means molds, molds mean formation.[24] Once formed, changes cannot be made. That is why noble men devote their full attention to this."

Zhonggong said, "In antiquity, when listening to cases of litigation, the ancients imposed punishment according to the facts of the situation and did not follow the heart. May I learn about that?"

Confucius replied: "In all cases, when listening to litigation involving the five punishments of mutilation, they had to weigh the odds by taking into consideration the feelings binding fathers and sons and by establishing the proper duties pertaining to rulers and subjects. They had to make distinctions by consciously discussing the weightiness or lightness of the situation and by cautiously divining the shallowness and depth of the intention. They had to compeletly understand the cases by making full use of their perception and understanding and by exerting their dedication and loving kindness. When the senior supervisor of corrections rectified punishments, clarified laws, and judged cases, he did so with three rounds of hearing. When there were allegations but no evidence, the cases were not heard. When considering crimes of implication, he veered toward light punishment. When extending pardon, he included even the more serious crimes. When in doubt over cases, he broadened the deliberation by sharing it with the multitude. If they were also in doubt, the defendants would be pardoned. In all cases, they formed their judgments by making comparisons with examples of great and small crimes from the past. That was why titles were always conferred at court, for it was a mark of favor shared with the multitude. Execution always took place in the marketplace, for the abandonment of the condemned was shared with the multitude. In ancient times, the lord's house did not keep persons who sufferd mutilating punishment. The high officers would not support them, and officers would not speak to them when they encounter him on the road. Banished to the four corners and left to their devices, they did not get to participate in government. No one wanted to let them live on."

[translator's note]
In this vision of law and order in antiquity, which overlaps with exhortations (not marked as Confucius's sayings) in *Record of Rituals* (*LJ* 1: 370–73), the imperative to "weigh the odds" in cases involving normative ties (father and son, ruler and subject) is built into broader claims for just punishment as the foundation of governance. In the slightly later *Kong Anthology*, there is greater emphasis on leniency in antiquity and on compassion and discernment in litigation in Confucius's responses to his disciples: "Punishments were few in antiquity; they are numerous in the present age"; "to keep the people in line through ritual propriety is like using reins in a horse-riding metaphor; to keep the people in line through punishments is like using whips in a horse-riding metaphor" (*KCZ* 4.77). When a Lu

minister consults Confucius on the appropriate punishment for a rebellious retainer, Confucius advises him: "There should be none. You didn't treat the retainer with ritual propriety, and that's why he left you. Now that he has returned of his own accord, his crime is erased by his return. Why should you pay back with punishment?" (*KCZ* 4.80).

Historical Arguments

Confucius is said to have expressed his moral judgments through his compilation or editing of the *Annals* (chapter 1, 1.66, 1.67). Comments on historical personages and events attributed to him in various early texts sometimes develop into debates on the question of legitimate political authority: What is the foundation of kingship? How should power be exercised? We will begin with the moral ambiguities surrounding the stories of the sage kings Yao and Shun, both praised in sayings attributed to Confucius. Around fourth century BCE, the legend arose that in antiquity Yao abdicated in favor of Shun, and Shun did the same in favor of Yu, the flood controller and founder of the Xia dynasty.[25] Yao and Shun, in addition to their appointment of worthy ministers and perfection of virtuous governance, exemplify political disinterestedness based on the recognition that the polity should be a justly and commonly shared realm (*tianxia wei gong* 天下為公) by passing the throne not to their own sons but to the most worthy men.

To fully develop the abdication plot, Shun needs a backstory. Why would Yao choose him? How should Shun prove his virtue? A commoner has no wherewithal to show his talent in government, and the only way for him to shine is through his family relations. How better to prove his mettle than to give him a villainous and undeserving family? Legends about the wickedness of his father the Blind Old Man, his mother, and his younger brother Xiang arose. Stories of the persecution of Shun by his parents and brother are elaborated in *Mencius*, often in the context of Mencius's disciples raising questions about Shun's ethical dilemmas. For example, is Shun being hypocritical when he pretends not to know his brother's murderous plots against him? Should he have enfeoffed his evil brother? Is it justified for him to flout ritual norms in not notifying his errant father when arranging his marriage? Shun's malevolent family highlights his virtue, inasmuch as his filial and fraternal feelings do not depend on worthy objects or reciprocity. Further, if Shun could influence his recalcitrant kin, it would imply his power to transform the entire polity (*Mencius* 4A.28).

The most pressing question raised by abdication is the creation of rival loci of authority. In the "Canon of Yao" (Yao dian 堯典) in the *Documents*, Yao tests and observes Shun by marrying his two daughters to Shun, sending Shun to implement the five fundamental teachings, putting Shun in various official positions, having Shun receive guests from four directions, and leaving Shun in the mountains to contend with wind, rain, and thunder. Yao as ruler is the one testing and judging Shun's fitness for office, but what is his role after his abdication? In lineal succession, the former ruler is the dead father. How should a ruler who ascends the throne through the abdication of another ruler treat his father and his predecessor? The hierarchy of ruler and subject, father and son, is threatened when the former emperor Yao and Shun's father, the Blind Old Man, have to pay obeisance to Shun at court. This scenario is discussed in *Mencius* (5A.4) through the merit of sayings attributed to Confucius:

2.25 Xianqiu Meng asked Mencius, "There is this saying: 'Regarding the man of the greatest virtue, the ruler cannot treat him as his subject, the father cannot treat him as his son.' When Shun as a ruler stood facing south, Yao led the lords to face north and pay obeisance at court, and the Blind Old Man also faced north and paid obeisance at court. When Shun saw the Blind Old Man, he showed great disquiet. Confucius said, 'At that moment, the entire realm under heaven was tottering dangerously!' I wonder whether those words were true?"

Mencius said, "No. Those were not the noble man's words, those were the words of uncouth rustics from Eastern Qi. Yao was growing old and Shun ruled on behalf of Yao. The 'Canon of Yao' said: 'After twenty-eight years, Yao died. The hundred clans grieved as if they had lost their parents. For three years, music fell silent within the four seas as the people mourned.' Confucius said, 'There are no two suns in the sky, even as there are no two kings for the people.' If, having become the Son of Heaven, Shun led all the lords under heaven to mourn Yao for three years, that would mean that there were two Sons of Heaven."

Xianqiu Meng said, "As for Shun not treating Yao as a subject, I have already received your instruction. It says in the *Odes*, 'For all under heaven, / there is no land that is not the king's land. / Follow the land to the water's edge, / There is no one who is not the king's subject.' Since Shun had already become the Son of Heaven, may I ask how it is possible that he did not treat the Blind Old Man as his subject?"

Mencius said, "As for this poem, that is not what is meant. The poet is toiling for the king's affairs and does not get to nurture his parents. He is saying, 'These are nothing but the king's affairs that should concern everyone, how does it happen that I alone am deemed worthy to bear the burden of toil?' That is why those who explain the meanings of the *Odes* do not let embellishment go against the phrasing, nor do they let the phrasing go against the intent. Use your imagination to meet the poet's intent: that's how you get it . . . When it comes to the highest level of being a filial son, nothing is greater than honoring his parents; when it comes to the highest level of honoring his parents, nothing is greater than bringing the entire realm under heaven to nurture them. Being the father of the Son of Heaven is the highest honor; bringing the entire realm to nurture one's parents is the highest form of nurturing. . . ."

[translator's note]
The first saying of Confucius quoted by Xianqiu Meng implies that Shun's treatment of his predecessor Yao and his father as subjects endangers the normative hierarchical order of ruler and subject, father and son. It is also quoted in *Mozi* as an example of Confucius's denigration of Shun and the abdication story (*MZ* 39.277). (Some scholars believe that the notion of sage rulers yielding their thrones to worthy commoners instead of their descendants originates among the Mohists, with their egalitarian ethos.) Mencius denies that Confucius said this and blames "uncouth rustics from Eastern Qi" for spreading such rumors. The state of Qi (present-day Shandong), situated to the east of Mencius's native Zou, is sometimes linked to fantastic stories.

Mencius maintains that Shun is merely a regent "ruling on behalf of" (*she* 攝) Yao and that he is not truly the Son of Heaven during the twenty-eight years between Yao's abdication and his death. This could imply that good governance is achieved through power sharing between a ruler retaining ultimate authority and a minister capable of governing on a ruler's behalf. To support the idea that Yao is still ruler after his abdication, Mencius quotes another saying by Confucius, which appears thrice in *Record of Rituals* to support arguments about indivisible political authority and unchallenged hierarchy. Note that Mencius's theory of Shun's "regency" in effect augments the vision of power sharing, despite his professed intention to defend Yao's royal status between the time of his abdication and his death.

Xianqiu Meng then quotes lines from an ancient poem about the limitless reach of sovereignty to suggest that Shun has to treat his father as his subject. Mencius chides Xianqiu Meng for being literal minded and argues that the poetic speaker is in fact expressing longing for his parents. According to Mencius, the poetic speaker is actually wondering why he alone has to be away from home to fulfill his military duty when other subjects of the king should be sharing the responsibility for defending the realm. Mencius's ingenious disquisition on misunderstood poetic intention—the first of its kind in the tradition and the progenitor of a poetics of indirectness as well as allegorical interpretations—turns lines that problematize filial piety into its ultimate affirmation.

Mencius finds it necessary to explain away the potential for creating rival loci of authority in the model of abdication, although, as we have seen, he in effect justifies it. While Mencius maintains that there is no contradiction between being simultaneously a deferential subject and a de facto ruler, between respecting paternal authority and exercising a ruler's authority, *Han Feizi* uses these potential contradictions to attack the abdication model outright in defense of his vision of the enlightened ruler's absolute power. By his time, the disastrous story of King Kuai of Yan (r. 320–314 BCE), who abdicated in favor of his minister Zi Zhi, was well-known. (Yan was plunged into turmoil and devastation with the fighting between Zi Zhi and King Kuai's son.) The supposed saying by Confucius dismissed by Mencius as the fabrication of "uncouth rustics" is affirmed by Han Feizi as representative of Confucius's views. He thus begins by attacking Confucius's presumed questioning of hierarchical order:

2.26 According to the records, "When Shun saw the Blind Old Man, he showed great disquiet." Confucius said, "At that moment, the entire realm under heaven was tottering dangerously! For the one who truly grasps the Way, the ruler cannot treat him as his subject, the father cannot treat him as his son."

Your servant submits: Confucius had not yet grasped the way of filial piety, fraternal duty, loyalty, and submission. If he is right, then is it true that he who grasped the Way could not serve his ruler as a subject when he advanced to the political realm, nor could he serve his father as a son when he withdrew to his private sphere? The reasons why a father wants to have a worthy son are that if the family is poor, he can enrich it; if the father is in distress, he can gladden him. The reasons why a ruler wants to have a worthy subject are that, if the state is in chaos, he can impose order; if the ruler is debased, he can elevate him. Now if there is a worthy son who does not serve his father, then his father is in a lamentable situation with his family; if there is a worthy subject who does not serve his ruler, then his ruler is in a perilous situation with his position. If so, then for a father to have a worthy son and for a ruler to have a worthy subject suffice precisely to bring them harm, how can they gain anything from it! As the saying goes, a loyal subject does not endanger his ruler, a filial son does not inveigh against his parents. . . .

The Blind Old Man was Shun's father, yet Shun exiled him. Xiang was Shun's younger brother, yet Shun put him to death. To exile one's father and kill one's younger brother cannot be called humane, to marry the sovereign's two daughters and through that gain control of the entire realm under heaven cannot be called righteous. To have no humaneness and righteousness cannot be called wisdom. It says in the *Odes*, 'For all under heaven, / there is no land that is not the king's land. / Follow the land to the water's edge, / There is no one who is not the king's subject.' If things are indeed as the poem describes, then Shun, in entering the political realm, turns his ruler into his subject, and in the family's context, turns his father into his subject, his mother into his maid servant, and takes as wives his lord's daughters . . . (*HFZ* 51.1153–54).

[translator's note]
No other extant sources mention Shun putting his younger brother Xiang to death, although some texts refer to Xiang's exile. Indeed, a sage king's punishment of guilty family members addresses questions of public good versus private ties, as noted previously in 2.14. While passage 2.26 focuses on how Shun threatens hierarchical order, other critiques of Yao and Shun in *Han Feizi* take issue with the very notion of virtuous governance through moral suasion, as in the following example, which also unfolds as an argument with Confucius:

2.27 Farmers at Mount Li encroached on areas beyond their fields' boundaries. Shun went there and plowed, and in a year the divisions between fields were settled and corrected. Fishermen by the river fought to occupy embankments. Shun went there and fished, and in a year the spirit of yielding grew. The potters of Eastern Yi made brittle vessels. Shun went there to make pottery, and in a year the vessels became durable. Confucius sighed, saying, "Plowing, fishing, and pottery were not Shun's official duties. Yet Shun went and did these things in order to correct misconduct. Shun indeed embodied the highest good! He personally took up hard labor and the people followed him. That is why we say that the sage's virtue can transform the people!"

Someone asked an expert in ritual and traditional learning, "At that moment, where was Yao?"

That person said, "Yao was the Son of Heaven."

"If so, why did Confucius consider Yao a sage? A sage exercising his illuminating discernment in a position of supreme power would rid the world of wrongdoing. Now if the farmers and the fishermen did not fight and the pottery was not brittle, how would Shun use his virtue to transform them? If Shun was correcting misconduct, then Yao was remiss. To honor Shun for being worthy is to negate Yao's illuminating discernment. To consider Yao a sage is to negate Shun's moral transformation of the people. One cannot have it both ways. A man from Chu who was selling shields and spears praised his ware: 'My shields are sturdy. Nothing can break through.' He also praised his spears: 'My spears are sharp. There is nothing they cannot break through.' Someone asked him: 'How about using your spears to break through your shields?' That person could not respond. An unbreakable shield and a spear that can break through anything cannot exist together in the world. Now Yao and Shun cannot both be praised: this is evident from the discourse of the spear and the shield."

Furthermore, the way Shun corrected misconduct meant that he stopped one transgression in one year and three transgressions in three years. There is a limit to Shun's lifespan but transgressions in the world are endless. To use what has a limit to pursue what is endless means that the transgressions that can be stopped are but few in number. The rules regarding reward and punishment can be made to prevail in the entire realm under heaven with such orders: "Those who carry out the law are to be rewarded; those who fail to do so are to be executed." If such orders arrive in the morning, transformations will take place by the evening. If they arrive in the evening, transformations will take place by the next morning. In ten days, this can be done within the seas, why would we need to wait a year? Still, Shun did not use this argument to persuade Yao to make the people follow him. Instead, he personally undertook all these tasks. Was he not deficient in the art of government? Moreover, to personally endure hardships and only then transform the people, that is something that even Yao and Shun would find difficult. Instead, to use a position of power to correct the behavior of one's subjects, that is something that even an average ruler would find easy. Those who want to bring order to the entire realm under heaven by letting go of what even the average ruler would find easy, and instead talk about what even Yao and Shun would find difficult, cannot be entrusted with the charge of government. (*HFZ* 36.845–47)

[translator's note]
A sage king instituting perfect rule would leave no room for another would-be sage king to prove his worth and receive the mandate. In any case, a sage ruler's moral transformation of his people is a slow process, if not an unattainable ideal. The use of laws and regulations, rewards and punishment, to control the people is much more practicable, according to Han Feizi. Elsewhere in *Han Feizi*, abdication myths are said to mask ruthless power struggles, with Shun "persecuting" (*bi* 偪) Yao, and Yu "persecuting" Shun (*HFZ* 44.978).[26] Given the drive to demystify the legends of Yao and Shun, it may come as a surprise that Yao's abdication is also presented as laudable in *Han Feizi* through implicit affirmation of Confucius's judgment, albeit with a twist:

2.28 Yao wanted to pass on rulership of the entire realm under heaven to Shun. Gun remonstrated with him, "This is inauspicious! How can you pass on rulership of the entire realm under heaven to a commoner!" Yao did not heed him, raised an army for a punitive expedition, and cut down Gun at the outskirts of Feather Mountain.[27] Gonggong also remonstrated with him, "How can you pass on rulership of the entire realm under heaven to a commoner!" Yao did not heed him, and again he raised an army for a punitive expedition, and banished Gonggong to the capital of the Dark Land. As a result, no one under heaven dared to say that rulership of the realm under heaven should not be passed to Shun. Confucius heard this and said, "For Yao to know Shun's worth was not the difficult part. But to go so far as to execute the ones who remonstrated and to insist on passing the throne to Shun, that was the difficult part." Alternatively, he said this:

"To not allow what he had doubts about to ruin what he discerned: that was the difficult part." (*HFZ* 34.788)

[translator's note]
In line with the celebration of the ruler's discernment and ability to override opposition in *Han Feizi*, Confucius is made to praise the punishment of remonstrating ministers. Gun and Gonggong are said to be executed and banished for their failures—not for opposing the abdicaton—in other early texts. The above passage also goes against the most common iteration of the stories about remonstration, which often presents rulers acceding to good advice and correcting their errors as laudable examples.

Another nodal point in ancient history that comes up often in philosophical debates is the Zhou conquest of Shang (ca. 1046 BCE). Legend has it that the last king of Shang, Zhòu, was a tyrant who indulged in all kinds of excesses and cruelty. Zhou, a subsidiary domain under Shang, flourished under the virtuous rule of King Wen and, under the leadership of his son King Wu, Zhou conquered Shang. In the *Analects* (19.20), Zigong remarks that Zhòu's reputation for wickedness might have outstripped reality, because a bad reputation tends to sink lower as it becomes a magnate for unsavory characters or stories of immorality. Confucius praises the music celebrating King Wu's martiality as "fully realizing beauty" but "not yet fully realizing goodness" (*Analects* 3.25), perhaps because of the violent Zhou conquest of Shang (see chapter 1, 1.31a, 1.54, translator's note).

The justification of deposing and killing the last Shang king is debated in Warring States texts. Mencius (1B.1) argues that Zhòu, by virtue of his violence and immorality, forfeits the right to be honored as a sovereign, and regicide in this case is just "the killing of a mere fellow" (*zhu yi fu* 誅一夫). Xunzi claims that "the army of humaneness and righteousness" (*renyi zhi bing* 仁義之兵) can rightfully cut down a tyrant like Zhòu, who can only be considered "a solitary fellow" (*dufu* 獨夫) (*XZ* 15.205, 18.239). Han Feizi, while regularly castigating Zhòu as the negative example of a bad ruler, also maintains that the Zhou conquest as a model for moral military action is an example of ancient history that cannot be replicated in his time. Celebrating raw power calculations, one story in *Han Feizi* even suggests that Zhòu, for all his iniquities, could have maintained his position had he not been deterred by the Zhou leader's embrace of "humaneness and righteousness" and decisively executed him (*HFZ* 33.737).

For more recent history, Warring States thinkers imagine political ideals as realized by strong leaders and sagacious ministers in a period when nominally subordinate domains became increasingly assertive and combative with Zhou decline. Various rulers from the seventh and sixth century BCE were believed to have become "hegemons" (*ba* 霸), leaders of interstate covenants who tried to maintain relative peace and stability with the blessing of the Zhou king (see chapter 1, 1.7, 1.17, 1.43a). One of them was Lord Wen of Jin (r. 636–628 BCE), whom Confucius describes as "flexibly tactical but not principled" (*jue er buzheng* 譎而不正) (*Analects* 14.15). In two anecdotes from *Han Feizi*, perspectives on the efficacy of virtue develops through Confucius's commendation of Lord Wen and the counterargument it provokes.

2.29 Lord Wen of Jin attacked Yuan and the army took supplies for ten days. He then made a pact with the high officers to overcome Yuan in ten days. They came to Yuan and besieged it for ten days, but Yuan did not fall. They beat the gong and withdrew, stopped the siege, and left. An officer who came out of Yuan said, "Yuan would fall in three days." Various officials and attendants remonstrated with Lord Wen, "Yuan is running out of food and has reached the limit of its strength. You, my lord, should just wait it out." The lord said, "I made a pact with the officers to overcome Yuan in ten days. If we do not leave, I will fail in good faith. To obtain Yuan and fail in good faith is not something I would do." He then stopped the siege and left. When the men of Yuan heard about this, they said, "To have a ruler like that with such good faith—how can we fail to submit to him!" They thus surrendered to the lord. When the men of Wen heard about this, they said, "To have a ruler like that with such good faith—how can we fail to follow him!" They thus surrendered to the lord. Confucius heard about this and recorded it, saying, "That he attacked Yuan and obtained Wei was because of his good faith." (*HFZ* 32.708–09)

[translator's note]
In another anecdote, Lord Wen of Jin receives opposite advice from two ministers, Jiu Fan and Hu Yan. Jiu Fan affirms the general importance of integrity and good faith but counsels deception and trickery, while Yong Ji insists on good faith because there is "no going back" despite temporary advantage.[28] The Jin ruler adopts Jiu Fan's advice and wins, but he ends up giving Yong Ji a greater reward. Lord Wen explains: "For Jiu Fan was

speaking about the expediency of the moment, while Yong Ji was speaking about the benefit for ten thousand generations" (*HFZ* 36.840). The anecdote continues with Confucius's comment and its refutation:

2.30 Confucius heard about this and remarked, "It is fitting that Lord Wen should attain hegemony! He understands both the expediency of the moment and the benefit for ten thousand generations."

[Han Feizi proceeds to refute Confucius.] One may say, "Yong Ji's response did not answer Lord Wen's question . . . Yong Ji's response was 'there is no going back': this was not a pertinent rejoinder. Furthermore, Lord Wen did not understand the expediency of the moment, nor did he understand the advantages for ten thousand generations. If one achieves victory in battles, then the state will be safe and one will have security, the army will be strengthened and one's authority will be established. What can exceed these even if there is no going back? Why be concerned that the benefit for ten thousand generations would not come about? If one fails to achieve victory in battles, then the state will fall and the army will be weakened, one will die and one's name will sink into oblivion. There would not be enough time even to exorcise the inauspiciousness over today's dead, how can one have the luxury to wait for the benefit of ten thousand generations? The benefit for ten thousand generations lies in today's victory, and today's victory lies in deceiving the enemy, that is all. Hence it is said: Yong Ji's response did not answer Lord Wen's question.

"Moreover, Lord Wen also did not understand Jiu Fan's words. When Jiu Fan said, 'one cannot have enough deception and trickery,' he was not talking about deceiving the people but deceiving the enemy. The enemy is the state one is attacking, what harm is there even if there is no going back?[29] Did Lord Wen give Yong Ji a greater reward because of his merit? But then the reason why Jin achieved victory over Chu and defeated the Chu army was because of Jiu Fan's scheme. Was it because Yong Ji excelled in his advice? But then Yong Ji only spoke about there being no going back later—there is no good advice here. Jiu Fan, on the other hand, had both merit and good advice; . . . the issue is military stratagem. Jiu Fan first gave good advice and later achieved victory in battle. Thus, Jiu Fan had two merits but received a lesser reward, while Yong Ji, without any merit, received a greater reward. 'For Lord Wen to have achieved hegemony, was that not fitting?' This shows that Confucius did not understand the principle of proper rewards." (*HFZ* 36.842–43)

The Master Said

At first glance the anecdotes in 2.29 and 2.30 seem to articulate opposite perspectives, with Confucius giving the last word in one case and being refuted in the other. Both, however, share a concern with the appearance of virtue and its tactical advantages: the only difference is that Confucius affirms it in one case and negates it in the other (and is refuted). Versions of the siege of Yuan story are told in *Zuo Tradition* (*Zuo* Xi 25.4, 1: 392–93), *Discourses of the States* (*GY* "Jinyu" 4.17, 376), *Mr. Lü's Annals* (*LSCQ* 2: 1294), *Huainanzi* (*HNZ* 12.399), and *New Order* (*Xinxu* 4.120). In probably the earliest version in *Zuo Tradition*, Jin troops retreat one day's march and Yuan surrenders, and there is no mention of Jin gaining other territories because of Lord Wen's demonstration of good faith. In *Huainanzi*, the story concludes thus: "That is why Laozi said, 'Intangible and dark, / there is essence in it. / Its essence is genuine, / there is good faith in it.' Hence 'Fine words can sell honor, / Fine deeds can raise a man above others' " (*HNZ* 12.399). Even as *Laozi* is invoked as an authoritative text in *Huainanzi*, Confucius is brought in as an authoritative figure that delivers the message in *Han Feizi*: namely, good faith pays. Lord Wen displays his trustworthiness through a tactical retreat, but he has also demonstrated that subjugating Yuan is well within his power.

The story on the opposite advice of Hu Yan and Yong Ji appears with variations in *Mr. Lü's Annals* (*LSCQ* 1: 780), *Huainanzi* (*HNZ* 18.603), and *The Garden of Eloquence* (*SY* 13.31). In *Mr. Lü's Annals*, Confucius comments, "To use deception when confronting a potential disaster suffices to repel the enemy; to honor the worthy upon his return suffices to repay virtue. Although Lord Wen cannot be principled from beginning to end, these acts suffice to make him hegemon" (*LSCQ* 1: 780). No other version includes a refutation of the reasoning behind elevating Yong Ji above Jiu Fan. That argument is typical of the pragmatic attention to political considerations in *Han Feizi*. Jiu Fan argues that "integrity" and "good faith" do not belong to the battlefield although they are the staples of ritual-minded noble men, implying their irrelevance for the hegemonic enterprise. The concluding interpretation of Jiu Fan's words reclaims "integrity" and "good faith" as something realized in the government of one's own state through deception and trickery practiced on the enemy. Although the argument with Confucius is purportedly about "the principle of proper rewards," the real issue is how the appearance and claim of virtue serve a ruthless concern with political efficacy and expanding state power.

The historical arguments above can use Confucius's sayings to launch counterarguments by registering misattribution or outright opposition. Whatever the scenario, Confucius has to speak. The same holds true for many of the other stories in this chapter, whether Confucius functions as the interlocutor, the empathetic interpreter, the exegete, the explainer of laws, or the defender of diverse positions. Arguing with Confucius means giving him a voice and developing implicitly or explicitly a dialogical structure in the justification of an intellectual position. The formula "the Master said" is often associated with the declarative mode and the affirmation of self-evident truths, but examples from this chapter reminds us of its rhetorical contexts and polemical functions.

CHAPTER III

Outsmarting Confucius (or His Followers)

I n *Balanced Discourses*, the Eastern Han skeptic Wang Chong turns his critical gaze to the *Analects*, part of a broader critique of earlier thinkers that include Mencius, Mozi, and Laozi. In the chapter "Questioning Confucius" (Wen Kong 問孔), he faults Confucius for his word choice (either too laconic or too ambiguous), raising doubts regarding Confucius's intention or rhetorical efficacy. In some cases, he also faults Confucius for inconsistencies or logical contradictions. For example, Confucius castigates his disciple Zai Yu for sleeping in the daytime: "Rotten wood cannot be carved; a wall of mud and dung cannot be trowelled" (*Analects* 5.10). Wang Chong considers this criticism excessive and inconsistent with Confucius's statement that "one should not seek the perfection of every talent in one man" (*Analects* 18.10). In another example, Wang Chong observes: Confucius declares that he "wants to live among the nine barbarian tribes," noting that the noble man can bring about moral and cultural transformation (*Analects* 9.14). Yet he also implies that barbarians cannot measure up to the central states (*Analects* 3.5). Wang Chong does not question classical learning and core precepts such as humaneness, proper duty, ritual propriety, or filial piety, mentions Confucius favorably hundreds of times, and affirms the Han view of Confucius as the "uncrowned king" expressing judgments of enduring value in the *Annals*. His skeptical tone may be directed against contemporary sacralization of Confucius as a semidivine being, or he may simply be vindicating his emphasis on clarity and

evidence. When he discusses Confucius's word choice or rhetorical strategies, he seems to imply that he can do it better.

Wang Chong's almost querulous tone taps into the impulse to push back
against the representation of Confucius as the all-knowing sage even while
abiding by his teachings. We see a similar duality in later examples. In 832,
the Tang emperor Wenzong ordered that actors and entertainers putting
up a skit "making fun of Confucius" (nong Kongzi 弄孔子) should be driven
out of the palace.[1] When we read such an account, the focus should not
only be on the suppression of "blasphemy." The interesting thing is that
such entertainment should coexist at all with a solemn discussion of the
merits of the Three Teachings (Confucianism, Daoism, Buddhism) taking
place at the palace at that time. Another ninth-century story describes how
the court jester Li Keji made jokes about Confucius being a woman, because
the phrase dai jia 待價, "waiting for the fair price or right offer" (that is,
recognition and the chance to implement his ideals) (Analects 9.13), is
homophonous with the phrase "waiting to give herself in marriage" (dai jia
待嫁).[2] Making fun of Confucius does not have to be subversive. In the following examples, only the Dunhuang ballad and the Taiping tract are
adversarial toward Confucius. In the other cases, competition with the sage
takes on the mood of harmless fun. Alternatively, the vitriol is directed
against the misguided followers of Confucius, often in the name of defending the true teachings of the sage.

Children and Women

It is not uncommon to find a humbled Confucius being criticized by
men of superior wisdom and converting to the latter's viewpoints in
texts with other worldviews or ideological stances, as seen in chapter 2.
But in some stories, Confucius is flummoxed or disparaged by unlikely
interlocutors such as children and women. Unlike the tone of serious
critique in Wang Chong's Balanced Discourses, these are often playful stories delivering merely glancing blows. In the following story from the
Daoist text Liezi (ca. third century CE), precocious children laugh at
Confucius:

3.1 Confucius was traveling eastward when he saw two children engaged
in a heated argument. One child said, "I think the sun is close to us when

it rises and is far away at midday." The other child said, "I think the sun is far away when it rises and is close to us at midday." One child said, "When the sun first rises, it is as big as the canopy of a carriage. By midday, it is like a bowl. Is it not because what is far away is small and what is close is big?" The other child said, "When the sun first rises, it is raw and cold. By midday, it is roiling hot. Is it not because what is close is hot and what is far away is cool?" Confucius could not decide between their arguments. The two children laughed and said, "Who says that you know a lot?" (*ZY* 799; *Liezi jishi* 5.168)

[translator's note]
Wang Chong describes this argument in "Disquisitions on the Sun" (Shuo ri 説日) in *Balanced Discourses* without the storytelling context (*LH* 32.493). Huan Tan's (ca. 40 BCE–32 CE) *New Disquisitions* (*Xinlun*, no longer extant) is said to have told this story. It also appears in Zhang Hua's *Record of Broad Knowledge of things* (*ZY* 770) and *Master of Golden Tower* (*Jinlou zi*) compiled by Xiao Yi (508–555) (*ZY* 910–11). *A New Account of the Tales of the World* (*Shishuo xinyu*, early fifth century, 12.3) features a precocious child who argues that the sun is both closer and farther than Chang'an. We may surmise that this is a familiar conundrum arising from contradictory answers to the question: "How far is the sun?" Confucius gets pegged to this story as the wise man who is also perplexed. In the following story (fifth–sixth century) from *Yin Yun's Tales* (*Yin Yun xiaoshuo*), two mulberry-picking girls take on the role of instructing Confucius.

3.2 Confucius left Wei and headed to Chen. On the way he saw two girls picking mulberry leaves. The Master said, "The southern branch is graceful, the northern branch is long." They answered, "The Master traveling in Chen will see his food all gone. He will not manage to thread the pearl with a nine-twists passage, and will have to ask us, the mulberry-picking girls, for a message."[3] The Master went to Chen, and the high officers there besieged him with troops. They ordered him to thread a pearl with a nine-twists passage and would only relieve his distress upon his success. The Master could not do it and sent Yan Hui and Zigong to go back and ask the girls. The girls' families falsely claimed that they had gone out and presented the two men with a melon. Zigong said, "A melon means that its seeds are inside." The girls thus came out and said, "Smear honey on the pearl. Tie a silk thread to an ant. The ant will take the silk thread through.

If it refuses to go, use fumes to smoke it." Confucius followed their words and thus managed to thread the pearl. It was then that Confucius ran out of food for seven days.[4]

[translator's note]
How exactly does one tie a silk thread to an ant? How likely is it that it can be coaxed to go through a pearl? Story interest hinges not on unanswerable questions (as in 3.1) but rather on the notion of improbable folkish knowledge unavailable to the elite. The trope of a girl besting male authority figures appears in the Vimalakīrti Sūtra (fifth century), where the Bodhisattva Mañjuśri is defeated in debate by the dragon girl. It is echoed in vernacular genres in the legend of the mantic competition between Master Zhou (whose name recalls the Duke of Zhou) and the girl Peach Blossom; a prime example is a fourteenth century play, *The Peach Blossom Girl Versus Master Zhou* (*Taohua nü dou Zhou gong* 桃花女鬭周公).[5] The defeated Master Zhou becomes homicidal, as does Confucius in the Xiang Tuo ballad.

In the more lighthearted story of 3.2, Zigong gains access to the mulberry-picking girls because he can solve the riddle of their absence. The word for seeds (*zi* 子) also means "children." In other words, Zigong, as Confucius's proxy, obtains the solution to a riddle by solving one himself. Riddles are thus a form of rhetorical competition. The same logic is evident in the following story collected in an early Tang encyclopedia (ca. seventh–eighth century):

3.3 We do not know where the roadside woman came from. Confucius encountered her while traveling. She was wearing a dark ivory comb in her hair. Confucius said to his disciples: "Who can obtain that?" Yan Hui said, "I can obtain it." He then went in front of the woman, knelt down, and said, "I have a mountain fit for wandering. A hundred kinds of grass grow on it. There are branches but no leaves. A myriad of animals gather there. We have drinks but no food, that is why we would like to borrow a net from you, my lady, to capture them." The woman took out her comb and gave it to him. Yan Hui said, "Why did you, my lady, take out your comb and give it to me without asking any questions?" The woman answered, "'A mountain fit for wandering': that is your head. 'A hundred kinds of grass grow on it. There are branches but no leaves': that is your hair. 'A myriad of animals gather there': those are your lice. 'To borrow a net to capture them': that is my comb. That is why I took out my comb and gave it to you. What is there to wonder at?" Yan Hui withdrew in silence. Hearing of this, Confucius said, "If even a woman's intelligence can be like this, how much more so when it comes to a man of learning!" (*ZY* 776).

[translator's note]
Confucius asking questions of the mulberry-picking girls can be said to exemplify his readiness to learn from all and sundry and Yan Hui's mission can be cast as a test of intelligence, but why would Confucius initiate the exchange with the girls or try to get the roadside woman's ivory comb? The very premise of 3.2 and 3.3 implies Confucius's impropriety. In stories about Confucius's encounters with clever women, the women's intelligence and rhetorical prowess that allow them to best Confucius or his disciples sometimes also suggest superior virtue. A good example is the following story, included in the chapter "Rhetorical Excellence" (Biantong 辯通) in *The Biographies of Notable Women* compiled by Liu Xiang (77–6 BCE) and in *Han's Exegesis* (*ZY* 504, *HSWZ* 1.4):

3.4 "The maiden of the Great Valley" refers to one who washed clothes by a path in the Great Valley. Confucius was traveling to the south and passing by a path of the Great Valley when he saw a maiden with a jade pendant washing clothes. Confucius said to Zigong, "The one washing clothes—do you think you can talk with her?" Taking out a goblet and giving it to Zigong, he said, "Make a speech to her and observe her intent." Zigong said to her, "I am a person from the northern periphery. Coming from the north to the south, we are about to head to Chu. Encountering such a hot day, my thoughts are set ablaze. I beg to have a drink of water, to save my heart from disarray."[6] The maiden said, "The path of the Great Valley is a secluded place. Its streams, one pure and one turbid, flow into the sea. If you want to take a drink, do so. Why ask this humble girl?" She received Zigong's goblet and, facing the current coming toward her, ladled water into it, threw it down, and tossed out the water. Turning to the same direction as the current, she ladled water into the goblet and filled it to the brim till it overflowed. She knelt down and placed it on the sand, saying, "According to ritual rules, I should not hand this to you personally."

Zigong returned and reported her speech. Confucius said, "I already knew it." He took out a zither, removed its tuning peg, and gave it to Zigong, saying, "Make a speech to her." Zigong went and said, "Earlier I heard your words, 'they were calming like the pure breeze.' Neither uncivil nor contrary, they covertly restored peace in my heart. We have a zither but no peg. Pray tune the notes with your art." The maiden said, "I am a person from the wilds of the periphery. Limited and untutored, I do not dither. Of the five notes I am ignorant, how can I tune the zither?"[7]

Zigong reported this to Confucius. Confucius said, "I already knew it. One should treat a worthy person one encounters like a respected guest." He took out five measures of hempen cloth and gave them to Zigong, saying, "Make a speech to her." Zigong went and said, "I am a person from the northern periphery. Coming from the north to the south, we are about to head to Chu. I have here five measures of hempen cloth. Not that I dare to suggest that they match your worth, but I beg to leave them by the water's side." The maiden said, "On the road is a traveler, who heaves a sigh that lingers. Sharing his resources and property, he is leaving them in the wilds of the periphery. I am quite young. How dare I receive your gift? You, sir, have not settled your betrothal with seemly haste. I, for my part, already had an eager man who asked about my name."[8]

Zigong told Confucius about this. Confucius said, "I already knew it. This is a woman who understands human feelings and knows ritual propriety."

It says in the *Odes*, "In the south are tall trees with little cover, / Where one cannot rest or find shelter. / The Han River has its roaming maidens, / To seek them is a hopeless endeavor." That is what is meant.

The encomium says, "Confucius sets out on a journey / to the south of the Great Valley. / He marvels at its maiden, / and wants to observe her manner. / Zigong goes back three times, / The maiden's words are deep and discerning. / The Master says she understands human feelings, / knows ritual propriety and is not guilty of licence." (*ZY* 723)

[translator's note]
Both Zigong and the maiden modestly describe themselves as hailing from the periphery: the far-off place where ritual and moral precepts are less defined or less well understood. Their encounter—almost a kind of muted courtship—is a testing ground or implicit competition for their respective knowledge of ritual propriety. True to the didactic intent of the texts in which this story is found, Confucius's authority is unchallenged. He is supposed to be the one setting up the tests for the maiden. He is the judge of her speech and conduct. The phrase "observe her intent" (*guan qi zhi* 觀其志)[9]

echoes the moments when Confucius asks his disciples to articulate their intent or ambition (see introduction, 4-12). Yet all the ingredients of a role reversal are already present. The maiden speaks like someone rebuffing the advances of an importune suitor. She seems to be wiser, more eloquent, and more vigilant about ritual propriety than Confucius and his disciple.

In *Kong Anthology*, Lord Pingyuan asks Confucius's descendant Zigao about the story told in 3.4 in in tandem with Confucius's meeting with Nan Zi (chapter 1, 1.20), implying that both involve impropriety in flouting the ritual separation of men and women. Zigao firmly refutes both stories. He opines that Confucius might have met Nan Zi in the context of sacrificial rituals, given the participation of the ruler's consorts in such rituals in ancient times (*KCZ* 13.297).[10] "As for the story about the Great Valley, it arose in recent times. It was probably the creation of those who transfer their own predilections to Confucius as they act out their desires" (*KCZ* 13.297–98).

Outsmarting Confucius

The tropes of the riddle, the rhetorical contest, the moral competition, and the potential role reversal persist in stories about Confucius's encounter with unexpected rivals. The ballad about Xiang Tuo, presented below, encompasses all these elements. Unlike the characters in the stories above, however, Xiang Tuo is more openly and deliberately adversarial. In Sima Qian's account of Confucius's life, "someone from Daxiangdang, a child" makes a comment about Confucius that can be interpreted as either matter of fact or sarcastic: "Great indeed is Confucius! He has broad learning but has not made a name for himself in anything" (chapter 1, 1.63). As mentioned in chapter 1, some commentators have identified this child as Xiang Tuo, the protagonist of the ballad translated here. Xiang Tuo is phonetically close to "Xiangdang," and Xiang Tuo is also sometimes referred to as "Great Xiang" or "Da Xiang" 大項, said to be related phonetically to the place name "Daxiangdang" 達巷黨,[11] although the connection seems to me tenuous and implausible. Almost all Han dynasty stone carvings of the meeting of Confucius and Laozi feature the child Xiang Tuo, often shown with a wheel, in the middle.[12] Several texts from about third century BCE to first century CE mention how "the seven-year-old Xiang

Tuo became Confucius's teacher" without providing details.[13] A few early medieval texts (ca. third–fifth century) mention that Xiang Tuo dies young. The ballad "Confucius and Xiang Tuo Asked Each Other Questions" 項託孔子相問書 was found among the trove of manuscripts discovered in the Dunhuang Caves in 1900. The ballad, with sections in partially rhyming prose and verse, features Confucius as the antagonist. The boy Xiang Tuo skillfully answers all the questions raised by Confucius. The latter, failing to solve the conundrums posed by Xiang Tuo and worsted in debates with him, kills the boy. (The verse describing the murder, included only in some versions, and the prose account of the exchange seem to come from different sources.) There are sixteen manuscript versions and three Tibetan translations of this text among Dunhuang materials, testifying to its popularity. Two of the Xiang Tuo manuscripts include the copying dates (943 and 936), but the provenance of the story could be much earlier.

3.5 Confucius and Xiang Tuo Asked Each Other Questions
孔子項託相問書[14]
Once upon a time, when Confucius was traveling east, he reached the foothills of Mount Jing and encountered three children on the road. Two of them were playing; one of them was not. Finding this strange, the Master asked, "Why don't you play?" The child answered: "Play big games and you kill each other, play small games and you wound each other. Playing does no good, so why bother? Clothes are torn; holes are born. Instead of tagging along to throw stones, I'd do better to pound grains at home.[15] From my father and mother above to my older and younger brothers below, my only wish is that they suffer no payback blow, for I fear rude indignities would follow. On this I have mulled well and quite a lot, and not playing is the conclusion I got. What is there to wonder about?"

Xiang Tuo, who had a special mien, then piled up earth to make a "city wall." Having done so, he sat inside. The Master said to the child, "Why are you not making way for my carriage?" The child answered, "Formerly, I heard that the sages had these words: for realms above, know the pattern of constellations; for realms below, know the geographical formations; for realms in the middle, know the human situations and emotions. From past to present, I've heard only of carriages making its way around city walls. Whoever heard of city walls making way for carriages?" At that moment, the Master could not come up with a reply. His carriage thus made its way around the "city wall." He sent someone to go down the road and ask: "Which family is this child from? What is his name?" The child replied, "Xiang is my surname, my given name is Tuo."

The Master said, "Despite your tender years, you know about big things." The child responded, "I have heard that three days after its birth, a fish swims in rivers and seas. Three days after its birth, a rabbit circuits three acres of land. Three days after its birth, a foal runs after its mother. Three days after its birth, a baby recognizes its parents. Heaven would have it so; it's all natural. Why speak about being big or small?"

The Master asked the child, "Do you know what hill has no rocks? What water has no fish? What gate has no lock? What carriage has no wheel? What cow has no calf? What horse has no foal? What blade has no ring? What fire has no smoke? What man has no wife? What woman has no husband? Which sun is inadequate? Which sun is excessive? What male has no female? What tree has no branch? What city has no governor? What person has no sobriquet?" The child answered, "An earthen hill has no rocks. Well water has no fish. The gate of emptiness has no lock. A sedan carriage has no wheel. A mud cow has no calf. A wooden horse has no foal. A chopping blade has no ring.[16] A firefly's fire has no smoke. An immortal has no wife. The Jade Maiden has no husband. The winter sun is inadequate. The summer sun is excessive. A loner male has no female. A dying tree has no branch. An abandoned city has no governor. A small child has no sobriquet."

The Master said, "Excellent! Excellent indeed! You and I should roam the world together. Would that be a good idea?" The child answered, "I am not going to roam. I have a stern father whom I need to serve. I have a kind mother whom I need to care for. I have an older brother whom I need to obey. I have a younger brother whom I need to instruct. That is why I cannot follow you and leave, sir."

The Master said, "I have a boardgame for double gammon set up in my carriage. How about we play a game of chance together?"[17] The child answered, "I do not play games of chance. When the Son of Heaven loves such games, wind and rain come at wrong moments. When the lords love such games, misrule prevails in government. When the clerks love such games, cases pile high with endless delay. When farmers love such games, their plowing and sowing miss the day. When students love such games, they forget to study the *Documents* and *Odes*. When children love such games, whips and lashes come their way. This is something that brings no benefits. Why should I bother to learn it?"

The Master said, "You and I could level differences in the entire world under heaven. Would that be a good idea?" The child answered, "The entire world under heaven cannot be brought to the same level. There are high mountains, there are rivers and seas. There are lords and ministers, there are servants and maids. That is why it cannot be brought to the same level."

The Master said, "You and I could level the high mountains, stop up the rivers and seas, abolish the lords and ministers, and do away with the servants and maids. The entire world under heaven would be swept of injustices, why would it not be brought to the same level?" The child answered, "Level the high mountains, and the beasts will have nowhere to rest. Stop up the rivers and seas, and the fish will have nowhere to go. Abolish the lords and ministers, and the people will contend over right and wrong. Do away with servants and maids—who will be at the gentlemen's beck and call?"

The Master said, "Excellent! Excellent indeed! Do you know why a pine tree grows in a house? Why reeds grow in front of the door? Why cattails grow on the bed? Why a dog barks at its master? Why a daughter-in-law sits with her mother-in-law waiting on her? Why a rooster turns into a pheasant? Why a hound turns into a fox?" The child answered, "The pine tree growing in a house is its pillar. The reeds growing in front of the door form its curtain. The cattails growing on the bed form its mat. A dog barks at its master because he has a guest by his side. A daughter-in-law sits with her mother-in-law waiting on her because [in her special state] she has just come under the flowers.[18] A rooster turns into a pheasant because it is in the hills and marshes. A hound turns into a fox because it is among mountain ranges."

The Master said to the child, "Do you know who are dearer? Are husbands and wives dearer? Are fathers and mothers dearer?" The child said, "Fathers and mothers are dearer." The Master said, "Husbands and wives are dearer. Living, they share the same beds and pillows. Dying, they share the same coffins. Their love and regard for each other are great indeed. How can they not be dearer to each other?" The child answered, "What sort of talk is this! What sort of talk is this! A person has a mother just like a tree has its roots. A person has a wife just like a carriage has its wheels. A carriage that is broken can be rebuilt—one is sure to get something new. A wife who dies can be replaced through remarriage—one is sure to get a worthy mate. When a tree dies, all its branches wither. When a mother dies, all her children become orphans. Is it not perverse to compare a wife to a mother?"

The child turned things around and asked the Master, "Why are swans and ducks able to float? Why are wild geese and cranes able to sing? Why are pines and cypresses evergreen through the seasons?" The Master responded, "Swans and ducks are able to float because of their square feet. Wild geese and cranes are able to sing because of their long necks. Pines and cypresses are evergreen through the seasons because of their stout hearts." The child countered, "Not so! Toads can sing, how can it be because of their long necks? Turtles can float, how can it be because of their square feet? *Hu* bamboos are evergreen through the seasons, how can it be because of their stout hearts?"

The Master asked Xiang Tuo, "Do you know how high is heaven? How thick is earth? How many beams does the sky have? How many pillars does the earth have? Where does wind come from? How does rain arise? From which corner does frost emerge? Whence does dew come?" The child answered, "The sky and the earth are a billion and 9,999 miles apart. The thickness of the earth is the same as its distance from the sky. Wind comes from Cangwu, rain from high places, frost from the sky, and dew from the hundred grass. Heaven has no beams, nor does earth have any pillars. Cloudy vapors from the four directions hold them up as if they were pillars. What is there to marvel at?"

The Master sighed, "Excellent! Excellent indeed! Only now do I know that the young ones should be held in awe."

The Master and Xiang Tuo exchanged questions and answers, and in every way the Master failed to measure up to Xiang Tuo. The Master made up his mind to kill Xiang Tuo and thus wrote this verse:

Sun Jing hung his head and pricked his thigh to stay awake.
Kuang Heng dug a hole in the wall for stealthy light's sake.
Deep love of valor defines Zilu's very character.
Zizhang's appetite for the classics one must register.[19]
At seven, Xiang Tuo's words never failed,
Answering Confucius, he indeed prevailed.
Xiang Tuo entered the mountains in pursuit of learning—
Hands pressed together, he spoke and turned to his parents:
"I will seek knowledge under a hundred-foot tree,
You don't have to remember where I will be."

His father and mother, getting on in years, became quite confused.
Confucius had them keep two cartloads of hay and was not refused.
The Master left, and with the passage of time year after year,
Xiang Tuo's parents could no longer hope that he would appear.
They took a hundred bundles of hay to be burned as fuel.
The rest became fodder for the cows, the sheep, and the mule.
All of a sudden, the Master came and demanded the hay.
Xiang Tuo's father and mother turned pale with dismay.
At that moment, they wanted to pay him double the price.
For each bundle, they would offer a golden ingot thrice.
"No need for gold or silver, I'll be bound—
Old lady, where is Xiang Tuo to be found?"
"My son left a long, long time ago,
To seek learning under a hundred-foot tree."
Once the Master heard what she said,
His heart was beyond all bounds glad.
He went into the mountains, riding a horse,
Scaling heights, crossing ridges, staying on course.
He measured every tree, but none was a hundred feet.
Over his legs, vines and creepers twined to meet.
The Master had his men dig away with a spade.
They reached underground, where a stone hall was found.
Inside the first set of gates, stone lions were shown.
Outside the second set were Vajradharas hewn from stone.
Entering the courtyard gate, he cocked his ear to listen:
On two sides, ranged like flying geese, were reciting students.
The Master drew his sword and hacked with wild fury,
But those people, all paired up, suffered no injury.
They turned into stone men and uttered no word of woe,
But with the iron sword slashing, blood began to flow.
With his remnant breath, Xiang Tuo clung to existence,
Called his mother, turned, and looked into the distance:
"Let my red blood be held in a pot of clay,
Bring it home and keep it for seven days."
The sight of her child's blood was hard for the mother to bear,
She held the pot next to a pile of feces and let it drip there.
In one day, in two days, bamboos began to take root.
In three days or four, dark green bamboos grew from the shoots.

The bamboos grew to a hundred feet, an awe-inspiring sight,
On every joint were mounted warriors, with a spirit king's might.
On their bodies were bows, daggers, and implements of war,
The precious swords by their waists gleamed like frost.
Right there and then, the two of them for victory vied,
Who could have known that Xiang Tuo had already died?
At that moment, the Master was filled with dread and fear—
Build a temple for Xiang Tuo in every county: let that be clear.

[translator's note]

In identifying the historical context for this work (beyond the classical sources listed earlier), scholars have turned to other Dunhuang materials, excavated texts, and earlier stories and joke books.[20] Dunhuang texts featuring Confucius answering a long series of questions or engaging in a lengthy exchange with his disciple Ziyu show marked affinities with our text.[21] The repetitions, the conundrums, the question-and-answer form are all typical of folk literature, while the catechismic format is common in exegetical and pedagogical literature. What might have been the ideological agenda here? Is Xiang Tuo supposed to represent another worldview? As early as the third century, he is identified as a Daoist figure. We have this surviving fragment from Xi Kang's (223–262) *Biographies of Lofty Recluses* (*Gaoshi zhuan*): "Confucius asked Xiang Tuo, 'Where do you live?' He said, 'The House of Myriad Flows.' He meant he was flowing with the myriad things, being one with them." Another fragment from Xi Kang's biography claims that both Xiang Tuo and Confucius studied with Laozi.

> Later, the Great Xiang, as a child, pushed the carriage with rush-covered wheels in a game. Confucius waited for him but passed by him without recognizing him. He asked, "Where does the Great Xiang live?" He said, "The House of the Myriad Flows." It was only when he went to the house that he knew that the child was Master Xiang. They made their acquaintance and engaged in discussion. (*ZY* 726)

Sage kings are said to wrap their carriage wheels with rushes for fear of harming the earth, the rocks and the vegetation on their way to perform the Feng and Shan sacrifices (*SJ* 28.20; *HS* 25A.1201). Carriages with rush-covered wheels are also used to bring honored men to the court because of its presumed comfort (*HHS* 83.2757). Xiang Tuo is also called Master Xiang and the Great Xiang. The hagiographical intent is obvious. Xiang Tuo came to be included in the pantheon of Daoist gods in some texts in the Daoist canon. According to Chen Yaowen (1573–1619) and Dong Sizhang (1586–1628), Xiang Tuo was honored as the god of children.[22] Official geographical compilations from the Ming and Qing dynasties mentioned temples devoted to Xiang Tuo in Shanxi.[23]

Xiang Tuo also enters the Buddhist pantheon. Perhaps in response to the Daoist notion that Laozi went to India to "convert the barbarians" (*hua Hu* 化胡), Chinese Buddhists told the story of Buddha sending his disciples to China to be reborn as sages to prepare the Chinese for Buddhist truth. Thus the *Sutra of Pure Acts of Dharma* (*Qingjing fa xing jing* 清淨法行經) declares: "The Buddha sent three disciples to teach and transform China: the Bodhisattva Gentle Child (Rutong pusa 儒童菩薩) is what they call Confucius; the Bodhisattva Pure Light (Jingguang pusa 淨光菩薩) is what they call Yan Hui; the Disciple of Great Light (Mahākāśyapa 摩訶伽葉) is what they call Laozi."[24] One sixth-century text quotes the *Sutra of the End of Dharma* (*Fa meijin jing* 法沒盡經) that claims that Laozi, Confucius, and Xiang Tuo are all bodhisattvas preparing the Chinese for conversion.[25]

There are other clues in the ballad that suggest Xiang Tuo's links with Buddhism. Xiang Tuo has "a special mien" (*you xiang* 有相), which may be associated with the manifestations (*xiang* 相) of Buddha and his followers. One of the conundrums refers to the "gate of emptiness," a byword for the Buddhist path. The hundred-foot tree may be connected to the bodhi tree, the site for meditation and enlightenment. The underground stone hall of Xiang Tuo is guarded by Vajradhara (*jingang* 金剛), a Buddhist guardian deity. Xiang Tuo's petrification reminds us that the Buddha's body is compared to stone. Indeed, the stone hall may recall contemporary Buddhist temple schools in Dunhuang. His endurance of violence and the "spirit king" vindicating him all have Buddhist echoes. One of the manuscripts was signed by a Buddhist who copied the text in a Buddhist temple in 943. Citing some of these Buddhist references, Zhang Chengjian concludes that the demonized Confucius in the ballad may reflect the tension between Buddhists and Confucian scholars during the Tang dynasty and the Five Dynasties.[26] There was ferocious persecution of Buddhists and widespread destruction of Buddhist temples in 845 and again in the 900s.

The Confucian allusions are also unmistakable. Confucius concludes at the end of his exchange with Xiang Tuo that "the young ones should be held in awe." The same expression appears in the *Analects* (9.23): "The young ones should be held in awe. How can we know that the generation of the future does not measure up to the present one?" Indeed, the whole exchange can be presented as the exegesis for that line—that is, it provides the backstory for explaining why Confucius makes that statement. After all, that is the modus operandi for the exegetical traditions of the *Odes* and the *Annals*: they purport to answer the question of why something was said or written, often by narrating a story. Other allusions to the *Analects* confirm Xiang Tuo as the embodiment of its teachings which Confucius tries to undermine. Confucius invites Xiang Tuo to join him and "roam the world together." Xiang Tuo refuses, citing his obligations as a son and a brother, echoing the *Analects* (4.19): "When your father and mother are alive, do not travel afar. If you have to travel, you must do so with a fixed goal." Xiang Tuo disparages games of chance, which Confucius encourages in the ballad but recommends only with biting sarcasm in the *Analects* (17.22): "Hard indeed it is to deal with those who gorge themselves with food all day long without using their minds! Aren't there ones who engage in games of chance and chess? To do things like that would be more worthwhile than doing nothing at all!" Xiang Tuo values filial piety more than conjugal affection; such arguments are implied in *Mencius* (4B.30), although according to "The Mean," "the Way of the noble man finds its beginning in the relationship between husband and wife."

Some references seem merely jocular, as when Confucius claims that pines and cypresses stay evergreen because of their "stout hearts" 心中強, recalling the Master's exclamation in the *Analects* (9.28): "It is only when it becomes cold that we know that pines and cypresses are the last to fade." Pines and cypresses symbolize the noble man's indomitable spirit that shines through adversities. Confucius in the ballad may imply that idea but also points to a more pedestrian explanation—pines and cypresses have a strong hardwood core—which leads to Xiang Tuo's refutation: *hu* bamboo stays evergreen although they are hollow in the middle and bend with the wind.

By contrast, the argument over "leveling differences in the entire world under heaven" (*ping que tianxia* 平却天下) contains the kernel of an important debate. The word translated as "to level" (*ping* 平) is polyvalent: it can also mean "to pacify" or "to bring peace and order." To bring peace and order to all under heaven (*ping tianxia* 平天下) is the ultimate goal of moral self-cultivation and its progressive extension to order for the family and the state, according to "The Great Learning" in the *Record of Rituals*. Mencius talks about "bringing peace and good governance to all under heaven" (*pingzhi tianxia* 平治天下) as his personal mission (*Mencius* 2B.12). Zhuangzi speaks of "making all things equal" (*qiwu* 齊物, *ZZ* 2), overcoming the opposition of even life and death, waking and dreaming, self and other; at the same time he decries futile efforts to efface the differences between things. The Daoist scripture *Canon of Great Leveling* (*Taiping jing*, ca. second–third century) explains its name as follows: "great" refers to the merit of heaven in covering everything; "leveling" refers to earth; earth can "nourish the myriad things" because it is level.[27] It states: "When heaven and earth bestow their generative and transformative powers equally, then the exalted and the debased, the great and the small, will be like one, and there is no more contention and judicial disputes."[28] The equality of dharma for the past, present, and future generations (*sanshi fa pingdeng* 三世法平等) is a recurrent refrain in Buddhist sutras. The word *ping* thus has major reverberations in Confucian, Daoist, and Buddhist teachings. In the ballad, Confucius's argument brings to mind the above quoted lines from the Daoist scripture,[29] while Xiang Tuo, reasserting the importance of social and political distinctions, echoes the Confucian emphasis on the fulfillment of normative social and familial roles through the rectification of names (see chapter 1, 1.9, 1.49; *Analects* 12.11, 13.3; *Mencius* 3A.3). In sum, Confucius and Xiang Tuo in the ballad become cyphers for a range of ideological positions, and not infrequently we find Xiang Tuo belittling Confucius by becoming the true exponent of Confucian ideas.

We do not find any mention of the story of Confucius and Xiang Tuo in extant Chinese texts from about the tenth century to the early sixteenth century. From the late sixteenth century onward, possibly as a result of a flourishing publishing industry, we know of a plethora of works retelling this story, often in primers or didactic texts that were produced in vast numbers until early twentieth century. They all exclude the verse section on the homicidal Confucius. Xiang Tuo as the precocious child and Confucius as one eager to learn from all and sundry (including children) are upheld as exemplars in texts such as the primer *Three-Character Classic*. The story also becomes widely known in Japan, Korea, and Vietnam.[30] Versions of the story also exist in Tibetan, Mongol, Thai, Manchu, Khmer, Vietnamese, Malay, and Javanese.[31] One famous version is included in the Japanese collection, *Tales from Past and Present* (*Konjaku monogatari shū* 今昔物語集, eleventh–twelfth century). Details localizing the story introduce interesting perspectives: in a later Khmer version, Confucius remarks that

Cau Thuk (Xiang Tuo) will become a bodhisattva; versions in Malay and Javanese add Islamic elements.[32]

Punishing Confucius

If the disparaged Confucius reflects the tensions between Buddhists and followers of Confucius, then we may expect a more troubled fate for the sage in a millenarian movement led by someone who, influenced by Christian tracts, believed that he was the son of God and younger brother of Jesus Christ: such was the claim of Hong Xiuquan (1814–1864), one of the leaders of the Taiping Rebellion (1850–1864), which spawned one of the most destructive civil wars in human history. The text that chronicles his rise, deifies him, and presents him as the unquestioned leader of the Taiping Rebellion, *The Taiping Heavenly Chronicle* (*Taiping tianri*, "announced" in 1848 and published in 1862), addresses him as the "Heavenly King" or "Lord." Spanning events from 1837 to 1847, the chronicle "comprises three major segments: a summary of the Book of Genesis and the story of Jesus Christ, the visionary journey made by Hong Xiuquan in Heaven, and Hong Xiuquan's proselytizing activities on earth."[33] Taken in a sedan chair on an eastward road to Heaven, Hong's belly is slit open upon arrival, and "the old was taken out and replaced by the new." The Heavenly Mother welcomes him and cleanses him in a river and presents him to his Heavenly Father, "who wore a tall hat, a black dragon robe, and had a flowing blonde beard reaching his abdomen." Hong is tasked with driving away a demon with a square head and red eyes from Heaven, but the deluded ones in Heaven want to run away with him. The Heavenly Father issues a decree to capture and bring back whoever wants to run away with the demon *and* to drive out whoever harbors evil intentions to assist the demon. Deliberations along these lines lead to a confrontation with Confucius:

3.6 They [the Heavenly Father and Hong Xiuquan] pondered the reasons why demons and evil spirits wrought havoc: everything could be traced to the many errors in Confucius's books of instruction. The Heavenly Father and Supreme Deity gave orders to have three kinds of books arrayed. He pointed them out for the Lord [Hong Xiuquan] to see and said, "Books like these are what are left behind, when earlier I descended to the mundane world, manifested my traces, and set forth warnings. These books are real; there are no errors in them. And books like these are what are left behind when earlier I sent your older brother Christ to descend to the mundane world to manifest his divine traces, give up his life to redeem sins, and act. These books are also real; there are no errors in them. Those books are what Confucius left behind—they are what you studied in the mundane world. They are full of errors; even you were corrupted by them just from studying them." The Heavenly Father and Supreme Deity thus reprimanded Confucius: "Why did you cause people to become so muddle-headed? It's because of you that the common people do not know me. Is it possible that your fame is even greater than mine?" Confucius started out by straining to make his case, but ultimately, he grew quiet and pensive and had nothing more to say. The Heavenly Elder Brother, Christ, also reprimanded Confucius: "You compiled these kinds of texts to teach people—even my own younger brother was led astray by your books just from studying them!" All the angels blamed him as well. The Lord also castigated Confucius: "You compiled these kinds of books to teach people— are you so good at writing books?" When Confucius saw that everyone in High Heaven was pinning blame on him, he secretly escaped from Heaven, hoping to leave together with the head of demons and evil spirits. The Heavenly Father and Supreme Deity thus sent the Lord and the angels to pursue Confucius, and they trussed Confucius up and brought him to the Heavenly Father and Supreme Deity. The Heavenly Father and Supreme Deity, in extreme fury, ordered the angels to whip him. Confucius knelt in front of Christ, the Heavenly Elder Brother, and again and again begged for forgiveness. The blows went on and on, and Confucius did not stop begging to be spared. The Heavenly Father and Supreme Deity, considering that his merit made up for his crimes, allowed him to stay in Heaven to enjoy his good fortune. But he was forever barred from descending to the mundane world.[34]

[translator's note]
Heaven here has a porous boundary with the human realm. Its depiction borrows from Buddhist imagery, and its fantastic battles recall *Journey to the West* (*Xiyou ji*). Despite his humiliation and punishment, Confucius, called here by the name Kong Qiu, is recognized for "merit that made up for his crimes" and allowed to stay in Heaven, although this tolerance also

seems to be a kind of confinement forestalling his influence in the human world. (Contrast this, for example, with the unrelenting logic that consigns Plato and Aristotle to Limbo, the first circle of hell, in Dante's *Divine Comedy*.) Perhaps this amounts to an awkward attempt to accommodate the Confucian legacy in the new Taiping order. In recounting Hong Xiuquan's forty-day sojourn in Heaven, the text makes no mention of his first encounter with Christianity through a Christian pamphlet, "Good Words to Admonish the World" (Quanshi liangyan) outside an examination hall in Guangzhou in 1836. "With this omission, *The Taiping Heavenly Chronicle* elides Hong Xiuquan's previous identity as a Confucian student."[35] That fact, however, is obliquely referred to in the passage quoted above: "even my own younger brother [i.e., Hong Xiuquan] was led astray by your books just from studying them!" Despite such vitriol, and despite the Qing general Zeng Guofan's (1811–1872) lamentation that the "crisis of civilization unprecedented since the beginning of time" brought about by the Taiping rebels made "our Confucius and Mencius wail bitterly in the Nine Springs," many Taiping tracts and documents setting forth the new Taiping order are filled with allusions and references to canonical classics in the Confucian tradition.[36]

Ambiguous Rebellion

If the homicidal Confucius in the Xiang Tuo ballad and the abject Confucius in the Taiping tract represent limit cases of "counter-tradition," what should we expect from scholars who identify with the ideals of Confucian thought but also express skeptical or heterodox views? From the twentieth century on, there have been assiduous attempts to recover "a counter-tradition from within"—that is, critical voices within the Confucian tradition that somehow "herald modernity." One of the most frequently lionized figures in this connection is the late Ming thinker Li Zhi (1527–1602), whose provocative attacks against the burden of ossified tradition and the hypocrisy of self-styled Confucian scholars were nevertheless mixed with fervent admiration of Confucius. Anticipating controversy, he gave titles such as *A Book to be Burned* (*Fenshu*) and *A Book to be Hidden* (*Cangshu*) to his writings.[37] He slit his throat in prison on May 6, 1602. His incarceration was the result of accusations that his heretical and aberrant writings and unconventional conduct undermined the mores of society. Li Zhi's "anti-Confucian" writings are often marked by humor, irony, and self-dramatizing display, as in the following examples:

3.7 "Praise of Liu Xie" 讚劉諧 [38]

There is a Master of the Learning of the Way who sports impressive shoes with high ridges, long sleeves and broad sashes, the headgear of Fundamental Principles, and the clothes of Normative Relationships. Picking up snippets of writings and snatches of discourses, he thinks he is truly a disciple of Confucius.

He once ran into Liu Xie. Liu Xie, a clever scholar, saw him and sneered, "This is someone who does not yet know anything about my older brother, Zhongni."

That man changed color and rose in anger: "'If Heaven had not brought Confucius into the world, the ten thousand ages would be like one long night.' What sort of person are you? How dare you call Confucius by his sobriquet 'Zhongni' and refer to him as your older brother?"

Liu Xie said, "Little wonder then that the sages of antiquity like Fuxi and those before him walked around by burning paper torches for light all day long!" That person grew quiet and stopped. But how could he have known that there was supreme wisdom in Liu's words!

Li Zhi heard about this and expressed his commendation: "These words are simple yet to the point, concise yet filled with deeper meanings. They can break down the snares of confusion and light up the sky! If Liu Xie's words are like this, one can imagine his fine character. For although this comes out of a joke of the moment, a hundred generations cannot alter the reach of its meaning."

[translator's note]
Liu Xie, a friend of Li Zhi, was a Ming dynasty scholar-official famous for "opposing those above him while not showing any lack of courtesy for those below him." "Learning of the Way" (*daoxue*) refers to the Song dynasty interpretation of the Confucian classics, often specifically Zhu Xi's (1130–1200) commentaries, which became the interpretation adopted as standard in the civil service examination. In an autobiographical account, Li Zhi describes his frustrations with Zhu Xi's commentaries: "I felt no affinities with Master Zhu's deep intentions."[39] "If Heaven had not brought

Confucius into the world, the ten thousand ages would be like one long night": these two lines, reportedly found on the pillar of a post station, are cited in the record of Zhu Xi's conversations with his disciples.[40] Liu Xie scoffs at these lines by reminding the reader of the centuries of civilization predating Confucius, but his "disrespectful" reference to Confucius as his older brother also implies closeness and affinity.

3.8 "Colophon on Confucius's Portrait at the Ganoderma Buddha Temple" 題孔子像於芝佛院 [41]

People all regard Confucius as the great sage, and I too regard him as the great sage. They all consider the teachings of Laozi and the Buddha as heresies, and I too consider them heresies. It is not that everyone truly knows about the great sage and heresies, it is what has become familiar through what they have heard from the teachings of their fathers and teachers. It is not that their fathers and teachers truly know about the great sage and heresies, it is what has become familiar through what they have heard from Confucian scholars of earlier generations. It is also not that Confucian scholars of earlier generations truly knew about the great sage and heresies; it is because they thought Confucius had uttered such words. When Confucius said, "Sagehood is not something I am capable of," people thought that he was being modest. When he said, "Attack the wrong beginnings," people thought that he must have been referring to Laozi and the Buddha.

Confucian scholars of earlier generations spoke about this on the basis of conjecture; fathers and teachers recite this by following inherited teachings; the young ones listen to this with a hazy lack of comprehension. Ten thousand mouths speak the same words, they cannot be challenged; a thousand years march to the same tune, there is no self-reflection. People do not say that they are "reciting his words in vain," but rather that they "already know him as a person." They do not say anything about "forcibly presenting 'not knowing' as 'knowing,'" but rather that it is "to regard what one knows as what one knows." By now, even if one has eyes, there is no wherewithal to use them!

What kind of person am I that I dare to say that I have eyes? I am also just following the multitude. Having followed the multitude in regarding Confucius as a sage, I have also followed the multitude in serving him. That is why I have followed the multitude in serving Confucius at the Ganoderma Buddha Temple.

★ ★ ★

[translator's note]

In 1580, Li Zhi ended his official career by resigning from his post as the prefect of Yao'an. After a sojourn in the Geng household with his friends and patrons that ended in discord, he moved into the Vimalakīrti Temple in 1587 and in the following year took up residence in the Ganoderma Buddha Monastery in present-day Hubei, so named because a Gano-derma (*zhi*, a kind of fungus considered auspicious) in the shape of Bud-dha was discovered at the site when construction for the monastery began. The colophon makes skillful and copious uses of sayings attributed to Confucius. According to *Mencius* (2A.2), "Confucius said, 'Sagehood is not what I am capable of, I am just one who is unflagging in learning and never tires of teaching.'" When Confucius confesses to imperfections or ignorance, Zhu Xi routinely tells us in his influential commentary that this is merely the sage's modesty—that is, his sagehood is beyond doubt. In other words, Confucius does not claim to be an all-knowing sage; it is posterity that has imposed this image on him. Mencius's words are prompted by his disciple Gongsun Chou's question: "Are you, Master, a sage?" Mencius is scandalized ("What are you saying!") and continues by pointing out that even Confucius does not claim to be a sage. By dis-claiming sagehood on behalf of Confucius, Mencius is in effect und`erlying his common ground with Confucius. Li Zhi is hinting at a similar rhetorical sleight of hand.

This rhetorical maneuver is spelled out more clearly in Li Zhi's response to a critic's sarcastic comment that he defies decorum as a kind of subtle Zen twist (*chanji* 禪機), that he perhaps justifies consorting with widows by invoking Confucius's meeting with Nan Zi (see chapter 1, 1.20, chap-ter 4, 4.2): "For the most part my heart is but that of an ordinary person in a mundane crowd. Even Confucius was but a mundane and ordinary kind of person. Anybody can meet Nan Zi, I too can meet Nan Zi, what does it have to do with Zen or subtle twist? Zilu could not understand, no won-der he was displeased that Confucius met her. How much more so for people a thousand years later! If anybody could meet Nan Zi, but the Master could not meet her, then there is for the Master an 'inevitable rejection of alternatives.' The Master has 'no inevitable rejection of alter-natives,' what is to prevent him from meeting her?"[42] To assert Confu-cius's "ordinariness" is to claim affinity with him; to defy decorum turns out to be another way to imitate the sage.

Li Zhi was attacked for his "heresies" (*yiduan* 異端). He wrote in a letter to his friend Jiao Hong (1540–1620): "Now the common run of humanity and all kinds of fake moralists band together to brand me as a heretic, so I figure I might as well become a heretic to spare them the bother of imposing an empty title on me."[43] The phrase translated as "heresies" appears in the *Analects*, where it means "wrong beginnings" or "divergent paths." The word translated as "attack" (*gong* 攻) also means "to work on." Confucius said, "To attack a problem from a wrong beginning—that is harmful indeed" (*Analects* 2.16). Some commentators take this as a warning against other teachings, such as those of Mozi and Yang Zhu. But since these thinkers postdate Confucius by a century or more, and since the scenario of rival thinkers disparaging each other's teachings was more characteristic of the fourth and third century BCE, the historical Confucius could not have intended such sectarian implications. (Whether this means a later dating for the *Analects* is another issue.) In any case, it would have been wildly anachronistic to infer Confucius's attack against "heresies" like Buddhism. In other words, Li Zhi decries intolerant and sanctimonious Confucian orthodoxy as being a far cry from Confucius. Confucius said to Zilu, "To regard what one knows as what one knows, and what one does not know as what one does not know—that is knowledge" (*Analects* 2.17). Li Zhi believes that by distilling from this saying only the blind certainty that "one knows what one knows," his contemporaries have given up on humility, intellectual honesty, and recognition of their limits.

One would expect from such a tirade against conformity that Li Zhi would set forth his different views. Yet the colophon begins and ends with his profession of "following the multitude" (*congzong* 從眾). His way of "following the multitude," however, is highly idiosyncratic and defies conventional boundaries: he is worshipping Confucius in a Buddhist monastery. Indeed, he might have brought the portrait of Confucius there. Elsewhere he referred to Confucius, Laozi, and the Buddha as "the three great sages" and opined that "the three teachings (Confucianism, Daoism, Buddhism) can be subsumed under Confucianism." Syncretism was in the air in the late sixteenth century, but Li Zhi also flaunted deliberate incongruities in his provocative sartorial choice: he shaved his head in keeping with Buddhist rules but kept his long beard; he lived in a Buddhist monastery but often favored Confucian robes and headgear.[44]

Confucius said in the *Analects* (9.3): "A ceremonial cap made of worsted linen is prescribed by ritual. Now silk is used. It is simpler, and I follow the multitude. For a subject to bow to a ruler below the dais is prescribed by ritual. Now he bows after ascending the dais. This is excessive pride. Even if I have to go against the multitude, I follow the rule of bowing from below." Earnestness and self-mockery are inexorably intertwined in Li Zhi's implicit allusion to "following the multitude." He may yet be immodestly imitating the sage, whose decision to follow certain rituals but not others is premised on judicious deliberation, not blind conformity. While his contemporaries may be "reciting his words in vain," Li Zhi knows, like Sima Qian, "what Confucius was like as a person" (chapter 1, 1.72). Just like Liu Xie, who calls Confucius his older brother, Li Zhi sometimes refers to Confucius as "my Master" or "our Confucius." According to tradition, King Wen of Zhou compiled the hexagrams of the *Classic of Changes* and Confucius explicated them. Li Zhi wrote: "In my opinion, the Master is what King Wen relies on for transmission, . . . and I am what the Master relies on for transmission."[45] Li Zhi implies that his own interpretation of Confucius's explication places him in a genealogy of sages despite, or perhaps because of, its unorthodox twists.

Li Zhi's sarcasm can be savagely comic. A joke book attributed to him includes "A Song of Laughter" (Hehe ling 呵呵令), which scoffs at gods and sages, including Confucius: "I also laugh at that old fellow Confucius: What is it about your mumble jumble on moral principles and fine writings? Those alive and kicking are done in for nothing."[46] But the barbs of jokes are trained much more frequently on pedantic Confucian scholars.[47] The following examples are from the "section on pedants" (fuliu bu 腐流部) in *Expanded Record of a Forest of Jokes* (Xiaolin guangji 笑林廣記), compiled by the Master of Play (Youxi zhuren 遊戲主人, 1791):[48]

3.9 Seeking Confirmation from Confucius 證孔子

Two Confucian scholars could not agree. Each took pride on being a true scholar of the Way and slandered the other as fake. They argued for a long time without reaching a solution and thus sought instruction from Confucius. Confucius came down the steps, bowed to them, and said, "My Way is very great. Why does it have to be the same always? You two gentlemen are both true scholars of the Way. I have always looked up to you. How could you be fake?" Both men were overjoyed and withdrew. The disciples of Confucius said, "How obsequious you are, sir!" Confucius said, "For people like this it's good enough to coax them and get them going. Why tangle with them?"

★ ★ ★

3.10 Paying His Respects at the Temple of Confucius 謁孔廟
A person who became a government student through connections and money paid his respects at the temple of Confucius. Confucius came down from his seat to pay his respects in return. The scholar said, "Today we have the ritual of a disciple paying his respects to the Master. You, sir, should just sit and receive the homage." Confucius said, "How dare I presume? You are the disciple of my elder brother Kong Square Hole.[49] I absolutely cannot receive your obeisance."

The following story by the eighteenth-century poet Yuan Mei, taken from his collection of strange tales, *Sequel to What the Master Did Not Speak About* (*Xu Zi bu yu*), mocks exegetes, scholars, and Confucian philosophers of various stripes who claim to interpret canonical texts and the teachings of Confucius. For the *qilin* or *lin* in the title, see chapter 1, 1.64. The *qilin* lamenting the misinterpretation of exegetes seems to be the cypher for Confucius himself.

3.11 "The *Qilin* Cried Out Against the Injustice It Suffered" 麒麟喊冤[50]
There was a scholar surnamed Qiu, a native of Wu. He had been studying the composition of examination essays since his earliest youth. After taking the examination several times without achieving success, he said in anger, "The Song Confucians misled me!" He thus burned all their expositions and the records of their discussions and devoted himself to evidential learning, honoring Zheng Xuan and Kong Yingda as sages and disdaining the two Cheng brothers and Zhu Xi.[51] His family was poor. Traveling for his studies in the Chu and Shu regions, he passed by Mount Emei. As he was sitting under an ancient pine tree and going over the *Commentary and Sub-commentary on Ceremonies and Rituals*, a white-browed tiger picked him up with its jaws and headed off. After proceeding for a few miles, it dropped Qiu into a deep valley and left. Qiu was penitent: "This must be retribution for turning against the Song Confucians."

Just as he was fretting, he saw that a stone gate was wide open on one side of the valley. Qiu entered and saw an imposing building with the name "Hall of Luminous Culture" on its beam. On both sides of the hall were ranged hundreds of thousands of books, their number unfathomably vast. Rummaging through the titles, Qiu was sure that the Six Classics would be honored as preeminent. Little did he expect that there was nothing of the sort even when he finished his search. He was mystified. A man clad in the cap and gown of antiquity appeared by his side, leaning against the door and just standing there. Qiu bowed and asked, "Which one is the god presiding at this place?" "Sage Cang" was the answer.[52]

Qiu asked, "Sage Cang invented writing, so it is fitting that there are hundreds of thousands of scrolls everywhere. The ancient Six Classics alone are missing. Why?"

The man in antique cap and gown replied, "These books have always been here, only they are called *Odes*, *Documents*, and *Zhou Changes*. They are not called Canonical Classics.[53] Ever since meddlers from the Han dynasty labeled them the Six Classics, men spun commentaries and subcommentaries that were filled with fabrication and fanciful nonsense. As a result, the Supreme Deity was sorely provoked and blamed Sage Cang for inventing writing, which built the steps leading to such horrors. From that point on, commentaries and subcommentaries have been banished from the Hall of Luminous Culture. That's why you couldn't find any with all your rummaging."

Qiu asked, "How did commentaries and subcommentaries rouse the anger of Heaven above?"

"It's a long story. Just be patient and listen. Don't you know that for the myriad kingdoms in the nine continents, there is only one Heaven? Ever since Pangu opened up the cosmos, through the eras of the three thearchs and five sovereigns, none failed to revere High Heaven, and Heaven too had been complaisantly enjoying the offerings of sacrificial bulls over several thousand years. Suddenly, at the end of Eastern Han, five demonic spirits sporting imperial headgear and dragon robes barged into the Heavenly Palace, each declaring its name. The one calling himself Raging Red Flames had a red face with a curly beard—his appearance was especially savage and sinister. There were in addition four of his brothers. The one wearing green was called Upward Spiritual Power; the one wearing yellow was called Holding Essential Knot; the one wearing white was called White Summoning Square; the one wearing black was called Mingling Light Discipline. Raising their eyebrows, with their heads held high, they made a horrific din. It was actually their wish to usurp the Supreme Deity's position and divide the realm into five kingdoms. When the Supreme Deity interrogated them and asked how they came by their names, they just stared and could not answer. The Supreme Deity ordered divine soldiers to capture them.

"Just as their battle was raging on with no resolution in sight, Sage Cang attended court in Heaven. He explained: 'The names of these five spirits all come from the diabolic words of omenology and apocrypha as transmitted by the disciples of Zheng Xuan from the Han dynasty.[54] Just summon Zheng Xuan, and they will submit without putting up a fight." Left with no alternatives, the Supreme Deity ordered the Messenger of the Nine Dark Realms to summon Zheng Xuan and his disciples to the celestial hall. Seeing that Zheng's deportment was sober and steady and that he could drink three hundred cups of wine without becoming inebriated, the Supreme Deity appointed him the administrator of the Hall of Luminous Culture.[55] Only then did the five demonic spirits submit and quiet down.

"Whatever propositions Zheng submitted to the heavenly throne were also decreed by the Supreme Deity as rules to be applied in the world. As time went by, there were among Zheng's ideas some that absolutely could not be put into practice.[56] Using 288 pieces of jade for the headgear of the Son of Heaven almost crushed his head. Having to wear a big fur cloak during the summer sacrifice to the spirit of the earth almost smothered the Son of Heaven. Being allowed only one meal a day and being able to eat again only when urged, the Son of Heaven almost died of hunger. The ritual prescription was to put 2.4 pints of rice in the mouth of the deceased as part of funeral ritual, and to put 4 pints of sorghum into the dead ruler's mouth and 4 pints of millet in the dead official's mouth. If clenched teeth could not be pried open with a horn spoon, then a small hole had to be drilled on the cheek to put the grain in. In all cases, the children and grandchildren of the deceased could not bear to do this. One piece of misinformation bred another, and rote practice without discernment lasted for almost a thousand years.

"One day, as the Supreme Deity was sitting in the Purple Wisteria Palace, he saw that an animal with the scales of a dragon and the mane of a horse had flown down from the clouds. It cried out about the injustice it had suffered: 'Your humble subject is a *qilin*. I don't eat live animals, nor do I step on vegetation, no matter how noxious it is. Everyone commends me as a benevolent animal, and I descend to the human realm only when a sage appears. Little did I expect that those buffoons, the Zheng fellow [Zheng Xuan] and the Kong fellow [Kong Yingda], would make up commentaries and subcommentaries: they claim that for the sacrifice to heaven, music can strike up only when a *qilin*'s hide is used as the drum cover. If their claim is true, then a *qilin* has to be killed every time a ruler offers sacrifice to Heaven. What crime is the *qilin* guilty of that it should suffer such persecution? This kind of talk was only good for fooling the bandits in yellow turbans—they would all bow down upon seeing old Zheng.[57] But if a *qilin* sees him, it would spit in his face for sure!'

"Before it finished speaking, they saw a beauty with cloud-like tresses and rainbow-colored ornaments descending from the sky. With several ladies in tow, she advanced slowly and gracefully. She knelt and said, 'I am Lady Jiang, the consort of a Zhou king. Back then, when the Zhou king went on ritual missions to encourage agriculture, I did not follow along. Now we have this preposterous Zheng fellow who claimed that when the Son of Heaven went about encouraging agriculture, he had to be accompanied by his queen. Women are delicate creatures of the inner chamber; their movements do not take them beyond the threshold. Does it make sense that they would brave frost and rain to come out and encourage agriculture? Wang Su of the Northern Wei dynasty once pointed this out as a mistake. Kong Yingda of the Tang dynasty fiercely berated Wang.[58] Factional partiality and scurrilous lies had come to this!'

"The various ladies made their case together, 'We are the wives of the lords and high officers of the southern states. When our husbands were away, our hearts were filled with worries. "Now that we have come together, / My heart can be at ease." This means peace of mind upon reunion—this is but a common emotion. Zheng glossed "coming together" (*gou* 覯) as "having intercourse" (*gou* 媾), meaning the heart was at ease after coitus. He glossed "The appointed time was the fifth day, / But he has not arrived on the sixth" by saying that women who had not had sexual congress for five days were sure to become sick with longing.[59] We are all delicately nurtured ladies of lords and princes, we should not be that lustful!'

"The *qilin* by their side stamped its feet and roared with laughter. The Supreme Deity asked what it was all about. The *qilin* said, 'These ladies only knew about blaming Zheng Xuan and did not think of blaming Dai Sheng.[60] Dai compiled the ritual classics; his crime was even greater. When I was in the Numinous Garden of King Wen of Zhou and wandering about with those 'lionhearted noble sons,'[61] I saw that there was no fixed number for King Wen's palace ladies: at the most there were twenty or thirty. There was no such thing as 'nine secondary wives, twenty-seven noble consorts, eighty-one ladies-in-waiting,'[62] and I never saw any rule such as 'using a golden ring to mark the presentation of a consort' or 'using a silver ring to mark the dismissal of a consort.'[63] King Wen toiled without a moment of leisure until the sun set. He 'embraced joy without becoming licentious,'[64] how could he have the time to have coitus with more than a hundred women over fifteen evenings? Dai Sheng was a corrupt official to begin with, he made up the canonical classics pertaining to the inner quarters of the palace to curry favor with benighted rulers. Then Zheng Xuan and his disciples followed along and made further fabrications. This led to the excesses of posterity: in the Sui dynasty palace, five piculs of kohl were consumed daily, and there were more than sixty thousand palace ladies during the Kaiyuan reign. In all such cases, Dai and Zheng were the instigators. Glossing the line 'Stoking disorder with slander, they accomplished nothing,' Zheng and his followers identified 'slander' as 'pounder,' claiming that it was thrust into a woman's vagina as punishment. This is an incident recorded in 'The Biographies of the Thirteen Princes Descended from Emperor Jing.'[65] The Three Dynasties did not have this kind of inhuman punishment.'

"Having heard this, the Supreme Deity was filled with regrets. He heaved a sigh and said, 'I have erred and appointed the wrong man!' He summoned Sage Cang and said, 'You, sir, invented writing, and it was fundamentally a great achievement that has brought benefit to thousands of generations. Great sages like the Duke of Zhou and Confucius all came through your gateway as disciples. How could we have known that the vulgar Confucian scholars of later times would abuse it to this extent! How can we save the situation?'

"Sage Cang said, 'We three brothers invented scripts together. All the scripts I compiled are vertical. The scripts compiled by younger brothers Jusong and Qulu either proceed horizontally leftward or rightward.[66] The ones going left or right are used in the eastern and western regions, and the one going downward is used in China. Now there is only one teaching in the east and the west, while the teachings in China are varied and clamorous to this extent! There is no choice but to summon those who 'find illumination in their heart and see their true nature'—those who try to master the Way of Buddha without ultimately succeeding—to manifest their superpower and make a clean sweep of people like that!'

"The Supreme Deity said, 'It sounds right to summon the Buddha, but why summon one who tries to master the Way of Buddha without ultimately succeeding?'

"Sage Cang said, 'There is no relationship of husband and wife or father and son for the Buddha; that was why Buddhism was considered heterodoxy. I am afraid many would not submit if he were to come to China. The only alternative is to find those who are immersed in the study of Buddhist texts in their youth and escape back to the camp of Duke of Zhou and Confucius in their prime—those who are 'Mohist in conduct but Confucian in name.' Only then would people be willing to submit to them. So-and-So of the Song dynasty is the best example of this.'[67]

"The *qilin* by his side objected, '"Chu was of course at fault, but Qi too has not hit upon the right way."[68] If one goes along with the Han Confucian scholars' notion of using drums covered with *qilin* skin for the sacrifice to Heaven, it would be rotten luck merely for the *qilin*—the Supreme Deity still gets to imbibe his fill. But to put Song Confucian scholars in charge of moral teachings is to have them gloss "the command of Heaven is called moral nature" by saying that Heaven just means Principle.[69] Since antiquity, we have only offered sacrifices to Heaven; there is no such things as offering sacrifices to Principle. Doesn't that mean the blood sacrifices to the Supreme Deity will be cut off in the future? Not only that, I am afraid the pointy-jawed Thunder God would also come and kick up a fuss!'

"The Supreme Deity said, 'Why?' He replied, 'Zhu Xi's comment on the two clauses "When presented with a sumptuous repast, Confucius would alter his expression and rise to his feet" puts it thus: "This was the ritual expressing respect for the host and not a response to the sumptuous repast." Commenting on the next line, "A sudden clap of thunder would certainly make him alter his expression," Zhu said that "it was reverent awe for the anger of Heaven."[70] Doesn't this next line imply that thunder was not what made the difference? From now on none would fear the Thunder God. How can the Thunder God be resigned to this!'

"The Supreme Deity smiled and said, 'There is something to what you said. But the cycles of vital energy have their own timely spans of rise and fall, and even I cannot decide their fate. Let's just summon those who "find illumination in their hearts and see their true nature" and test their skills and competence!' Not long after, he saw Sage Cang leading Song Confucian scholars up the steps of the celestial hall. There were some wearing flowing robes and tall caps and holding the Circle of Supreme Polarity; there were some with their eyes closed, pointing to their hearts and claiming to be "constantly reverent and vigilant"; there were some appreciating flowers and the moon and prided themselves on being "natural and spontaneous."[71] The last four men carried a big bucket with a thousand straws on their shoulders and said, 'This is the bucket of straws.[72] Ever since the death of Confucius and Mencius, none had the power to carry this bucket on their shoulders. Han Yu from the Tang dynasty presumed to carry the bucket on his shoulders, but I ferreted out his correspondence with the Monk Dadian and got incontrovertible evidence of deviance and have overturned *his* bucket.[73] How could Zheng Xuan and Kong Yingda amount to much! Would they dare to make trouble for us?' Before they finished speaking, Raging Red Flames, White Summoning Square, and the other three demonic spirits could indeed be seen crawling through a hole in the wall, and the furor of battle abated as they made their escape. The Supreme Deity was overjoyed and thus ordered these four to take over for the time being as administrators in the Hall of Luminous Culture. This explains the abeyance of Han learning and the absence of commentaries and sub-commentaries in the Hall of Luminous Culture."

Qiu asked, "If that is the case, why are commentaries and subcommentaries by Song Confucians not collected and arranged on the shelves?"

"Having erred once, how can we err again? I am afraid that the Song Confucians will ultimately not occupy this seat of preeminence for too long. Right now, Lu Jiuyuan, Wang Yangming, and the scholars of the current dynasty, including Yan Yuan, Li Gong, and Mao Qiling, all find fault with them."[74]

Just as they were talking, they were suddenly greeted by the sound of bells and drums, and Sage Cang could be heard transmitting the divine decree from within: "I ordered the white tiger to carry Scholar Qiu here. My original intention was to abandon him to the jackals and tigers because I abhorred how he took such great pride in Han learning and poured contempt on the hundred schools; it was like "taking control of the Son of Heaven to issue order to the various lords."[75] Now I hear that he has already repented. We can bestow on him a cup of tea brewed with the mists and clouds of the hills and lead him out of the mountain, so that he can recount who he has heard and enlighten his generation."

The one in the ancient cap and gown led Qiu through roads along winding streams. Qiu asked, "According to Sage Cang, we cannot follow the path of Han learning. According to the *qilin*, Song Confucians are also not worth emulating. But then to which place can I return as my home?"

The spirit said, "The significance of timeliness in the hexagram Following is great indeed![76] Scholars and noble men take action by judging the times,[77] that's why we say that those who follow Heaven will flourish. It's just like using the gods to establish moral teachings. The god Lord Jiang having gone into decline; the god Lord Guan naturally rose to prominence[78]— these are self-evident facts that we can see for ourselves. When Han learning was flourishing, Wang Bi of Jin dynasty wrote his commentary on the *Changes* and cursed Zheng Xuan for having been an old slave. Zheng Xuan revealed himself in broad daylight and immediately took Wang Bi's life.[79] Yuan Dan once said, "People these days would rather say that Confucius was wrong. They would avoid criticizing the errors of Zheng Xuan and Kong Yingda at all costs."[80] That was also because he was afraid of being haunted by Zheng Xuan. Now that the cycle of his vital energy has declined, his ghost no longer has numinous power. And few speak about Zheng Xuan and Kong Yingda! When Song learning was flourishing, the Yuan dynasty offered sacrifices to Zhu Xi, so much so that Genghis Khan was called by name during his sacrifice to Zhu Xi, who was honored as being equal to Heaven. When the first Ming emperor ascended the throne, he appointed Song Lian and three other scholars to lecture on the classics—they were all puny disciples of Zhu Xi. So, the line of transmission continued, and *Complete Meanings of the Four Books* gained currency for the entire realm under heaven.[81] Men of intelligence and insights, all tied up, have all followed its teachings and no longer study anything else. Yang Shen once said, 'There are worms that echo what they hear. Confucian scholars of these days are all echo worms of Song Confucian scholars.'[82] If you do not become an echo worm, how can you attain success in the examination and repay the beneficence of your ruler and your father?"

Qiu said, "Does that mean that the Supreme Deity also likes examination essays?"

The one in ancient cap and gown laughed aloud: "The Supreme Deity is not a licentiate scholar, why does He need examination essays? Not only does the Supreme Deity's domain have no examination essays, Langhuan Cave and the Two Yóu Mountains, divine realms filled with books, are also devoid of this rotten stuff. Tiny characters on small plates—ancient books are for their part not unsightly like that."

Qiu said, "But then why did the examination system produce so many heroic and talented men?"

The spirit said, "Scholars are like marine creatures: One could catch them by fishing, shooting, and also by throwing a net. The big ones are sea dragons and giant turtles, the little ones are breams and carps—they are all bred by the sea, they do not become different because they are fished, shot, or netted. Through the ages, for renowned ministers raised to office through exegetical scholarship on canonical classics, we have so-and-so; for renowned ministers raised to office through poetry, poetic exposition, or disquisitions, we have so-and-so; for renowned ministers raised to office through examination essays, we have so-and-so. How can heroic and talented men be limited by the rules of selection and thus sink into oblivion? Look how Lü Meng was plucked from the ranks of bandits and Guo Ziyi rose up from the fetters of the law.[83] There are notable men even among bandits and criminals, let alone those taking the examination!"

Qiu asked what the Supreme Deity was partial to.

"He loved poetry and the belles-lettres." Qiu asked how he knew this.

"Just think: When the Supreme Deity finished building the White Jade Tower, why did He not summon sober moralists like Ma Liang or Jing Dan to write an account of it? Why did He have to summon the young and giddy Li He? For the Master of the Lotus City, the Immortal Shrine beyond the seas, why did He not summon Zhou Dunyi, the Cheng brothers, Zhu Xi, or those who gathered disciples and lectured on moral principles? Why did He summon Bai Juyi, who loved wine and women, and the wild and impulsive Shi Manqing?"[84]

Qiu suddenly saw the light and was awakened. He bowed low again and said, "If it is as you said, Divine One, then I will abandon Han learning and Song learning and apply myself to poetry and the belles-lettres. How about that?"

The divine one said, "You are mistaken again! Humans are endowed with different strengths and weaknesses. The talent for creative writing is like water. If there is indeed a source, it will naturally become rivers and waterways. Evidential learning and lectures on moral teachings are like fire. Those who have nothing inside have to attach themselves to something—only then can they illuminate meanings, just as fire has to be attached to firewood and coals. You are not endowed with anything in your nature, how can you not look around uncertainly like a suspicious mouse? Furthermore, since you are already steeped in Han learning, let me ask you: What is the name of the rice for the consumption of emperors and kings?" Qiu could not answer.

The divine one said, "Glossing the line 'We wash the grain, slosh, slosh,' Zheng Xuan said, 'Pound it and sift it so that it can become refined grain.' For one peck of coarse-grained millet, pound away a picul and it becomes half-coarse grains, remove another 0.8 picul and it becomes refined grains, remove another 0.9 picul and it becomes imperial fare. Imperial fare is what rulers eat.[85] Just think: When the grains are pounded eight or nine times, where do the husks and outer layers of bran go? Heaven deliberately gives birth to this kind of men who satiate themselves with husks and coarse bran. They either fixate on the details of evidential scholarship or indulge in the grand talk of ultimate principles. Each follows his predilection and skills, and each gravitates to his ranks. I often see Confucius, Buddha, and Laozi meeting in Heaven. They smile at each other, bow, and pass by each other, never exchanging a word. This is the reason for the capaciousness of heaven and earth."

Upon hearing this, Qiu changed color and his countenance was like dead ash. He seemed to want to linger and was reluctant to leave. The divine one said, "Have done already! You were carried in the tiger's jaws and dropped into the mountain valley next to its streams. The *Commentary and Sub-commentary on Ceremonies and Rituals* is more than half eaten up by bookworms. Why don't you make haste and go back?" Qiu bowed again before leaving the cave. He is still alive.

Elusive Counter-Traditions

The picture of Confucius, Laozi, and Buddha passing each other by with a smile wordlessly in heaven in Yuan Mei's story conveys a kind of aspiration for peaceful coexistence or even sympathetic convergence. The hexagram Sui (Following) reveals Yuan Mei's belief in flexibility and timeliness in interpreting Confucius's teachings. It was probably the reason why he named his garden Sui yuan 隨園 (Following Garden). His final comparison of poets with scholars leaves little doubt that he considers the former superior, though they form an exclusive club of superior sensibility that leaves no room for unworthy aspirant like Qiu. This is very much in line with Yuan Mei's widely celebrated image as the free-spirited poet emphasizing spontaneity and "natural sensibility" (*xingling* 性靈). He wrote in one poem dated 1791: "I don't turn back before the gates of Kong and Zheng; / Nor do I bother to tarry at the feast of Cheng and Zhu. / Setting sail, crossing straight to River Yi in the east, / I seek Ziyou among the ranks of culture and learning." 鄭孔門前不掉頭，程朱席上懶勾留. 一帆直渡東沂水，文學班中訪子游.[86] He has no patience for Han and Tang exegetes (Zheng Xuan, Kong Yingda) or Song philosophers (the Cheng brothers, Zhu Xi), but wants to head straight to the source of Confucius's wisdom. River Yi recalls Zeng Dian's joy bathing in River Yi and chanting odes (see the introduction). Ziyou is Confucius's disciple commended for his culture and learning in the *Analects* (11.3) and here symbolizes a kind of fusion of ethics, learning, and aesthetics. Yuan Mei may also want to claim a special affinity with Ziyou because the latter is the only disciple of Confucius from the south (the ancient state of Wu), and Yuan hailed from Hangzhou and lived in Nanjing.

The scathing critique of various exegetical traditions here is also a self-conscious display of erudition. In other words, Yuan is positioning himself as the superior exegete, and similar critiques of Han and Song commentaries and of the very notion of "classic" appear in Yuan's jottings, letters, and essays. For example, most of the canonical interpretations he ridicules in the above story can be found almost verbatim in an entry titled "Far-Fetched Errors in Exegetical Commentaries on the Classics" (Jingzhu miuwu 經注謬誤) in a collection of his jottings (*YM* 13: 3–6). In his preface to a book on the principles of historical writings, he regards the sacralizing notion of "canonical classics" (*jing* 經) as ultimately obfuscating: "In antiquity there were historical writings but no canonical classics" (*YM* 5: 211–12). Here "historical writings" (*shi* 史) encompass records, documents, and accounts of the words and institutions of the ancients. Yuan Mei also questions the idea that Confucius played an active role in compiling and editing the classics (see chapter 1, 1.52–1.67). He claims to be following Confucius's injuction to "learn as much as possible while leaving blank what is doubtful" (*Analects* 2.18) in developing his skeptical attitude (*YM* 6: 469–70). He declares upon ruminations on inconsistencies and the grounds for skepticism in the classics: "Personally washing both eyes with autumnal water, / I've never been deceived by the ancients my whole life" 兩眼自將秋水洗, 一生不受古人欺 (*YM* 10: 693).

The analogy of creativity with water and exegetical obsession with fire in the story is also developed in Yuan's letter to his friend Cheng Jiyuan, where fire is not only dependent but also destructive: "At its utmost reach, it will have set the plains ablaze; it will have burned up big locust trees. Yet ultimately what it will have obtained are nothing but ashes." Unlike writers who "learn for their own sakes" (*weiji* 為己), evidential scholars "learn for the sake of others" (*weiren* 為人) because they are parsing meanings on behalf of others (*YM* 7: 593).[87] He wrote in a letter to the scholar and poet

Hui Dong (1697–1758): "There are pitfalls in Song learning, and even more so in Han learning. Song scholars are preoccupied with the metaphysical, that is why their theory of mind and nature comes close to being abstruse and empty. Han scholars are preoccupied with the tangible, that is why their commentaries are full of fabrications" (*YM* 6: 346). Yuan Mei skewers both the questionable historical details in Han exegetical scholarship and the speculative abstractions in Song Neo-Confucianism.[88]

Yuan Mei lived during the height of Qing philology, which drew on Han exegetical scholarship (Han Learning). At the same time, Song Neo-Confucianism remained influential, not least because Zhu Xi's commentary on the Four Books was part of the examination system. The notion of a sagely lineage or "Genealogy of the Way" (*Daotong* 道統), derisively depicted as "a bucket or straws" (*daotong* 稻桶) through a homophonic pun in the above story, presumes the insistence on the continuous transmission of correct interpretations and breeds intolerance of differences. It fuels the mutual recriminations of adherents of "Han Learning" and "Song Learning." By dismissing the notion of *daotong*, Yuan Mei is actually better equipped to see the merits and drawbacks of both sides. Despite his criticism, Yuan Mei drew on both "Han Learning" and "Song Learning" in his writings and often defended one to the partisans of the other in his letters. Likewise, his condemnation of examination essays as "rotten stuff" and orthodox interpretations of the Four Books as suffocating should not obscure his complete mastery of such compositions and exegetical traditions. He was repeatedly successful in the examinations and gained his *jinshi* degree at the age of twenty-four.

Like the jokes about Confucius and Li Zhi's satire, Yuan Mei's criticism of the Confucian tradition is rooted in unwavering commitment to its fundamental values and deep reverence of Confucius. He claims to be "skeptical about the classics to maintain his faith in the sage" (*YM* 6: 347). Yuan Mei mentions Confucius more than two hundred times in his collected writings. As noted earlier, elite barbs are usually trained on Confucius's misguided interpreters rather than on the sage himself. Women and children outsmarting Confucius feeds on the carnivalistic spirit of challenging authority figures without turning into real reversals. It is only when opposition taps into rival religious systems, as in the case of the Xiang Tuo ballad and the Taiping Chronicle, that we have rumbles of counter-traditions.

CHAPTER IV

Settling Scores with Confucius

In June 1898, the scholar Kang Youwei (1858–1927) presented his *Study of Confucius's Remaking of Institutions* (*Kongzi gaizhi kao* 孔子改制考) to the Guangxu emperor (r. 1847–1908). This provided the theoretical justification of the so-called Hundred Days Reforms (June 11–September 21, 1898), whereby the emperor and a group of committed intellectuals led by Kang and his student Liang Qichao (1873–1929) sought to push reforms through edicts and thereby create legal, educational, military, administrative, and financial institutions inspired by European and Japanese models. Kang proclaimed Confucian precedents for these reforms found in canonical classics and also envisioned turning his brand of Confucianism into an organized state religion. The reforms came to naught when Empress Dowager Cixi (1835–1908), the de facto ruler, supported by conservative forces, locked up the emperor and executed the reformers she could find. Kang and Liang managed to flee to Japan.

On June 16, 1921, in his preface to a collection of essays by the scholar Wu Yu (1871–1949), Hu Shi (1891–1962), the champion of the New Culture Movement, praised Wu by comparing him to a street sweeper cleaning up "Confucian dust and grime." Wu Yu's theme was "the unfitness of the Way of Confucius for modern life"; he had written two years earlier about Confucian rituals and moral teachings that "eat up people," echoing Lu Xun's short story, "Diary of a Madman" (1918). Hu Shi paired Wu Yu with his colleague at Beijing University, Chen Duxiu (1879–1942), another vociferous critic of Confucius and cofounder of the Chinese Communist Party, quoting with approval Chen's rebuttal of those who blamed Confucius's followers and interpreters for distorting the sage's teachings but sought to defend their fundamental validity. Hu Shi concludes, "Precisely because for two thousand years, repressive (literally, cannibalistic) rituals, teachings, rules, and regulations have hung up the shop sign of Confucius, this shop sign—no matter whether it is an authentic or fake one—has to be taken down, crushed, and burnt! I am going to introduce to all Chinese youths Mr. Wu Youling (Wu Yu): this old hero from Sichuan who single-handedly attacked Confucius Inc.!"[1]

A lot had happened in the twenty-three years separating these two events. The Qing dynasty, and along with it the whole imperial system, collapsed with a series of uprisings that started in October 1911. The last Qing emperor abdicated in February 1912. The Qing military commander Yuan Shikai (1859–1916) became the president of the nascent republic and promptly showed his dictatorial intention. In December 1915, Yuan restored the monarchy and declared himself emperor, only to abdicate after eighty-three days in face of strong opposition. The fact that in 1914 Yuan ordered the resumption of the worship of Confucius in schools and temples and that various warlords invoked the figure of Confucius—as Lu Xun pointed out in his essay "Confucius in Modern China" (see below)—seems to taint the sage by association. In the meantime, a new generation of intellectuals tried to "save China" by remaking its culture. In 1915, Chen Duxiu founded the journal *New Youth* (*Xin qingnian*); one of its mantras was to establish vernacular Chinese as the medium of expression. Lu Xun published "Diary of a Madman" in the April 2, 1918, issue of *New Youth*. In this story, the madman's diary excoriating wonted traditional virtues and rules as "cannibalistic" is written in the vernacular, while the narrator's preface, which tells of the madman's "descent into paranoia" and "recovery," is written in classical Chinese. The bifurcation establishes the vernacular as the language mercilessly confronting national malaise and rejecting the burden of tradition.

The New Culture Movement soon took a political turn; anger over the allies' recognition of Japanese claims to German concessions in Shandong at the Versailles Peace Conference sparked widespread protests, starting with some three thousand Beijing students demonstrating at Tiananmen on May 4, 1919. The May Fourth Movement had numerous and at times contradictory crosscurrents, weaving patriotic fervor and anti-imperialism with a broader quest for cultural transformation, personal freedom, science, and democracy. Included in the following are the critiques and reappraisals of Confucius by several May Fourth intellectuals. It is important to remember, however, that these writers were often steeped in the values they set out to dismantle, and that their arguments were sometimes determined by political and polemical contexts, which means that they might express different views elsewhere.

The whiplash from Kang Youwei's reinvention of Confucius to the tide of tirades against Confucius during the May Fourth period in some ways typifies how culture wars and proxy wars have unfolded through the figure of Confucius in the modern period. In 1934, under the leadership of Chiang Kai-shek (1887–1975), the newly resurgent Nationalist Party (KMT or GMD), which had unified in China in 1927 and had tried to eradicate the Chinese Communist Party (CCP), launched the New Life Movement, which borrowed tactics from contemporary fascist movements in Europe but also invoked Confucius as "the leader of Chinese national culture." Perhaps because the promotion of Confucius was intertwined with the KMT-CCP struggle for power, the Communist Party had been suspicious of Confucian teachings as "old ideology" since its advent to power in 1949. Mao Zedong (1893–1976) liked to profess his admiration for the First Emperor of Qin (r. 221–210 BCE), who is remembered among other things for having "burnt books and buried alive experts of ritual and traditional learning." The anti-Confucian rhetoric rose to fever pitch during the Cultural Revolution (1966–1976). One of its most bizarre episodes was the "anti–Lin Biao / anti-Confucius" propaganda campaign. Lin Biao (1907–1971), Mao's would-be successor, died under mysterious circumstances. The fact that Lin had a calligraphy scroll with lines from the *Analects* in his bedroom fed the grist for the propaganda campaign, which was driven by power struggles among party leaders. The rehabilitation of Confucius in China since the 1980s is part of a process of "normalization," while the active promotion of Confucius in contemporary China is packaged as a kind of cultural nationalism.

Confucius and Marx

Guo Moruo (1892–1978) was a notable and prolific writer whoses corpus encompasses poetry, plays, fiction, essays, autobiography, and historical and archaeological schoalrship on oracle bones, archaeology, and early Chinese history and thought. He studied in Japan from 1914 to 1923. During this period, he immersed himself in the study of languages and literatures—he learned Japanese, German, and English—although he was enrolled in medical school. He won early fame for his vernacular free verse steeped in Romanticism and was one of the cofounders of the Creation Society, one of the most important literary groups in the 1920s. In an essay on the spirit of traditional Chinese culture (1923), Guo lauded Confucius for his dynamism, individuality, self-realization, and his perfect harmony of body and mind, comparing his life to "a beautiful piece of poetry. . . . He had the strength of a Samson." (Recall the references to Confucius's physical strength in some early sources, see chapter 1, 1.1, translator's note.) Guo saw in Confucius "a genius combining Kant and Goethe." (Guo published his translation of *The Sufferings of Young Werther* in 1922 and returned intermittently to his translation of *Faust.*) In other words, Guo remade Confucius in his image or, more precisely, the image of his Romantic ideal, combining his pantheism, sentimentalism, and hero-worship.

Guo went to Japan again in 1924 and started translating *Social Organization and Social Revolution (Shakai soshiki to shakai kakumei* 社会組織と社会革命) by the Japanese Marxist economist Hajime Kawakami (1879–1946). He declared himself a thorough convert to Marxim in a letter dated August 9, 1924. Leo Ou-fan Lee observed that Guo's Marxism in the 1920s "is much more akin to the theories of the 'young Marx'—the more voluntaristic and revoluntary Marx from the *Philosophical and Economic Manuscripts* to the *Communist Manifesto*—than to those of the 'old Marx' of *Das Kapital*." Guo declared his intention to translate *Das Kapital*, but the project never materialized. Guo's story, "Marx Enters the Temple of Confucius," is a half-ironic, half-serious exploration of the possible common grounds between Marxism and Confucian teachings. It was published in Shanghai on December 16, 1925, in the literary magazine *Floods (Hongshui* 洪水).[2]

Guo participated in the Northern Expedition (1926–27), the united front of the Nationalist Party (KMT) and the Chinese Communist Party (CCP) against the warlords in northern China. When the alliance broke down and the KMT persecuted the communists, Guo fled to Japan in 1928, and for the next nine years wrote and translated extensively while in exile in Japan. During the second Sino-Japanese War (1937–45), he was active in the second united front of the KMT and CCP, eventually casting his lot with the latter. After 1949, Guo rose to the highest echelons of power and courted controversy because of his sycophancy toward Mao Zedong and his readiness to adapt his opinions to political expediency. Even opportunism and political dexterity could not save him from tragedy, however. Two of his sons committed suicide during the Cultural Revolution (in 1967 and 1968); one was driven to take his own life because of persecution by Red Guards.

4.1 Guo Moruo, "Marx Enters the Temple of Confucius" 馬克斯進文廟

On the fifteenth day of the tenth month, the day after the sacrifice to Confucius, Confucius and his most esteemed disciples, Yan Hui, Zilu, and Zigong, were eating cold pork from a pig's head at the Temple of Confucius in Shanghai.[3] Four young bigwigs, bearing a vermilion sedan chair, barged straight into the temple.

Zilu first saw this, and in spite of himself became furious. He threw down his chopsticks, preparing to step up and intervene. Confucius hastily stopped him, saying, "Yóu, your love of valor exceeds mine, but nowhere can I find the right talent!"[4]

Zilu had no choice but to suppress his anger.

Turning his head, Confucius called out to Zigong and asked him to receive the guests.

The vermilion sedan chair was let down in front of the Sage's hall. A crab-faced Westerner with a full beard emerged from it.[5]

Zigong came forward to welcome him and led this Westerner up the hall. The four sedan bearers followed behind.

Thus, hosts and guests, nine of them, greeted each other on equal terms in the hall.

Confucius was the first to say his own name. Only when he turned around and asked the guest's name did he realize that this bearded and crab-faced man was Karl Marx.

The name of this Karl Marx had long since reached Confucius because his popularity had recently rose to such a high pitch. Confucius had always been a person who honored the worthy and loved learning. Look: in his lifetime he learned rituals from Laozi, he learned to play the zither with music master Xiang, and he studied music with Chang Hong.[6] For anyone skilled in anything, not only would Confucius not offend him, but he would also try to learn from him with true humility. Only in this way could Confucius become Confucius! He is not like us moderns who shut the door against everything, arbitrarily claiming to know what we do not know anything about! Once Confucius heard that it was Marx coming, he involuntarily exclaimed in surprise and delight:

"Ah! Ah! To have a friend coming from afar—isn't that a joy?[7] Mr. Marx, what an exceptional pleasure it is to have you come! Truly an exceptional pleasure! Having come to our humble temple, what advice would you bestow on us?"

Without any polite demur, Marx then opened his mouth—needless to say, he was speaking the language of shrike-tongued southern barbarians.[8] For Confucius to understand what he was saying, he had to totally rely on the translation of the sedan bearers. Confucius's words were also translated before they could be understood by Marx.

Marx said, "I have come especially to learn from you. Our ideas have already reached your country and I hope they can be realized in China. But recently some people claim that my ideology is different from your teachings, and therefore in China, where your thought prevails, there is no chance that my ideas can be put into practice. That is why I have come directly to seek advice: What exactly is your thought? How is it different from my ideas? Furthermore, how great is this difference? It is my earnest hope that you can instruct me in detail on these questions."

Having heard Marx's speech, Confucius nodded repeatedly to show his agreement, then he responded: "My way of thinking is not very systematic. For as you know, science did not yet exist in my lifetime, and I had no understanding of logic.[9] If it is necessary to first bring different strands together to summarize my thought, I wouldn't be able to sort out the one main clue, and I am afraid we will have to betray your great expectations. So, by my reckoning, it would be better if you first speak about your ideology, and I will then match it against my ideas. Although your ideology has long since spread to China, I still don't really understand what it is all about, because none of your books have been translated into Chinese."

"How—if none of my books has been translated—how can people talk up a storm and raise such furor with my ideas?"

"I heard that to talk about your ideas one does not need your books. All one needs to do is to read a few Japanese and European journals.[10] Isn't it so? You men of the new age!" (Making a public show of his improbable flair for levity, he directed this question to the four bigwigs. But these men of the new age showed no chink in their armor. They did not translate Confucius's words literally, what they produced in their translation was the following: "However, many of us can read your works in the original. Just take the several gentlemen here: they reach the epitome of excellence in their German and economics!" In this way, Marx and Confucius were fooled by these four bigwig scholars.)

"That is good," Marx said. "So long as they can read the original, that is good."

"It is such a rare opportunity to have you come here personally. Time is short, and we can't very well invite you for a lecture. Inviting famous people to give lectures is a very fashionable thing these days. But at least we can ask you to talk to us."

"Fine, fine. Then I will just talk and speak about my ideology. But before I do so, I cannot but explain the premises of my thought. I unconditionally affirm this world and human existence—that is to say, I am different from most proponents of religion who look upon human existence as illusory or sinful. Since we are born into this world, what we should investigate is how we should live in order to achieve the greatest happiness, and what our world should be like to make it suitable for our existence. I am standing in this world and speaking of this world. On this point I diverge from religionists or mystics. On this point I must ask you: How does your way of thinking compare to mine? If on this starting point we are already at odds, then we are basically going on different paths, and we do not have to continue our conversation."

Just as Marx finished speaking, Zilu piped up without waiting for Confucius to open his mouth:

"Yes! Our Master also emphasizes using things advantageously and enriching livelihood.[11] Our Master is most concerned about the people's livelihood. That is why he said, 'The great virtue of heaven and earth is the generation and sustenance of life.'"[12]

"Yes," Confucius continued, "One can say that our starting point is identical. But you want the present world to be suitable for our existence. So, what sort of world can be suitable? What sort of world will facilitate for our existence the highest level of happiness? You must surely have this kind of ideal world in mind. What is your ideal world like?"

"You are asking about my ideal world? Excellent! Excellent! You asked well! Many people take me for a materialist. They all consider me some sort of bird and beast, someone who cares just about material needs and is devoid of ideals. Actually, I am, as you implied in your question, someone who has the loftiest and most far-reaching ideal. I am afraid I am an extreme idealist! In my ideal world, we exist therein by having the myriad people, each individually, fully developing their talents in a state of freedom and equality. Every person can give his or her best without hoping for recompense, every person can have a guaranteed livelihood without worrying about hunger and cold. We call this the communist society, whose principle is 'from each according to his ability, to each according to his needs.'[13] If such a society can be realized, wouldn't it be a paradise on earth?"

"A-ha! Yes!" This time even the dignified Confucius could not help applauding and cheering in appreciation. "This ideal society of yours and my world of great common good converge without any planning on our part. Allow me to recite an old passage that I wrote: 'When the great Way prevailed, all under heaven was justly and commonly shared. The worthy ones were chosen; the able ones were commended. Good faith was emphasized and harmony cultivated. That was why people loved as parents not only their own parents, nor did they nourish as children only their own children. In this way, the old were provided for in their final years, the able-bodied ones were employed, the young had the support for growing up, and widowers, widows, orphans, the childless, the disabled, and the sick were all taken care of. Men have their proper work; women have their homes. They disliked the wastefulness of having goods discarded on the ground, yet it did not matter whether they or others kept them. They disliked not personally exerting themselves, yet it did not have to be for their own advantage. That was why schemes and machinations dwindled and did not develop, and banditry, larceny, disorder, and delinquency did not arise. Thus, the outer gates were not closed. This is what we call the great common good.'[14] Isn't this completely the same as your ideal?"

Confucius drew out his voice as he recited this passage that filled him with pride. When he recited the two lines, "They disliked the wastefulness of having goods discarded on the ground, yet it did not matter whether they or others kept them. They disliked not personally exerting themselves, yet it did not have to be for their own advantage," he swayed his head back and forth with special exhilaration, showing a state of self-hypnosis. But Marx remained very calm. He did not seem to regard this speech of Confucius as being particularly noteworthy. At this moment, Confucius was perhaps in his eyes at the most a "utopian socialist?" And so, he lectured on as if he were standing at the lectern and continued to talk about his theory.

"However"—Marx placed great emphasis on this contrastive conjunction—"my ideal is different from the utopias championed by some. My ideal is not fabricated or imaginary. It is also not attainable with one leap. We first prove with historical evidence that it is possible for society's production to progressively increase in value, and then show how this wealth that progressively increases in value is gradually concentrated in the hands of a few people. This causes the ills of scarcity and impoverishment, and contention and struggles in society become prevalent and unceasing."

"Ah, yes, yes." Confucius had not quite awakened from his sense of being intoxicated with his own ideas, so he only nodded again and again in agreement. "I already said a long time ago, 'They should not worry about poverty but about inequitable distribution; they should not worry about a scarce population but about its peace and contentment!' "[15]

"No! No! My ideas and yours are ultimately different. I am worried about both poverty and inequitable distribution, both a scarce population and its peace and contentment. You have to understand: equity is not possible with the plight of scarcity, and poverty is the basis of discontent. That is why although I am opposed to the concentration of private property in a few hands, I do not dare to oppose the increase in production. Not only do I not oppose it, I promote it wholeheartedly. That is why we put prodigious efforts into the abolition of private property and simultaneously put prodigious efforts into increasing society's productive power. Only when production increases can we share in its enjoyment, only then can we develop our abilities and character in contentment and with a single-minded focus, in equality and with selfless devotion. The momentum of the power to do so, needless to say, are the people who support the abolition of private property, or should we say the proletariat. The formal structure of this power uses the state as its unit in the beginning, and it will progress and become international. Proceeding in this manner, we can all each fully satisfy our needs, both in material and spiritual terms. Only then can human existence reach the highest happiness. So, my ideal comes with definite steps toward fulfillment and is based on solid evidence."

"Yes! Yes!" Confucius is still nodding and agreeing. "I have also said things like: 'The people are already numerous, enrich them.'[16] I also talked about 'having sufficient food and sufficient weapons, and the people will trust you' as the principle of government.[17] (When he came to this, Confucius turned his head and asked Zigong, 'I remember I said this to you, didn't I?' Zigong only nodded.) I also said, 'If a true king is to arise in our generation, then the greatest good will certainly be achieved after another generation.'[18] I also said, 'Qi can change and reach the level of Lu, Lu can change and reach the level of the Way.'[19] I also said, 'He who wants to illuminate bright virtue for all under heaven must first achieve good governance in his state.'[20] To respect and uphold the importance of material well-being is basic to traditional Chinese thought: In the 'eight concerns of government' in 'The Great Plan,' food and goods rank first.[21] Master Guan also stated, 'Only when the granaries and barns are filled can the people know ritual propriety and regulations; only when they have sufficient food and clothing can they know the meanings of glory and shame.'[22] In that sense my thought and, further, the traditional thought of our country, is basically the same as yours. It is always about first raising production and then considering distribution. That was why I said, 'They disliked the wastefulness of having goods discarded on the ground, yet it did not matter whether they or others kept them.' I have always despised merchants, only this disciple of mine (the Master again turned his head and pointed to Zigong) persisted in not heeding my command.

I often told him not to get involved in business, yet he insisted on not listening to me—but he's really good at making money![23] People should understand that we lived in an era before science developed, so our methods for producing wealth were rather primitive. We had to emphasize regulating the uses of resources in the context of our limited capacity for producing wealth—this was because of the constraints of our times![24] However, perhaps regulating the uses of resources is still an important issue even now? At the moment when we don't even have enough rice to go around for everyone, we should not be letting a few people feast on sea cucumbers and shark fins."

"Oh, yes!" Only at this point did Marx heave a sigh. "I did not realize that more than two thousand years ago, in the far east, I already had an old comrade like you! You and I think along the same lines. Why do some people say that my ideas do not match yours, or that they are incompatible with the situation in China and therefore cannot be put into practice in China?"

"Alas!" At this point Confucius suddenly heaved a long sigh. This sigh of his was really long, so long that it sufficed to totally expel the frustrations repressed in his heart for over two thousand years. "Alas!" Confucius continued after his long sigh, "How can they realize your ideas? Even I have already been eating cold pork from the pig's head at this place for over two thousand years!"

"What? Do you mean that Chinese people cannot put your ideas into practice?"

"Never mind putting them into practice—that is too much to hope for! If they manage to at least understand, your followers will not oppose me, and my followers will not oppose you."

"Well, in that case I will . . ."

"What are you going to do?"

"I will go back and look for my wife."

At this point, if this were the Confucius as imagined by Confucian moralists, he would certainly have thundered away in indignant rage and castigate this Marx, who could only think of his wife, as being no different from birds and beasts.[25] But the Sage does not prohibit what cannot be helped in human emotions. Not only did our Sage, Confucius, not castigate Marx, he asked him enviously:

"Mr. Marx, do you have a wife?"

"How could I not? My wife and I shared goals and ideals. Moreover, she is very beautiful!"[26]

Once the topic turned to his wife, the somewhat brusque Marx blew her up into an ideal, just as he blew his ideology up into an ideal.

Seeing how complacent Marx seemed, the Master exhaled with melancholy and heaved a long sigh, "Everyone has a wife, I alone am without one!"[27]

Zigong's tongue had been itching to move for quite a while, so he chimed in hastily at this moment, "All within the four seas are his wives. Why should the Master worry about not having a wife?"[28]

It was not for nothing that Zigong was the only mighty rhetorician among Confucius's disciples. He repackaged Confucius's words and deliberately turned them into a joke.

The mystified one was Marx. Only after a round of questioning did he realize that Confucius had been divorced of his own accord.[29] He felt that this Confucius was becoming more interesting.

Turning around, Confucius said to Marx, "But then I treat the aged in my family with the respect due to the aged and extend that treatment to the aged in other people's families. I treat the young in my family with care due to the young and extend that to the young in other people's families.[30] I treat my wife with the feelings due to a wife and extend that to other people's wives, so your wife is actually like my wife."

Marx is so shocked that he shouted out, "Hey, Mr. Confucius,[31] I only promote the public ownership of property, but you are openly promoting the uninhibited sharing of wives! Your thinking is more dangerous than mine! Well, I do not dare to trouble you any further!"[32]

Once Marx finished speaking, he hurriedly called for the four bigwigs and beat a hasty retreat from the scene of confrontation, as if that wife of his, who remained in Europe, was in danger of being shared by Confucius.

The Master and his disciples stood in the hall and saw Marx's sedan chair being borne and leaving from the main west gate. Yan Hui, who from beginning to end had seemed like a dunce, finally said this:

"With one comment a noble man can prove his wisdom, and with one comment he can show his lack of it. The Master of today is not the Master of yesterday.[33] Why did you make such a nonsensical comment?"

The Master smiled with delight, "I was just joking earlier."

And so, everyone laughed. After a while, they returned to their places and started chewing anew the cold pork from a pig's head that they had been eating earlier.

[translator's note]
"I was just joking earlier": How far does the joke go? Is Confucius only referring to his somewhat indelicate joke about "sharing wives"? Does the joke extend to the entire preceding discussion, especially when we recall the unreliability of the four bigwig translators? Confucius's line alludes to the *Analects* (17.4):

> When the Master went to Wuchen, he heard the sound of stringed instruments and singing. He broke into a smile and said, "Why use an ox-cleaver to slaughter a chicken?" Ziyou [the governor of Wucheng] responded: "Formerly I heard this from you, Master: 'Noble men who learn the Way will cherish the people; commoners who learn the Way will be easy to manage.' " The Master said, "Disciples! What Yan [Ziyou] said was right. I was just joking earlier."

Ziyou might have shown exaggerated zeal, but Confucius basically approves of his principle of promulgating ritual and music whenever possible, and even his criticism is belied by his pleasure. "Joking" here implies approval despite minor quibbles. The same may be said of Confucius's last line in Guo Moruo's story. Guo may simply be using it to introduce a sense of ironic distance vis-à-vis inevitable over-simplifications in this wishful vision of reconciling Marxim and Confucian thought.

The idea of "the great common good" (*datong* 大同), the ideal supposedly shared by Marx and Confucius, is found in the chapter "The Course of Riutal" (Liyun 禮運) in *Record of Rituals*. After the abeyance of the great Way and the great common good, self-interest prevailed, but the sage kings of antiquity, the usual heroes of Confucian discourse, still managed to uphold a lesser version of good order (*xiaokang* 小康), whose elaboration, increasingly concerned with ritual rules, laws, and political order, takes up most of "The Course of Ritual." In his *Commentary on The Course of Riutal* (*Liyun zhu* 禮運注), Kang Youwei reversed the emphasis of the original text and expatiated on the great common good, which he described as "the true transmission of Confucius's subtle message" (*weiyan zhenchuan* 微言真傳)—not something lost in the distant past, but the ideal future and the goal of historical progression.[34] Kang dated this text to 1884, but it might have been written later. From about 1892 to 1901, Kang wrote his *Treatise on the Great Common Good* (*Datong shu* 大同書), which outlined his vision of an ideal world based on absolute equality and the common good, erasing the boundaries of the nation-state, race, class, property, family, gender, and species. Sections of the text were published in 1913 and 1919, but the entire text was not published until 1935, eight years after Kang's death.

Was Guo Moruo influenced by Kang Youwei? Perhaps it is not necessary to identify a specific link, for the modern reverberations of the notion of the great common good were very much in the air in early twentieth century China. Sun Yat-sen (1866–1925), the leader of the 1911 revolution, explained his doctrine of "People's Livelihood" (Minsheng 民生, one of the Three People's Principles) as "actually socialism, also called communism, and none other than the great common good." Li Dazhao (1889–1927), who cofounded the Chinese Communist Party with Chen Duxiu in 1921, believed that democracy is a necessary step toward the great common good in the world. In a letter to Li Jinxi dated August 23, 1917, Mao Zedong wrote, "The great common good is our goal." In his essay, "On the People's Democratic Dictatorship" 論人民民主專政 (June 30, 1949), Mao implicitly acknowledged Kang's treatise as the imperfect avatar of Chinese communism: "Kang wrote *Treatise on the Great Common Good*, but he did not and could not find the road leading to the great common good." Mao was to invoke the idea of the great common good during the Collectivization Campaign in 1958.[35]

To counter the charge of being no more than a "utopian socialist," Confucius enumerates his sayings on the people's economic well-being and also quotes *Master Guan* (*Guanzi*), which drew new attention in the Republican period because of its economic focus. *Guanzi* contains lore and arguments associated with the Qi minister Guan Zhong (d. 645 BCE) and was collated by Liu Xiang (77–6 BCE) based on economic, political, legal, military, and moral discourses in circulation from about the fourth to the first century BCE. In the *Analects*, Confucius expresses both criticism and commendation of Guan Zhong (*Analects* 3.22, 14.16, 14.17). The quotation from *Guanzi*, along with Confucius's other sayings on effective governance and economic prosperity, present Confuius as a practical thinker intent on improving people's livelihood, despite the satirical tone of the above piece. This focus on economic well-being became a more radical empathy with the people's struggles in the image of Confucius Guo propounded in his scholarly writings from the 1930s and 1940s, some of which were collected in *The Bronze Age* (*Qingtong shidai* 青銅時代, 1945) and *Ten Critiques* (*Shi pipan shu* 十批判書, 1945).

On August 5, 1973, Mao Zedong addressed a classical poem to Guo Moruo praising the First Emperor of Qin, decrying Confucius, and attacking Guo's *Ten Critiques*. Guo responded by writing another classical poem, "Spring Thunder" 春雷, on February 7, 1974. He compares Mao's decrees to the rumble of spring thunder that rouses dragons. "You affirm the Qin Emperor's merit; it has lasted a hundred generations, / You announce the verdict on Kong Second, whose crimes defy atonement" 肯定秦皇功百代, 判宣孔二有餘辜. Guo declares that the great error of his *Ten Critiques* is "as bright as flames" 明如火.

Confucius and the New Woman

Treatise on the Great Common Good advocates equal rights for the sexes, which Kang Youwei sees as fundamental to the erasure of other barriers and boundaries. Commenting on the meeting of Confucius and Nan Zi in the *Analects* (6.28) (see also chapter 1, 1.20), Kang Youwei argues that Confucius, acting according to the Way of the great common good (*datong*), sees each individual as equal and independent agents and can thus meet Nan Zi with no qualms. Zilu, on the other hand, is ruffled because he adheres to a lesser version of good order (*xiaokang*). Kang's student Tan Sitong

(1865–1898), one of the martyrs of the Hundred Days Reform, interprets *ren* 仁 (the highest good) as a moral force and grand compassion that breaks down boundaries between men and women (among other barriers), and thus, in his *Learning of the Highest Good* (*Ren xue* 仁學, 1897), upholds the meeting of Confucius and Nan Zi as exemplary. In 1903, a woman under the pseudonym of "Hero from Northern Chu" (Chubei yingxiong 楚北英雄) published "A Fervent Manifesto of Women's Rights in China" 支那女權憤言 in *Hubei Students* (*Hubei xuesheng jie* 湖北學生界), a journal established by Hubei students studying in Japan. She argued that the meeting of Confucius and Nan Zi proved that Confucius recognized women's rights and that he would have supported or at least acquiesced to equal rights for women in the modern era. One of the most interesting modern iterations of Nan Zi and her encounter with Confucius is *Confucius Meets Nan Zi* 子見南子, a "one-act tragicomedy" (*dumu beixi ju* 獨幕悲喜劇) by Lin Yutang (1895–1976).[36]

Lin Yutang was a prolific essayist, novelist, and translator who published extensively in both Chinese and English. On November 30, 1928, Lin published *Confucius Meets Nan Zi* in the literary magazine *Raging Currents* (*Benliu*) run by Lu Xun (1881–1936) and Yu Dafu (1896–1945). In the play, Nan Zi speaks like a modern woman defending emotions and sensual pleasures; she champions "The Society for the Study of the Six Arts" open to both men and women. Confucius, initially confident, becomes torn between "the ritual of the Duke of Zhou" and "the ritual of Nan Zi," especially after Nan Zi lifts the curtain separating them and treats him and Zilu to a musical performance by herself and several singing girls. Confucius finally leaves declaring, "I have to save myself first!" The implication is that he does not know how else to extricate himself from the intellectual and emotional quagmire stirred up by Nan Zi. This all-too-human Confucius starkly contrasts with the lofty sage in Tanizaki Jun'ichirō's (1886–1965) retelling of the Nan Zi encounter as the battle between carnality and spiritual ideals in his short story, "Qilin" 麒麟 (1910).

4.2 Lin Yutang, *Confucius Meets Nan Zi* (1928)

CAST OF CHARACTERS

QU BOYU

CONFUCIUS

MI ZIXIA   An official, a favorite of Lord Ling of Wei and Nan Zi,
   Zilu's brother-in-law
ZILU   Confucius's disciple
NAN ZI   Principal consort of Lord Ling of Wei
YONGQU   eunuch
Four singing girls, one attendant

Time: The fourteenth year of Lord Ding of Lu [496 BCE]
Place: The audience chamber of the Wei ruler [Lord Ling of Wei]. There
are a few benches and chairs, on one of them is seated a man from Lu. He
is a tall man of impressive build, about fifty years old, with a high forehead, broad cheeks, penetrating eyes, and a faint beard. Sitting opposite
him is an elegant, white-haired old man. He is short, but his eyes are even
more penetrating and awe-inspiring. The corners of his lips curl upward
slightly; his smile reveals a toothless mouth. His chin juts out and seems to
convey the disdain and equanimity of a cynic who has seen through the
ways of the world. Even so, there is a stirring vigor about him. The former
is Confucius. The latter is Qu Boyu. Although the room is grandly and
beautifully decorated with elaborate screens, silk curtains, bejeweled shades,
and embroidered drapery, its ambience is somber and oppressive, judging
from the bolt upright way the two are sitting. Confucius's mien is vigilant
and solemn, as if he is about to face a great foe, but Qu Boyu seems much
calmer.[37]

QU BOYU (*feeling bored and impatient*): When is Zilu coming?
CONFUCIUS: A-yóu? He is always late. But if he is late, he does always
   apologize for being late. You can't blame him.
QU BOYU: Why should I blame him! I figure this whole thing has been
   finagled by him and Mi Zixia. Add to that your impressive virtue and
   great renown, sir, success is certain.
CONFUCIUS (*draws himself up respectfully, hastily replies*): You are too kind,
   sir, too kind. A noble man seeks to implement the Way and no more. I
   don't care about anything else . . .
QU BOYU (*as if he didn't hear anything*): I heard that the salary is forty thousand measures of grain—no, sixty thousand, the same as what you, sir,
   received in Lu?[38]
CONFUCIUS: I don't care about that at all! Not in the least! This is just a
   matter of showing . . . eh . . . a measure of appropriate—respect. For a

noble man—he will draw close when he is met with respect and ritual propriety; when the proper ritual declines, he leaves. I don't care about that at all . . . a measure of appropriate . . . for me, from the very beginning, there is no inevitable affirmation or inevitable rejection of alternatives.[39]

QU BOYU: But of course! But then none of us is a gourd (*Confucius steals a glance at Qu Boyu*)—how could we be strung up and not be eaten?[40] (*Both reveal a smile*) I like being upfront and call a spade a spade. Furthermore, I have been thinking—(*points to the attendant and calls out*) Bring tea!—about this, I think we can very well do something together about this. There is nothing exceptionable in the lord's character. Minister Kong is quick-witted and loves learning, and he is not ashamed of seeking advice from those inferior to him. You, sir, have a sound understanding, and you have Zilu to help you. And Scribe Qiu is also here.[41] We all count as old friends, friends who have bonded over the way of proper duty. Among your followers you also have Zigong. The Wei state is populous and prosperous. More likely than not, it will yet turn out to be the auspicious beginning of a great enterprise.

CONFUCIUS (*solemnly*): Precisely. A noble man who lives by the emolument of his lord must plan on his behalf.[42] King Wen and King Wu started their enterprises at Feng and Hao, and their territories did not exceed a hundred *li*,[43] and now . . .

QU BOYU (*ignoring him*): However, what matters most is the Lady of Wei. But Mi Zixia (*showing disdain*) and she are really intimate, and Mi Zixia's wife and Zilu's wife are sisters,[44] that is why I am willing to encourage this affair. The one coming toward us—isn't that Zilu?

(*Zilu enters running. He is about forty. Seeing his two seniors, he rushes forward to bow. Qu Boyu too hastens forward, showing great cordiality. Confucius also stands up and smiles at Zilu with great cordiality and benignity.*)[45]

ZILU: The gatekeeper is a scoundrel. How could he not have recognized me? We got into a row, and it was only when I drew my sword that he apologized. My apologies. I fear I made you wait for quite a while?

QU BOYU: Not at all!

CONFUCIUS (*simultaneously*): Quite! (*Zilu stares at him. Confucius changes his tune.*) Not too long.

ZILU: Mi Zixia and I made an arrangement, and he will be here soon. He said he had something to discuss with you, sir. (*Confucius frowns.*) Yes, I suppose all the negotiations have been satisfactorily concluded. But I wonder what else he has to say. Sixty thousand measures of grain, as it was in Lu.

CONFUCIUS (*frowning even more*): A-yóu, when it comes to what a noble man speaks about, there is no room for negligence, and that is all.[46] A noble man serves in government when he should serve, and withdraws when he should withdraw.[47] To be like Boyi and Shuqi and insist on not becoming an official is of course too obdurate and uncompromising,[48] but it is also not necessary to insist on becoming an official. Draw close when treated with ritual propriety, leave when the proper ritual declines. For me, there is no inevitable affirmation or inevitable rejection of alternatives.

ZILU: Your humble servant misspoke. Please forgive me, sir. Of course, whether a noble man advances or retreats should depend on the flourishing or decline of ritual propriety. It is just that with sixty thousand measures of grains, the Wei ruler's regard for the proper ritual cannot said to be insignificant.[49] I have been thinking on your behalf, sir, and your future has to be in Wei. As for becoming an official, you have to do that. "Having excelled in learning, one should serve in government."[50] What would a gentleman do if he does not serve in government?[51] If there are no officials between heaven and earth, how can there be a ruler? If all under heaven refuse to serve as officials, how can anyone still act as a "ruler?" If we do away with fathers and rulers, wouldn't we sink to the same level as birds and beasts?[52] If a noble man does not become an official, who would become an official? That is why for a noble man to become an official is his proper duty. It is by becoming an official that a noble man carries out his proper duty, and the great principles governing rulers and subjects are thereby sustained.[53] That is why becoming an official fulfills the heaven-ordained duty for rulers and subjects.

QU BOYU: Zilu, you are gabbing away again!

CONFUCIUS: No, I actually found this interesting. This is a problem I am thinking about right now. Recently, I have been quite taken with the idea of leaving everything and becoming a recluse. It's just that what A-yóu was saying was judicious and persuasive. But then there are easy ways and hard ways of serving as an official, this is what the young and inexperienced Yóu still has not figured out.

(QU BOYU *smiles and says nothing.*)

CONFUCIUS (*asks suddenly*): How old is the Lady of Wei?

ZILU: About thirty or so! This hardly matters.

CONFUCIUS: Hmm? (*frowns*) I heard that the Wei ruler always heeds her counsel. Is that true?

ZILU: Everything, everything. He heeds everything she tells him.

CONFUCIUS: In that case, she is really powerful?

ZILU: Yes.

CONFUCIUS: She—does the lady like to talk?

ZILU: Master, your question is really curious. Everyone says that she loves to talk. But why does that matter?

CONFUCIUS (*covers his mouth*): Does she receive guests?

(*Zilu's countenance changes color.*)

(*Qu Boyu laughs loudly. Zilu becomes very embarrassed. Confucius looks unmoved.*)

QU BOYU (*quiets down and smiles, mutters to himself*): One advocates becoming an official but understands nothing about becoming an official. One understands how to become an official but advocates that one does not have to become an official.

(*Confucius looks at Qu Boyu. The two understand each other.*)

CONFUCIUS: A-yóu, come here. Let me explain to you. Didn't you say that the Wei ruler heeded everything that his wife said?

ZILU: Everything.

CONFUCIUS: Didn't you just say that the lady is very powerful?

ZILU: Yes, Master.

CONFUCIUS: In that case, isn't the government of Wei in the hands of the lady?

ZILU: Even your salary, Master, was negotiated between Mi Zixia and the lady. But the lady is just behind the scene. The person occupying the throne and holding the reins of government is still the Wei ruler.

CONFUCIUS: A-yóu, how uncouth you are![54] Truly, you are too inexperienced.

dum—di, dum—di, dum
di, dum—di, di, dum—

(While humming and pacing in the room, he turns his head, as if he suddenly grasps something, and, stretching out his fingers, says to Zilu):

This is what I meant by the difference between the easy ways and the hard ways of serving as an official.

(He turns his head again, chanting and pacing.)

dum—di, dum—di, dum
di, dum—di, di, dum—di, dum—
The mouths of those women
can drive away fine men.
Those women with their entreaties
can bring death and defeat.[55]

ZILU *(his eyes following the movement of Confucius's feet)*: May I be instructed about the meaning of the poem you sang, Master?

(Mi Zixia enters tiptoeing behind Confucius. Zilu sees him but Confucius does not.)

CONFUCIUS: This is talking about the difficulties of serving as an official. The mouths of those women can drive away fine men. . . . *(Zilu purses his mouth to signal to Confucius, but Confucius does not notice.)* Those women with their entreaties . . . *(He suddenly sees Mi Zixia next to him and Zilu signaling, he continues with unhurried ease.)* . . . can make you withdraw your feet.

dum—di, dum—di, dum—

(Qu Boyu and Zilu laugh out loud. Confucius chants slowly and then stops.)

MI ZIXIA *(smiling)*: Confucius looks really happy today. Hehe! I have been really remiss! I have kept you waiting for too long, sir. My apologies, my apologies!

CONFUCIUS: It is not worth mentioning. On the contrary, we are the ones causing you inconvenience, sir.

(Mi Zixia pulls Zilu aside and they speak privately. Confucius chats with Qu Boyu, as if he has not noticed anything, but he is totally focused on the expressions of Zilu and Mi Zixia. Both look troubled. Zilu and Mi Zixia agree among themselves and turn around. Zilu walks ahead, but gazes at Confucius with great embarrassment.)

MI ZIXIA *(his face wreathed in smiles)*: It is a great honor for the state of Wei to have you, Master, condescend to visit our humble domain. Both the Lord and Lady of Wei very much hope to have you, Master, assist in government. The Lady—eh—the Lord of Wei has long heard of your endeavors—how you discourse on the highest good and proper duty, cultivate rituals and music, how you honor the sage kings Yao and Shun as ancestors and transmit their teachings, how you make manifest the rules of Kings Wen and Wu,[56] trying to govern the world by the right Way. He wishes you to serve as his minister.

CONFUCIUS (*looking glad, but all of sudden becoming solemn*): How dare I not follow the ruler's command!

MI ZIXIA: The Lady—eh—the Lord has agreed to have everything arranged as you wish. However, although Wei is descended from Kangshu, we have long ignored the ritual and music of the former kings. The mores of the times are not what they used to be, and morality has sadly declined. Outside the Eastern Gate and by the River Qi, men and women consort together, and one hears a lot about lascivious words and unseemly conduct.[57] Perhaps you, sir, would not take it amiss?

CONFUCIUS (*as if suddenly determined*): Alas! The mores of the times are not what they used to be. It is the same everywhere. The state of Wei has an enlightened ruler on the throne and has worthy men like you, Mi Zixia, and his honor Qu to assist in government, (*he smiles at Qu Boyu and Mi Zixia. Both demur politely but eye each other with dislike and suspicion*) that is already a very good situation. How do I dare to take offense at anything? Hehe!

MI ZIXIA (*relieved*): If that's the case, we can hope for your honor's acquiescence if Lady Nan Zi has a request?

(*All three of them—Zilu, Qu Boyu, and Mi Zixia—look intently at Confucius's expression.*)

CONFUCIUS (*with apparent unconcern but also showing a hint of pleasure*): How dare I accept such a compliment! How dare I! I will certainly follow your command.

MI ZIXIA (*looks at Zilu; Zilu looks at him*): This—this, (*suddenly looks directly at Confucius*) Lady Nan Zi wants to have a face-to-face discussion with you!?

(*Mi Zixia and Zilu both seem quite tense. Qu Boyu suppresses his laughter with difficulty.*)

CONFUCIUS (*carelessly, speaking loudly with ease*): This is nothing to worry about. I was wondering what you're proposing! Haha, whoo—oo—haha! Face-to-face discussion? Lady Nan Zi wants to have a face-to-face discussion with me? We can see that she has a fervent love of the Way. This is truly admirable!

(Qu Boyu's lips curl upward slightly, but no laughter escapes him. Zilu falls silent for quite a while. Mi Zixia also says nothing for that duration. The silence makes everyone embarrassed.)

CONFUCIUS *(deliberately breaking the silence, slaps Zilu on the shoulder)*: A-yóu! Haha! A-yóu! Why are you transfixed like this!

(Zilu raises his heard and takes a look at Confucius, but he does not utter a word and bows his head in silence for quite a while.)

CONFUCIUS *(sternly and severely)*: A-yóu! How can you be so far-fetched and wrong-headed![58] A noble man who enters a state has to find out about its government, and how is he going to hear about this government if not from the women? A noble man acts by assessing opportunities, and fashions what is suitable according to the changing times.[59] How can you be so far-fetched and wrong-headed? Your understanding of the Way can only be considered entry into the chamber, you have not yet ascended the hall![60]

(Zilu does not answer and only throws a look at Mi Zixia. He heaves a sigh and becomes silent again.)

MI ZIXIA *(with a smile)*: The Master agrees to meet Lady Nan Zi, that cannot be better. I will go back and report this. However, the lady's thinking is very new and she doesn't quite believe in all this talk about the separation and distinctions between men and women. That is why her comportment may not fully correspond to the rituals of the Duke of Zhou. I hope you, sir, will not snicker at this when you meet. She is very fond of heart-to-heart conversations with men. Her discourse is elevated and defies constraints, her wit is sharp and effortless, and her ways of thinking are original and breathtaking. She has none of the conventional airs of ladies of the inner chamber. So, may I invite the lady to come out?

CONFUCIUS *(his courage somewhat diminished, with some confusion and uncertainty)*: It's all fine. For me, there is no inevitable affirmation or inevitable rejection of alternatives.

(Mi Zixia takes his leave and withdraws from the back chamber behind the curtain. Zilu and Confucius look at each other.)

CONFUCIUS: Yóu, why are you not saying a word?

ZILU: In the inner chambers of the Lord of Wei, he observes no separation from his kinswomen.[61] Have you heard about that?

CONFUCIUS: I have not heard of that.

ZILU: Then you are going to hear about that soon—or perhaps you will see it with your own eyes *(stops for a moment)*. Master!

CONFUCIUS: What now?

ZILU: Lady Nan Zi has one thing to say. Mi Zixia was too embarrassed to broach the subject.

CONFUCIUS: What is it?

ZILU: Mi Zixia was sure that you, Master, will agree to meet Nan Zi, that was why he did not bring this up. Lady Nan Zi said that she really looked up to—eh—really admired your learning.

CONFUCIUS (*surprised*): She—looks up to—me? (*He smiles.*)

ZILU: This was because she heard the Ducal Son Qumou talk about you. At first, she wanted to write a letter to you . . .

CONFUCIUS: She—writes a letter—to me?

ZILU: Yes. She wants to invite you for tea . . .

CONFUCIUS: To invite me—for tea!

ZILU: She said she also had some grand plan to start some sort of "Society for the Study of the Six Arts." She wants to gather the Ducal Son Qumou, Mi Zixia, Wang Linguo, Qinzu, and some of her kinswomen in her house to discuss the classics, ritual, and music and have an intellectual exchange. (*Confucius stares in amazement and is tongue-tied. Zilu ignores him.*) Later, Mi Zixia told her that it would not be necessary. She thus asked Zixia to convey the message, and so she didn't write the letter. She also said, "Noble men from four directions who condescend to wish for fraternal amity with our humble ruler must have an audience with our ruler's lady."[62] Although your learning is what she looks up to, everything about procedure and remuneration have to be decided only after the interview. I suppose the sixty thousand measures of grain would not be an issue—but she did say this about the interview. Mi Zixia was really too embarrassed to bring this up, that's why he didn't. (*Confucius ponders over this.*) I think we have a difficulty here. Lady Nan Zi is young and beautiful . . . (*Zilu looks at Confucius, and their eyes meet. Confucius is listless and impassive. Zilu is dejected and melancholy.*)

CONFUCIUS (*suddenly beating his chest with indignation*): A-yóu! If I err in any way, may Heaven abandon me! May Heaven abandon me![63]

QU BOYU: Zilu! You are too stuck in your ways. It was only when I was fifty that I realized that I had erred for forty-nine years, and when I was sixty, my views changed again.[64] What harm is there to meet her?

ZILU: We cannot say that. Lady Nan Zi is a free spirit, by nature unconventional. Her words, conduct, and deportment deviate in many ways from the Master's teachings about the rituals of the Duke of Zhou.

Relying on the favor she enjoys, she is willful, impolitic, and volatile, all jovial one moment and offended the next. When the Master has an interview with Nan Zi, if he does not remonstrate, he will have no wherewithal to rectify ritual impropriety and correct musical deviance and set up good examples for the people. If he remonstrates and is not heeded, and if verbal altercations arise, both sides may be cornered, unable to step back and save face. Even if he does not suffer the sad fate of Bi Gan and Xie Ye, he would have no choice but to leave in a huff. He would ultimately not be able to fulfill his ambition to govern a state according to the Way so that it can attain hegemony and the ideals of the sage kings.

CONFUCIUS: Why bother to dredge this up? Xie Ye was a fool, he brought upon himself the calamity of his execution. The case of Bi Gan and the tyrant Zhòu was different. In terms of kinship, Bi Gan was Zhòu's uncle; in terms of office, Bi Gan served as his junior tutor. His earnest, loyal heart was set on preserving the ancestral temple. That was why he had to brave death to make his point. He was hoping that with his death Zhòu would be moved to repent. His motive was based on the highest good. Lord Ling of Chen and his ministers flaunted their licentiousness. When it came to Xie Ye, his position was just that of a junior high officer, and he had no blood ties with the Chen ruler. Trusting in the ruler's regard for him, he did not leave the Chen court, and with his puny self, pitted his life against the wicked ones. This is what wise men would not do. For him to end up being killed—wasn't it what he deserved? And no good came of his death. How can I be as foolish as Xie Ye?[65]

ZILU: Master, you are also in your way an unconventional free spirit.[66] This is what we call "serving in government when the circumstances were acceptable."[67] You will go forward when it is acceptable, and you will withdraw when it is acceptable. There is no hard and fast rule forbidding this, and sacrifice is also uncalled for. Even so, this is still an obstacle when it comes to your ambition to implement the Way. That is why I would ultimately advise you against meeting her. But then the situation has come to this, so we don't have a choice. She insists on meeting you, and you have no way to get around that. She may very well invite you, Master, to attend archery sessions or to ride the carriage with her to get some fresh air. She really likes to parade herself as she flamboyantly goes around town in her carriage. Often, in late spring evenings, she would do so sitting next to the Lord of Wei, or she would come with Mi Zixia to the banks of River Qi to listen to the people singing "mountain songs." But there is one more thing you have to be careful about when you talk to her.

CONFUCIUS: About what?

ZILU: Master, you have probably heard about the heir apparent Kuaikui fleeing from the state.

CONFUCIUS: Hmm!

ZILU: Kuaikui is now at Zhao Jianzi's establishment. The other day I asked you, "The Wei ruler wants you to stay and take charge of government. What would be your first priority?" You said, "It would probably be the rectification of names? If names are not rectified, words will not follow reason, etc., etc." Now the heir apparent is on the run because he's at loggerheads with Lady Nan Zi. There is of course no "rectification of names" in their cases.[68] If you mention the Kuaikui affair in front of Lady Nan Zi, you will stoke her anger for sure. This is a rather delicate matter.

CONFUCIUS: Did Kuaikui really flee because of the incident with Lady Nan Zi?

ZILU: Certainly. There is absolutely no doubt. It's best not to mention the name of the heir apparent in front of the lady.

CONFUCIUS (*unmoved*): Then I will deal with it may own way!

(*Qu Boyu takes Zilu by the hand.*)

QU BOYU: Let us leave now! The lady wants to see only Confucius. . . .
(*The two of them take turns to withdraw. Qu Boyu, imitating Confucius's earlier tune, sings in a low voice. Clasping his hands behind his back, he leaves the room slowly.*)

The mouths of those women
can drive away fine men,
Those women with their entreaties
can bring death and defeat.

(*The two men leave. Confucius sits, dazed, on a chair. After a moment's silence, there is suddenly the sound of a jade bracelet falling to the ground, making a clear chime. What follows is the voice of a woman talking and laughing. It is quiet and gentle, sweet and lovely, and does not suggest a frivolous or shallow character. In a moment, the beaded curtains stir, and the eunuch Yongqu comes out.*)

YONGQU (*entering to report*): My lady, please take your seat!

(*Nan Zi comes out and takes her seat behind silk curtains. One can vaguely discern a fair, small face. Her chignon is piled high on her head, with bangs on her forehead and fringes on two sides. By the fringes are a pair of heavy earrings. She wears a very grand and beautiful dress with embroidery in deep blue. The eunuch stands next to her in attendance. Confucius hastens forward to bow with his forehead touching the ground, knocking it audibly. Simultaneously Mi Zixia comes out and stands on the right side of the curtains. The lady's girdle jade and pendants tinkle melodiously.*)

NAN ZI: Master, please rise. (*Confucius stands up.*) Please take a seat. (*Confucius reverentially sits down on a chair close by, both grateful and tense.*) I have long admired you, sir, such is your glorious renown.

CONFUCIUS (*rising slightly*): How dare I accept such a compliment! How dare I!

NAN ZI: Your great reputation has stirred a deep yearning in this humble consort. Not having the chance to meet you has been a source of great regret. Now you have condescended to visit us. My heart is overjoyed, and I am only sorry that it has taken so long for this meeting to take place. Now we would like to offer you a pair of white jade discs as a small token of our deep admiration. (*She gives a pair of jade discs to Yongqu.*)

CONFUCIUS (*hastily gets on the ground and bows with his forehead touching the ground*): I do not dare to decline a gift bestowed by the ruler. (*He stretches out his hands to receive the jade and returns to his seat.*)

NAN ZI: Master, do you like the jades or not?

CONFUCIUS: I like them, of course.

NAN ZI: I too like them. Master, which kind do you like more? White jade? Agate jade? Or jadeite jade?

CONFUCIUS (*cannot come up with an answer right away and seems to be at a loss*): White jades are good.

NAN ZI: I think green jadeite jades are the most beautiful. One can make them into earrings, girdle pendants, or rings; in all cases they have a lovely luster.

CONFUCIUS: Yes, yes. White jade has its merits, as does jadeite jade. In sum, both are wonderful. All jades are wonderful and lovely.

NAN ZI: How so?

CONFUCIUS (*feeling at ease*): Jades are lovely because they can be compared to the virtues of a noble man. It has a gentle warmth and lustrous glow: that is benevolence. It has a dense and compact pattern: that is intelligence. It is firm and uncompromising: that is righteousness. It is modest and has no sharp edges: that is ritual propriety. It defies all efforts to bend it: that is courage. It has these five virtues, that is why it is lovely.[69]

NAN ZI: Hmm! (*Stops for a moment, turning her head toward Mi Zixia.*) Zixia, what do you think about jade?

MI ZIXIA: I just love the tinkling music the jade pendants make when you wear them.

NAN ZI: Fie! Mind your manners in front of the Master. (*She moves to another seat, and the tinkling jade pendants make another round of music.*)

MI ZIXIA: Didn't I say so?

(*Nan Zi laughs. And because of that Mi Zixia laughs, and so does Yongqu. Confucius follows suit and also laughs.*)

NAN ZI (*to Confucius*): Do you see the purple markings on that pair of jade discs? There is this pattern, about the size of a fingerprint. It really looks like some ancient characters and strange graphs . . . (*Confucius turns them around and looks.*) . . . No, turn them around, it is at the tip . . . (*Confucius is still turning them around, yet he cannot find it; Mi Zixia runs over and also cannot find it.*) . . . naw, that side! (*Nan Zi becomes impatient and calls for Yongqu.*) Raise the curtains! (*Confucius and Mi Zixia both turn around and raise their heads. Confucius is startled and his countenance changes color. Nan Zi leaves her seat and comes to Confucius's side. Confucius hastens to stand up.*) . . . bring them to me . . . at this end, doesn't this look like the graph for "hand?" (*She bows her head and looks with Confucius. Mi Zixia presses close and looks with interest. Yongqu also comes closer. The four of them surround the jade disc, looking at it together.*) . . . naw, look how fine and bright this purple pattern is . . . look, isn't it lovely? . . . And there is this dot here that makes it look like the graph for "shen," wouldn't you say it is wondrous? . . . (*To Confucius*) This pair is my favorite, that is why I dared to offer it . . . (*She seems to finish speaking. Mi Zixia and Yongqu step back. Nan Zi goes and is about to return to her original position. She takes the jade discs and wants to give them back to Confucius. Confucius is about to receive them but does not. Nan Zi lets go, and with a clear "chink" the discs fall to the ground. Nan Zi is startled.*) . . . oo—ah—oo-ch! (*She becomes flushed and stamps her foot.*) What a pity! (*Yongqu rushes forward to pick up the jades. Nan Zi and Confucius look at each other for a while, and Nan Zi smiles.*) It does not matter, sir. It is just a pity to have this pair ruined. Tomorrow we will send someone to bring you another pair, sir. (*She returns to her original position.*)

NAN ZI (*to Yongqu*): There is no need to let down the curtains. Otherwise, it will always be neither here nor there. The speaker cannot articulate with satisfaction and the listener cannot hear clearly.

(*Everyone falls silent for a while.*)

NAN ZI: Master, for you to bring your august presence to our humble domain is a point of great pride and honor to the Lord of Wei and me. We are also hoping that you will stay here for a long time and give us the benefit of your instruction. The lord and I are both great admirers of your character and learning. I am especially eager to make progress in my studies by learning from you.

CONFUCIUS: How dare I accept such fulsome compliments! How dare I!

NAN ZI: Did you, sir, just returned from the Pu settlement?

CONFUCIUS: Yes.

NAN ZI: I heard that there was some sort of incident in Kuang. Is that true?

CONFUCIUS: Yes. The men of Kuang thought I was Yang Hu and arrested me.

NAN ZI: How could they have been so unreasonable?

CONFUCIUS: It's because they really hated Yang Hu, and I look a bit like Yang Hu, hence the misunderstanding.[70]

NAN ZI: Which Yang Hu? Is that Yang Huo from your exalted state of Lu, the one who sent you a ham?

CONFUCIUS: That was him. He didn't send me a ham. He sent me braised pork shanks.

NAN ZI: Then I got the story wrong. Even so, this shows that he understood ritual propriety better than Ji Huanzi. I heard that Ji Huanzi didn't send the pork shanks, and that was why you left Lu. Is that true? (*Confucius nods.*) I heard that Yang Hu made sure you were out before he sent the pork shanks, and you also went to thank him only when you guessed that he would not be home. Did this really happen?[71]

CONFUCIUS: That was the man.

NAN ZI: Is Yang Hu a bad man?

CONFUCIUS: A very bad man. That is why I am not willing to stay in the state of Lu.

NAN ZI: Then why did you have to go and bow in thanks?

CONFUCIUS: When a high officer bestows a gift on an officer, if the latter does not get to receive it at his house, he will have to bow at the gates of the former. This is the ritual of the former kings.

NAN ZI: If you have to bow in thanks, why did you have to wait till he was not home?

CONFUCIUS: I had no choice.

NAN ZI: Hmm! Sir, what is your judgment of the mores and popular sentiments in the state of Wei?

CONFUCIUS: Very good. Very good. It is a beautiful and prosperous place. Although it only counts as a state of a thousand chariots,[72] if its ruler can instruct his people in ritual propriety, order will prevail between the old and the young, as will correct distinctions between men and women. Put the people to use in a timely fashion, promote the right music and restore ritual propriety, in three months one can transform the people and change their customs, in a year one can achieve hegemony, in three years one can attain ideal kingship.[73]

NAN ZI: Is that really so?

CONFUCIUS: Why would I mislead you? In time past King Wen began his enterprise at Feng and King Wu at Hao. Their territories were no more than a hundred *li*, and they were able to become kings of the entire realm under heaven. This happened because the Duke of Zhou instituted proper rituals and musical forms. Assisting King Cheng, he was so dedicated that he suffered his meals and baths to be constantly interrupted.[74] He treated worthy men, be they ever so humble, with great respect, and all under heaven turned to Zhou.

NAN ZI: Where does this ritual come from?

CONFUCIUS: In the old days, King Yao . . .

NAN ZI: Fie!

CONFUCIUS (*stops for a moment, then starts talking again*): In the old days, King Shun . . .

NAN ZI: Fie (*as if she suddenly understands*)! You must not take offense, sir. I am not making light of your words. I just thought that since Yao and Shun lived about two thousand years ago, their bones should probably have rotted by now!

CONFUCIUS: Yes, but this ritual traces back to high antiquity, transforming the legacy of Yao and Shun. Through the Xia and Shang dynasties, there were attenuations and additions, until it was instituted by the Duke of Zhou.

NAN ZI: The reason why I am asking is this: Because I figure that your coming, sir, is the opportunity of a lifetime not to be missed on any account, I want to create a "Society for the Study of the Six Arts." Or we can also call it the "Society for the Discussion of National Learning." You, sir, will lead and instruct us. We will meet right here on the first and fifteenth of the month, and the format does not have to be fixed. We will just be like students studying together. You, sir, will lecture on the *Odes*, the *Documents*, ritual, and music. As for the refreshments and other things, I will try my best to provide them, that goes without saying. Last night I asked the Lord of Wei about this, he fully supported the idea and also promised to attend the meetings. Sometimes we can change the format, perhaps we can practice archery, zither-playing, sword dance, or horse riding. In sum, we will cover all six arts—ritual, music, archery, charioteering, writing, mathematics. Zilu will surely be pleased. What do you think, sir?

CONFUCIUS: Excellent! Excellent!

NAN ZI: But I still have another notion for which I must seek your instruction, sir. If we have this society, then I will certainly want to participate personally, and I will also certainly invite several kinswomen to join. For one thing, coeducation will save your time, otherwise you will have to teach us, the women, separately.[75] Second, regarding the refreshments, I will be able to oversee the arrangements personally and you will be spared the inconvenience of suffering service below par. I can assure you that the food will taste just right, and the temperature of the room will be optimal. Third, if men and women gather in the same hall to exchange views and discuss important questions, we will reap the benefit of casting our net wide. The research will be much livelier and more interesting than what you get when you segregate men and women, outer and inner quarters. Fourth, the bond between men and women is the beginning of all normative relationships.[76] No aspect of ritual propriety is more important than the interactions between men and women. If they study together, they can get into some practice; it would be much more effective than poring over words on the page. Sometimes I see you scholars quite dazed in front of women and absolutely tongue-tied. It is truly tiresome, and it's all because you don't understand the rituals of interaction between men and women and lack practice. Fifth, in the classics of the ancient kings, there is no lack of references to the mores of society or the concerns of the inner chamber. This kind of folk songs and folk customs are precisely the province of us women. For example, for odes with lines such as "In the seventh month, the Fire Star flows past, / In the ninth month, we are tasked with making winter clothes,"[77] we women recite them with greater fluency than men and can give a better exposition than even you, Master, if I may be so bold. What's more, there are all these stories about women in the classics, and if it is left to men, who don't understand women's psychology, to build their discourse on them, it would just mean injustice for these women. Take for example the tyrant Jie—obsessed with his own pleasure, he locked up Bao Si, regarding her as his toy. Bao Si was a woman of temperance and was not guilty of licentiousness. She just did not like to talk or laugh. King Jie insisted on her laughter and cooked up this harebrained and childish game of starting beacon fires as a joke. How could Bao Si not laugh? You must know that Bao Si was laughing at the stupidity of men, not at the beacon fires.[78] Later, with the fall of the dynasty and the destruction of the country, men who took over the critique turned things around and put all the blame on Bao Si. What was Bao Si's crime that she should be slandered and reduced to total ignominy? If we let women join the discussion, I think we can expatiate on new meanings on many points. Sixth, of course men may excel in sword fight, riding, or archery, but can you say that we have no merit in zither, chess, calligraphy, or painting? Even when it comes to riding or sword fight, you need us cheering and clapping on the side, for only then would your swords move with flourish or your horses race fast. Wouldn't you say so? As for all this talk of the distinctions between men and women, I am a bit skeptical whether it was in reality some attempt to change the system in the name of antiquity. On theoretical grounds, I absolutely refuse to accept it. Do you agree with my thinking?

CONFUCIUS: Aw . . . aw . . . aw!

NAN ZI: Sir, what do you think? Am I right?

CONFUCIUS (*reluctantly*): The distinctions between men and women come from the legacy of the Three Dynasties and was established by the Duke of Zhou.

NAN ZI: This way of organizing a coeducational "Society for the Study of the Six Arts"—do you, sir, consider it a good plan?

CONFUCIUS (*smiling*): The refreshments will surely be good! (*falls silent again*)

NAN ZI: What about clothing and headgear?

CONFUCIUS: Of course, they should be neat and proper.

NAN ZI (*pondering*): Ah! Sometimes I think—eat, drink, clothes, headgear—they are what make up the true meaning of life. Take Yongqu, for example, his entire life is about serving me tea. Just think: Is the true meaning of his life about serving tea? Or is it what he eats, drinks, and wears as clothes and caps? That's why I thought if there is enough satisfaction about what one eats, drinks, and wears as clothes and caps, the meaning of life may just get fuller.

CONFUCIUS (*admiringly*): Lady Nan Zi, I have not expected women to have such deep understanding and lofty thinking. But your four words, "eat, drink, clothing, headgear," should be changed to "eat, drink, men, women."[79]

NAN ZI: So, you approve of the Society of the Six Arts?

CONFUCIUS (*feeling a new interest*): With you, my lady, overseeing the whole thing, I should naturally abide by your command. But still, I am afraid that violations of ritual propriety may arise between men and women. I beg you, my lady, to forestall such developments.

NAN ZI: There you go again. I think "eat, drink, men, women" constitute the true meaning of life—they are the source of the river of life. It is only when we get bountiful and unending irrigation from this source of the river that human existence can flourish. The ties between men and women form the deepest love in human life. When this deepest love stirs, it is manifested as poetry. You need to have poetry before you can have literature. Have you heard of the odes from our state of Wei?

CONFUCIUS: I have.

NAN ZI: Aren't they good?

CONFUCIUS: Very good!

NAN ZI: Do you know why our odes and those from Bei and Yong are the best? It's because those men and women who don't understand ritual propriety are stirred by the deepest emotions and are moved to express them during their rendezvous under the mulberry and as they make pledges by the corner of the city walls, so having coeducational students in the "Society for the Study of the Six Arts" is not just about the excellence of what we eat, drink, and wear, it will bring great benefits for literature and poetry. (*She stops for a moment.*) Should we go for a drive? Would that be a good idea? The weather is glorious now. When dusk falls, we should take the carriage and get some air by the banks of

River Qi and listen to the singing of men and women. As the sun is setting, we can return via the Dun Mound.[80] That will be really interesting.

CONFUCIUS (*somewhat embarrassed*): All right! This is the command of Heaven!

NAN ZI: I often go out with the Lord of Wei in a carriage to take the air and listen to our people singing. Their songs are really interesting.

(*Someone knocks on the door outside. Yongqu hastens forward to open the door and sees that it is Zilu. Zilu stands outside the door and asks to see Confucius. Yongqu enters.*)

YONGQU: Zilu requests to see the Master.

(*Confucius goes out, the two speak in the low voice on the other side of the door.*)

ZILU: How is your affair going, sir?

CONFUCIUS (*sighing*): It's not going to work. Let us leave our fate to Heaven!

ZILU: What happened?

CONFUCIUS (*shaking his head*): Nan Zi's way of thinking is too new. Those not sharing the same Way cannot seek each other's counsel.[81] She is set on organizing the "Society for the Study of the Six Arts" that you mentioned. She wants it to be coeducational. I figure I should just go along for a while, but sooner or later I will have to go!

(*Zilu falls silent for a while. Suddenly, they hear melodious music coming from the room. Nan Zi has already taken a lute and is humming a low tune. Confucius returns to the room.*)

NAN ZI: Is that Zilu? Why not invite him to enter?

CONFUCIUS: He thought since he had no special business, he shouldn't dare to presume.

NAN ZI: Invite him to enter!

(*Confucius comes out and invites Zilu to enter with him together. Zilu sees Nan Zi and bows. She stops playing.*)

NAN ZI: Just now I invited the Master to go driving with me and get some air. We are going to listen to the people's mountain songs. Can you join us?

ZILU (*politely*): It is my great honor to receive this command from you, my lady. I do not dare to fail to obey.

NAN ZI (*again plucking the strings of the lute to make a ding-dong sound*): Just think: a late spring evening, when the moon shines bright and the stars are sparse, a group of men and women are singing and chanting poems at the bridge by the River Qi. Just look—

The waters of the River are wide and deep.
Northward it flows, with a majestic sweep.
In fishing nets dropping with splashing sounds,
Sturgeons and paddle fish swish and swirl,
While reeds and sedges rise high.
The ladies following her are resplendent,
The officers in her retinue are valiant.[82]
What an impressive picture of people living in peace!

NAN ZI (*a bit tipsy*): I think sadness crowds out joy in human existence!
The poets are right—

The crickets are in the hall,
The year is soon coming to an end!
If we do not enjoy ourselves now,
The days and months will pass us by![83]

Zilu!

ZILU (*as if waking up all of a sudden*): My lady!

NAN ZI: Just now I talked to the Master about establishing a learned society. We want only six or seven gentlemen and ladies of commensurate age and artistic achievements. Together we will study ritual, music, and the Six Arts. The meetings will take place on the first and fifteenth day of the month. The Lord of Wei and I will host, and the Master will preside. On top of the pursuit of learning, we will feast and make merry. What do you say?

ZILU (*hesitant, with mixed emotions of shock and elation*): The Lord of Wei and you, my lady, are both champions of literature and learning. If in addition we get the Master to teach us ritual and music, then the enlightened ruler and the worthy minister will be gathering in the same hall. Truly this will be a grand occasion hard to come by in a thousand years!

NAN ZI: Excellent! The other day I composed a song based on the lyrics created by our people in Wei. Today I met the Master for the first time. I beg leave to play the song as a gift celebrating our meeting!

(*Nan Zi turns to Confucius and Zilu and smiles. Confucius looks very grave, as if at a loss. Dazed and confused, Zilu nods and agrees that it's a good idea. Nan Zi reclines on her chair, the lute in the hand. Her appearance seems almost too free and easy. She plays the tune of "Under the Mulberry," moving her lips and humming. The music is free-spirited yet melancholy.)*

NAN ZI: Summon the singing girls!

(Yongqu acknowledges the command and leaves. Nan Zi again sings and chants in a low voice. Zilu is ill at ease and does not know whether he should sit or stand. Confucius is lost in thought. All of a sudden, he seems to have awakened and becomes vigilant.)

CONFUCIUS *(in a low voice to Zilu)*: I have decided to leave Wei.

(Nan Zi is unrestrained and at ease, neither registering anything nor asking any questions.)

ZILU: Is this because you do not share the same Way?

CONFUCIUS: I have my fears. I have my fears.

(Zilu understands.)

NAN ZI *(chants)*:

Her hands are like soft white rush,
Her skin is like cool ointment,
Her neck is like larvae,
Her teeth are like melon seeds.
Who is this?
The sister-in-law of the Lord of Xing.

ZILU: The sister of the heir in Qi.

CONFUCIUS: The wife of the Lord of Wei.[84] *(Suddenly aware that he misspoke, he rises in shock.)* Oo—ah—oo!

NAN ZI *(laughing wildly)*: Haha! Master, I don't deserve such high praise!

(Confucius and Zilu are both rather shamefaced and embarrassed.)

YONGQU *(smiling)*: I have never heard this poem recited this way in reverse order.

(Yongqu and the singing girls enter together.[85] Their clothes are splendid and bewitching. Confucius and Zilu rouse themselves. Nan Zi sits up, holding the lute.)

NAN ZI: Music is the Master's specialty. We look forward to your instruction and corrections!

(She plays the "Mulberry" tune again and sings along. Melodious and sonorous, the music is the epitome of desolate beauty. The singing girls dance to the tune, sometimes chiming in and sometimes stopping. Confucius and Zilu cannot stop looking. They are entranced and yearn for the music but also show unease and melancholy. Mi Zixia, however, is totally natural and does not seem to be troubled at all.)

NAN ZI (*sings*): Where should I gather the dodder?
In the fields of Mei.
SINGING GIRLS (*chiming in*): Who are you longing for?
The lovely Meng Jiang!
(*Together*): She is to meet me under the mulberry,
Has invited me to the upper story,
And will see me off by the banks of River Qi!

(*The singing girls dance. Nan Zi throws the lute to Yongqu, takes off her robe and dances.*)

NAN ZI (*sings*): Where should I gather the avena?
To the north of Mei.
SINGING GIRLS (*chiming in*): Who are you longing for?
The lovely Meng Yi!
(*Together*): She is to meet me under the mulberry,
Has invited me to the upper story,
And will see me off by the banks of River Qi!

(*Nan Zi and the singing girls dance together. Yongqu plucks the lute.*)

NAN ZI (*sings*): Where should I gather the brassica?
To the east of Mei!
SINGING GIRLS (*chiming in*): Who are you longing for?
The lovely Meng Yong!
(*Together*): She is to meet me under the mulberry,
Has invited me to the upper story,
And will see me off by the banks of River Qi![86]

MI ZIXIA (*expressing great enthusiasm*): Marvelous, marvelous!
ZILU: My lady, you sang and danced so well. You are truly talented. I am
filled with heartfelt admiration.
NAN ZI: You're too kind! We are but a mockery of the real thing! (*She suddenly fixes her gaze on Confucius, who seems to be deep in thought.*) Master,
we seek your instruction.
CONFUCIUS (*as if waking up from a dream, heaves a slow sigh*): I did not realize
that music and dance can be this excellent! (*He recovers his original
demeanor.*) My lady, you must be tired!

NAN ZI: Not at all!

CONFUCIUS: Thank you! Thank you!

NAN ZI: Let us consider this the gift I offer in order to bow to the Master as a teacher! (*She bows to Confucius with a beaming smile.*) I trust you will agree to lead the "Society for the Study of the Six Arts!" (*Confucius does not respond.*) No? You do not agree? (*Her lovely voice and expression move Confucius.*)

CONFUCIUS (*muttering to himself*): I am fifty-six, and only now do I understand the arts and recognize human existence for what it is. Yes, only this counts as true poetry, true ritual, true music. Other types of odes and hymns,[87] other kinds of bowing and yielding are all meaningless, they are but empty decorations.

NAN ZI (*looks pleased*): I am unworthy of the Master's excessive praise. Well then, we will count this as your agreement. The day after tomorrow we will go driving and take the air. You have to come! We will withdraw for now!

MI ZIXIA: My lady, you are tired. Please withdraw for now!

NAN ZI: When you come the day after tomorrow, please make sure that you and Zilu arrive on time. (*She continues with appealing sincerity.*) The Lord of Wei and I will be waiting for you at home. Do come! You have to come! Good-bye!

(*Nan Zi, Mi Zixia, Yongqu, and the singing girls leave behind the curtain. Zilu and Confucius look at each other. After Nan Zi leaves, the mutual gaze continues.*)

ZILU: What is the lady's intention? You can perhaps stay in Wei?

CONFUCIUS (*with a rejoinder that does not answer the question*): If it were not for my belief in the Duke of Zhou, I would believe in Nan Zi.

ZILU: In that case, the Master can stay?

CONFUCIUS (*with determination*): No!

ZILU: Is this because Nan Zi does not understand ritual propriety?

CONFUCIUS: Nan Zi has Nan Zi's own version of ritual propriety. It is not something that you people can understand.

ZILU: In that case, why don't we just stay here?

CONFUCIUS: I don't know, I have to think about this . . . (*pondering*) . . . If I listen to Nan Zi, if I am transformed by Nan Zi, her ritual, her music . . . erasing the separation and distinctions between men and women, everything liberated, following the course of nature . . . (*for a fleeting moment he shows a wild joy*) . . . Ah . . . (*as if he discovers a new world*) . . . no (*his face suddenly seems old, somber, and solemn*). No! I am leaving!

ZILU: Whereto?

CONFUCIUS: I don't know. I will leave Wei. I absolutely have to leave Wei!

ZILU: Master, aren't you going to implement the Way and save all the people under heaven?

CONFUCIUS: I don't know. I have to save myself first.

ZILU: You are really leaving?

CONFUCIUS: Leaving! I must leave! I will leave sooner or later! (*He appears haggard and bows his head slowly. He props his forehead with one hand and leans the other hand on his knees, forming a curved shape.*)

(*Next to him, Zilu stands straight and stares at Confucius in a daze. In the silence, Confucius's long sigh is faintly audible—the sighing stops—then silence.*)

(The End)

Lin Yutang's note: According to "The Hereditary House of Confucius" in *Historical Records*, after about a month, Confucius left Wei. Three years later, he returned to Wei. Having left Wei, he headed toward Jin without achieving concrete results. He returned again to Wei.

[translator's note]

In "The Hereditary House of Confucius," Confucius returns to Wei several times, possibly as a result of Sima Qian's attempt to accommodate different stories or versions of the same story set in Wei. Here Lin Yutang implies that Confucius circles back to Wei because he feels a secret affinity with "the Way of Nan Zi." The quasi-conversion of Confucius marks him as a potential champion of the pet causes of the New Culture Movement.

The descendants of Confucius had for centuries remained a powerful clan in Shandong. In the 1920s, members of the Kong clan had close ties with the warlord Zhang Zongchang (1881–1932) and therefore viewed the advancing troops of the Northern Expedition with some trepidation. Their fears were somewhat allayed when Chiang Kai-shek paid his respects at the Confucius Temple in May 1928, announcing the Nationalist government's support of Confucian teachings in order to "fundamentally eradicate Communism." In August 2028, the Kong clan petitioned the government to retain its hereditary lands and priveleges while renouncing the ducal title for its leader. On August 30, 1928, Lin Yutang wrote a public letter of protest to Kong Xiangxi (1880–1967), the minister of finance in the Nationalist government and a self-declared seventy-fifth generation descendant of Confucius. Two months later, he wrote *Confucius Meets Nan Zi*. Both Lin's play and its performance (especially in Confucius's hometown) may be seen as gestures of protest against the claims of the Kong clan to special powers and privileges.

Confucius Meets Nan Zi was performed in Nanjing and Shanghai without incident. But in June 1929, the performance of the play in a teacher's college in Shandong—it was situated between the Confucius Temple and the official residence of the Kong lineage—led to vociferous protest from Confucius's descendants, who accused the students and teachers putting up the play as well as the college president of defaming the sage. Government ministers and leading intellectuals got involved in the controversy. Opposing factions within the resurgent Nationalist Party that had just unified the country attacked and defended the Kong clan. The president of the teacher's college, Song Huanwu, Lin Yutang's classmate at Peking University, was eventually "reassigned" to another university, and the students involved in the play were suspended. Lu Xun published the private and public documents related to the case and stated his own firm defense of the play in a newspaper article on July 26, 1929. Lin Yutang later included these materials in his collection *The Endless Wilds* (*Dahuang ji* 大荒集). The Nan Zi affair thus became a fuse for debating the weight of tradition, the definition of Confucius's cultural legacy, modernization, state control over education and cultural expression, and the role of women and of intellectuals in society and politics.[88] Lin Yutang published an English version of the play in *Confucius Saw Nancy and Essays About Nothing* in 1937. Note that in Lin Yutang's other English publications introducing the values of Chinese civilization to an English readership (for example, *The Wisdom of Confucius*, 1938), he leaves behind the satirical mode and presents a much more positive image of Confucius.

The Uses and Misuses of Confucius

In his postscript to his compilation of the documents on the Nan Zi case (August 11, 1929), Lu Xun lamented the litigious tactics of "the sage's descendants" and their power in "the sage's territory." Lin Yutang's letter to Kong Xiangxi also opposed the sacralization of Confucius and the preservation of special privileges for his descendants, but his play is ultimately less strident, suggesting a potential rapport between Confucius and Nan Zi. This resonated with Lin's interest in humor, reconciling differences, and the option of detachment from politics. Lin Yutang and Lu Xun were allies in the Nan Zi affair, but their friendship frayed in August 1929 over a trivial misunderstanding.

Lu Xun, widely recognized as one of the most important writers in modern China, leaped into prominence with the publication of "Diary of a Madman" in 1918. His writings became more explicitly political from the 1920s onward with the waves of political violence devastating the country. Some of his students were among the forty-seven protestors killed by the warlord Duan Qirui (1865–1936) in an unarmed demonstration in Beijing on March 18, 1926. Mao Zedong hailed him as "the sage of modern China," although Lu Xun never joined the Communist Party and was more of a sympathizer and fellow traveler. "Confucius in Modern China," first written in Japanese, was published in the May 1935 issue of the Japanese journal *Kaizō* 改造 (*Reformation*). (Lu Xun studied in Japan from 1904 to 1909 and was fluent in Japanese.) The essay was translated into Chinese by Yiguang 亦光 and published in the journal *Zawen* 雜文 (*Miscellaneous Writings*) in July 1935. Lu Xun revised it and included it in his *Second Collection of Essays from Qieqie Pavilion* (*Qiejie ting zawen erji* 且介亭雜文二集). He wrote in the postscript to that collection: "At that time the descendants of the sage were offering sacrifices to their ancestor with great exhilaration in the capital." The New Life Movement promoting Confucian values under the aegis of the Nationalist government led by Chiang Kai-shek was then at its height. In "Confucius in Modern China," Lu Xun is ultimately less interested in defining "what was wrong with Confucius" than in the misuses and misappropriation of Confucius—the inevitable compromises that result from the sage's cooptation by virtue of being embedded in power structures through the ages.

4.3   Lu Xun, "Confucius in Modern China" 在現代中國的孔子 (April 29, 1935)[89]

According to a recent report in the newspapers in Shanghai, General He Jian, the chairman of Hunan Province, sent a portrait of Confucius, a long-cherished item in his collection, as a congratulatory gift to the Temple of Confucius, the construction of which was recently completed at Yushima.[90] To be honest, the common people in China know next to nothing about what Confucius looks like. Since antiquity, every county is sure to have a Temple of the Sage, or a Temple of Letters, but usually there is no statue of the Sage inside. When it comes to painting or sculpting figures that deserve to be worshipped, the general principle is to create something more magnificent than the average person. But when it comes to a figure that most deserves to be worshipped, such as a sage like Confucius, then it seems even the very existence of an image becomes blasphemous, and it would be better not to have any at all. This is not entirely unreasonable. Confucius did not leave any photograph, so naturally we cannot know his real appearance. Although there are occasional references in the textual traditions, one cannot say for sure whether they spring from pure fabrication. If one is to create a new sculpture from scratch, then there is no recourse but to let the sculptor give free rein to his imagination, which is even more worrisome. That was why Confucian scholars finally adopted the attitude of "all or nothing" à la Brand.[91]

However, if we are speaking of paintings, one may still come across them sometimes. I have seen them thrice. Once as an illustration in *Sayings from the House of Confucius*, once as an image that adorned the first page of the *Pure Critique*, a newspaper published in Yokohama when Liang Qichao was fleeing for his life in Japan—it was exported from Japan back into China.[92] There was also the occasion when I saw the picture of Confucius meeting Laozi carved on a Han dynasty tombstone.[93] As for my impression of what can be gleaned of Confucius's image in these pictures: This gentleman was a very thin old man dressed in a long robe with wide sleeves. He was wearing a sword at his waist or perhaps holding a staff under one of his arms. His bearing was awe-inspiring. If you were sitting and attending to him by his side, you would have to sit bolt upright and would no doubt suffer from joint pain after two or three hours.[94] If you are a mere mortal, you would probably be anxious to escape.

Later, I once traveled to Shandong. During the moments when the uneven roads bothered me, I suddenly thought of our Confucius. It occurred to me that the Sage who appeared so impressive and cognizant of the Way was but sitting on a simple, rickety carriage, being tossed and tumbled, as he rushed about in those parts. There was something quite comical about this idea. Needless to say, such associations were atrocious. In other words, they bordered on irreverence. I am afraid they would certainly not arise if one were a follower of Confucius. But at that time, there were many young people who harbored wayward thoughts like mine.

I was born in the final years of the Qing dynasty. Confucius had already been saddled with the horribly grand title of "Supreme Sage of Perfect Accomplishment, King of the Manifestation of Culture."[95] It goes without saying that it was an era when the Sagely Way controlled everything in the entire country. For those who studied, the government made them study designated books, that is, the Four Books and the Five Classics.[96] It made them follow designated interpretations, made them write essays in a designated style, that is, the so-called eight-part essay.[97] Furthermore, it made them express designated views. However, while these Confucian scholars, who repeated the same ideas over and over again, might know everything about the world that was square,[98] they knew nothing when it came to the spherical earth. Thus, when they fought wars with France and England, which was not mentioned in the Four Books, they suffered defeat. Was it because they thought self-preservation made more sense than dying while worshipping Confucius? Or was there some other reason? In any case, at that time the government and bureaucrats who had whole-heartedly honored Confucius began to be shaken in their convictions. They poured government money into the translation of books by foreign devils. Among the scientific classics were *On the Heavens* by Herchel, *Introduction to Geology* by Lyell, *On Minerals and Rocks* by Dana.[99] Even now one can find these remnants from that era lying around in bookstores with old books.

But reactions against this were inevitable. The so-called embodiment and representative of Confucian learning, Xu Tong, came on the scene at the very end of the Qing dynasty.[100] Not only did he denounce even mathematics as the learning of foreign devils, he also denied the existence of Spain and Portugal: although he acknowledged that countries such as France and England existed in the world, he definitely refused to believe that Spain and Portugal existed. According to him, France and England came to demand concessions from China so many times that even they became embarrassed, so they made up the names of new countries to continue doing the same thing. He was the instigator and orchestrator behind the scene during the notorious Boxer Uprising of 1900. But the Boxers were totally defeated, and Xu Tong also committed suicide. The government again regarded the politics, law, technology, and learning of foreign countries as something worth understanding and emulating.

It was at that time that I yearned to go to Japan to study. I attained my goal, and the place where I started studying was the Kōbun Gakuin established by Kanō sensei in Tokyo.[101] At this place, Misawa Rikitarō sensei taught me that water was made up of oxygen and hydrogen. Yamanouchi Shigeo sensei taught me which part of the shell of mollusks was called the "mantle." One day, the overseer of the academy, Ōkubo sensei, gathered everyone and said, "Because you are all followers of Confucius, today we are going to the Temple of Confucius at Ochanomizu[102] to pay our respects." I was really taken aback. I still remember what I thought then: it was precisely because I despaired of any answer coming from Confucius and his followers that I came to Japan. But then was I to worship him again? For a moment I felt this was all very strange. Furthermore, I think this feeling was by no means limited to me alone.

For Confucius, however, the misfortune of being misunderstood in his own country did not begin in the twentieth century. Mencius criticized him as "the timely among sages." If we have to translate this into modern Chinese, then there is really no option other than "the modern Sage."[103] As far as he himself is concerned, this is of course not a particularly dangerous honorific, but still, it is not a title that should be wholeheartedly welcomed. But perhaps it was not like this in reality. Confucius became settled in his role as "the modern Sage" only after his death. He suffered quite a lot when he was alive. He rushed about here and there, and although he once served in the exalted position of police chief in Lu,[104] he soon lost his position and became unemployed. Furthermore, he was disdained by powerful ministers, scorned by recluses in the wilds, and was even besieged by a violent mob, becoming all shriveled from starvation. Although he collected three thousand disciples, only seventy-two counted for something, and then there was only one among them that he could trust. One day, Confucius said in frustration: "My Way is not implemented. I want to go on a raft and take to the sea. And the one who would follow me—would it not be Yóu?"[105] Later, when Zilu [Yóu] was locked in combat with his enemies, his cap-string was cut off, but he truly lived up to our expectations of him. Even at that moment, he did not forget the lessons he learned from the Master, so he said, "When a noble man dies, he does not remove his cap."[106] Even as he tied his cap-string, he was hacked to pieces. Having lost the only disciple he could trust, Confucius was of course very devastated. It was said that once he heard the news, he sent word to the kitchen to throw out the sauce made from minced meat.[107]

I think we can say that Confucius fared a bit better after his death. Since he could no longer prattle about his views, all kinds of powerful people have been using all kinds of white powder to put cosmetics on him, elevating him to a terrifying height. But compared to Shakyamuni who was imported into China later, he actually seemed very pitiful. It is true that every county has a Temple of the Sage or a Temple of Letters, but they appear lonely and neglected. Ordinary people do not go there to worship. If they go to a place of worship, it would be either a Buddhist temple or a Daoist temple. If you ask the common folk who is Confucius, they will of course answer that he is the Sage, but they are only acting as the phonograph of those who wield power. They also respect and cherish paper with writing on it, but that is because of the superstition that they will be struck by lightning if they fail to do so.[108] The Temple of Confucius at Nanjing is of course a bustling place, but that is on account of the varieties of amusements and teashops there. It is said that when Confucius compiled the *Spring and Autumn Annals*, ministers fomenting disorder and miscreant sons quaked in fear.[109] But if you ask people now, almost no one can name any of these ministers fomenting disorder or miscreant sons subjected to the unsparing attacks of Confucius's brush. If you mention such categories, many would think of Cao Cao, but that is a lesson not taught by the Sage but by the nameless authors of fiction and plays.[110]

In sum, Confucius in China is elevated to great heights by those wielding power. He is the Sage of those powerful people or those who aspire to become powerful people. He does not have much of a relationship with the common people. But when it comes to the Temple of the Sage, the enthusiasm of those powerful people lasts but a moment. Because they are already harboring other goals while honoring Confucius, it is a tool that becomes useless once they attain their goals. If they do not attain these goals, then this tool is even more useless. Thirty or forty years ago, those who had designs on attaining power, that is, those who wanted to become officials, all studied the Four Books and the Five Classics and wrote eight-part essays. Other people called these texts and compositions categorically "the gate-knocking brick." What this meant was that once these scholars achieved success in the examination, all these texts and writings would be forgotten, just like the brick used to knock on the gate. Once the gate is opened, this brick would also be forgotten. The truth is, ever since Confucius died, he has always been used as "the gate-knocking brick."

If we look at recent examples, this becomes even clearer. From the beginning of the twentieth century, Confucius had been suffering a run of bad luck. But in the age of Yuan Shikai, he was again remembered.[111] Not only were the sacrificial rituals restored, they even made some strange costumes for the sacrificants to wear. What came along with this was the attempted restoration of the monarchical system. However, ultimately that gate did not open in response to the knock, and Yuan Shikai died outside the gate. What remained were the northern warlords. When they felt that they were gradually reaching the end of the road, they also used Confucius to knock on other gates of happiness. On one side we had General Sun Chuanfang, who controlled the provinces of Jiangsu and Zhejiang, and who cut down ordinary people in a cavalier fashion when he was on the road, restoring the pitch-pot ritual.[112] And then there was General Zhang Zongchang, who bore his way into the Shandong province, and who had so much money and so many troops and concubines that even he himself lost count—he reprinted the Thirteen Classics.[113] Furthermore, he looked upon the Way of the Sage as something that could be sexually transmitted like venereal disease, and so he took a certain descendant of Confucius as his son-in-law. However, the gates of happiness were still not opened by anyone.

These three persons all looked upon Confucius as a brick, but the times have changed, and that was why they unmistakably failed. Not only did they themselves failed, but they also dragged down Confucius and put him in an even more tragic situation. They were barely literate, but perversely droned away on subjects like the Thirteen Classics, that was why people found it comical and ludicrous. The gap between their words and their actions was too great; this provoked even greater disgust. Being already disgusted by the monk, abhorrence extends to his cassock. The fact that Confucius was being used and instrumentalized for a certain purpose could be seen even more clearly, and so the desire to knock him down became even stronger. That was why when Confucius was decked out with supreme dignity and solemnity, the essays and books finding faults with him were bound to appear.

Even Confucius had his flaws, and under ordinary circumstances nobody cares, because the Sage is after all human, and so this is something excusable. But if the followers of the Sage step up and talk nonsense, arguing that the Sage acts this way or that way, and that you too have no choice but to act this way or that way, people would not be able to help laughing. Five or six years ago, the performance of *Confucius Meets Nan Zi* stirred up a controversy. In that play, Confucius appears on the stage. By the standards of the Sage, he is of course somewhat lacking in gravitas[114] and does seem a bit silly and slow, but as a character, he is actually an appealing and sympathetic person. But the descendants of the Sage were extremely outraged and took the issue all the way to court and the seat of government. This was because the venue of the performance was actually Confucius's hometown. At that place, the Sage's descendants multiplied exponentially, having become a class enjoying special privileges that put Shakyamuni and Socrates to shame. However, perhaps that was precisely why the youths who lived there and who were not the Sage's descendants could not help but put up a performance of *Confucius Meets Nan Zi*.

As for the ordinary people, especially the so-called unenlightened masses, although they call Confucius the Sage, they do not feel that he is the Sage. Regarding Confucius, they have reverence but no sense of affinity. But I am afraid there may not be another group in the world who can understand Confucius as well as the unenlightened masses of China. Make no mistake, Confucius did plan outstanding ways of governing the state, but those were all for the sake of governing the people. They were methods of government devised on behalf those wielding power, none of them were for the sake of the people themselves. This is what is meant by the line "ritual protocols do not go down to the common people."[115] For Confucius to have become the Sage of the powerful and finally transformed into a "gate-knocking brick" cannot after all be considered an injustice. One cannot say that Confucius has no relationship at all with common people. But to say that there is no affinity—I am afraid that is but to put it mildly. Not to draw close to the Sage for whom one has no affinity is a matter of course. Try this any time: try to put on some torn and tattered clothes, keep your feet bare, and run out to the Temple of Perfect Accomplishment and see what will happen. I am afraid it will be like going by mistake into the fancy cinemas of Shanghai or the first-class compartment of the tram: you will be driven out right away. Everyone knows that this is the proper province of people with means and clout. Even the unenlightened masses would not be unenlightened to the extent of committing such a faux pas.

[translator's note]
"Confucius in Modern China" was written a year before Lu Xun's death. "Kong Yiji," one of Lu Xun's first vernacular stories, was written sixteen years earlier. I have reversed the chronology here so that "Kong Yiji" can be juxtaposed with "The Sunny and Cheerful Kong Yiji," a rap song from 2023. As I mentioned in the introduction, copybooks with characters in

red that children traced when they learned to write begin with lines that contain "Kong Yiji" (Kong the second son, that is, Confucius). The name Kong Yiji thus echoes Confucius's name and is associated with a rudimentary Confucian education. The town is called Luzhen, recalling Confucius's birthplace in Lu. Kong Yiji's degradation debases familiar tropes from the tradition: the scholar's frustration, exegesis as learning, the promise of education, the failure of recognition, and the gulf between self and society. The youthful, unsympathetic, and unreflective narrator draws attention to the absence of a viable alternative to Kong Yiji's mode of being. The rap song by Gui Shange turns "the sunny and cheerful Kong Yiji" (2023) into ironic despair over dashed hopes and the voice of protest against the inequities of society. It became popular quickly but was soon scrubbed from websites in China.

The Fate of a Degraded Scholar

4.4 Lu Xun, "Kong Yiji" 孔乙己 (March 1919)
The setup of the wineshops at Luzhen was different from other places: They all had a counter shaped like a square ruler facing the street. Under the pane were cabinets storing hot water ready to warm the wine at any moment. Laborers often spent four copper coins to buy a bowl of wine at noon or in the evening when they were done with work—this was more than twenty years ago, now the price for a bowl has risen to ten copper coins. They would lean against the other side of the counter, quaffing the warm liquor before calling it a day. If they were willing to spend an extra copper coin, they could buy a plate of boiled salted bamboo shoot or beans flavored with aniseed to go down with the drink. If they could come up with more than ten copper coins, they would be able to buy a meat dish. But these patrons were mostly of the short garment variety and probably could not afford such extravagance. Only those wearing long gowns would saunter into the room next to the shop, ask for wine and proper dishes, and sit down to drink slowly.

I had been working as an attendant at the Xianheng Wineshop near the town entrance since the age of twelve. The headwaiter said I looked too awkward and could not be trusted with the clients sporting long gowns, so I should just make myself useful outside. Now when it came to the customers wearing short garments, although it was easy enough to deal with them, there was no lack of nagging and bothersome ones among them. Those people often insisted on inspecting how the wine was ladled from the tawny pitcher. It was only after they had checked that the bottle had no water at the bottom and had personally watched the bottles lowered into the hot water that their minds were set at rest. Under such strict surveillance, it was very hard to mix water into the wine. So, after a few days, the headwaiter claimed I could not manage that job. Fortunately, the person who recommended me for the job in the first place had some say and I could not be dismissed outright. As a result, I was assigned to the boring task of warming the wine and nothing else.

From that point on I stood at the counter the whole day focusing on my duty. I was not remiss but could not help feeling the monotony and tedium. The headwaiter looked forbiddingly fierce, and the customers were not particularly friendly—there was no room for any fun. It was only when Kong Yiji came to the shop that I could laugh a bit, that is why it still stays in my memory.

Kong Yiji was the only one drinking while standing and yet wore a long gown. A very tall man, he had a pale face with traces of scars often discernible between wrinkles and a matted grey beard. Although he wore a long gown, it was dirty and tattered, as if it had not been mended or washed for ten years or more. When he talked, his speech was full of archaisms like "ergo, wherefore, inasmuch, alas," which meant he was only half understood. Since his surname was Kong, people took their cue from the half-understood line, "the supreme great man, Kong the second son (*yi*) on his own (*ji*)," on trace-the-red character sheets and gave him the nickname "Kong Yiji." Whenever Kong Yiji came to the shop, all the men who were drinking looked at him and laughed. Some shouted, "Kong Yiji, you have new scars on your face!" He did not answer and turned to the waiter behind the counter, "Warm me two bowls of wine, and I want a plate of aniseed beans." Then he doled out nine copper coins. The others deliberately bellowed in a loud voice, "You must have been stealing again!" Kong Yiji stared with wide-open eyes and said, "How can you baselessly besmirch someone's spotless reputation thus?" "What spotless reputation? The other day these very eyes saw you strung up and beaten after having stolen books from the He family." Horribly flushed, with blue veins protruding on his forehead, Kong Yiji argued, "Peculating books cannot be considered theft . . . peculating books! . . . A scholar's affairs—can this be considered theft?" He then continued with a string of incomprehensible words, something like "noble men persevere in dire straits,"[116] something like "and thus it was," et cetera, which roused the crowd's boisterous mirth: everyone inside and outside the shop were in high spirits.

I heard people say behind his back: Kong Yiji actually studied but ultimately did not become a government student and had no clue how to make a living; he thus became poorer and poorer, so much so that he was almost reduced to beggary.[117] Fortunately, his calligraphy was respectable, so he squeaked by as a copier. What a pity that he had a deplorable trait—namely, laziness. Before a few days of copying had gone by, he would vanish, along with the books, paper, brush, and inkstone he was using. When this happened a few times, no one asked him to do copying anymore. With no other recourse, Kong Yiji could not help but resort now and then to stealing. But his conduct in our shop was superior to all the others—that is, he never owed money for too long. Even if now and then he had no cash and had to have his name recorded on the board, he was sure to clear his debt in less than a month, and Kong Yiji's name would be erased from the board.

Having quaffed half a bowl of wine, Kong Yiji's flushed face gradually returned to normal. Someone by his side asked, "Kong Yiji, are you really literate?" Kong Yiji looked at the man asking the question and it was obvious that he did not deign to make his case. The others pressed on, "How did it happen that you couldn't even manage to nab even a fraction of a licentiate degree?" Kong Yiji immediately gave every indication of disconsolation and unease. His face became ashen, and he mumbled something. But this time it was all something along the lines of "ergo, wherefore, inasmuch, alas," and he was no longer comprehensible. At that moment, everyone burst out laughing: everyone inside and outside the shop were in high spirits.

At such moments, I was allowed to join in the laughter: the headwaiter would certainly not take me to task for that. Furthermore, whenever the headwaiter saw Kong Yiji, he would often ask that same question to provoke the mirth of others. Kong Yiji realized that it was not possible to hold his own with them, so he had no choice but to talk to the children. He said to me once, "Have you studied?" I nodded slightly. He said, "If you have studied . . . well, let me set you a test. How do you write the graph for aniseed?" I pondered: Would someone not better than a beggar have the right to test me? So, I turned away and no longer paid him any attention. Kong Yiji waited for a long while and said with great earnestness, "You did not know how to write it? . . . Let me teach you. Remember! You should remember all these words. You need them for the account books when you become a headwaiter in the future." I mused privately: there were still many steps between me and the headwaiter! Moreover, our headwaiter never put aniseed on the accounts. Amused and impatient, I said indifferently, "Who needs your instruction? Isn't it just the graph for *hui*, as in *laihui*, meaning to go back and forth, underneath the grass radical?" Showing great delight, Kong Yiji rapped the counter with the long nails of his two fingers and nodded, "That's right! That's right! . . . Do you know that there are four ways to write the graph *hui*?" I got even more impatient and scampered off with puckered lips. Kong Yiji had dipped his fingernails into the wine and was just about to write the graphs on the counter. Seeing how I utterly lacked enthusiasm, he sighed and seemed to consider this a great pity.

There were several occasions when the children in the neighborhood, having heard the laughter, came for the excitement, and made a circle surrounding Kong Yiji, who then gave them aniseed flavored beans, one for each. Having finished their share of the beans, the children still did not scatter, their eyes fixed on the plate. Kong Yiji became nervous, stretched out five fingers to cover the plate, and bent low to say, "Not many, I don't have that many." He drew himself straight, looked again at the beans, and shook his head, "Not many! Not many! Should he have many? Not many, indeed."[118] The gang of children thus scattered in laughter.

It was thus that Kong Yiji kept others in high spirits. But then, even without him, people passed their days just fine.

One day, perhaps two or three days before Mid-Autumn Festival, just as the headwaiter was slowly making calculations for the accounts, he took down the board and said all of a sudden, "Kong Yiji has not shown up for a long while. He still owes nineteen copper coins!" Only then did I realize that he had indeed not come for quite a while. One who was drinking said, "How can he come? . . . His legs have been broken from a beating." The headwaiter said, "Oh!" "He just stuck to his stealing. This time around, he lost his head and actually stole from Provincial Graduate Ding. Now could *his* family's stuff be filched with impunity?" "And then what happened?" "What happened? He first wrote out the confession, and that was followed by a beating. The beating lasted through a good part of the night, and then his legs were broken." "And then?" "Then his legs were broken from the beating." "What happened then when his legs were broken?" "What happened? . . . Who knows? Perhaps he died." The headwaiter asked no more and returned to his accounts with slow deliberation.

After Mid-Autumn Festival, the autumn wind became brisker by the day, and soon enough it was close to early winter. I sat next to the fire all day long and still had to put on a padded coat. One day, there wasn't any customer, and I was just sitting with my eyes shut. Suddenly I heard a voice: "Warm me a bowl of wine." Although the voice was extremely low, it was very familiar. I looked around but there was no one. I stood up and looked outside, and Kong Yiji was sitting there facing the threshold beneath the counter. His face was sallow and thin, and he no longer looked like anything. He was wearing a ragged padded jacket and sitting cross-legged on a rush bundle tied to his shoulder with coarse ropes. He saw me and said again, "Warm me a bowl of wine." The headwaiter also poked his head out, saying, "Is that Kong Yiji? You still owe nineteen copper coins!" Utterly crushed, Kong Yiji raised his face and said, "This . . . let me clear my debt next time. For now, I have cash. Give me the good stuff." The headwaiter resumed his normal manner and said to him with a smile, "Kong Yiji, you are stealing again!" But this time he did not make any effort to argue and only said, "Don't make fun of me!" "Make fun of you? If you didn't steal, how could your legs have been broken from the beating?" Kong Yiji said in a low voice, "I fell and broke my legs, I fell, fell . . ." His eyes seemed to be pleading with the headwaiter to say no more. By then, several men had gathered, and they laughed, along with the headwaiter. I warmed the wine and brought it outside, leaving it on the threshold. He took out four copper coins from his torn pocket and put them in my hands. I saw that his hands were all muddy and realized that he had crawled his way here with his hands. It did not take long for him to finish the wine. Sitting, he then used his hands to slowly crawl away in the midst of the others' chatter and laughter.

Since then, a long time passed without any sighting of Kong Yiji. When it came to the year's end, the headwaiter took down the board and said, "Kong Yiji still owes nineteen copper coins!" By Double Fifth next year, he said again, "Kong Yiji still owes nineteen copper coins!" But he did not say anything when it was Mid-Autumn Festival. And we did not see him again as the year drew to its end.

To this day I have never seen him again—perhaps Kong Yiji had indeed died.

4.5 Gui Shange, "The Sunny and Cheerful Kong Yiji" 陽光開朗孔乙己 (2023)

I put on a tattered long gown
And head straight to the wineshop at Luzhen.
I hail the waiter: Warm me two bowls of wine,
Add a plate of aniseed beans for nine copper coins.
I invite scorn with talk of "ergo, wherefore, inasmuch, alas,"
and before I know it, my face is all flushed:
Why do you besmirch my spotless reputation thus?
I take a sip and continue to argue with them:
Camel Xiangzi dies because
He doesn't work hard enough pulling the rickshaw.
Every single work by Lu Xun
Touches untouchable topics.
The days of Chen Sheng and Wu Guang were not easy
Because they could not be practically and solidly busy.[119]
Finally, the customers turn their gaze to me
And ask me: After all, what are you supposed to be?
I look at my long gown and say I am
The sunny and cheerful Kong Yiji.
The sunny and cheerful Kong Yiji.
With his outrageous writing style
He confronts me: Would you submit or not?
The sunny and cheerful Kong Yiji,
The sunny and cheerful Kong Yiji.
Even if I have to dump my labor into the river,
I am not selling it to you for cheap,
The sunny and cheerful Kong Yiji,
The sunny and cheerful Kong Yiji.
You drive your Lamborghini,
But mock me for not working hard enough,
The sunny and cheerful Kong Yiji,
The sunny and cheerful Kong Yiji.
The rotten old society

What does it have to do with me?[120]
Although I wash my face every day,
My pockets are cleaner than my face.
I have no choice but to wear my long gown,
Copying books for the masters, it's an endless round.
I thought the work was some easy fix,
Not realizing that it's actually nine-nine-six.
When the job's done, the "hostile demand for salary"
Led to the arrest of hungry me by the police.
Why is this Old Society with myriad flaws
Totally devoid of labor laws?
Why is the dignity of we ordinary people
So easily trampled by the privileged few?[121]
For all these unhinged stories and encounters,
None dares now to give any answers.
Finally, the customers turn their gaze to me
And ask: Why aren't you afraid in the least?
I smile and say: Because I am
The sunny and cheerful Kong Yiji,
The sunny and cheerful Kong Yiji.
The weak and powerless twiggy squiggle
Has long given up the struggle.
The sunny and cheerful Kong Yiji,
The sunny and cheerful Kong Yiji.
Time has worn down the sharp corners,
Leaving behind only a few scars.
The sunny and cheerful Kong Yiji,
The sunny and cheerful Kong Yiji.
Optimism becomes my fangs and claws,
Under the mask, tears are brimming over.
The sunny and cheerful Kong Yiji,
The sunny and cheerful Kong Yiji.
You ask me whether I am blessed or not,
I just want to give a profane retort.
The sunny and cheerful Kong Yiji,
The sunny and cheerful Kong Yiji.
All the curses, doubts, rebuttals, and ridicule,
What do they have to do with me?

Studying is for the sake of the Rise of China,
Not for becoming a delivery man or courier.
Everyone, when they're done listening,
Make a show of their heedless laughter,
Except for that stupid SB—
The sunny and cheerful Kong Yiji,
The sunny and cheerful Kong Yiji.
Tear down this wall of rot and blight
And seek the True Way's ray of light.
The sunny and cheerful Kong Yiji,
The sunny and cheerful Kong Yiji.
On those "comments carefully retooled"—
How much hot blood that is hard to cool?
The sunny and cheerful Kong Yiji,
The sunny and cheerful Kong Yiji.
Kongming is my ideal,
My fate as Shang Yang is sealed.[122]

Coda: The Scholar's Garb

The first line of "The Sunny and Cheerful Kong Yiji" refers to Kong putting on his "tattered long gown." In Lu Xun's 1919 story, Kong Yiji's "tattered long gown" symbolizes his pathetic attempt to cling to the dignity of a Confucian scholar in a society where he has become irrelevant, useless, and despicable. "Kong Yiji literature," referring to the expressions of discontent from unemployed or underemployed young people, gains some traction on the Chinese internet in 2023. Refusing to take a job beneath one's education and training is likened to "Kong Yiji not being able to take off the long gown." The image of Kong's "tattered long gown" taps into long-standing issues in the Chinese tradition about the relationship between external markers of roles and attributes and their fulfillment in terms of character and conduct. It also brings to mind debates about notions of adaptability (*yin* 因) and the judicious weighing of circumstances (*quan* 權) in Confucian teachings, and the relationship between political power and ethical principles implied by ritual prescriptions. What is the line between timely (*shi* 時) action and opportunism? The first Han emperor, Liu Bang (d. 195 BCE), was initially disdainful of Confucian scholars and hated the "scholar's garb" (*rufu* 儒服) of Shusun Tong (d. 188 BCE), who thus changed his costume to a short jacket in the Chu style and won the emperor's approval (*SJ* 99.12).[123] In his final comments, Sima Qian commends Shusun Tong for "changing with the times" (*SJ* 99.22) but seems to be implicitly criticizing him for his compromises and opportunism.

In "The Conduct of Scholars" (Ruxing 儒行) in the *Record of Rituals*, when Lord Ai of Lu asks Confucius whether he dons the scholar's garb, Confucius replies, "I lived in Lu in my youth, and wore clothes with wide sleeves. In later years, I stayed in Song and wore their ritual caps. I have heard: The noble man's learning is broad, and he wears the costume of his region. I do not know anything about donning a scholar's garb" (*LJ* 3: 1398, see also *KZJY* 5.43). Confucius disclaims any special garb for a classical scholar and implicitly refutes charges of pride and rigidity. Instead, he modestly claims to be wearing what is customary for specific regions, reminding us of Mencius's claim that Confucius is "the timely among sages." Confucius proceeds to expatiate on the virtuous conduct (*xing* 行) of scholars as manifested in their dignity, courage, resolution, and moral purpose. This passage may belong to a broader discussion on whether and how adopting different styles of clothing is associated with a focus on inner strength and timely action.

The connection between costume and conduct is also discussed in *Mozi*. Gong Meng, wearing a scholar's gown, asks Mozi whether costume (*fu* 服) determines conduct or vice versa. Mozi in response observes that the famous rulers of Qi, Jin, Chu, and Yue sport different types of clothing, yet all achieve good governance, and concludes that "conduct does not depend on costume" (*MZ* 12.435–36). In *Kong Anthology*, Zigao (identified as Kong Chuan, a descendant of Confucius) presents himself to Lord Pingyuan in a long gown with wide sleeves, but also proceeds to emphasize that the scholar's garb is "not uniform," for the official's court robes, the military commander's armor, and the long gown for day-to-day use can all be considered proper costumes for the Confucian scholar, who should be defined as one who "encompasses all excellences, masters the six arts, and does not deviate from the centered Way in movement or quietude" (*KCZ* 13.296). To argue that the scholar's costume takes many forms is thus to insist on a more capacious understanding of the man of learning and ritual expertise and thereby expand his possible spheres of action.[124]

Both "The Conduct of Scholars" in *Record of Rituals* and the exchange between Gong Meng and Mozi in *Mozi* consider whether "conduct" or "costume" may claim a determinative priority. The scholar's garb thus highlights the question of authenticity, the relationship between the true and the false, interiority and externalization. An anecdote from *Zhuangzi* brings this to the fore:

> Zhuangzi had an audience with Lord Ai of Lu. Lord Ai said, "Lu has many scholars, but few of them can be compared to you, sir." Zhuangzi said, "Lu has but few scholars." Lord Ai said, "Everyone in the state of Lu wears the scholar's garb. How can you say there are few of them?" Zhuangzi said, "I have heard: The scholar wears a round cap because he understands the timing of heaven. His feet are shod in square shoes because he understands the shape of the earth. He dons the cut jade pendant to remind himself that affairs have to be cut through decisively. The noble men who realize the Way may not necessarily put on the garb; those who put on the garb may not necessarily know the Way. If you, my lord, do not believe this, why don't you issue an order for the whole state: 'For those who put on the garb without having realized the Way, their crime will be punishable by death.' Lord Ai thus issued the order for the whole state. Five days passed and none dared to put on the scholar's garb. Only one man in the scholar's garb stood at the lord's gate. The lord then summoned him and asked him about affairs of the state. A thousand twists and myriad turns failed to exhaust his power to respond. Zhuangzi said, "Even in the state of Lu, there is but one scholar. How can one say that there are many?" (*ZZ* 21.717–18)

In the above passage from *Zhuangzi*, *ru* refers to men of learning and expertise who have realized the Way. To take the outward indices of their garb seriously is to consider absolute claims of profound knowledge and moral probity. No wonder only one brave man rises to the challenge and meets the demand for inexhaustible knowledge on "affairs of the state." Ironically, Lord Ai by his very question implies that Zhuangzi may be the real *ru* or the one who can judge who qualifies as a real *ru*.

Confucius speaks of "the scholar by the standards of noble men" (*junzi ru* 君子儒), as distinct from "the scholar by the standards of petty men" (*xiaoren ru* 小人儒) (*Analects* 6.13). Xunzi discusses the "great scholar" (*daru* 大儒), the "correct scholar" (*yaru* 雅儒), the "vulgar scholar" (*suru* 俗儒), "the debased scholar" (*jianru* 賤儒) (*XZ* 6.67, 8.89–91), "the paltry scholar" (*louru* 陋儒) (*XZ* 1.8), "the unregulated scholar" (*sanru* 散儒) (*XZ* 1.9), and "the pedantic scholar" (*furu* 腐儒) (*XZ* 5.53). Wang Chong expatiates on "the culturally accomplished scholar" (*wenru* 文儒) who wrote books (*LH* 82.1150–52) and "the standard scholar of the world" (*shiru* 世儒) who focused on exegesis (*LH* 82.1150–52). All these distinctions and gradations suggest that the protean transformations of Confucius are echoed in ways of defining and adjudicating the *ru*, whose changing meanings encompass the classist, the scholar, the ritual expert, the person of learning and principles, the adherent to virtues enunciated in the canonical classics, and the follower of Confucius.

For the modern period, questions and judgments regarding the role and authenticity of the *ru* pertain to the intellectual. In the case of Lu Xun's "Kong Yiji," for example, it would be the narrator and implied author who has to answer the challenge of the scholar's garb. What is the relationship between the callous teenage narrator and the implied author? Perhaps even the discontent of the "Kong Yiji literature" on the Chinese web in 2023 continues to be rooted in questions on the role and definition of the intellectual. It is precisely this kind of resonance and reverberations that clarify the importance of tracing how stories about Confucius unfold over a wide temporal arc.

Notes

Introduction

1. Among the numerous examples are *CDB*; Herrlee G. Creel, *Confucius: The Man and the Myth* (J. Day Co., 1949); Qian Mu, *Kongzi zhuan* (Jiuzhou chubanshe, 2011); Annping Chin, *The Authentic Confucius: A Life of Thought and Politics* (Scribner, 2007); Li Ling, *Sang jia gou: wo du Lunyu* (Shanxi renmin chubanshe, 2007); Li Ling, *Qu sheng nai de zhen Kongzi: Lunyu zongheng du* (Sanlian shudian, 2008).

2. There are many studies of how the images and representation of Confucius change over time. See, for example, Zhang Hongsheng, *Kongzi de xingxiang jiqi wenxue jingshen* (Liwen wenhua shiye jigou, 1995), chapter 1; Lionel Jensen, *Manufacturing Confucianism: Chinese Traditions and Universal Civilizations* (Duke University Press, 1997); Thomas Wilson, ed., *On Sacred Grounds: Culture, Society, Politics, and the Formation of the Cult of Confucius* (Harvard University Asia Center, 2002); Lin Cunguang, *Lishi shang de Kongzi xingxiang—zhengzhi yu wenhua yujing xia de Kongzi he ruxue* (Qi Lu shushe, 2004); Zhu Weizheng, "Lishi de Kongzi he Kongzi de lishi," in *Zouchu zhong shiji—cong wan Ming dao wan Qing de lishi duanxiang* (Zhonghe chuban youxian gongsi, 2009); Michael Nylan and Thomas Wilson, *Lives of Confucius: Civilization's Greatest Sage Through the Ages* (Random House, 2010); Huang Chun-chieh, ed., *Dong Ya shiyu zhong de Kongzi xingxiang yu sixiang* (Guoli Taiwan daxue chuban zhongxin, 2015); Lee Long-Shien, "*Zhuangzi Liezi* zhong de Kongzi xingxiang," *Dongya guannian shi jikan* 8 (June 2015): 311–41; Lee Long-Shien,

"Xian Qin Han chu zajia wenxian zhong de Kongzi xingxiang," *Zheng Da zhongwen xuebao* 29 (June 2018): 127–74; Julia Murray, *The Aura of Confucius: Relics and Representations of the Sage at the Kongzhai Shrine in Shanghai* (Cambridge University Press, 2021); Zhao Lu, *Weird Confucius: Unorthodox Representations of Confucius in History* (Bloomsbury, 2024).

3. On Confucius's birth sequence as the second son, see chapter 1, 1.1, translator's note. The earliest extant reference to these lines are found among Dunhuang manuscripts (ca. 8th–11th century).

4. The *Analects* has spawned extensive commentaries, heated debates on dating, and numerous translations. For discussions of some of these translations, see Alice W. Cheang, "The Master's Voice: On Reading, Translating, and Interpreting the *Analects* of Confucius," *The Review of Politics* 62, no. 3 (Summer 2000): 563–81; David Schaberg, "'Sell it! Sell it!': Recent Translations of *Lunyu*," *Chinese Literature: Essays, Articles, Reviews* 23 (December 2001): 115–39; Michael Nylan, ed., *The Analects, Confucius: A Norton Critical Edition*, trans. Simon Leys (Norton, 2014), xxiii–lxiii. For some hypotheses on the origins and composition of the *Analects*, see E. Bruce Brooks and A. Taeko Brooks, *The Original Analects: Sayings of Confucius and His Successors: A New Commentary by E. Bruce Brooks and A. Taeko Brooks* (Columbia University Press, 1998); Li Dongjun, *Kongzi shenghua yu ruzhe geming* (Zhongguo renmin daxue chubanshe, 2004), 69–75; Michael Hunter, *Confucius Beyond the Analects* (Brill, 2017); Michael Hunter and Martin Kern, eds., *Confucius and the Analects Revisited: New Perspectives on Composition, Dating, and Authorship* (Brill, 2018). On the formal and intellectual implications of its "scene of instruction," see Wiebke Denecke, *The Dynamics of Masters Literature: Early Chinese Thought from Confucius to Han Feizi* (Harvard University Asia Center, 2010), 90-127. On commentaries on the *Analects* and their relationship to intellectual history, see Daniel K. Gardner, *Zhu Xi's Reading of the Analects: Canon, Commentary, and the Classical Tradition* (Columbia University Press, 2003); John Makeham, *Transmitters and Creators: Chinese Commentators and Commentaries on the Analects* (Harvard University Asia Center, 2003); Matsukawa Kenji, *Rongo no shisōshi* (1994), trans. Lin Ching-chang et al. as *Lunyu de sixiang shi* (Wanjuan lou tushu gongsi, 2004); Tang Minggui, *Lunyu xue shi* (Zhongguo shehui kexue chubanshe, 2009). For collections of sayings attributed to Confucius beyond the *Analects*, see Sun Xingyan (1753–1818), *Kongzi jiyu jiaozhu*, ed. Guo Yi, 3 vols. (Zhonghua shuju, 2017); and *ZY*.

5. Historians have questioned the prominence of Confucius during the Western Han and whether state sponsorship of classical learning and Confucian activities was consistent or effective. See Michael Nylan, "A Problematic Model: The Han Synthesis Then and Now," in *Imagining Boundaries: Changing Confucian Doctrines, Texts, and Hermeneutics*, ed. Kai-wing Chow, On-cho

Ng, and John Henderson (State University of New York Press, 1999), 17–56; Michael Loewe, "Confucian Values and Practices in Han China," *T'oung Pao* 98 (2012): 1–30; Michael Loewe, "Attitudes to Kongzi in Han Times," *Journal of Asian History* 55, no. 1 (2021): 1–30; Michael Loewe, "The *Rulin* of Han Times and Their Relation to Kongzi," *Journal of Asian History* 55, no. 2 (2021): 183–215. Cf. chapter 4, n123.

6. Julia Murray and Lu Wensheng, *Confucius: His Life and Legacy in Art*, ed. J. May Lee Barrett (China Institute, 2010), 15, 25n15.

7. The text refers to them here by their style names: "Zilu, Ran You, Gongxi Hua, and Zeng Xi," and later Confucius addresses them by their given names. I have retained the use of the style name only for Zilu (Zhong Yóu) to minimize confusion.

8. Zeng Dian appears in a less flattering light as a violent father in received texts dating from first century BCE to early third century (*HSWZ* 8.383; *SY* 3.6; *KZJY* 15.228-29) and in the excavated text "The Scholar's Words" 儒家者言, where his unjustified corporal punishment of his docile son Zeng Shen is told to highlight the latter's filial piety. See Tian Zhizhong, *Zhuzi lun Zeng Dian "qixiang" yanjiu* (Zhongguo shehui kexue chubanshe, 2020), 10.

9. *HSWZ* 7.343, 9.411; *SY* 15.13; *KZJY* 8.88-89.

10. On interpretations of this passage, see Wu Daofang, "Jingxue shi shiye zhong Zeng Dian zhi zhi de duowei jiedu—jian ping *Lunyu* Xianjin 'Shi zuo' chanshishi de deshi," *Zhongguo zhexue shi* (2009): 5–12; Jiang Yean Liang and Wu Te-Ling, "Kongzi weihe zantong Zeng Dian: zhujie fazhan yu dianfan zhuanyi zhi chutan," *Changgeng keji xuekan* 22 (December 2014): 97–122; Lü Shih-hao, "Cong shijian jiaodu lun 'Lunyu Xianjin' 'Shizuo' zhang de yiyi," *Dong Wu lishi xuebao* 33 (2015): 1–44; Liu Huanwen, "Lunyu 'Sizi shizuo' zhang yanjiu" (MA thesis, Qufu shifan daxue lishi wenhua xueyuan, 2015); Feng Xueqin, " 'Zeng Dian chuantong' 'shenmi chuantong' yu 'zhuguan pai'—rujia shenmei xingshang xue chuantong jiqi shijian fangfa," *Meiyu xuekan* 9, no. 6 (December 2018): 67–75; Chen Hui, "Zeng Dian zhi zhi yu rujia zhengjiao lixiang," *Zhongguo zhexue shi*, no. 4 (2020): 60–66, 107; Tian Zhizhong, *Zhuzi lun "Zeng Dian qixiang" yanjiu*; Chen Zhiyang, "Zeng Xi yanzhi de zhenyi yu Kongzi 'Yu Dian' de zhenxiang," *Zhongguo wenhua yanjiu* (Summer 2024): 76–94.

11. *LY* 3: 1043. The breeze would have made the cold even more unbearable, and Wang Chong glosses *feng* 風 (breeze or wind) as *feng* 諷 (chant). Wang Chong follows another recension of the *Analects*, where *gui* 歸 (return) appears as *kui* 饋 (offer food), which is tied to sacrifice. The Tang poet and scholar-official Han Yu (768–824) also raises the issue of water temperature and proposes the emendation of *yu* 浴 (bathe) as *yan* 沿 (go along the banks of the river) (*LY* 1:1043).

12. *CDB* 1: 321–22, 369.

13. "Biographies of Wang Chong, Wang Fu, Zhongchang Tong," in *HHS* 49.1644.

14. *Lunyu zhushu,* with commentaries by He Yan (195–249) and Xing Bing (932–1010), 11.102a, in *Chongkan Songben Shisan jing zhushu fu jiaokan ji,* ed. Ruan Yuan et al. (1815) (Yiwen yinshuguan, 1965).

15. The phrase is derived from the chapter "The Conduct of Scholars" (Ruxing 儒行) in *Record of Rituals* (*LJ* 3: 1406).

16. Cheng Hao and Cheng Yi, *Er Cheng ji* (Zhonghua shuju, 1981), 136, 396.

17. *Lunyu jizhu,* 131–32, in *Dianjiao Sishu zhangju jizhu,* with commentaries by Zhu Xi (1130–1200) et al. (Zhonghua shuju, 2003); *LY* 3: 1048. On how Zhu Xi's views on "Zeng Dian's aura" change over time, see Tian Zhizhong, *Zhuzi lun "Zeng Dian qixiang" yanjiu,* 67–185.

18. The Ming scholar Yang Shen (1488–1559) claimed that Zhu Xi regretted his comment on his deathbed (*LY* 3: 1048). For questions on this claim, see Tian Zhizhong, *Zhuzi lun "Zeng Dian qixiang" yanjiu,* 184–85. Zhu Xi singled out "The Great Learning" (Daxue 大學) and "The Mean" (Zhongyong 中庸), both chapters from the *Record of Rituals* (*Liji*), and assigned them independent status. They were grouped with the *Analects* and *Mencius* as the Four Books and became the core texts in the imperial civil service examination.

19. Wang Yangming [Wang Shouren], "Moonlit Night: Chanting Poems with Various Disciples at Heavenly Spring Bridge, Two Poems" 月夜二首：與諸生歌於天泉橋, in Wang Shouren, *Wang Yangming quanji,* 2 vols. (Shanghai guji chubanshe, 1992), 1: 787.

20. The remark, recalled by Qian Dehong (1532 *jinshi*), is quoted in Huang Chi-li, "Yeyan Tianquan qiao: yige Wang men jiti jiyi anli de kaocha," *Ehu yuekan* 491 (May 2016): 24.

21. On music in the Confucian tradition, see "Record of Music" (Yue ji) in *Record of Rituals* (*LJ* 3: 975–1039).

22. See, for example, Wang Guowei (1877–1927), "Kongzi zhi meiyu zhuyi" (1904), in *Xiandai Zhongguo meiyu wenxian xuanbian yu daodu 1900–1960,* ed. Guo Huanling (Shandong wenyi chubanshe, 2023), 1–13; Xu Fuguan, *Zhongguo yishu jingshen* (Xuesheng shuju, 1984), 17–19; Chen Zhaoying, *Rujia meixue yu jingdian quanshi* (Huadong shifan daxue chubanshe, 2008), 27.

23. See Yan Yuan's (1635–1704) critique of the Song Neo-Confucian reading of this passage, *Yan Yuan ji* (Zhonghua shuju, 1987), 209; the comments of the Qing poet and scholar-official Yuan Mei (1716–1797) (*LY* 3: 1050). The late Qing novel *Lovers and Heroes* (*Ernü yingxiong zhuan*), by Wen Kang (b. 1794), elaborates this reading and argues that the exchange between Dian and Confucius amounts to an implicit rebuke of Dian. See Wen Kang, *Ernü yingxiong zhuan,* ed. Rao Bin, ann. Miu Tianhua, 2 vols. (Sanmin shuju, 1999), chapter 39,

725–29. According to *Analects* 17.4, Confucius "broke into a smile" when discussing the role of music in government, see chapter 4, 243.

24. See the comments by Huang Zhen (1213–1281) (*LY* 3: 1048–49), Yang Shen (*LY* 3: 1048), Yuan Mei (*LY* 3: 1050), and Qian Mu, *Lunyu xinjie* (Sanlian shudian, 2002), 299–300.

25. Mou Zongsan, *Cong Lu Xiangshan dao Liu Jishan* (Jilin chuban jituan, 2010), 182. On humor in the *Analects*, see Christoph Harbsmeier, "Confucius Ridens: Humor in the *Analects*," *Harvard Journal of Asiatic Studies* 50, no. 1 (1990): 131–61.

26. Yang Shuda, *Lunyu shuzheng* (Shanghai guji chubanshe, 2007), 272; Chen Zhiyang, "Zeng Xi yanzhi de zhenyi," 94.

27. Zhang Taiyan, "Lun zhuzi xue," in *Zhang Taiyan zhenglun xuanji*, ed. Tang Zhijun, 2 vols. (Zhonghua shuju, 1977), 1: 291. In that essay, Zhang postulated three versions of Confucius: as historian, as educator, and as "national goody two shoes," who "was not adamant when it came to morality, not adamant also when it came to ideals, and deemed as acceptable whatever could get things done with expediency." Zhang later recanted and acknowledged he was just trying to discredit Kang Youwei's (1858–1927) version of Confucius.

1. Chronicling Confucius

1. According to *Gongyang Tradition*, Confucius was born in the eleventh month of the twenty-first year of Lord Xiang (552 BCE). *Guliang Tradition* claims that he was born in the tenth month of that year.

2. See *Shiben bazhong*, comp. and comm. Song Zhong, ed. Qin Jiamo et al. (Shangwu yinshuguan, 1957), 20, 27–29, 31, 51, 105, 162; *Qianfu lun*, by Wang Fu, ann. Wang Jipei, ed. Peng Duo (Zhonghua shuju, 1997), 31.431–35; *KZJY* 39.525–27. Song rulers were descendants of the Shang royal line. The Song minister Kongfu Jia (d. 701), named as one of Confucius's forbears in *Qianfu lun* and *KZJY* (39.527), was killed by Hua Du, another Song minister (*Zuo Huan* 2.1, 1: 74–75). Kong Fangshu is said to have fled to Lu to escape the Hua lineage's persecution (*KZJY* 39.527). Cui Shu is skeptical (*CDB* 264–65).

3. See the comments by Sima Zhen (679–732) and Zhang Shoujie (7th c.) (*SJ* 47.5–6).

4. The name of Confucius's mother is given as Zhengzai in the *Record of Ritual* (*LJ* 1:291).

5. One *chi* in this period is about 19 cm.

6. See the comments of Liang Yusheng (1745–1819) and Cui Shi (1852–1924) (*SJ* 47.6–7).

7. Cui Shi comments: This is Sima Qian's way of honoring Confucius as a sage who received the command from heaven (*SJ* 47.6). In addition to the stories

of Jian Di and Jiang Yuan, Confucius refers to the story of Yu (founder of Xia dynasty) being born from his mother's back, but he goes on to affirm the greater virtue of the sage king Shun in the excavated text "Zigao." On Confucius in excavated texts, see *KJY* 3: 793–1003; Scott Cook, "Confucius in Excavated Warring States Manuscripts," in *A Concise Companion to Confucius*, ed. Paul Goldin (John Wiley and Sons, 2017), 35–51. Sima Qian tells the stories of the miraculous birth of the Shang and Zhou ancestors (*SJ* 3.2, 4.2) and also that of Liu Bang (r. 206–195 BCE), the founder of Han. His mother dreams of intercourse with a spirit as her husband sees a dragon hovering over her when she becomes pregnant with Liu Bang (*SJ* 8.4).

8. *Chunqiu wei yan Kong tu* 春秋緯演孔圖, in *ZY* 962. Confucius is called the "Dark Sage" 玄聖 because of this connection with the Black God; see Li Xian's annotations in Ban Gu's biography in *Hou Hanshu* (*HHS* 40B.1376).

9. The notion of law and order also includes calendrical calculations; see Xu Xingwu, "Zuowei pifu de xuansheng suwang: chenwei wenxian zhong de Kongzi xingxiang yu sixiang," in *Dongya Lunyu xue: Zhongguo pian,* ed. Huang Chun-chieh (Taida chuban zhongxin 2009), 154–55.

10. "Sang zhong" 桑中; see *Shijing zhuxi*, ann. Cheng Junying and Jiang Jianyuan (Zhonghua shuju, 2017), 1: 142–45.

11. On sacred places associated with Kongsang in Chinese mythology, see Robert Henricks, "On the Whereabouts and Identity of the Place Called 'K'ung-sang' (Hollow Mulberry) in Chinese Mythology," *Bulletin of the School of Oriental and African Studies* 58, no.1 (January 1995): 69–90.

12. Wang Genlin, Huang Yiyuan, and Cao Guangfu, eds., *Han Wei Liuchao biji xiaoshuo daguan* (Shanghai guji chubanshe, 1999), 224.

13. For a transcription and discussion of texts from Lord Haihun's tomb, see Zhu Fenghan and Ke Zhonghua, eds., *Haihun jiandu chulu* (Beijing daxue chubanshe, 2020). For a translation and discussion of the text on the mirror screen, see Mark Csikszentmihalyi, "The Haihunhou Capsule Biographies of Kongzi and His Disciples," *Early China* 45 (2022): 341–74. The mirror screen text also has *chou* 疇 (field), which can be a variant of *dao* 禱 (pray, as in the received text) but can also be read as follows: "They (Confucius's parents) cultivated fields at Ni Hill" 疇於尼丘, see Csikszentmihalyi, "The Haihunhou Capsule," 349–50. Huo Guang (d. 68 BCE) put Liu He on the throne after the sudden death of Emperor Zhao (r. 87–74 BCE), but Huo deposed him after twenty-seven days and replaced him with Emperor Xuan (r. 74–48 BCE).

14. *Shuowen jiezi zhu*, Xu Shen. Ann. and comm. Duan Yucai (1735–1815) (Shanghai guji chubanshe, 1981), 8A.44a.

15. Duan Yucai suggests that the original graph for "Ni" should be 坭, the embankment that keeps the water in, see *Shuowen jiezi zhu*, 8A.44b-45a.

16. According to *Sayings* (*KZJY* 39.528), Confucius was three when his father died. Fang lies to the east of Qufu.

17. In the *Analects* (15.1), Confucius says he is familiar with "sacrificial vessels" (*zudou* 俎豆) but knows nothing about military affairs. See also 1.33.

18. This landmark is mentioned several times in *Zuo Tradition*, where it is often associated with oaths of imprecation.

19. Confucius's grandson Zisi explains why his son should not wear mourning for his mother because she has been "sent away" (that is, divorced) and is no longer Zisi's wife. When asked why he deviates from the practice of his "illustrious ancestor" (*xian junzi* 先君子), Zisi implies that the latter could set his own rules because of his great virtue (*LJ* 1: 166–67). If this "illustrious ancestor" is Confucius's son Boyu, it would mean that Confucius divorced his wife (*LJ* 1: 185; cf. chapter 4, 242), but if it refers to Confucius, it means that Confucius's mother was not properly recognized for some reason by her husband Shuliang He's lineage. Qian Mu argues that the divorced wife refers to Shuliang He's sonless first wife, see Qian Mu, *Kongzi zhuan*, in *Qian Mu xiansheng quanji* (Jiuzhou chubanshe, 2011), 6: 6. Two entries in the *Record of Rituals* mention that Zisi's mother died in Wei (*LJ* 1: 120, 1: 296); some commentators take this to mean that she was divorced or remarried after Boyu died. Hence the assertion that "for three generations, men of the Kong lineage (Confucius, his son Boyu, his grandson Zisi) divorced their wives" (*KZJY* 662).

20. *Lienü zhuan jinzhu jinyi*, comp. Liu Xiang, ann. Zhang Jing (Shangwu yin-shuguan, 1994), 1.11. Oliver Weingarten notes this parallel in "Recent Monographs on Confucius and Early Confucianism," *T'oung Pao* 97 (2011): 178.

21. Zheng Xuan glosses *shen* 慎 (translated as "caution") as *yin* 引, a kind of implement for the funeral (instead of the burial) ceremony (*LJ* 1: 171).

22. The implication is that they repair the grave mound before returning.

23. Cf. *KZJY* 43.648, 44.655.

24. *Record of Rituals* often assigns divergent customs to different dynasties (Xia, Shang, Zhou), as does Zheng Xuan in his annotations (e.g., *LJ* 1: 163, 1: 166–67, 1: 169, 1: 172, 1: 196, 1: 208, 1: 219, 1: 226, 1: 254, 1: 258–59, 1: 262, 1: 292–93). See also *Sayings* (*KZJY* 42.602, 43.623, 43.634, 43.650–52).

25. For definitions of the ideal *shi* 士 that focus more specifically on personal moral qualities, see the *Analects* (4.9, 8.7, 12.20, 13.28, 14.2). For some other important passages defining *shi* in early texts, see *XZ* 29.400, 31.407; *LSCQ* 2: 1020; *DDLJ* 1: 52–53; *KZJY* 9.126). On *shi* in preimperial China, see Yu Ying-shih, *Shi yu Zhongguo wenhua* (Shanghai renmin chubanshe, 2003), 3–114. Cf. Matthias Richter, "Roots of Ru 儒 Ethics in Shi 士 Status Anxiety," *Journal of American Oriental Society* 137, no. 3 (July–September 2017): 449–71.

26. D. C. Lau disputes the identification of Yang Hu and Yang Huo, see D. C. Lau, trans. and ed., *Confucius: The Analects* (Penguin Books, 1979), 213–14. Cf. Qian Mu, *Xian Qin zhuzi xinian* (Dong da tushu gongsi, 1990), 13–15; *CDB* 278.

27. It is possible to punctuate this passage differently and regard the twice-uttered phrase, "it cannot," as Confucius's responses to Yang Hu's questions.

28. Ji Wuzi, head of the most powerful lineage in Lu, died in 535 BCE. His son, Ji Pingzi, succeeded him.

29. *GY* "Luyu" 2.20, 216. Both "Fufu He" and "Zheng Kaofu" combine the given names (He, Zheng) with the style names (Fufu, Kaofu).

30. Alternatively, "like a mask worn in exorcism rites" (*ZY* 611). Apocryphal texts mention other strange physical traits: see *ZY* 978; *CDB* 266; Xing Yitian, *Hua wai zhi yi: Handai Kongzi jian Laozi huaxiang yanjiu* (Sanmin shuju, 2018), 122–24; Zhou Yutong, *Kongzi, Kong sheng he Zhu Xi*, ed. Zhu Weizheng (Renmin chubanshe, 2012), 84. A *Shiben* fragment mentions that Confucius has forty-nine remarkable traits and names some of them; see Li Ling, *Qu sheng naide zhen Kongzi: Lunyu zongheng du* (Sanlian shudian, 2008), 57–58. An account by a descendant of Confucius in the fifty-first generation (*Kong shi zuting guangji* 孔氏祖庭廣記) also enumerates forty-nine remarkable traits; cf. *ZY* 781. According to Li Ling, *Qu sheng naide zhen Kongzi*, 59n2, nine *chi* and six *cun* equals 221.76 cm., or 7 ft., 3 in.

31. Similar formulations are found in *XZ* 27.380 and *YZCQ* 5.347.

32. Xing Yitian, *Hua wai zhi yi*.

33. This echoes the comparison of wisdom texts and the sages' words to "dregs" (*zaopo* 糟粕) in the chapter titled "Way of Heaven" (Tiandao 天道) in *Zhuangzi* (*ZZ* 13.490–91).

34. See *ZZ*, chapters 12, 13, 14, 21, 22.

35. Versions of this story appear in *Balanced Discourses* (*LH* 80.1117–18) and *Liezi* or *Master Lie* (*LZ* 4.122–23).

36. The account from Lord Haihun's tomb states that Confucius was thirty in Zhao 6 (536 BCE) although it gives the same dates for Confucius's birth and death as in *Historical Records*.

37. See, e.g., *HFZ* 37.882, *ZZ* 21.719, *HNZ* 13.450, *LSCQ* 1: 803, *HSWZ* 7.282, *SY* 2.9, 11.10. *Mencius* (5A.9) dismisses such stories as mere rumors.

38. Eric Henry, "The Motif of Recognition in Early China," *Harvard Journal of Asiatic Studies* 47, no. 1 (June 1987): 5–30.

39. Chen Renxi (1581–1636), one of the commentators included in *Shiji pinglin*, notes the break but tries to justify it as deliberate distancing. See *Shiji pinglin*, Sima Qian. Comp. Ling Zhilong (17th c.), with additions by Li Guangjin (17th c.) and Arii Shinsai (1830–1889). 5 vols. (Diqiu chubanshe, 1992), 47.1511.

40. Cf. the summary in *SJ* 47.44–45.

41. In his account of these events in "The Hereditary House of Lu," Sima Qian notes that Qi instates Lord Zhao at Yun and Lord Zhao eventually dies at Ganhou in Jin (*SJ* 33.46–48). See also *Zuo* Zhao 26.3, 3: 1656–57; *SJ* 47.46.

42. Ironically, the Chen (Tian) lineage, which claimed descent from Shun and might have brought this music to Qi, would eventually usurp Qi rule.

43. In the analogous passage in *Master Yan's Annals* (*YZCQ* 8.491), Nixi appears as Erji.

44. Variants of these final two clauses appear in *Mozi* (*MZ* 39.272), *Master Yan's Annals* (*YZCQ* 8.491), and Sima Tan's summary of the main points of the Six Schools (*SJ* 130.10).

45. The key issue is the nature and fulfillment of social roles rather than the function of language. On ways to think about "the rectification of names" and definitions in early Chinese thought, see Carine Defoort, "How to Name and Not to Name: That is the Question in Early Chinese Philosophy," in *Keywords in Chinese Culture*, ed. Wai-yee Li and Yuri Pines (Chinese University of Hong Kong Press, 2020), 3–36.

46. Indeed, the idea that rulers "cannot use" (*buyong* 不用) Confucius becomes a refrain in this chapter; see Chen Renxi's comment (*Shiji pinglin* 47.1507).

47. *Zuo* Ding 5.4, 3: 1762–63 (505 BCE). Ji Huanzi was Ji Pingzi's son and the most powerful minister in Lu.

48. Tang Gu glosses *fenyang* 墳羊 (written in some recensions of *GY* as 羵羊) as "the sheep which cannot yet be identified as male or female" (see Tang Gu's comment, cited in *SJ* 47.22).

49. Wei Zhao glosses "spirits" as "rulers," whose dominion over mountains and rivers also means control of their spirits (see Wei Zhao's comment, in *GY* "Luyu" 2.18, 214). Kuaiji Mountain is the supposed site of Yu's burial.

50. Lu defeated Chang Di in 616 BCE (*Zuo* Wen 11.5, 1: 522–23).

51. Cf. *SY* 18.18, *KZJY* 15.242–44, *HNZ* 13.458–59.

52. Liu Zongyuan (773–819) describes 1.10 as "slandering the sage" (see Liu Zongyuan's comment, in *Shiji pinglin* 47.1513). Some scholars emend "did not speak" as "did not usually speak" in the *Analects* (7.21) to accommodate passages like 1.10.

53. The last line is found in "Xici xia" 繫辭下; see *Zhouyi zhushu*, comm. Wang Bi (226–249) and Han Kangbo (332–380), 8.179, included in *Chongkan Songben Shisan jing zhushu fu jiaokan ji*, ed. Ruan Yuan et al. (1815) (Yiwen yinshuguan, 1965). This anecdote also appears in *Sayings* (*KZJY* 18.276).

54. Cited in Chen Miaoru, "Biji xiaoshuo zhong de 'Kongzi chuanshuo' jiqi tese," *Zhongguo Wenhua daxue zhongwen xuebao* 37 (March 2019): 39.

55. According to *Zuo Tradition*, Yang Hu intends to put himself forward as the head of the Meng lineage (*Zuo* Ding 8.10, 3: 1784–85).

56. Reading *wen* 溫 as *yun* 蘊, following Takigawa (*SJ* 47.25).

57. Zhou started out in the west and Lu was situated to its east.

58. Gongshan's rebellion could have been the result of the decision to reduce the city walls of the major lineages. To separate those two events would help to explain how Confucius's sympathy shifts. See *CDB* 284; Edward Slingerland, trans., *Confucius/Analects: With Selections from Traditional Commentaries* (Hackett, 2013), 203. Alternatively, if the temporal distance is erased, one would have to choose between the accounts of Gongshan summoning Confucius and that of Confucius directing moves that drive Gongshan to rebellion.

59. See Jin Lüxiang's (1232–1703) comment (cited in *LY* 4: 1533).

60. In *Zuo Tradition*, Gongshan Buniu is shown to have some redeeming traits (*Zuo* Ai 8.2, 3: 1880–81).

61. Wang Fuzhi, *Sishu xunyi*, in *Chuanshan quanshu*, 16 vols., ed. *Chuanshan quanshu* bianji huiyuan hui (Yuelu shushe, 1998), 7: 906.

62. *Zuo Tradition*, *Gongyang*, and *Guliang* mention Zhongcheng (central city). On the interpretation of *zhongdu* as "middle-sized city," see *Zuo* 1: 7–8.

63. Lu was in present-day Shandong, and the other lords were in states west of Lu.

64. According to Wang Su (195–256), these refer to mountains and forests, rivers and marshes, mounds and low hills, banks and flat land, plains and marshland (*KZJY* 1.3).

65. Lords come to meetings with chariots (*bingche* 兵車) and, much more rarely, carriages (*chengche* 乘車). The latter indicates the expectation of amity and accord. Qi-Lu tensions built up prior to Jiagu because Lu was vacillating between Qi and Jin (*CDB* 281).

66. This is the ritually proper way for a subject to walk to indicate respectful urgency in the presence of rulers. I have omitted the words "with small steps" in translating subsequent repetition of the term *qujin* 趨進 ("to hasten forward with small steps") for stylistic reasons.

67. See, e.g., comments in Ye Mengde (1077–1148), *Shilin xiansheng Chunqiu zhuan*, 19.15a–16b, in *Tongzhi tang jingjie*, comp. Nara Singde, 1673 edition (Harvard-Yenching Library Rare Books); Cui Shu's refutation of the account in *Guliang* and *Historical Records* (*CDB* 280–83).

68. Note that Limi (called Liju in 1.14, 1.17, and 1.17a) is dismissive of Confucius, while in 1.14 he regards Confucius as a major threat that necessitates a preemptive strike.

69. The so-called barbarians were living in close proximity with groups identified as "central states" in this period, despite the model of center and margins invoked in diplomatic speeches; see Wai-yee Li, "Cultural Identity and Cultural Difference in Zuozhuan," special issue on "Cultural Others in Traditional Chinese Literature," ed. Wai-yee Li, *Journal of Chinese Literature and Culture* 7, no. 1 (June 2020): 7–33; and Wai-yee Li, "Hua Yi zhi bian / Hua

Yi zhi bian: cong *Zuozhuan* tanqi," *Lingnan xuebao* 13 (December 2020): 19–50.

70. See, e.g., *HNZ* 11.346, *HSWZ* 10.438, *SJ* 32.9.

71. These lines (except the last) also appear in *Mr. Lü's Annals* (*LSCQ* 1: 383–84).

72. Some scholars believe that one *zhi* equals three *zhang* (693 cm), others argue that it is over five *zhang*, or just over 10 m. If the latter is correct, then one hundred *zhi* would be 1.5 km. Cf. *Zuo* Yin 1.4, 1: 7–8: the Zheng minister Zhai Zhong urges Lord Zhuang of Zheng to curb the power of his younger brother, "For the wall of an outlying city to exceed one hundred *zhi* is a danger for the capital."

73. See 1.13, 1.13a.

74. This summary of Confucius's achievements also appears (with variations in details and wording) in *XZ* 8.77; *LSCQ* 2: 989; *Xinxu* 1.3–4; *KZJY* 1:12.

75. Some read *ze* 澤 ("giving it luster") as *shi* 釋, "explaining it away."

76. See, e.g., *CDB* 286–87; Qian Mu, *Xian Qin zhuzi xinian*, 25–26; Xu Fuguan, "Yige lishi gushi de xingcheng qiji yanjin—lun Kongzi zhu Shaozheng Mao," in Xu Fuguan, *Rujia zhengzhi sixiang yu minzhu ziyou renquan*, ed. Xiao Xinyi (Xuesheng shuju, 2013); D. C. Lau, *Confucius: The Analects*, 187–94; Xia Changpu, "Zi wei zheng yan yong sha—lun Kongzi zhu Shaozheng Mao," in Xia Changpu, *Rujia yu ruxue tanjiu* (Da'an chubanshe, 2014), 87–124. Shaozheng Mao does not appear in other contexts in early texts.

77. See the *Analects* (2.3), discussed in chapter 2, 179-80.

78. This account also appears in *Sayings* (*KZJY* 19.293). In *Zither Music* (*Qin cao*, ca. third century), Confucius is credited with various songs (*ZY* 743–46). On the occasion of leaving Lu, he is said to have sung "The Song of Mount Turtle," comparing Mount Turtle to the Ji lineage: "I want to look at Lu, / But Mount Turtle blocks my view. / I don't have an axe, / What can I do about Mount Turtle?" (*ZY* 744). Confucius's song in 1.17 is quoted in Lin Yutang's play, see chapter 4, 251.

79. For a discussion of versions of this story, see Wai-yee Li, "Anecdotal Barbarians in Early China," in *Between Philosophy and History: Rhetorical Uses of Anecdotes in Early China*, ed. Sarah Queen and Paul van Els (State University of New York Press, 2017), 113–44.

80. Note that the story is dated to the reign of Lord Ai, when according to Sima Qian this event is dated to the reign of Lord Ding. Liju should not be referring to the Lu ruler by his posthumous honorific.

81. As a posthumous honorific, "Ling" usually conveys a negative judgment. Lord Xiao is identified as the Ousted Lord of Wei; see 1.34.

82. The unit of measure is unstated and debated by scholars (*SJ* 47.36). Cui Shu finds the bald statement of salary jarring in the world of fifth century BCE and incongruous with Confucius's character (*CDB* 289).

83. Sima Zhen believes that Gongsun Yujia is carrying weapons to threaten Confucius (*SJ* 47.36), but it is more likely Gongsun Yujia goes in and out to exercise surveillance.

84. On this figure in various early texts, see Oliver Weingarten, "The Figure of Yan Zhuoju 顏涿聚 in Ancient Chinese Literature," *Monumenta Serica: Journal of Oriental Studies* 63, no.2 (December 2015): 229–61.

85. Ning Wuzi is mentioned in *Zuo Tradition* in events dated to 632 and 623 BCE, long before the birth of Confucius. The Ning lineage was decimated in 546 BCE. He is highly praised in the *Analects* (5.10) as a wise man who shows his wisdom when good governance prevails in his state but hides it when disorder takes over.

86. The different meanings of *ming* 命 as lifespan, command, and destiny are combined in the story of Lord Wen of Zhu (d. 615 BCE), who decides to move his capital to Yi even though the result of divination proclaims that such a move would benefit the people but not the ruler, see *Zuo* Wen 13.3, 1: 531–32; David Schaberg, "Command and the Content of Tradition," in *The Magnitude of Ming: Command, Allotment, and Fate in Chinese Culture*, ed. Christopher Lupke (University of Hawai'i Press, 2005). For *ming* as command, see also 1.18a.

87. *Lienü zhuan* 8.12. The virtuous wife of Lord Ling in the chapter "Wise and Good" (*Lienü zhuan* 3.1) may refer to another woman.

88. Straw dogs might have been used as a kind of ritual scapegoat. Cf. *Laozi* 5: "Heaven and earth have no benevolence and use the myriad creatures as straw dogs. The sage has no benevolence and uses the myriad clans as straw dogs."

89. On Li Ling's interpretation of this term, see Li Ling, *Qu sheng naide zhen Kongzi*, 158–68.

90. But no extant text mentions Wu obtaining control over three Chen settlements.

91. *Zuo* Zhao 20.4, 3: 1572–78; Ding 8.7, 3: 1782–83; 9.4, 3: 1792–93; 10.4, 3: 1798–99; 13.1, 3: 1808–09; 14.1, 3: 1812–15.

92. Cf. *Zuo* Cheng 12.2, 2: 660–61: "In writing, 'stop' and 'dagger-axe' make 'martial.' " 夫文，止戈為武.

93. The lines about the disappearance of mythical animals are found with some variations in *HNZ* 8.246; *DDLJ* 2: 1329; *LSCQ* 1: 678. The *qilin* is the same as the *lin* in 1.64.

94. I have used a diacritical mark to distinguish the city Qī 戚 from the state of Qí 齊. They should not be confused with the small state Qǐ 杞 mentioned in 1.52. On Kuaikui, see 1.20.

95. See the arguments of Zhu Xi and Quan Zuwang (1705–1755) (*SJ* 47.58; *LY* 3: 1356–58); Qian Mu, *Xian Qin zhuzi xinian*, 46; Cui Shu (*CDB* 301–03).

96. In *Sayings*, Zilu quotes this as a former saying by Confucius (*KZJY* 20.298).

97. See John Makeham, "Between Chen and Cai: *Zhuangzi* and the *Analects*," in *Wandering at Ease in the Zhuangzi*, ed. Roger Aimes (State University of New York Press, 1998), 75–100; Andrew Meyer, "The Frontier Between Chen and Cai: Anecdote, Narrative, and Philosophical Argumentation in Early China," in *Between Philosophy and History*, ed. Sarah Queen and Paul van Els, 65–91; Chen Xiaoming, "Kongzi e yu Chen Cai zhihou," *Zhongshan daxue xuebao* 44, no. 6 (2004): 147–54.

98. See 1.59; *Analects* 10.8.

99. Following Chen Qiyou's emendation of the text (*LSCQ* 2: 1076). The original has "If the food is clean, we can offer it as sacrifice," but Confucius is not supposed to know at this point that the food is not clean.

100. Following Chen Qiyou's emendation (*LSCQ* 2: 1077).

101. This line appears in *Laozi*.

102. Meyer, "The Frontier Between Chen and Cai," 78.

103. Makeham, "Between Chen and Cai."

104. Confucius tells his disciples to board the tall man's carriage upon seeing its cracks "periodically opening" (like a fish's gills) (*ZY* 923). The story is also found in the Buddhist anthology *Pearls in the Garden of Dharma* (*Fayuan zhulin*, 32.668), included in *Taishō shinshū Daizōkyō* (Xin wenfang, 1983), vol. 52. On fantastic tales featuring Confucius, see Chen Miaoru, "Biji xiaoshuo zhong de 'Kongzi chuanshuo' jiqi tese"; Lu Zhao, *Weird Confucius: Unorthodox Representations of Confucius in History* (Bloomsbury, 2024), 35–74.

105. Sima Guang (1019–1086) refers to that passage as the programmatic affirmation of the hierarchy of ruler and subject in his comprehensive history. See *Zizhi tongjian*, Sima Guang et al., with phonetic glosses by Hu Sanxing, ed. Biaodian *Zizhi tongjian* xiaozu (Guji chubanshe, 1956), 1.4. The argument about the inviolability of "ritual objects" and "names" is repeated in *Zuo* Zhao 32.4, 3: 1724–25.

106. *Luan* 亂 ("disorder") can also mean "final strains," as in the *Analects* (8.15), but here it seems to refer specifically to Zhou decline. The two words *zhi luan* 之亂 also disrupt the parallelism and might have been added by mistake.

107. In *Han's Exegesis*, "Osprey" is lauded as "the foundation of heaven and earth" (*HSWZ* 5.229). According to Mao Tradition, "Osprey" praises the virtuous consorts of Zhou. See also "The Mean": "The Way of the noble man finds its beginnings in the relationship between husband and wife" 君子之道, 造端乎夫婦; see *Zhongyong zhangju*, 23, in *Dianjiao Sishu zhangju jizhu*, comm. Zhu Xi et al. (Zhonghua shuju, 2003); "Xici xia": "The essences of male and female intersect and the myriad things are generated and transformed 男女構精,萬物化生, *Zhouyi zhushu*, 8.170. In a set of excavated bamboo strips designated by the title "Confucius's Discourse on the Odes" (Kongzi shilun 孔子詩論, ca. 4th–3rd century BCE), "Osprey" is said to be about "correction" (*gai* 改),

depicting sensual attraction that ends in a ritually proper marriage celebrated with bells and drums (*KJY* 3: 908–09).

108. Slingerland, trans., *Confucius/Analects*, 98. On the *Analects* (chapter 10) and ritual prescriptions, see Arthur Waley, *Three Ways of Thought in Ancient China* (G. Allen and Unwin, 1939), 21.

109. These ritual prescriptions about meat and mat also appear as "fetal instruction" for pregnant women; see Oliver Weingarten, "Confucius and Pregnant Women: An Investigation Into the Intertextuality of the 'Lunyu,' " *Journal of American Oriental Society* 129, no. 4 (2009): 608–13.

110. "The way of the dark sage and uncrowned king" is associated with Daoist nonaction and transcendence in *Zhuangzi* (*ZZ* 13.457). But in the Confucian tradition, Confucius as *suwang* (uncrowned king) refers to how he, despite not being a king, could claim supreme authority (or even hypothetical political authority), laying down laws for posterity through the *Annals* (see *HNZ* 9.313); see also Dong Zhongshu's memorial to the throne (*HS* 56.2609); *SY* 5.2; *LH* 39.609, 80.1122; *KZJY* 39.531; Hung Chun-yin, "Lun Kongzi suwang shuo de xingcheng yu fazhan zhuxiang," *Xing da zhongwen xuebao* 20 (December 2006): 101–40; Hans Van Ess, "Kongzi suwang he Chunqiu chuantong," in *Shengyu lun Lin jing: 2018 Chunqiu xue luntan lunwen ji* (Foguang daxue, 2018), 1–14.

111. Legend has it that there are three locust trees outside the Zhou court. The three highest ministers face the three locusts during court audience. The first Han emperor, Liu Bang, hailed from Feng and Pei.

112. Red Pine and Qiao are both names of immortals.

113. Chen Sheng (d. 208 BCE) and Xiang Yu (d. 202 BCE) rose up against Qin and paved the way for Han success. The Year Star is Jupiter, whose movements were thought to portend important events. "Five stars gathered at the East Well Asterism" is said to be the sign that Liu Bang received the mandate (*HS* 26.1301).

114. Cf. *ZY* 720, 978–79. On Confucius as the Black God, see 1.1b. "Red Liu" 赤劉 (the Red Emperor Liu) parallels with "Black Qiu" 玄丘 (the Black God Confucius). *Mao* 卯 and *jin* 金 are constituent components of the character *liu* 劉.

115. Zhou Yutong, *Kongzi Kong sheng he Zhu Xi*, 86–87, 98.

116. The color black is associated with the element water in the theory of the five phases. On "five stars" and kingship, see n113 above.

117. There are obvious mistakes here. Lord Ding reigned for sixteen years (509–495 BCE). The capture of the *lin* is dated to the fourteenth year of Lord Ai (481 BCE).

118. *Zhuzi yulei*, comp. Li Jingde, ed. Wang Xingxian (Zhonghua shuju, 1986), 83.2172.

119. Commentary on the judgments of the hexagram Great Holdings (*Dayou*) in *Changes*. See Richard John Lynn, trans., *The Classic of Changes: A New Translation of the I Ching as Interpreted by Wang Bi* (Columbia University Press, 1994), 222.

120. Liu Shipei, *Liu Shipei shixue lunzhu xuanji*, ed. Wu Guoyi and Wu Xiuyi (Shanghai guji, 2006), 522. Cf. Martin Kern, "Kongzi as Author in the Han," in *Confucius and the Analects Revisited: New Perspectives on Composition, Dating, and Authorship*, ed. Michael Hunter and Martin Kern (Brill 2018), 268–307.

121. The term *suwang* appears twice in *Historical Records* (*SJ* 3.7, 6.89); in neither case does it refer to Confucius. Cf. n110 above.

122. One *qing* is the equivalent of about 16.5 acres. The Qing scholar Yan Ruoqu (1636–1704) argued that the discussion of rituals could not have taken place at the gravesite and emended *zhong* 冢 as *jia* 家 (*SJ* 47.89). The translation here follows Yan's emendation. Note that Sima Qian also mentions ritual discussions taking place at the former abode of Confucius in his final comments (1.72).

123. On the extent of Confucian influence on Han political culture, see the introduction n5, and chapter 4, n123.

124. See Thomas Wilson, ed., *On Sacred Grounds: Culture, Society, Politics, and the Formation of the Cult of Confucius* (Harvard University Asia Center, 2002); Michael Nylan and Thomas Wilson, *Lives of Confucius: Civilization's Greatest Sage Through the Ages* (Random House, 2010), 149–50.

125. Nylan and Wilson, *Lives of Confucius*, 24. See also Yang Yi, "*Lunyu* nei wai de shikong kaoyi," in *Dongya hanxue yanjiu xuehui shinian ji*, ed. Li Jikai, Yang Xiao'an, and Jiang Shujun (Shanxi Shifan daxue chuban zongshe, 2020).

126. See the *Analects* (9.30); *Mencius* 1A.7, 4A.17; *Chunqiu fanlu yizheng*, ann. Su Yu (Zhonghua shuju, 1992), 3.59, 4.74–75; Yang Xiong, *Fayan yishu*, comp. and comm. Wang Rongbao (Zhonghua shuju, 1987), 8.249. On the notion of *quan* 權, see Griet Vankeerberghen, "Choosing Balance: Weighing (Quan) as a Metaphor for Action in Early Chinese Texts," *Early China* 30 (2005–2006), 47–89.

127. Cui Shu links this specifically to the textual interventions of Zhang Yu (d. 8 CE) and broadens his critique to skepticism regarding the *Analects*, especially its last five chapters (*CDB* 284–86).

128. See, e.g., Robert G. Henricks, "The Hero Pattern and the Life of Confucius," *Journal of Chinese Studies* 1, no. 3 (October 1984): 241–60; Stephen Durrant, *The Cloudy Mirror: Tension and Conflict in the Writings of Sima Qian* (State University of New York Press, 1995), 29–45; Wu Zhenxun, "Shengren xushi yu shensheng dianfan: Shiji Kongzi shijia xilun," *Qinghua xuebao* 39, no. 2 (June 2009): 227–59; Zhang Dake and Chen Xi, *Zhisheng xianshi Kongzi* (Shangwu yinshuguan, 2018).

129. Kai Vogelsang, "Beyond Confucius: A Socio-historical Reading of the *Lunyu,*" *Oriens Extremus,* 49 (2010): 29–61. See also the discussion of the term *shengren* 聖人 in Li Ling, *Qu sheng naide zhen Kongzi,* 144–57.

130. Wai-yee Li, "The Letter to Ren An and Authorship in the Chinese Tradition," in Stephen Durrant, Wai-yee Li, Michael Nylan, and Hans Van Ess, *The Letter to Ren An and Sima Qian's Legacy* (University of Washington Press, 2016), 96–124.

131. The identification of these "sage rulers" with Han rulers becomes explicit in *Chunqiu fanlu* and He Xiu's commentary; see Sarah Queen, *From Chronicle to Canon: The Hermeneutics of the Spring and Autumn According to Tung Chung-shu* (Cambridge University Press, 1996); Michael Loewe, *Dong Zhongshu, a "Confucian" Heritage and the* Chunqiu fanlu (Brill, 2011); Joachim Gentz, "The Past as a Messianic Vision: Historical Thought and Strategies of Sacralization in the Early Gongyang Tradition," in *Historical Truth, Historical Criticism, and Ideology: Chinese Historiography and Historical Culture from a New Comparative Perspective,* ed. Schmidt-Glintzer, Achim Mittag, and Jörn Rüsen (Brill, 2005), 227–54; Wai-yee Li, *The Readability of the Past in Early Chinese Historiography* (Harvard University Asia Center, 2007), 411–21.

2. Arguing with Confucius

1. For a succinct discussion, see Michael Nylan and Thomas Wilson, *Lives of Confucius: Civilization's Greatest Sage Through the Ages* (Random House, 2010), 29–66.

2. Xiao Gongquan, *Zhongguo zhengzhi sixiang shi,* 2 vols. (Lianjing chuban gongsi, 2022), 1: 120; Michael Nylan, "Kongzi and Mozi, the Classicists (Ru 儒) and the Mohists (Mo 墨) in Classical-Era Thinking," *Oriens Extremus* 48 (2009): 1–20.

3. Yao yielded the throne to Shun and Shun to Yu. Abdication of the throne to the worthy is upheld by some as the highest political virtue, but this means that the descendants of Yao and Shun could not lay claim to any territory.

4. Cheng Tang was the first king the Shang dynasty; King Wu was an early Zhou king. The last Zhou king ended his rule in 256 BCE, which may date this chapter to early third century BCE or later.

5. According to Sima Qian, Zilu's cap is decorated with the model or pattern of a rooster, and he wears at his waist a boar-shaped pendant; both animals signify valor and a combative spirit (*SJ* 67.10). Zilu died as a result of being embroiled in internecine power struggles in the state of Wei; see chapter 1, 1.68, translator's note.

6. There are forty-six stories featuring Confucius and twenty-six stories featuring Zhuangzi. See Chen Xiaoming, "Kongzi e yu Chen Cai zhihou," *Zhongshan daxue xuebao* 44, no. 6 (2004): 148.

7. Jie and Zhòu are the tyrannical last rulers of Xia and Shang; Guan Longfeng and Prince Bigan are righteous men who try to remonstrate with them. Confucius claims that the latter two mix high principles with the concern for reputation.

8. Yao and Yu are sage kings, but even they engage in endless wars that cause widespread destruction because they want to gain territories.

9. The Ming Confucian thinker Wang Ji (1498–1583), a follower of Wang Yangming, argues that Zhuangzi grasps the main idea about Confucius, as can be seen with "Zeng Dian and his ilk," cited in Yang Rubin, *Rumen nei de Zhuangzi* (Lianjing chuban gongsi, 2016), 130.

10. John Makeham, "Between Chen and Cai: *Zhuangzi* and the *Analects*," in *Wandering at Ease in the Zhuangzi*, ed. Roger Aimes (State University of New York Press, 1998), 75–100; Hsu Sheng-hsin, " 'Zhuangzi zun Kong lun' xipu zongshu: Zhuang xue shi shang de linglei lijie yu yuedu," *Taida zhongwen xuebao* 17 (2002): 21–66; Yang Rubin, *Rumen nei de Zhuangzi*; Fang Yong, *Zhuangzi xue shi: zengbu ban*, 6 vols. (Renmin chubanshe, 2017), 1: 319–38, 2: 194–236, 2: 479–522, 3: 30–123, 3: 197–221, 3: 344–409; Michael Nylan, "Zhuangzi: Closet Confucian?" *European Journal of Political Philosophy* 16, no. 4 (2017): 411–29; Fang Yonghan, "Ru shi zhi nan, zhi Kong shen ye—yi Zhuangzi 'Renjian shi' chongtan Zhuangzi zun Kong," *Taida wen shi zhe xueba* 97 (2022): 1–32.

11. Yang Xiong, *Exemplary Figures / Fayan*, trans. Michael Nylan (University of Washington Press, 2013), 79–80; Fang Yong, *Zhuangzi xue shi*, 1: 334–38.

12. Su Shi, "Account of Temple of Zhuangzi," in *Su Shi wenji biannian jianzhu*, comp. Li Zhiliang, 6 vols. (Ba Shu shushe, 2011), 2: 103–07; Fang Yong, *Zhuangzi xue shi*, 2: 216–36. See also Li Zhi's letter to Lu Tianpu (from *Xu Fenshu* 續焚書) in Li Zhi, *Li Zhi wenji*, ed. Zhang Jianye, 7 vols. (Shehui kexue chubanshe, 2000), 1: 5.

13. See, e.g., Zhang Taiyan, *Zhangshi congshu: bielu* (Shijie shuju, 1958); Qian Mu, *Zhuang Lao tongbian* (Sanmin shuju, 1991), 29, 132, 149, 146, 206, 220; Guo Moruo, *Shi pipan shu*, in *Guo Moruo quanji*, 30 vols. (Renmin wenxue chubanshe, 1982–92), 2: 143–47; Tang Junyi, *Zhongguo zhexue yuanlun* (Xuesheng shuju, 1986), 104; Xu Fuguan, *Zhongguo yishu jingshen* (Xuesheng shuju, 1984), 92.

14. See Arthur Waley, *Three Ways of Thought in Ancient China* (G. Allen and Unwin, 1939), for the characterization of *fajia* as "realist." For a comprehensive introduction to *fajia*, see Yuri Pines, ed., *Dao Companion to China's Fa Tradition: The Philosophy of Governance by Impartial Standards* (Springer, 2024).

15. In *HFZ* (30.587), Shang Yang is said to "use punishment to remove punishment" (*yi xing qu xing* 以刑去刑")—that is, punish minor infractions with severity in order to promote a law-abiding society that will not need recourse to punishment.

16. Confucius held no official post in Wei. For his disciple Zigao's (Gao Chai) involvement in Wei politics, see *Zuo* Ai 15.5, 3: 1938–39.

17. In the received version of *Han Feizi*, Confucius's comment does not immediately follow the story, as it does in *Garden of Eloquence* (*SY* 14.22) and *Sayings* (*KZJY* 8.94). See Chen Qiyou's annotations (*HFZ* 33.724, 727).

18. Zigong implies that Confucius did not respond because the answers were too self-evident.

19. Shuxiang does not put his brother to death but would have if he were still alive. He "kills" his reputation.

20. Sima Qian includes Shi She in his chapter on worthy officials (*SJ* 119.6–7), see also *LSCQ* 2: 1247; Liu Xiang's (77–6 BCE) *New Order* (*Xinxu*), in Lu Yuanjun, ed., *Xinxu* (Shangwu yinshuguan, 1991), 7.243. For other examples of how the conflict between filial piety and loyalty toward the ruler result in suicide, see the story of the Chu noble Qiji (*Zuo* Xiang 22.6, 3: 1098–1101) and the story of Shenming in *The Garden of Eloquence* (*SY* 4.10) and *Han's Exegesis* (*HSWZ* 10.462).

21. Bian Zhuangzi, a Lu man praised for his valor in the *Analects* (14.12) and *Xunzi* (27.378), is said to have run away three times from the battlefield while his mother was still alive. He becomes a brave warrior and dies in battle only after her death (*HSWZ* 10.447, *Xinxu* 8.281).

22. Fan Gai (d. 548 BCE) was a Jin minister from an earlier generation. The legal code he promulgated was replicated and cast on cauldrons in 513 BCE.

23. On the transcription and interpretation of this passage, see the essays collected in Zhu Yuanqing and Liao Mingchun, *Shang bo guan cang Zhanguo Chu zhushu yanjiu xubian* (Shanghai shudian chubanshe, 2004), 105–188; Scott Cook, "A Brief Look at the Shanghai Museum Manuscript 'The State of Lu Suffered a Great Drought,' " in *Bone, Bronze, and Bamboo: Unearthing Early China with Sarah Allan*, ed. Constance A. Cook, Christopher J. Foster, Susan Blader, Amy Matthewson, Gail Patten (State University of New York Press, 2024), 215–32. A similar passage in *Master Yan's Annals* has Yan Ying remonstrating with the Qi ruler against offering sacrifices to the spirits of mountains and rivers (*YZCQ* 1:55). The drought ends when the Qi ruler takes responsibility and exposes himself in the wilds for three days as penance. On the ruler's appropriate self-recrimination during a natural disaster, see also *Zuo* Zhuang 11.2, 1: 164–67. On policies of frugality and redirecting resources in such cases, see *Zuo* Xi 21.3, 1: 350–51.

24. The words for punishment (*xing* 刑) and models (*xing* 型,俪) are homophonous in modern Chinese. The metallurgical metaphor implies that punishment (or its threat) molds the people.

25. On the debates surrounding the idea of abdication, see Yuri Pines, "Disputers of Abdication: Zhangguo Egalitarianism and the Sovereign's Power," *T'oung Pao* 91 (2005): 243–300; Sarah Allan, *The Heir and the Sage: Dynastic Legend in Early China*. Revised and expanded edition. (State University of New York Press, 2016).

26. According to *Bamboo Annals* (*Zhushu jinian*), Shun imprisons Yao and prevents him from seeing his son Danzhu.

27. Gun is the father of Yu, the controller of floods to whom Shun passes the throne. Gun is a failed official executed by Yao (or Shun, in some accounts) (*SJ* 1.29, 1.41, 2.3).

28. "No going back" (*wufu* 無復) in the sense that one cannot reclaim lost trust, but the phrase also means that the enemy would not be deceived again and the advantage cannot be repeated.

29. That is, there is no need to reclaim trust with the enemy. There is also the double meaning that the defeated enemy state cannot come back (*wufu*).

3. Outsmarting Confucius (or His Followers)

1. *Jiu Tangshu*, comp. Liu Xu (887–946) (Zhonghua shuju, 1975), 17B.544.

2. Using a series of puns, Li Keji "proves" that the Budda, Laozi, and Confucius were all women; see *Taiping guangji*, comp. Li Fang (925–996) et al. (Zhonghua shuju, 1961), 252.1958–59. On jokes based on the *Analects*, see He Yuming, "Talking Back to the Master: Play and Subversion in Entertainment Uses of the *Analects*," in *The Analects / Confucius: A Norton Critical Edition*, trans. Simon Ley, ed. Michael Nylan (Norton, 2014), 248. In the *Analects* (9.13), Confucius compares himself to a beautiful jade waiting for a fair offer.

3. The exchange consists of four seven-character lines rhyming in the pattern of *aaba*.

4. Wang Genlin, Huang Yiyuan, and Cao Guangfu, eds. *Han Wei Liuchao biji xiaoshu daguan* (Shanghai guji chubanshe, 1999), 1023.

5. See Anonymous, "The Song of Peach Blossom's Competition in Magic with Master Zhou," trans. Wilt Idema, in *Taiwan Literature: English Translation Series, no. 31/32, Taiwan Gezai*, ed. Kuo-ch'ing Tu and Robert Backus (US-Taiwan Literature Foundation, 2013), 83–116; Wilt Idema, "Expert in Yin and Yang and the Eight Trigrams: The Girl Peach Blossom," in *Divine Interventions*,

trans. and ed. Wilt Idema and Stephen West (Cambria Press, forthcoming). I thank Wilt Idema for the reference.

6. The translation of *tantan* as "ablaze" is based on the reading of *tan* 譚 as loan word for *qian* 燂. The last line means literally "to quell (or press down) my heart." Zigong's speech consists of partially rhyming four-character lines.

7. The phrase *wuxin* 無心 (rendered as "I do not dither") here means "I do not set my heart on just anything" or "I do not let my attention wander." It can also imply "I have no deliberate intention (of attracting your attention)" or "I am not interested." Both Zigong and the maiden speak with mostly rhyming four-character lines.

8. Asking a woman's family about her name is the first step of the betrothal process.

9. This phrase is used in *Biographies of Notable Women*. See *Lienü zhuan jinzhu jinyi*, comp. Liu Xiang, ann. Zhang Jing (Shangwu yinshuguan, 1994), 6.6, 226–27. In *Han's Exegesis*, the analogous expression is "observe her words" (*guan qi yu* 觀其語).

10. Many commentators find fault with Zigao's argument (*KCZ* 13.305–08).

11. Liu Changdong, "Kongzi Xiang Tuo xiangwen shu kaolun—yi Dunhuang Hanwen ben 'Kongzi Xiang Tuo xiangwen shu' wei zhongxin," *Sichuan daxue xuebao* 125, no. 2 (2003): 61–71.

12. Xing Yitian, *Hua wai zhi yi: Handai Kongzi jian Laozi huaxiang yanjiu* (Sanmin shuju, 2018).

13. *Zhanguo ce*, comp. Liu Xiang (Shanghai guji chubanshe, 1978), "Qin ce," 282; *HNZ* 19.654; *LH* 78.1076–77.

14. Huang Zheng and Zhang Yongquan, eds., *Dunhuang bianwen jiaozhu* (Zhonghua shuju, 1997), 357–69.

15. But Xiang Tuo is, of course, outside the home.

16. "The gate of emptiness" can also be rendered as "an empty gate." "An empty gate" or the gate of an empty house does not need a lock. The gate of emptiness also means Buddhist renunciation. The Buddhist way has no lock because it poses no obstacles. A mud cow is used to symbolize the beginning of spring plowing during early spring sacrifices. A wooden horse is a toy and can also mean the protection afforded by inoffensive passivity (*SY* 16.203). Broad swords and knives are both *dao* 刀 (translated as "blade" here) in Chinese. Swords have rings on their hilts but not chopping knives.

17. The game *shuanglu* 雙陸 (translated here as "double gammon") was a board-game involving the use of dice popular during the Tang dynasty. *Bo* 博 (usually translated as "gamble") is mentioned in the *Analects* (17.22), it may be a game of dice or a kind of chess game.

18. Zhang Hongxun believes this refers to the wedding night: a new bride is allowed a few days of grace before she has to serve her in-laws. See Zhang

Hongxun, " 'Kongzi Xiang Tuo xiangwen shu' chengchuan yanjiu," *Minjian wenxue luntan*, no. 6 (1986): 35–43. Huang Zheng and Zhang Yongquan argue that this means childbirth, citing a Buddhist sutra describing how Buddha's mother holds on to a sprig of flowers when Siddhartha (the earthly incarnation of Buddha) was born; see Huang Zheng and Zhang Yongquan, *Dunhuang bianwen jiaozhu*, 363, n47.

19. The Han dynasty scholar Sun Jing tied his hair to the beam to prevent himself from dozing off. Su Qin (3rd century BCE) pricked his thigh with an awl to stay awake to study. Kuang Heng (1st century) was a poor scholar who made a hole in the wall to study by the light from his neighbor's house. Confucius's disciple Zilu was famous for being brave and impetuous. Zizhang asks Confucius many questions on morality and politics in the *Analects*. The beginning four lines thus present exemplars who are determined to learn and eventually achieve great things. They are implicitly contrasted with the precocious Xiang Tuo, whose wisdom is inborn.

20. Zhang Hongxun, " 'Kongzi Xiang Tuo xiangwen shu' chengchuan yanjiu."

21. See the discussion of "Confucius Answering Questions" 孔子備問書 in Zheng Acai, "Dunhuang xieben 'Kongzi beiwen shu' chutan," *Dunhuang xue*, no. 17 (1991): 99–128; and the discussion of fragments from "The Tang Manuscript of the Dialogue Between Confucius and Ziyu" 唐寫本孔子與子羽對話雜抄 in Zhang Hongxun, " 'Kongzi Xiang Tuo xiangwen shu' chengchuan yanjiu," 33–34.

22. Chen Yaowen, *Tian zhong ji*, and Dong Sizhang, *Guang bowu zhi*, cited in Liu Changdong, "Kongzi Xiang Tuo xiangwen shi kaolun," 63–64.

23. Kim Bunkyō, "Xiang Tuo kao: Kongzi de chuanshuo," *Zhongguo wenxue xuebao*, no. 1 (2010): 9–10. Kim advances the intriguing hypothesis that Xiang Tuo is Confucius's metaphorical son and double.

24. Shi Dao'an, *Er jiao lun*, *Guang Hongming ji*, comp. Shi Daoxuan, in *Taishō shinshū Daizōkyō* , vol. 52 (Xin wenfang, 1983).

25. Kim Bunkyō, "Xiang Tuo kao," 13. The extant sutra with a similar name, *Fa miejin jing* 法滅盡經, does not contain this passage.

26. Zhang Chengjian, "Shenghua yu mohua de Kong fuzi: Dunhuang 'Kongzi Xiang Tuo xiangwen shu' kaoping," *Wenzhou daxue xuebao*, no. 3 (1990): 44–49.

27. *Taiping jing hejiao*, ed. Wang Ming (Zhonghua shuju, 1960), 718.

28. *Taiping jing hejiao*, 683.

29. See Zhang Chengjian, "Shenghua yu mohua de Kong fuzi," 49.

30. Kim Bunkyō, "Xiang Tuo kao," 7–8.

31. Michel Soymié, "L'entrevue de Confucius et Hiang T'o," *Journal Asiatique* (1956): 311–392; Henri Chambert-Loir, "Confucius Crosses the South Seas," *Indonesia* 99 (2015): 67–107.

32. Chambert-Loir, "Confucius Crosses the South Seas," 76.

33. Huan Jin, *The Collapse of Heaven: The Taiping Civil War and Chinese Literature and Culture, 1850–1880* (Harvard University Asia Center, 2004), 57–58. For the text of *Taiping Heavenly Chronicle*, see Luo Ergang, ed., *Taiping tianguo wenxuan* (Shanghai renmin chubanshe, 1956), 137–51. For its discussion, see Huan Jin, *The Collapse of Heaven*, 55–65.

34. Luo Ergang, *Taiping tianguo wenxuan*, 139–40.

35. Huan Jin, *The Collapse of Heaven*, 64.

36. Zeng Guofan led the Xiang army that played a key role in suppressing the Taiping Rebellion. The quoted lines are from Zeng's "Proclamation of Punitive Expedition Against the Cantonese Bandits" 討粵匪檄. See Zeng Guofan, *Zeng Guofan quanji* (Hebei renmin chubanshe, 2016), 38–39. On allusions to Confucian classics in Taiping tracts, see Liu Xuezhao, "Taiping tianguo yu chuantong wenhua lueyi," *Guangxi shifan daxue xuebao*, no. 38 (2002): 103–08.

37. Rebecca Handler-Spitz, *Symptoms of an Unruly Age: Li Zhi and Cultures of Early Modernity* (University of Washington Press, 2017); Handler-Spitz, Haun Saussy, and Pauline Lee, eds., *A Book to Burn and a Book to Keep (Hidden): Selected Writings* (Columbia University Press, 2016); Handler-Spitz, Haun Saussy, and Pauline Lee, eds., *The Objectionable Li Zhi: Fiction, Criticism, and Dissent in Early Modern China* (University of Washington Press, 2020).

38. Li Zhi, *Fenshu*, in *Li Zhi wenji*, ed. Zhang Jianye, 7 vols. (Shehui kexue chubanshe, 2000), 1: 121.

39. "A Brief Account of Zhuowu" 卓吾論略. See Li Zhi, *Fenshu*, in *Li Zhi wenji*, 1: 78.

40. The word order is slightly different in the original: "The ten thousand ages would have always been like night" 萬古長如夜 (instead of 萬古如長夜). *Zhuzi yulei*, comp. Li Jingde, ed. Wang Xingxian (Zhonghua shuju, 1986), 93.2350.

41. Li Zhi, *Xu Fenshu*, in *Li Zhi wenji*, 1: 94–95.

42. Li Zhi, "Response to Zhou Liutang"; see Li Zhi, *Fenshu*, in *Li Zhi wenji*, 1: 255. Li Zhi's friendship with Mei Danran, the widowed daughter of the famous scholar-official Mei Guozhen, bred speculations of impropriety. Mei Danren had embraced Buddhism, and in their correspondence Li Zhi addressed her as "Master Danran." On Confucius's saying that "there is no inevitable affirmation or inevitable rejection of alternatives," see chap. 1, 1.65, *Analects* 18.8; chapter 4, 4.2.

43. Li Zhi, *Fenshu*, in *Li Zhi wenji*, 1: 7.

44. Handler-Spitz, *Symptoms of an Unruly Age*, 69–87.

45. Li Zhi, "Letter to a Friend"; see Li Zhi, *Xu Fenshu*, in *Li Zhi wenji*, 1: 37.

46. This song is incorporated into "Preface to An Expanded Treasury of Jokes" (*Guang Xiaofu* xu 廣笑府序), questionably attributed to Feng Menglong

(1574–1646). See Nie Fusheng, *Feng Menglong yanjiu* (Xuelin chubanshe, 2002), 342–43.

47. Many of these jokes are based on puns, see He Yuming, "Talking Back to the Master."

48. Youxi zhuren, *Xiaolin guangji* (Gu Wu xuan chubanshe, 2021), 23, 30–31. Many of the jokes appear in earlier joke books from the Ming and Qing dynasties.

49. Chinese coins had a square (*fang* 方) hole in the middle. The word *kong* 孔 also means "hole." Kongfang xiong 孔方兄 thus means "Elder Brother Square Hole."

50. *Xu Zi bu yu* 續子不語, *juan* 5, in *YM* 12: 99–105.

51. The Han dynasty scholar Zheng Xuan (127–200) wrote authoritative commentaries on canonical classics. Kong Yingda (574–648) compiled subcommentaries based on Zheng's exegesis. The two Cheng brothers refer to the Neo-Confucian thinkers Cheng Yi (1033–1107) and Cheng Hao (1032–1085). The Four Books with Zhu Xi's commentary, which often quotes the Cheng brothers, became the basic texts for the civil service examination after 1313. "Evidential learning" flourished between the seventeenth and nineteenth century and refers to scholarly trends that emphasized philology and textual criticism.

52. Cang Jie is the legendary figure that invented writing. See chapter 2, 2.17.

53. On the five Confucian classics, see Michael Nylan, *The Five "Confucian" Classics* (Yale University Press, 2001). On the evolution and definition of the category, see David Schaberg, "Classics (Jing)," in *The Oxford Handbook of Classical Chinese Literature (1000 BCE–900 CE),*" ed. Wiebke Denecke, Wai-yee Li, and Xiaofei Tian (Oxford University Press, 2017), 170–83. Yuan Mei justified his skepticism of the classics and pointed out that the notion of the classics did not exist in antiquity in his letters to Hui Dong (*YM* 6: 345–48).

54. Apocryphal and omenological texts purport to interpret the classics and are sometimes mentioned in Kong Yingda's subcommentary. The five spirits appearing in apocryphal interpretations of the *Annals* are related to the theory of five phases (*wu xing* 五行), mapped to five colors (red, green, yellow, white, black), five elements (metal, wood, water, fire, earth), four seasons plus midyear, and four directions plus the center; see Gu Jiegang, *Qin Han de fangshi yu rusheng* (Shanghai guji chubanshe, 1998); Wang Xiaoming, *Chunqiu wei yu Handai sixiang shijie* (Ba Shu shushe, 2020), 257–64. In *Sayings*, Confucius discusses the five phases (*KZJY* 24.341).

55. At a farewell feast for Zheng Xuan organized by the warlord Yuan Shao (d. 202), three hundred guests take turns to toast Zheng, who consequently drains three hundred cups from morning to evening but maintains his mild and

restrained demeanor. See "Another Biography of Zheng Xuan" (Zheng Xuan biezhuan 鄭玄別傳), cited by Liu Jun (462–521) in his commentary to *A New Account of Tales of the World* (*Shishuo xinyu* 世說新語), in *Shishuo xinyu jianshu*, comp. Liu Yiqing et al., ann. Yu Jiaxi, ed. Zhou Zumo et al., 2 vols. (Huazheng shuju, 1984), 189–90.

56. What follows are absurd ritual prescriptions found in Zheng Xuan's commentary and Kong Yingda's subcommentary on *Record of Rituals* and the *Odes*. Cf. *YM* 13: 3–6.

57. The insurrection by rebels with yellow turbans (184–185) hastened the end of the Han dynasty. According to Fan Ye's (398–446) *Later Han History* (*Hou Hanshu*), Zheng Xuan encountered thousands of Yellow Turban rebels during his journey, but they bowed down to him with respect and would not enter his county, such was the respect he inspired (*HHS* 35.1209). On the debate about using a *qilin*'s hide as drum cover, see *YM* 13: 3.

58. Kong Yingda refutes Wang Su (464–501) in his subcommentary on "Extensive Fields" 甫田 in *Odes*. See *Maoshi zhushu*, comm. Zheng Xuan and Kong Yingda, 4.470–71, in *Chongkan Songben Shisan jing zhushu fu jiaokan ji*, eds. Ruan Yuan et al. (1815) (Yiwen yinshuguan, 1965). It is standard exegetical practice for the author of a subcommentary (*shu* 疏) to endorse and elaborate the commentary (*zhu* 注) it builds on, so in this case Kong Yingda has to refute Wang Su in support of Zheng Xuan.

59. The ladies are referring to the exegesis of "Grasshoppers" 草蟲 and "Gathering Green" 采綠 in *Odes*. See *Maoshi zhushu*, 1.51, 15.513. Cf. *YM* 13: 3.

60. Dai Sheng (ca. 1st century BCE to 1st century CE) is traditionally credited with compiling with the *Record of Rituals*. For Yuan Mei's critique of Dai Sheng, see his second letter to Hui Dong (*YM* 6: 347).

61. This is a line from "The feet of the *qilin*" 麟之趾 in *Odes*. It compares "lion-hearted noble sons" 振振公子 to the *qilin*. See *Maoshi zhushu*, 1.45.

62. See the chapter titled "Marriage Ritual" in *Record of Rituals* (*LJ* 3: 1422).

63. See the Mao commentary to "Fair Maiden" 靜女 in *Odes*, see *Maoshi zhushu*, 2.105. Yuan Mei names these details as instances of fanciful but interesting Han interpretations in his jottings (*YM* 13: 16).

64. This is Confucius's judgment of "Ospreys" 關雎, the first piece in *Odes* (*Analects* 3.20).

65. The line in question is from "Zhao's Compassion" 召旻 in *Odes*. The word *zhuo* 椓 (a wooden baton or pounder) in the original is probably a loan word for *zhuo* 諑 (slander). The idea that a piece of wood was used to destroy a woman's vagina is elaborated in the comments of Zheng Xuan and Kong Yingda. See *Maoshu zhushu*, 18.698. Zhaoxin, the jealous consort of Liu Qu (d. 70 BCE), Prince of Guangchuan, mutilated a rival's corpse and thrust a wooden baton into its vagina, an episode told in "The Biographies of the

Thirteen Princes Descended from Emperor Jing" in *History of the Han (Hanshu)* by Ban Gu (32–92) (*HS* 53.2429). Cf. *YM* 13: 4.

66. According to a text on calligraphy by Wei Heng (d. 291), Cang Jie 倉頡 and Ju Song 沮誦, officials in the court of the Yellow Emperor, create writing by observing the traces left by birds. See Wei Heng, "Four Modes and Their Calligraphic Style" (Siti shushi 四體書勢), *Quan Jin wen*, in *Quan shanggu Sandai Qin Han Sanguo Liuchao wen*, comp. Yan Kejun, 4 vols. (Zhonghua shuju, 1991), 2: 1629–30. In the Buddhist anthology *Fayuan zhulin*, Fan 梵 (Sanskrit) creates the script that goes rightward, his younger brother Qulu 佉盧 creates the script that goes leftward, while the youngest brother Cang Jie creates the script that goes downward. See *Fayuan zhulin*, 9.352, in *Taishō shinshū Daizōkyō*, vol. 53 (Xin wenfang, 1983). Qulu is a deity and Qulu shizha 佉盧虱吒 is mentioned as one of the Indian languages. "Qulu" is used to designate Manchu in Yuan Mei's autobiographical poem, "Song of Master Zicai, Shown to Zhuang Niannong" 子才子歌示莊念農 (*YM* 1: 294). Yuan Mei failed the examination in Manchu in 1742 and was demoted from the Hanlin Academy to become a magistrate in Jiangnan.

67. This may be referring to the Song dynasty poet and scholar-official Su Shi, who was interested in Buddhism but also deeply committed to Confucian values.

68. These lines are spoken by Lord Nonexistent 無是公 to disparage the accounts of Chu and Qi gardens described by Master Fiction 子虛 and Master Fantasy 烏有先生 in Sima Xiangru's (179–117 BCE) "Poetic Exposition of Shanglin" 上林賦, which Sima Qian includes in his biography of Sima Xiangru (*SJ* 117.3002–43).

69. The cited line is from "The Mean." Song Confucian scholars equate Heaven with *li* 理, variously translated as principle, coherence, reason. See *Zhongyong zhangju*, 17, in *Dianjiao Sishu zhangju jizhu*, comm. Zhu Xi et al. (Zhonghua shuju, 2003).

70. Zhu Xi's comment on the *Analects* (10.25). See *Lunyu jizhu*, 121, in *Dianjiao Sishu zhangju jizhu*. Yuan Mei is making fun of Zhu Xi's tendency to abstract a higher principle from concrete situations.

71. To "find illumination in one's heart and see one's true nature" (*mingxin jianxing* 明心見性) is a Buddhist term incorporated into the vocabulary of Neo-Confucian moral self-cultivation. The Neo-Confucian thinker Zhou Dunyi (1017–1073) wrote "Explanation of the Diagram of the Supreme Polarity" (Taiji tu shuo 太極圖說). In *Categories of Master Zhu Xi's Sayings* (*Zuzi yulei* 朱子語類), being "constantly reverent and vigilant" (*chang xingxing* 常惺惺) is the mental preparation for moral effort, and being "natural and spontaneous" (*huopopo di* 活潑潑地) is a kind of second nature upon full internalization of moral precepts. Both phrases recur in the text.

72. "The bucket of straws" (*daotong* 稻桶) is homophonous with "the Genealogy of the Way" (*daotong* 道統). Zhu Xi first used the term "the Genealogy of the Way" in his 1189 preface to "The Mean" (*Zhongyong zhangju* xu 中庸章句序), see *Zhongyong zhangju*, 14–16, in *Dianjiao sishu zhangju jizhu*. The four men carrying "the bucket of straws" may refer to the Neo-Confucians Zhou Dunyi, Cheng Yi, Cheng Hao, and Zhu Xi, often named by Zhu Xi's followers as key figures in "the Genealogy of the Way" after Mencius. Yuan Mei criticizes the exclusionary impulse behind the proposition of "the Genealogy of the Way" in his letter to Lei Cuiting (*YM* 6: 334–36).

73. In "The Origins of the Way" (Yuandao 原道), Han Yu (768–824) describes how the essential moral teachings were passed on from Yao, Shun, Yu, Tang, King Wen, King Wu, Duke of Zhou, Confucius, to Mencius, with whom it breaks off. Han implicitly places himself as the one who continues "the Genealogy of the Way" without using that term. Although he criticized Buddhism, he befriended the Buddhist Dadian when he was exiled to Chaozhou. Zhu Xi criticized Han Yu for consorting with Buddhists, see *Zhuzi yulei* 139.3305. In Zhu Xi's estimation, Han Yu "understood the broad principles" but failed to follow through with actual effort, being overly concerned with literary excellence (*Zhuzi yulei* 137.3255–57).

74. Zhu Xi's contemporary Lu Jiuyuan (1139–1193) opposed Zhu Xi's views and argued that "mind" and "principle" are the same. Wang Yangming's (1472–1529) "learning of mind-and-heart" further cements the identification of "mind" and "principle." Yan Yuan (1635–1704) and Li Gong (1659–1733) advocated "practical learning" and opposed the abstruse philosophical speculations of Song and Ming Confucian scholars. Mao Qiling (1623–1716) compiled *Corrections of Erroneous Interpretations of the Four Books* (*Sishu gaicuo* 四書改錯), which attacks Zhu Xi for his supposed errors.

75. Various warlords at the end of the Han dynasty (e.g., Cao Cao) are described with this phrase—the idea is to assert supremacy over rivals by claiming to represent the highest authority.

76. This is part of the statement on the hexagram Sui 隨 (Following) in the *Changes*. Yuan Mei's famous garden is called Sui yuan 隨園.

77. *Zuo* Yin 11.3, 1: 62–63.

78. Lord Jiang refers to Jiang Ziwen, an official of dubious repute who became a god. See Gan Bao, *Soushen ji*, in Wang Genlin et al., *Han Wei Liuchao biji xiaoshuo daguan*, 311–13. From about the tenth century on, the general Guan Yu (d. 220) was honored as a god.

79. Yin Yun (471–529) told this story in his collection of tales, see Wang Genlin et al., *Han Wei Liuchao biji xiaoshuo daguan*, 1035–36. The historical Wang Bi (226–249) died at twenty-three from an epidemic.

80. Yuan Dan (635–729) was a Tang dynasty scholar official.

81. Rulers are not addressed by their names but by various honorifics. The officiant at the sacrifice called Genghis Khan by his name to show deference for Zhu Xi. Song Lian (1310–1381) was a Confucian scholar and minister in the court of the first Ming emperor. *Complete Meanings of the Four Books (Sishu daquan* 四書大全, 1415) was compiled by Hu Guang (1370–1418) on imperial order. It includes commentaries by Zhu Xi and a few others. It became the official textbook for the civil service examination.
82. Yang Shen (1488–1559) was a famous scholar and polymath.
83. Lü Meng (178–219) was a general who contributed to the rise of the southern Kingdom Wu. Guo Ziyi (697–781) played a key role in ending the An Lushan Rebellion (755–763).
84. Ma Liang (187–222) and Jing Dan (1st century CE) were both famous Confucian scholars from the Han dynasty. In his biography of the poet Li He (790–816), the poet Li Shangyin (813–858) recounts how Li He, on his deathbed, sees a divine envoy who summons him to compose an account of the White Jade Tower in heaven. The story of how Shi Manqing (Shi Yannian, 994–1041) became the god of Lotus City after death is told in Ouyang Xiu's (1007–1072) *Liuyi's Poetic Conversations (Liuyi shihua)* and the poem "Lotus City" 芙蓉城 by Su Shi.
85. The cited line is from "Giving Birth to the People" 生民 in the *Odes*. It describes the preparation of grains for sacrifice to Lord Millet, the Zhou ancestor. The explanation that follows Zheng Xuan's commentary is from Kong Yingda's subcommentary; see *Maoshi zhushu*, 17.59.
86. "Following My Moods" 遣興, 20th of 24 quatrains, in *YM* 4: 870.
87. Cf. *Analects* 14.25. Yuan compares writers to magical steeds and shooting stars flying over mountains and seas, and contrasts them with evidential scholars, whom he likens to tailors taking measurement and dealers checking accounts, fighting over every inch and cent (*YM* 15: 25).
88. See Yuan Mei's letters to Hui Dong (*YM* 6: 345–48), Yin Sichuan (*YM* 6: 372–72), and Cheng Jiyuan (*YM* 6: 375–80), and his disquisition on Song Confucians ("Song ru lun" 宋儒論) (*YM* 6: 414–16). Cf. Lin Shin-shin, "Yuan Mei de jingxue taidu—dui Han Song xue de jiantao," *Hanxue yanjiu jikan* (2007.4): 17–46.

4. Settling Scores with Confucius

1. See Hu Shi's preface in Wu Yu, *Wu Yu wenlu* (Ya dong tushuguan, 1921), 6–7. "Attacked" (*da* 打) is often misquoted as "brought down" (*dadao* 打倒) in the retelling of this incident.
2. Leo Ou-fan Lee, *The Romantic Generation of Modern Chinese Writers* (Harvard University Press, 2014), 193–94. On Guo's 1923 essay, see Lee, *The Romantic*

Generation, 186; Pu Wang, *The Translatability of Revolution: Guo Moruo and Twentieth Century Chinese Culture* (Harvard University Asia Center, 2018), 283. Guo Moruo, "Ma Kesi jin Wen miao" (Marx Enters the Temple of Confucius), in *Guo Moruo quan ji*, 30 vols. (Renmin wenxue chubanshe, 1982–1992), 10: 161–69. On Guo as a translator, see Pu Wang, *The Translatability of Revolution*, which includes a concise discussion of how Guo positions himself as a translator of both Marx and Confucius (281–83).

3. When the scholar and poet Zhu Yizun (1629–1709) was asked to cut out a long love poem (rumored to be about his illicit love for his sister-in-law) from his collection in order to preserve his reputation, he said that he would not do so for the sake of "cold pork from a pig's head in the Temple of Confucius." The somewhat irreverent reference to "cold pork" here indicates the neglect of Confucius in the 1920s. It may also imply that Confucius has always been misunderstood.

4. *Analects* 5.7: " 'My Way is not implemented. I want to go on a raft and take to the sea. And the one who would follow me—would it not be Yóu?' Upon hearing this, Zilu was happy. The Master said, 'Yóu's love of valor exceeds mine, but nowhere can I find the right talent.'" In other words, Zilu's valor alone does not equip him to "take to the sea" with Confucius. The last line has other interpretations: "but nowhere does he (Zilu) use his judgment [to manage his valor]"; "Where is the timber [for the raft] to be found?" The word *cai* 材 can mean "talent," "materials," or "timber." It can also be the loan word for *cai* 裁, to judge, to measure.

5. Xunzi describes Confucius as having a "crab-like face," see chapter 1, 1.5, translator's note.

6. See chapter 1, 1.6, for Confucius's meeting with Laozi; see 1.31 and 1.31a for Confucius receiving instruction from music master Xiang.

7. *Analects* 1.1.

8. Mencius chides Chen Xiang for turning against Confucian teachings and becoming a follower of the teachings of the agrarian Xu Xing, "a shrike-tongued southern barbarian" (*Mencius* 3A.4). See chapter 1, 1.70a.

9. The first generation of modern Chinese scholars who tried to write the history of Chinese philosophy often perceived (and felt the need to justify) a lack of system and logical rigor in Chinese thought; see, for example, the works of Hu Shi and Feng Youlan (1895–1990).

10. In an article from the April 1, 1921, issue of the journal *The World of Youths* (*Shaonian shijie* 少年世界), Guo Moruo attacked those who "swallowed whole a few books newly translated in Japan without digesting them and then passed themselves off as the warriors of the New Culture Movement" (90). But Guo himself came to understand Marxism through Japanese scholarship.

11. "Correcting virtue," "using things advantageously," and "enriching livelihood" are called the three concerns of government (*Zuo* Wen 7.8, 1: 506–07). The same phrases appear in "The Counsel of Great Yu" 大禹謨 in the *Documents*.

12. The "Appended Commentary" in the *Changes*. See *Zhouyi zhushu* 8.166, in *Chongkan Songben Shisan jing zhushu fu jiaokan ji*, ed. Ruan Yuan et al. (1815) (Yiwen yinshuguan, 1965).

13. This slogan was common in the socialist movement before Marx but was popularized by Marx in his *Critique of the Gotha Programme* (1875). The Gotha Programme was a proposed party platform manifesto for the congress of the Social Democratic Worker's Party of Germany, which was to take place in the town of Gotha. The humanistic vision of a free and complete development of individualities echoes Guo Moruo's own vision of a future Communist utopia, though it is realized through the efforts of individuals who sacrifice their freedom and individuality. See Guo Moruo, "Wenyi lunji xu" 文藝論集序 (dated November 29, 1925), in *Guo Moruo quanji*, 15: 146; Lee, *The Romantic Generation*, 194.

14. Confucius's speech is found in the chapter "The Course of Ritual" (Liyun 禮運) in *Record of Rituals* (*LJ* 2: 581–82).

15. *Analects* 16.1. On the transposition of the words *pin* (poverty) and *gua* (scarce population) in the original quote, see *LY* 4: 1464–65.

16. *Analects* 13.9. In an exchange between Confucius and Ran Qiu regarding the healthy size of the population in Wei, Confucius says that the next step is to enrich people and then to instruct them.

17. *Analects* 12.7. The quote continues: When Zigong asks which of the three (food, weapons, trust) has to be sacrificed if one is forced to dispense with one of them, Confucius says, "Forego the weapons." When asked about the unhappy choice between food and trust, Confucius says, "Forego the food. Death comes to all since the beginning of time, but a state cannot stand without the trust of the people."

18. *Analects* 13.12. The original has *ru* 如 (if) instead of *shi* 世 (generation): "If a true king is to arise, then the greatest good will certainly be achieved after one generation." "A true king" (*wangzhe* 王者) is a king who fulfills the ideals of kingship.

19. *Analects* 6.24. "With one change, Qi can reach the level of Lu. With one change, Lu can reach the Way." As noted in chapter 1, 1.14 (translator's note, after passage 1.14d), Qi and Lu are sometimes juxtaposed in Warring States and Han texts as examples of pragmatic, even opportunistic adaptability versus strict, sometimes outmoded adherence to ritual norms. Here Qi is presented as inferior in ritual propriety and moral cultivation.

20. See "The Great Learning." This and the above four quotes are supposed to show how Confucius envisions gradations and concrete steps for transforming society.

21. "The Great Plan" is a chapter in the *Documents*.

22. *Guanzi jiaozhu*, comp. Li Xiangfeng, ed. Liang Yunhua (Zhonghua shuju, 2004), 3 vols., 1: 2, 3: 1432. There was a new wave of interest in Guanzi scholarship during the Qing dynasty and in the Republican period. Guo Moruo annotated *Guanzi* and published it in 1956.

23. The idea that of the four classes of people—officers or gentlemen, farmers, artisans, merchants—merchants rank at the bottom first appears in late Warring States writings. In the *Analects*, Confucius says nothing about merchants and only notes Zigong's success in "increasing assets" (*Analects* 11.19). Sima Qian lauds Zigong's mercantile success, speaks admiringly of how rulers treat him as an equal (*fenting kangli* 分庭抗禮) and suggests that he is the one who spreads Confucius's fame (*SJ* 129.12).

24. On Confucius's concern with regulating the uses of resources, see chapter 1, 1.9.

25. On the opposition between the attraction of virtue and the seductive wiles of women, see chapter 1, 1.17, 1.20. "Confucian prudery" often came up in writings during this period.

26. Marx attacked bourgeois marriage ("The bourgeois sees in his wife a mere instrument of production") but had a long, conventional, and by all account happy marriage with Jenny von Westphalen (1814–1881).

27. *Analects* 12.5: "Sima Niu said with sadness, 'Everyone has brothers, I alone have none.'"

28. In response to Sima Niu's lament (see n27), Zixia responds that for the noble man who is unfailingly respectful and abides by ritual propriety in his interaction with others, "all within the four seas are his brothers. How can a noble man worry about not having brothers?" (*Analects* 12.5).

29. On the notion that Confucius divorced his wife, see chapter 1, n19.

30. *Mencius* 1A.7. In the original context, this is Mencius's injunction to King Hui of Liang as he urges such empathy as the basis of political authority.

31. Literally, Mr. Kong Second. Recall that the "Zhong" in Confucius's sobriquet (Zhongni) refers to his birth sequence as the second son (chapter 1, 1.1, translator's note).

32. Detractors of communism in that period claimed that communism was also about "sharing wives" (*gong qi* 共妻). Note that in Plato's *Republic*, the wives and children of the "Guardians" are held in common. In *Treatise on the Great Common Good* (*Datong shu* 大同書) (see the translator's note, 244), Kang Youwei abolishes marriage and the family: men and women with equal rights

enter into contractual relationships that can be renewed and abrogated based on consent. See Kang Youwei, *Datong shu*, in *Kang Youwei quanji*, ed. Jiang Yihua, Zhang Ronghua, 12 vols. (Renmin daxue chubanshe, 2007), 7: 77, 163–64.

33. In the *Analects* (19.25), Zigong chides Chen Ziqin for presuming to suggest that Zigong is no less worthy than Confucius: "With one comment a noble man can prove his wisdom, and with one comment he can show his lack of it." Yan Hui's line about his changeful master echoes the beginning of "The Discourse on Making Things Equal" in *Zhuangzi*, when Yancheng Ziyou says to his master, Nanguo Ziqi: "The one who is leaning against the table now is not the one who leaned against it in olden days" (*ZZ* 2.45). "Daily renewal" (*rixin* 日新), discussed in "The Great Learning," is supposed to be the crux of moral self-cultivation. In *Zhuangzi*, Confucius is said to have changed sixty times in sixty years: in that context, transformation is about responding to endless changes of the world in a timely fashion. Here the valence of self-transformation is of course negative instead of positive.

34. Kang Youwei, *Liyun zhu*, in *Kang Youwei quanji*, 5: 553–54.

35. Sun Zhongshan, *Sun Zhongshan wenji*, ed. Meng Qingpeng (Tuanjie chubanshe, 1997), 231; Li Daozhao, *Li Dazhao quanji*, ed. Zhongguo Li Dazhao yanjiuhui, 5 vols. (Renmin chubanshe, 2013), 2: 347; Mao Zedong, *Mao Zedong zaoqi wengao*, ed. Zhonggong Zhongyang wenxian yanjiushi (Hunan renmin chubanshe, 1990), 88–89.

36. See Kang Youwei, *Datong shu*, in *Kang Youwei quanji*, 7: 163–64; Kang Youwei, *Lunyu zhu*, in *Kang Youwei quanji*, 6: 423; Tan Sitong, *Renxue*, in *Tan Sitong quanji*, ed. Cai Shangsi and Fang Xing (Zhonghua shuju, 1981), 364; Xia Xiaohong, *Wan Qing wenren funü guan (zengding ben)* (Beijing daxue chubanshe, 2016), 72–73; Lin Yutang, *Lin Yutang mingzhu quanji*, 30 vols. (Dongbei Sifan daxue chubanshe, 1994), 13: 268–90; for the documents related to the controversy surrounding the play, see *Lin Yutang mingzhu quanji*, 13: 291–314.

37. Qu Boyu was a wise man in Wei known for his timely withdrawal from politics. Liu Yutang calls Confucius "Kong Qiu" in the play to indicate rejection of his automatic "sacralization." Mi Zixia is said to be Lord Ling of Wei's lover in some account. The word for favorite (*bi* 嬖) implies improper intimacy. Cf. chapter 1, 1.18, 1.20. He is also called Mi Zi in the play, but I have regularized his name as "Mi Zixia." The chairs and benches here, as well as the mention of tea, horse riding, and paper ("words on the page") below, are anachronistic: these things did not exist in 5th-century BCE China.

38. See chapter 1, 1.18.

39. *Analects* 18.8; chapter 1, 1.65. The line implies Confucius's judiciousness and adaptability. In the play, however, it is repeated to suggest his evasiveness.

40. *Analects* 17.7; chapter 1, 1.29.

41. Minister Kong refers to Kong Yu or Kong Wenzi, see the *Analects* (5.15); chapter 1, 1.33a, 1.50. Scribe Qiu, also called Scribe Yu, is described as being straight "like an arrow" 如矢 irrespective of the political situation. By contrast, Qu Boyu would only serve in a government run on sound principles (*Analects* 15.7).

42. Zilu believes that he has to risk death to defend Kong Kui (Kong Wenzi's son) because he receives emolument from the latter (*Zuo* Ai 15.5, 3: 1938–41).

43. See chapter 1, 1.12, 1.46.

44. See chapter 1, 1.18a.

45. The historical Zilu was nine years younger than Confucius (*SJ* 67). Confucius is described as "cordial" and "benign" (*Analects* 1.10).

46. *Analects* 13.3; chapter 1, 1.49. The original context of that line is Confucius's discussion of the "rectification of names."

47. *Mencius* 2A.2.

48. For Boyi and Shuqi, see the *Analects* (7.5, 18.8); *SJ* 61; chapter 1, 1.43, 1.49a, 1.65.

49. The word *li* 禮 means both "gift" and "proper ritual."

50. *Analects* 19.13.

51. The word translated here as "gentleman" is *shi* 士 (see chapter 1, 1.3b), which is homophonous with *shi* 仕, "to serve in government."

52. See *Mencius* 3B.9. Mencius criticizes Yang Zhu's philosophy of self-interest as "doing away with rulers" and Mozi's doctrine of universal love as "doing away with fathers." "To do away with fathers and rulers is to become birds and beasts."

53. This echoes the *Analects* (18.7), see chapter 1.40a.

54. *Analects* 13.3; see chapter 1, 1.49.

55. Chapter 1, 1.17. Confucius chants this song when he feels that he can no longer hope to gain the Lu chief minister Ji Huanzi's attention since the latter has become engrossed with the women musicians that Qi sends to Lu.

56. These lines referring to Yao, Shun, King Wen, and King Wu are from "The Mean," one of the Four Books.

57. Kangshu was the younger brother of King Wu of Zhou. The "Airs of Wei" in the *Odes* contains many love songs which are criticized by some commentators as licentious. "Outside the Eastern Gate" and "by the River Qi" are the setting for some of these songs.

58. Zilu accuses Confucius of being "far-fetched" (*yu* 迂) when he talks about the rectification of names in Wei (*Analects* 13.3). See also chapter 1, 1.49. *Yu* also implies being old-fashioned and inflexible.

59. Similar formulation appears in *HNZ* 13.431; *LSCQ* 2: 936.

60. Confucius describes Zilu's understanding of his teachings as admirable though not complete—"He has ascended the hall, but he has not yet entered the chamber" (*Analects* 11.15). It is not clear whether Lin Yutang misremembers the quote or reverses it deliberately.

61. *SY* 8.18; *KZJY* 13.188. In a conversation between Confucius and Lord Ai of Lu, Confucius praises Lord Ling of Wei as the worthiest ruler among his contemporaries. Lord Ai is skeptical, citing the Wei ruler's disregard for proper boundaries between men and women in his inner chambers. In other words, the Wei ruler violates ritual prescriptions and consorts freely (or has improper sexual relations) with his kinswomen. Confucius responds by enumerating the worthy men in the Wei court. Those names (Qumou, Linguo, Qingzu) will appear later in Zilu's speech. Qumou is the younger brother of Lord Ling of Wei.

62. Chapter 1, 1.20.

63. *Analects* 6.28; chapter 1, 1.20.

64. Confucius praises Qu Boyu as one who chooses withdrawal in an age of disorder (*Analects* 15.7). Versions of Qu Boyu's lines appear in *Zhuangzi* and *Huainanzi* (*ZZ* 4.165, 25.905; *HNZ* 1.25): his changing views respond to a world in flux and embody the power of Daoist transformations. Zhuangzi also commends Confucius for his transformations in similar lines (*ZZ* 27.952–53).

65. The exchange here overlaps with that between Zigong and Confucius in *Sayings* (*KZJY* 19.291–92). In *Zuo Tradition*, the Chen ruler and two ministers of Chen have adulterous relations with Xia Ji. They each wear her intimate garments under their court robes and banter about their liaisons. The Chen minister Xie Ye remonstrates with Lord Ling and is killed. Confucius criticizes Xie Ye for lacking sound judgment (*Zuo* Xuan 9.6, 1: 626–27). Xie Ye is remembered either as a paragon of loyalty (e.g., *SY* 1.4; *HSWZ* 7.299) or as a cautionary tale against rash interference (e.g., *SY* 9.1; *HFZ* 44.918; *KZJY* 19.291–92).

66. Zilu uses the same term, *xiaosa* 瀟灑, to describe both Confucius and Nan Zi.

67. Mencius describes how Confucius served "when he hoped to see what could be done, when the circumstances were acceptable, and when he was supported by the court" (see chapter 1, 1.17c) and relates the second to his experience in the court of Lord Ling of Wei (*Mencius* 5B.4).

68. See the *Analects* (13.3); chapter 1, 1.20, 1.34, 1.49. Kuaikui tries to assassinate Nan Zi, his father's wife, when confronted with stories about her adulterous liaisons. He flees Wei when the assassination fails. Their "names" are not correct because the son does not act like a son and the mother does not act like a mother.

69. Closely analogous passages are found in *Xunzi* (*XZ* 30.403–04), *Record of Rituals* (*LJ* 3: 1466), and *Sayings* (*KZJY* 36.466).

70. See the *Analects* (9.5, 11.23), chapter 1, 1.19.

71. On Ji Huanzi's failure to send Confucius sacrificial meat, see *Mencius* 6B.6, chapter 1, 1.17. On Yang Hu's gift, see the *Analects* (17.1), chapter 1, 1.3c.

72. That is, a midlevel state, not among the most powerful.

73. In the *Analects* (13.10), Confucius declares that if any ruler would employ him, he should achieve something in twelve months and bring his plans to fruition in three years.

74. Literally, "he spit out his food three times during one meal, and three times he grasped his hair during one bath" (*HSWZ* 3.167; *SY* 10.2). On the humble beginnings of Kings Wen and Wu at Feng and Hao, see chapter 1, 1.12.

75. Datong University in Shanghai was the first to become coeducational in China in 1918. Other better-known universities made tentative beginnings with coeducation in the 1920s, but controversies remained.

76. This is a refrain in the classics. See, e.g., "The Mean": "The Way of the noble man finds its beginnings in the relationship between husband and wife" 君子之道，造端乎夫婦. Also see the *Changes*: "The essences of male and female intersect and the myriad things are generated and transformed" 男女構精，萬物化生; "It is only when we have husband and wife that we have fathers and sons; it is only when we have fathers and sons that we have rulers and subjects" 有夫婦然後有父子，有父子然後有君臣. This idea is often invoked as legitimation in the defense of literature celebrating romantic love. Cf. chapter 1, n107.

77. "Seventh Month" 七月 in the *Odes* describes a cycle of agrarian labor.

78. Bao Si is said to be the consort of King You of Zhou (not the tyrant Jie), who, according to legend, starts beacon fires signaling military emergency to summon the lords as a joke in order to make the unsmiling Bao Si laugh.

79. "Eat, drink, men, women: these are the great desires of humans" (*LJ* 2: 607; *KZJY* 32.423). The context is how ritual propriety regulates desires and aversions.

80. "Under the mulberry" and "the corner of the city walls" are places for romantic assignations in the *Odes*. The River Qi and Dun Mound are both mentioned in "Airs of Wei" in the *Odes*.

81. *Analects* 15.40.

82. These lines are from "The Tall Lady" 碩人 in the "Airs of Wei" in the *Odes*.

83. The lines are from "Crickets" 蟋蟀 in the "Airs of Tang" in the *Odes*.

84. These are lines from "The Tall Lady," but the sequence is scrambled. This poem is said to praise the virtuous wife of Lord Zhuang of Wei, whose natal state is Qi. In the play, this becomes Nan Zi's song about herself.

85. Here the text has "the singing girl," but according to the "cast of characters," the author seems to have planned to have four singing girls on stage.

86. "Under the Mulberry" in the "Airs of Yong" in the *Odes*.

87. The sections "Great Odes" and "Hymns" in the *Odes* deal more with political themes, dynastic destiny, rituals, and sacrifices. To regard the "Airs" of the states as "folksongs" was an argument advanced by many leading intellectuals, including Hu Shi, Chen Duxiu, Zheng Zhenduo (1898–1958), and Gu Jiegang (1893–1980), in the 1910s and the 1920s.

88. See Diran John Sohigian, "Confucius and the Lady in Question: Power Politics, Cultural Production and the Performance of *Confucius Saw Nanzi* in China in 1929," *Twentieth-Century China* 36, no. 1 (January 2011): 23–43; Zheng Haoyue, " 'Zi jian Nan Zi' an zhong Lu Xun yu Lin Yutang de sixiang fenqi," *Zhongguo xiandai wenxue yanjiu congkan* no. 1 (2021), 64–75.

89. Included in Lu Xun, *Qiejie ting zawen erji*, in *Lu Xun quanji*, ed. Lu Xun xiansheng jinian weiyuanhui (Renmin wenxue chubanshe, 1973), 20 vols, 6: 17–21.

90. Yushima is the name of a street in Tokyo. The Yushima Temple of Confucius is the largest of its kind in Japan. Puyi (1906–1967), the last Chinese emperor who became the nominal ruler of Manchukuo (1932–1945), the puppet regime created by imperial Japan, participated in the ceremony for the reopening of this temple in 1935. The ritual reform in 1530 replaced sculptural images of Confucius with inscribed tablets in temples of Confucius. See Julia Murray, *The Aura of Confucius: Relics and Representations of the Sage at the Kongzhai Shrine in Shanghai* (Cambridge University Press, 2021), 89.

91. In Ibsen's play *Brand* (written in 1865 and first performed in Stockholm in 1867), the eponymous hero, idealistic and uncompromising, lives by the belief in "all or nothing." Ibsen was very popular among intellectuals in the Republican period.

92. Liang Qichao was a major intellectual, journalist, and political figure in modern China. He was a leader of the Hundred Days Reform in 1898. After its collapse, he fled to Japan. In the final decades of the Han dynasty (second century), the discourse of reform-minded intellectuals attacking corrupt forces at court was called "pure critique" (*qingyi* 清議). Liang implicitly upheld these Han intellectuals as his models.

93. Lu Xun owned a rubbing of the image of Confucius meeting Laozi from the Wu Liang Shrine. See Lu Xun Museum ed., *Lu Xun cang tuoben quanji* (Xiling chubanshe, 2014), 100–101. Cf. chapter 1, 1.6, 1.6a.

94. Confucius's disciples are sometimes described as "seated in attendance upon the master" (*shizuo* 仕坐) in the *Analects* and *Record of Rituals*; see the introduction, 4. This was before chairs were introduced, so "sitting" is really kneeling and putting one's weight on one's heels while keeping a straight back.

95. Confucius was given the title of "King of the Manifestation of Culture" by the Tang court (739). Successive dynasties conferred new titles on him. In 1645, he was honored by the first Qing emperor as "Supreme Sage of Perfect Accomplishment, Foremost Teacher of the Manifestation of Culture."

96. See the introduction, n18. The Five Classics refers to the *Odes*, the *Documents*, the *Changes*, *Record of Rituals* and other ritual texts, the *Annals* and their commentary traditions.

97. The "eight-part essay," also called the "eight-legged essay," was the prescribed format for examination essays during the Ming and Qing dynasties.

98. Some ancient texts (e.g., *Huainanzi*) assert that "heaven is round and the earth is square."

99. This refers to F. W. Herchel's (1792–1871) work on astronomy, C. Lyell's (1797–1875) introduction to geology, and J. D. Dana's (1813–1895) book on minerology and geology.

100. Xu Tong (1819–1900) was a staunch Neo-Confucian scholar who espoused extreme antiforeign sentiments.

101. Kōbun Gakuin 弘文學院 means "Academy for the Promotion of Culture." Kanō Jigorō (1860–1938) was a famous intellectual and educator and the founder of judo. Among the famous Chinese students who studied at Kōbun Gakuin were Lu Xun, Chen Duxiu, the writer Xu Shoushang, the woman revolutionary Qiu Jin, the historian Chen Yinke, and his brother Chen Hengke, an accomplished painter.

102. A place in Tokyo, the name means literally "water for tea." This temple dated from 1690 and was destroyed during the Kantō earthquake of 1923. Lu Xun begins his essay by referring to its reconstruction in 1935.

103. Mencius calls Confucius "the timely among sages" (*Mencius* 5B.10) to praise his flexibility and capacious understanding. Cf. chapter 1, 1.65, translator's note. Lu Xun infuses negative valence into this comment by linking "timeliness" to opportunism.

104. Confucius was the supervisor of corrections in Lu (chapter 1, 1.13).

105. *Analects* 5.7; see n4 above.

106. *Zuo* Ai 15.5, 3: 1940–41. Zilu died during the internecine conflict in Wei (chapter 1, 1.68, translator's note). The noble man is mindful of his dignity and ritual propriety even when facing death.

107. Being hacked to pieces and turned into "minced meat" (*hai* 醢) was one of the most extreme punishments in ancient China. Confucius asks to have a pot of minced meat covered up when he hears the news that Zilu suffers such a punishment, finding the reminder of Zilu's fate unbearable (*LJ* 1: 169).

108. The belief that paper with writing should be treated with respect may be interpreted as a "Confucian" idea, but Lu Xun suggests that the motivating factor is actually based on superstition.

109. *Mencius* 3B.9; see chapter 1, 1.66.

110. *Three Kingdoms* and other works of fiction and drama often cast the poet and statesman Cao Cao (155–220) as a villain.

111. As mentioned earlier, in 1914 Yuan Shikai ordered that the worship of Confucius be resumed in schools and temples. When Lu Xun returned to China in 1912, he worked for some years at the ministry of education. His role in the ministry meant that he had to participate in the sacrifices to Confucius; his task might have been to hand over the sacrificial items to the chief sacrificant. Minoru Takeuchi quotes the relevant entries in Lu Xun's diary. See Minoru Takeuchi, trans., Cheng Ma, *Zhongguo xiandai wenxue pingshuo* (Zhongguo wenlian chubanshe, 2002), 242–45.

112. In pitch-pot (*touhu* 投壺), the players took turns tossing arrows into a narrow-necked vase or pot. The rules are given in the chapter titled "Pitch-pot" in the *Record of Rituals*. Sun Chuanfang (1885–1935) was a protégé of Yuan Shikai and a warlord.

113. Zhang Zongchang was a warlord with a power base in Shandong, see translator's note for *Confucius Meets Nan Zi* (269). He was notorious for his ruthlessness. The Five Classics of the Han were the basis for the "Nine Classics" of the Tang dynasty and ultimately for the set of "Thirteen Classics" devised in the Song dynasty. The Thirteen Classics included the original five with each of their exegetical traditions counted as separate works, plus the *Analects*, *Mencius*, a short work on filial piety, and a dictionary.

114. According to Minoru Takeuchi, the phrase in the Japanese original was "romantic" (*fengliu* 風流), but upon the translation of this essay into Chinese by Yiguang, Lu Xun probably suggested the change to "lacking in gravitas" (*qian wenzhong* 欠穩重); see Minoru Takeuchi, *Zhongguo xiandai wenxue pingshuo*, 238.

115. A line from the *Record of Rituals* (*LJ* 1: 81).

116. Chapter 1, 1.41; *Analects* 15.2. "Kong Yiji" is included in Lu Xun, *Nahan*, in *Lu Xun quanji*, 1: 292–97.

117. Those who passed the lowest level of the examination system became "government students" and received a stipend.

118. Confucius said of himself, "Being of a lowly station in my youth, I thus became adept at many plebian tasks. Should a noble man have many such skills? Not many, indeed" (*Analects* 9.6).

119. Lao She's (1899–1966) *Camel Xiangzi* (1937) describes the struggles and wrenching degradation of a rickshaw puller. Chen Sheng and Wu Guang were commoners who started the insurrection (209 BCE) that brought down the Qin dynasty. Xiangzi, Chen, and Wu, are all lionized figures in the PRC. If we imagine the patrons speaking the lines about Xiangzi, Chen, and Wu, then "Kong Yiji" is being put in the same category and he in response compares

himself to Lu Xun. If "Kong Yiji" is the speaker impugning these figures, then making light of victimhood is one way to stay "sunny and happy."

120. The original contains a swear word.

121. "The privileged few" is literally "the meat eaters." In its locus classicus, the meat eaters are powerful people at court who are "base and unable to make long-range plans" (*Zuo* Zhuang 10.1, 1: 160–61).

122. Kongming or Zhuge Liang (181–234) is remembered as a supreme strategist and loyal minister, but in official historiography he is credited with "legalist methods" in the administration of the kingdom of Shu. Shang Yang (390–338 BCE) was a Qin minister responsible for legal, military, and administrative reforms in Qin. The key legalist text, *Book of Lord Shang* (*Shang jun shu*), is named after him. Shang Yang was quartered by his political enemies.

123. On Han political culture and its relationship with Confucianism, see Gu Jiegang, *Qin Han de fangshi yu rusheng* (Shanghai guji chubanshe, 1998); Anne Cheng, "What Did It Mean to Be a Ru in Han Times?" *Asia Major*, Third Series, 14, no. 2 (2001): 101–18; Li Dongjun, *Kongzi shenghua yu ruzhe geming* (Zhongguo renmin daxue chubanshe), 2004; Lin Tsung-shun, *Handai ruxue biecai—diguo yishi xingtai de xingcheng yu fazhan* (Guoli Taiwan daxue chuban zhongxin, 2013); Wu Hsiao-yun, *Dao yu zheng zhijian—Zhou Qin zhiji de Kongzi lunshu* (Xin wenfeng chuban gongsi, 2022). See also the sources cited in the introduction, n5.

124. On the term *ru*, variously translated as "classical scholar," "ritual expert," "expert in ritual and traditional learning," and "Confucian scholar," and its early meanings, see Zhang Taiyan, "Yuan Ru," in *Guogu lunheng* (Guangwen shuju, 1977), 151–55; Hu Shi, "Shuo ru," in *Hu Shi zuopin ji*, 19 vols. (Yuanliu chubanshe, 1986), 15: 6–98; Nicholas Zufferey, *To the Origins of Confucianism: The "Ru" in Pre-Qin Times and During the Early Han Dynasty* (Peter Lang, 2003); Nicholas Zufferey, "On the Ru and Confucius," in *The Analects / Confucius: A Norton Critical Edition*, trans. Simon Leys, ed. Michael Nylan (Norton, 2014), 129–40; Xu Zhongshu, "Lun jiagu wen zhong suojian de ru," in *Xu Zhongshu wencun* (Jiangsu renmin chubanshe, 2016), 270–82; Matthias Richter, "Roots of Ru 儒 Ethics in Shi 士 Status Anxiety," *Journal of American Oriental Society* 137, no. 3 (July–September 2017): 449–71; Yang Rubin, *Yuan ru: cong Di Yao dao Kongzi* (Guoli Qinghua daxue chubanshe, 2020).

Works Cited

Works cited by title in the text are listed below by their titles; works preceded by initials in the front matter abbreviation list are included below and alphabetized by their initials.

Allan, Sarah. *The Heir and the Sage: Dynastic Legend in Early China*. Revised and expanded edition. State University of New York Press, 2016.

Anonymous. "The Song of Peach Blossom's Competition in Magic with Master Zhou." Trans. Wilt Idema. In *Taiwan Literature: English Translation Series 31/32 Taiwan Gezai*, ed. Kuo-ch'ing Tu and Robert Backus, 83–116. US-Taiwan Literature Foundation, 2013.

Brooks, E. Bruce, and A. Taeko Brooks. *The Original Analects: Sayings of Confucius and His Successors: A New Commentary by E. Bruce Brooks and A. Taeko Brooks*. Columbia University Press, 1998.

CDB Cui Shu 崔述. *Cui Dongbi yishu* 崔東壁遺書. Ed. Gu Jiegang 顧頡剛. 2 vols. Shanghai guji chubanshe, 2013.

Chambert-Loir, Henri. "Confucius Crosses the South Seas." *Indonesia* 99 (April 2015): 67–107.

Cheang, Alice W. "The Master's Voice: On Reading, Translating, and Interpreting the *Analects* of Confucius." *The Review of Politics* 62, no. 3 (Summer 2000), 563–81.

Chen Hui 陳慧. " 'Zeng Dian zhi zhi' yu rujia zhengjiao lixiang" "曾點之志"與儒家政教理想. *Zhongguo zhexue shi* 中國哲學史, no. 4 (2020): 60–66, 107.

Chen Miaoru 陳妙如. "Biji xiaoshuo zhong de 'Kongzi chuanshuo' jiqi tese" 筆記小說中的「孔子傳說」及其特色. *Zhongguo Wenhua daxue zhongwen xuebao* 中國文化大學中文學報, no. 37 (March 2019): 23–46.

Chen Xiaoming 陳小明. "Kongzi e yu Chen Cai zhihou" 孔子厄於陳蔡之後. *Zhongshan daxue xuebao* 中山大學學報 44, no. 6 (2004): 147–54.

Chen Zhaoying 陳昭瑛. *Rujia meixue yu jingdian quanshi* 儒家美學與經典詮釋. Huadong Shifan daxue chubanshe, 2008.

Chen Zhiyang 陳志揚. "Zeng Xi yanzhi de zhenyi yu Kongzi 'Yu Dian' de zhenxiang" 曾晳言志的真義與孔子「與點」的真相. *Zhongguo wenhua yanjiu* 中國文化研究 (Summer 2024): 76–94.

Cheng, Anne. "What Did it Mean to Be a Ru in Han Times?" *Asia Major*, Third Series, 14, no. 2. (2001): 101–18.

Cheng Hao 程顥 and Cheng Yi 程頤. *Er Cheng ji* 二程集. Zhonghua shuju, 1981.

Chin, Annping. *The Authentic Confucius: A Life of Thought and Politics.* Scribner, 2007.

Chunqiu fanlu yizheng 春秋繁露義證. Ann. Su Yu 蘇輿. Zhonghua shuju, 1992.

Chunqiu Gongyang zhuan zhushu 春秋公羊傳注. Comm. He Xiu 何休 and Xu Yan 徐彥. Ed. Diao Xiaolong 刁小龍. Shanghai guji chubanshe, 2014.

Chunqiu wei yan Kong tu 春秋緯演孔圖. In *ZY* 962.

Cook, Scott. "A Brief Look at the Shanghai Museum Manuscript 'The State of Lu Suffered a Great Drought.' " In *Bone, Bronze, and Bamboo: Unearthing Early China with Sarah Allan*, ed. Constance A. Cook, Christopher J. Foster, Susan Blader, Amy Matthewson, and Gail Patten, 215–32. State University of New York Press, 2024.

——. "Confucius in Excavated Warring States Manuscripts." In *A Concise Companion to Confucius*, ed. Paul Goldin, 35–51. John Wiley and Sons, 2017.

Creel, Herrlee G. *Confucius: The Man and the Myth.* J. Day Co., 1949.

Csikszentmihalyi, Mark. "The Haihunhou Capsule Biographies of Kongzi and His Disciples." *Early China* 45 (2022): 341–74.

DDLJ Da Dai Liji huijiao jizhu 大戴禮記彙校集注. Ann. and comm. Huang Huaixin 黃懷信. 2 vols. San Qin chubanshe, 2005.

Defoort, Carine. "How to Name or Not to Name: That Is the Question in Early Chinese Philosophy." In *Keywords in Chinese Culture*, ed. Wai-yee Li and Yuri Pines. Chinese University of Hong Kong Press, 2020.

Denecke, Wiebke. *The Dynamics of Masters Literature: Early Chinese Thought from Confucius to Han Feizi.* Harvard University Asia Center, 2010.

Durrant, Stephen. *The Cloudy Mirror: Tension and Conflict in the Writings of Sima Qian.* State University of New York Press, 1995.

Fang Yong 方勇. *Zhuangzi xue shi: zengbu ban* 莊子學史：增補版. 6 vols. Renmin chubanshe, 2017.

Fang Yonghan 方湧漢. "Ru shi zhi nan, zhi Kong shen ye—yi Zhuangzi 'Renjian shi' chongtan Zhuangzi zun Kong" 入世之難，知孔深也—以《莊子。人間世》重探莊子尊孔. *Taida wen shi zhe xuebao* 臺大文史哲學報 97 (2022): 1–32.

Fayuan zhulin 法苑珠林. In *Taishō shinshū Daizōkyō* 大正新脩大藏經, vol. 53. Xin wenfang, 1983.

Feng Xueqin 馮學勤. "'Zeng Dian chuantong' 'shenmi chuantong' yu 'zhuguan pai'—rujia shenmei xingshang xue chuantong jiqi shijian fangfa" "曾點傳統" "神秘傳統" 與 "主觀派"—儒家審美形上學傳統及其實踐方法. *Meiyu xuekan* 美育學刊 9, no. 6 (December 2018): 67–75.

Gan Bao 干寶. *Soushen ji* 搜神記. In Wang Genlin 王根林, Huang Yiyuan 黃益元, and Cao Guangfu 曹光甫, eds. *Han Wei Liuchao biji xiaoshuo daguan* 漢魏六朝筆記小說大觀. Shanghai guji chubanshe, 1999.

Gardner, Daniel K. *Zhu Xi's Reading of the Analects: Canon, Commentary, and the Classical Tradition.* Columbia University Press, 2003.

Gentz, Joachim. "The Past as a Messianic Vision: Historical Thought and Strategies of Sacralization in the Early Gongyang Tradition." In *Historical Truth, Historical Criticism, and Ideology: Chinese Historiography and Historical Culture from a New Comparative Perspective*, ed. Helwig Schmidt-Glintzer, Achim Mittag, and Jörn Rüsen, 227–54. Brill, 2005.

Gu Jiegang 顧頡剛. *Qin Han de fangshi yu rusheng* 秦漢的方士與儒生. Shanghai guji chubanshe, 1998.

Guanzi jiaozhu 管子校注. Comp. Li Xiangfeng 黎翔鳳. Ed. Liang Yunhua 梁運華. 3 vols. Zhonghua shuju, 2004.

Guliang zhuan 穀梁傳. Comm. Fan Ning 范甯 and Yang Shixun 楊士勛. In *Chongkan Songben Shisan jing zhushu fu jiaokan ji* 重刊宋本十三經注疏附校勘記, ed. Ruan Yuan 阮元 et al (1815). Taipei: Yiwen yinshuguan, 1993.

Guo Moruo 郭沫若. *Guo Moruo quanji* 郭沫若全集. 30 vols. Renmin wenxue chubanshe, 1982–1992.

——. "Ma Kesi jin Wen miao" 馬克斯進文廟 [Marx Enters the Temple of Confucius]. In *Guo Moruo quanji*, vol. 10.

——. *Shi pipan shu* 十批判書. In *Guo Moruo quanji*, vol. 2.

GY *Guoyu* 國語. Ed. Shanghai Shifan daxue guji zhengli yanjiusuo 上海師範大學古籍整理研究所. Shanghai guji chubanshe, 1978.

Han Feizi shiping 韓非子釋評. Ann. and comm. Zhu Shouliang 朱守亮. 4 vols. Wunan tushu chuban gongsi, 1992.

Handler-Spitz, Rebecca. *Symptoms of an Unruly Age: Li Zhi and Cultures of Early Modernity.* University of Washington Press, 2017.

Handler-Spitz, Rebecca, Haun Saussy, and Pauline Lee, eds. *A Book to Burn and a Book to Keep (Hidden): Selected Writings.* Columbia University Press, 2016.

——. *The Objectionable Li Zhi: Fiction, Criticism, and Dissent in Early Modern China.* University of Washington Press, 2020.

Harbsmeier, Christoph. "Confucius Ridens: Humor in the Analects." *Harvard Journal of Asiatic Studies* 50, no. 1 (1990): 131–61.

He Yuming. "Talking Back to the Master: Play and Subversion in Entertainment Uses of the *Analects*." In Michael Nylan, ed. *The Analects / Confucius: A Norton Critical Edition*, trans. Simon Leys, 243–58. Norton, 2014.

Henricks, Robert G. "The Hero Pattern and the Life of Confucius." *Journal of Chinese Studies* 1, no. 3 (1984): 241–60.

——. "On the Whereabouts and Identity of the Place Called 'K'ung-sang' (Hollow Mulberry) in Chinese Mythology." *Bulletin of the School of Oriental and African Studies* 58, no. 1 (January 1995): 69–90.

Henry, Eric. "The Motif of Recognition in Early China." *Harvard Journal of Asiatic Studies* 47, no. 1 (June 1987): 5–30.

HFZ Han Feizi xin jiaozhu 韓非子新校注 (*Master Han Fei: Edition with Revised Annotations and Commentary*). Ann. and comm. Chen Qiyou 陳奇猷. Shanghai guji chubanshe, 2000.

HHS Hou Hanshu 後漢書. Fan Ye 范曄. Zhonghua shuju, 1973.

HNZ Huainanzi 淮南子. Ann. Liu Wendian 劉文典. Zhonghua shuju, 1989.

HS Hanshu 漢書. Ban Ku 班固. Ann. Yan Shigu 顏師古. Taipei: Dingwen shuju, 1986.

Hsu Sheng-hsin 徐聖心. "'Zhuangzi zun Kong lun' xipu zongshu: Zhuang xue shi shang de linglei lijie yu yuedu" 「莊子尊孔論」系譜綜述：莊學史上的另類理解與閱讀. *Taida zhongwen xuebao* 臺大中文學報17 (2002): 21–66.

HSWZ Han shi waizhuan jianshu 韓詩外傳箋疏. Comp. Han Ying 韓嬰. Ann. Qu Shouyuan 屈守元. Ba Shu shushe, 2011.

Hu Shi 胡適. "Shuo Ru" 說儒. In *Hu Shi zuopin ji* 胡適作品集, vol. 15. 19 vols. Yuanliu chubanshe, 1986.

Huan Jin. *The Collapse of Heaven: The Taiping Civil War and Chinese Literature and Culture, 1850–1880.* Harvard University Asia Center, 2024.

Huang Chi-li 黃繼立. "Yeyan Tianquan qiao: yige Wang men jiti jiyi anli de kaocha" 夜宴天泉橋：一個王門集體記憶案例的考察. *Ehu yuekan* 鵝湖月刊 491 (May 2016): 18–32.

Huang Chun-chieh 黃俊傑, ed. *Dong Ya shiyu zhong de Kongzi xingxiang yu sixiang* 東亞視域中的孔子形象與思想. Guoli Taiwan daxue chuban zhongxin, 2015.

Huang Zheng 黃征 and Zhang Yongquan 張湧泉, eds. *Dunhuang bianwen jiaozhu* 敦煌變文校注. Zhonghua shuju, 1997.

Hung Chun-yin 洪春音. "Lun Kongzi suwang shuo de xingcheng yu fazhan zhuxiang" 論孔子素王說的形成與發展主向. *Xing da zhongwen xuebao* 興大中文學報 20 (December 2006): 101–40.

Hunter, Michael. *Confucius Beyond the Analects.* Brill, 2017.

Hunter, Michael, and Martin Kern, eds. *Confucius and the Analects Revisited: New Perspectives on Composition, Dating, and Authorship.* Brill, 2018.

Idema, Wilt. "Expert in Yin and Yang and the Eight Trigrams: The Girl Peach Blossom." In *Divine Interventions*, trans. and ed. Wilt Idema and Stephen West. Cambria Press, forthcoming.

Jensen, Lionel M. *Manufacturing Confucianism: Chinese Traditions and Universal Civilizaions*. Duke University Press, 1997.

Jiang Yean Liang 江衍良 and Wu Te-Ling 吳德玲. "Kongzi weihe zantong Zeng Dian: zhujie fazhan yu dianfan zhuanyi zhi chutan" 孔子為何贊同曾點：註解發展與典範轉移之初探. *Changgeng keji xuekan* 長庚科技學刊 22 (December 2014): 97–122.

Jiu Tangshu 舊唐書. Comp. Liu Xu 劉昫. Zhonghua shuju, 1975.

Kang Youwei 康有為. *Datong shu* 大同書. In *Kang Youwei quanji* 康有為全集, vol. 7, ed. Jiang Yihua 姜義華 and Zhang Ronghua 張榮華. 12 vols. Renmin daxue chubanshe, 2007.

——. *Liyun zhu* 禮運注. In *Kang Youwei quanji*, vol. 5.

——. *Lunyu zhu* 論語注. In *Kang Youwei quanji*, vol. 6.

KCZ *Kongcong zi jiaoshi* 孔叢子校釋. Ann. Fu Yashu 傅亞庶. Zhonghua shuju, 2011.

Kern, Martin. "Kongzi as Author in the Han." In *Confucius and the Analects Revisited: New Perspectives on Composition, Dating, and Authorship*. Ed. Michael Hunter and Martin Kern, 268–307. Brill, 2018.

Kim Bunkyō 金文京. "Xiang Tuo kao: Kongzi de chuanshuo" 項橐考：孔子的傳說. *Zhongguo wenxue xuebao* 中國文學學報1 (2010): 1–19.

KJY *Kongzi jiyu jiaozhu* 孔子集語校注. 3 vols. Ann. Sun Xingyan 孫星衍. Ed. Guo Yi 郭沂. Zhonghua shuju, 2018.

KZJY *Kongzi jiayu jiaozhu* 孔子家語校注. Ann. Gao Shangju 張尚舉, Zhang Binzheng 張濱鄭, and Zhang Yan 張燕. Zhonghua shuju, 2021.

Lau, D. C., trans. and ed. *Confucius: The Analects*. Penguin Books, 1979.

Lee, Leo Ou-fan. *The Romantic Generation of Modern Chinese Writers*. Harvard University Press, 2014.

Lee Long-Shien 李隆獻. "Xian Qin Han chu zajia wenxian zhong de Kongzi xingxiang" 先秦漢初雜家文獻中的孔子形象. *Zhengda zhongwen xuebao* 政大中文學報 29 (June 2018): 127–74.

——. "*Zhuangzi Liezi* zhong de Kongzi xingxiang" 《莊子》、《列子》中的孔子形象. *Dong Ya guannian shi jikan* 東亞觀念史集刊 8 (June 2015): 311–41.

LH *Lunheng jiaoshi* 論衡校釋. Wang Chong 王充. Ann. Huang Hui 黃暉. Zhonghua shuju, 1990.

Li Dazhao 李大釗. *Li Dazhao quanji* 李大釗全集. Ed. Zhongguo Li Dazhao yanjiuhui 中國李大釗研究會. 5 vols. Renmin chubanshe, 2013.

Li Dongjun 李冬君. *Kongzi shenghua yu ruzhe geming* 孔子聖化與儒者革命. Zhongguo renmin daxue chubanshe, 2004.

Li Ling 李零. *Qu sheng nai de zhen Kongzi: Lunyu zongheng du* 去聖乃得真孔子：論語縱橫讀. Sanlian shudian, 2008.

———. *Sang jia gou: wo du Lunyu* 喪家狗：我讀論語. Shanxi renmin chubanshe, 2007.

Li, Wai-yee. "Anecdotal Barbarians in Early China." In *Between Philosophy and History: Rhetorical Uses of Anecdotes in Early China*. ed. Sarah Queen and Paul van Els, 113–44. State University of New York Press, 2017.

———. "Cultural Identity and Cultural Difference in *Zuozhuan*." Special issue: *Cultural Others in Traditional Chinese Literature*, ed. Wai-yee Li. *Journal of Chinese Literature and Culture* 7, no. 1 (June 2020): 7–33.

———. "Hua Yi zhi bian / Hua Yi zhi bian: cong Zuozhuan tanqi" 華夷之辨・華夷之辯：從《左傳》談起. *Lingnan Journal of Chinese Studies* 嶺南學報 13 (December 2020): 19–50.

———. "The Letter to Ren An and Authorship in the Chinese Tradition." In Stephen Durrant, Wai-yee Li, Michael Nylan, and Hans Van Ess, *The Letter to Ren An and Sima Qian's Legacy*. University of Washington Press, 2016.

———. *The Readability of the Past in Early Chinese Historiography*. Harvard University Asia Center, 2007.

Li Zhi 李贄. *Fenshu*. In *Li Zhi wenji* 李贄文集. Ed. Zhang Jianye 張建業. 7 vols. Shehui kexue wenxian chubanshe, 2000.

Lienü zhuan jinzhu jinyi 列女傳今註今譯. Comp. Liu Xiang 劉向. Ann. Zhang Jing 張敬. Shangwu yinshuguan, 1994.

Lin Cunguang 林存光. *Lishi shang de Kongzi xingxiang—zhengzhi yu wenhua yujing xia de Kongzi he ruxue* 歷史上的孔子形象—政治與文化語境下的孔子和儒學. Qi Lu shushe, 2004.

Lin Shin-shin 林心欣. "Yuan Mei de jingxue taidu—dui Han Song xue de jiantao" 袁枚的經學態度—對漢宋學的檢討. *Hanxue yanjiu jikan* 漢學研究集刊 no. 4 (2007): 17–46.

Lin Tsung-shun 林聰舜. *Handai ruxue biecai—diguo yishi xingtai de xingcheng yu fazhan* 漢代儒學別裁—帝國意識形態的形成與發展. Guoli Taiwan daxue chuban zhongxin, 2013.

Lin Yutang 林語堂. *Confucius Saw Nancy and Essays About Nothing*. Shanghai Commercial Press, 1937.

———. *Zi jian Nan Zi* 子見南子 (*Confucius Meets Nan Zi*). In *Lin Yutang mingzhu quanji* 林語堂名著全集, vol. 13. 30 vols. Dongbei shifan daxue chubanshe, 1994.

Liu Changdong 劉長東. "Kongzi Xiang Tuo xiangwen shi kaolun—yi Dunhuang Hanwen ben 'Kongzi Xiang Tuo xiangwen shu' wei zhongxin." 孔子項橐相問事考論—以敦煌漢文本《孔子項橐相問書》為中心. *Sichuan daxue xuebao* 四川大學學報 125, no. 2 (2003): 61–71.

Liu Huanwen 劉煥文. "Lunyu 'Si zi shizuo' zhang yanjiu" 論語「四子侍坐」章研究. MA thesis. Qufu shifan daxue lishi wenhua xueyuan, 2015.

Liu Shipei 劉師培. *Liu Shipei shixue lunzhu xuanji* 劉師培史學論著選集. Ed. Wu Guoyi 鄔國義 and Wu Xiuyi 吳修藝. Shanghai guji chubanshe, 2006.

Liu Xiang 劉向. *Xinxu* 新序. Ann. Lu Yuanjun 盧元駿. Shangwu yinshuguan, 1991.

Liu Xuezhao 劉學照. "Taiping tianguo yu chuantong wenhua lueyi" 太平天國與傳統文化略議. *Guangxi Shifan daxue xuebao* 廣西師範大學學報 38 (2002): 103–08.

LJ Liji jijie 禮記集解. Ann. and comm. Sun Xidan 孫希旦. Ed. Shen Xiaohuan 沈嘯寰 and Wang Xingxian 王星賢. 3 vols. Zhonghua shuju, 1998.

Loewe, Michael. "Attitudes to Kongzi in Han Times." *Journal of Asian History* 55, no. 1 (2021): 1–30.

——. "'Confucian' Values and Practices in Han China." *T'oung Pao* 98 (2012): 1–30.

——. *Dong Zhongshu, a "Confucian" Heritage and the* Chunqiu fanlu. Brill, 2011.

——. "The *Rulin* of Han Times and Their Relation to Kongzi." *Journal of Asian History* 55, no. 2 (2021): 183–215.

LSCQ Lüshi chunqiu jiaoshi 呂氏春秋校釋. Ann. Chen Qiyou 陳奇猷. Shanghai guji chubanshe, 2002.

Lü Shih-hao 呂世浩. "Cong shijian jiaodu lun 'Lunyu Xianjin' 'Shizuo' zhang de yiyi" 從時間角度論《論語。先進》「侍坐」章的意義. *Dong Wu lishi xuebao* 東吳歷史學報 33 (2015): 1–44.

Lu Xun 魯迅. *Nahan* 吶喊. In *Lu Xun quanji* 魯迅全集. Vol. 1. Ed. Lu Xun xiansheng jinian weiyuan hui 魯迅先生紀念委員會. 20 vols. Renmin wenxue chubanshe, 1973.

——. *Qiejie ting zawen erji* 且介亭雜文二集. In *Lu Xun quanji*, vol. 6.

Lu Xun Museum, ed. *Lu Xun cang tuoben quanji* 魯迅藏拓本全集. Xiling chubanshe, 2014.

Lunyu jizhu 論語集注. In *Dianjiao Sishu zhangju jizhu* 點校四書章句集注. Comm. Zhu Xi 朱熹 et al. Zhonghua shuju, 2003.

Lunyu zhushu 論語注疏. Comm. He Yan 何晏 and Xing Bing 邢昺. In *Chongkan Songben Shisanjing zhushu fu jiaokan ji*, ed. Ruan Yuan et al. (1815). Yiwen yishu guan, 1965.

Lu Zhao. *Weird Confucius: Unorthodox Representations of Confucius in History*. Bloomsbury, 2024.

Luo Ergang 羅爾綱, ed. *Taiping tianguo wenxuan* 太平天國文選. Shanghai renmin chubanshe, 1956.

LY Lunyu jishi 論語集釋. Comp. Cheng Shude 程樹德. Ed. Cheng Junying 程俊英 and Jiang Jianyuan 蔣見元. 4 vols. Zhonghua shuju, 2014.

Lynn, Richard John, trans. *The Classic of Changes: A New Translation of the I Ching as Interpreted by Wang Bi*. Columbia University Press, 1994.

LZ Liezi jishi 列子集釋. Ann. Yang Bojun 楊伯峻. Zhonghua shuju, 1979.

Makeham, John. "Between Chen and Cai: *Zhuangzi* and the *Analects*." In *Wandering at Ease in the Zhuangzi*, ed. Roger Aimes, 75–100. State University of New York Press, 1998.

——. *Transmitters and Creators: Chinese Commentators and Commentaries on the Analects*. Harvard University Asia Center, 2003.

Mao Zedong 毛澤東. *Mao Zedong zaoqi wengao* 毛澤東早期文稿. Ed. Zhongguo zhongyan wenxian yanjiu shi 中國中央文獻研究室. Hunan renmin chubanshe, 1990.

Maoshi zhushu 毛詩注疏. Comm. Zheng Xuan 鄭玄 and Kong Yingda 孔穎達. In *Chongkan Songben Shisan jing zhushu fu jiaokan ji*, ed. Ruan Yuan et al. (1815). Yiwen yinshuguan, 1965.

Matsukawa Kenji 松川健二. *Rongo no shisōshi* 論語の思想史 (1994). Trans. Lin Ching-chang [Lin Qingzhang] 林慶彰 et al., as *Lunyu sixiang shi* 論語思想史. Wanjuan lou tushu gongsi, 2004.

Meyer, Andrew. "The Frontier Between Chen and Cai: Anecdote, Narrative, and Philosophical Argumentation in Early China." In *Between Philosophy and History: Rhetorical Uses of Anecdotes in Early China*, ed. Sarah Queen and Paul van Els, 63–91. State University of New York Press, 2017.

Mou Zongsan 牟宗三. *Cong Lu Xiangsan dao Liu Jishan* 從陸象山到劉蕺山. Jilin chuban jituan, 2010.

Mozi jijie 墨子集解. Ann. and comm. Zhang Chunyi 張純一. Guji shudian, 1988.

Murray, Julia. *The Aura of Confucius: Relics and Representations of the Sage at the Kongzhai Shrine in Shanghai*. Cambridge University Press, 2021.

——. "'Idols' in the Temple: Icons and the Cult of Confucius." *The Journal of Asian Studies* 68, no. 2 (2009): 371–411.

Murray, Julia, and Lu Wensheng. *Confucius: His Life and Legacy in Art*. Ed. J. May Lee Barrett. China Institute, 2010.

MZ Mozi jiangu 墨子閒詁. Ann. and comm. Sun Yirang 孫詒讓. Ed. Sun Yikai 孫以楷. Huazheng shuju, 1987.

Nie Fusheng 聶付生. *Feng Menglong yanjiu* 馮夢龍研究. Xuelin chubanshe, 2002.

Nylan, Michael. *The Five "Confucian" Classics*. Yale University Press, 2001.

——. "Kongzi and Mozi, the Classicists (Ru 儒) and the Mohists (Mo 墨) in Classical-Era Thinking." *Oriens Extremus* 48 (2009): 1–20.

——. "A Problematic Model: The Han Synthesis Then and Now." In *Imagining Boundaries: Changing Confucian Doctrines, Texts, and Hermeneutics*, ed. Kai-wing Chow, On-cho Ng, and John B. Henderson, 17–56. State University of New York Press, 1999.

——. "Zhuangzi: Closet Confucian?" *European Journal of Political Philosophy* 16, no. 4 (2017): 411–29.

Nylan, Michael, ed. *The Analects, Confucius: A Norton Critical Edition*, trans. Simon Ley. Norton, 2014.

Nylan, Michael, and Thomas Wilson. *Lives of Confucius: Civilization's Greatest Sage Through the Ages*. Random House, 2010.

Pines, Yuri. "Disputers of Abdication: Zhanguo Egalitarianism and the Sovereign's Power." *T'oung Pao* 91 (2005): 243–300.

Pines, Yuri, ed. *Dao Companion to China's Fa Tradition: The Philosophy of Governance by Impartial Standards.* Springer, 2024.

Qian Mu 錢穆. *Kongzi zhuan* 孔子傳. In *Qian Mu xiansheng quanji* 錢穆先生全集, vol. 6. 70 vols. Jiuzhou chubanshe, 2011.

——. *Lunyu xinjie* 論語新解. Sanlian shudian, 2002.

——. *Xian Qin zhuzi xinian* 先秦諸子繫年. Dong da tushu gongsi, 1990.

——. *Zhuang Lao tongbian* 莊老通辯. Sanmin shuju, 1991.

Qianfu lun 潛夫論. Wang Fu 王符. Ann. Wang Jipei 汪繼培. Ed. Peng Duo 彭鐸. Zhonghua shuju, 1997.

Quan shanggu Sandai Qin Han Sanguo Liuchao wen 全上古三代秦漢三國六朝文. Comp. Yan Kejun 嚴可均. 4 vols. Zhonghua shuju, 1991.

Queen, Sarah. *From Chronicle to Canon: The Hermeneutics of the Spring and Autumn According to Tung Chung-shu.* Cambridge University Press, 1996.

Richter, Matthias. "Roots of Ru 儒 Ethics in Shi 士 Status Anxiety." *Journal of the American Oriental Society* 137, no. 3 (July–September 2017): 449–71.

Schaberg, David. "Classics (Jing)." In *The Oxford Handbook of Classical Chinese Literature (1000 BCE–900 CE)*, ed. Wiebke Denecke, Wai-yee Li, and Xiaofei Tian, 170–83. Oxford University Press, 2017.

——. "Command and the Content of Tradition." In *The Magnitude of Ming: Command, Allotment, and Fate in Chinese Culture*, ed. Christopher Lupke. University of Hawai'i Press, 2005.

——. "'Sell it! Sell it!': Recent Translations of *Lunyu*." *Chinese Literature: Essays, Articles, Reviews* 23 (December 2001): 115–39.

Shi Dao'an 釋道安. *Er jiao lun* 二教論. In *Guang Hongming ji* 廣弘明集, comp. Shi Daoxuan 釋道宣. In *Taishō shinshū Daizōkyō*, vol. 52. Xin wenfang, 1983.

Shiben ba zhong 世本八種. Comp. and comm. Song Zhong 宋衷. Ed. Qin Jiamo 秦嘉謨 et al. Shangwu yinshuguan, 1957.

Shiji pinglin 史記評林. Sima Qian. Comp. Ling Zhilong 凌稚隆, with additions by Li Guangjin 李光縉 and Arii Shinzai 有井進齋. 5 vols. Diqiu chubanshe, 1992.

Shijing zhuxi 詩經注析. Ann. Cheng Junying 程俊英 and Jiang Jianyuan 蔣見元. 3 vols. Zhonghua shuju, 2017.

Shishuo xinyu jianshu 世說新語箋疏. Comp. Liu Yiqing 劉義慶 et al. Ann. Yu Jiaxi 余嘉錫. Ed. Zhou Zumo 周祖謨 et al. Huazheng shuju, 1984.

Shuowen jiezi zhu 說文解字注. Xu Shen 許慎. Ann. and comm. Duan Yucai 段玉裁. Shanghai guji chubanshe, 1981.

SJ *Shiji huizhu kaozheng (Shiki kaichū kōshō)* 史記會注考證. Sima Qian 司馬遷. Comp. Takigawa Kametarō 瀧川資言. Wenxue guji kanxing she, 1955.

Slingerland, Edward, trans. *Confucius/Analects: With Selections from Traditional Commentaries.* Hackett, 2013.

Sohigian, Diran John. "Confucius and the Lady in Question: Power Politics, Cultural Production and the Performance of *Confucius Saw Nanzi* in China in 1929." *Twentieth-Century China* 36, no. 1 (January 2011): 23–43.

Soymié, Michel. "L'entrevue de Confucius et Hiang T'o." *Journal Asiatique* (1956): 311–92.

Su Shi 蘇軾. "Account of Temple Zhuangzi" 莊子祠堂記. In *Su Shi wenji biannian jianzhu* 蘇軾文集編年箋注. Comp. Li Zhiliang 李之亮. 6 vols. Ba Shu shushe, 2011.

Sun Xingyan 孫星衍, comp. *Kongzi jiyu jiaozhu* 孔子集語校注. Ed. Guo Yi 郭沂. 3 vols. Beijing: Zhonghua shuju, 2017.

Sun Zhongshan 孫中山 [Sun Yat-sen 孫逸仙]. *Sun Zhongshan wenji* 孫中山文集. Ed. Meng Qingpeng 孟慶鵬. Tuanjie chubanshe, 1997.

SY Shuoyuan shuzheng 說苑疏證. Liu Xiang 劉向. Comp. Zhao Shanyi 趙善詒. Huadong shifan daxue chubanshe, 1985.

Takeuchi, Minoru 竹內実, trans. Cheng Ma 程麻. *Zhongguo xiandai wenxue pingshuo* 中國現代文學評說. Zhonguo wenlian chubanshe, 2002.

Taiping guangji 太平廣記. Comp. Li Fang 李昉 et al. Zhonghua shuju, 1961.

Taiping jing hejiao 太平經合校. Ed. Wang Ming 王明. Zhonghua shuju, 1960.

Taishō shinshū Daizōkyō 大正新脩大藏經. Xin wenfeng, 1983.

Tan Sitong 譚嗣同. *Tan Sitong quanji* 譚嗣同全集. Ed. Cai Shangsi 蔡尚思 and Fang Xing 方行. Zhonghua shuju, 1981.

Tang Junyi 唐君毅. *Zhongguo zhexue yuanlun* 中國哲學原論. Xuesheng shuju, 1986.

Tang Minggui 唐明貴. *Lunyu xue shi* 論語學史. Zhongguo shehui kexue chubanshe, 2009.

Tian Zhizhong 田智忠. *Zhuzi lun Zeng Dian "qixiang" yanjiu* 朱子論曾點「氣象」研究. Zhongguo shehui kexue chubanshe, 2020.

Van Ess, Hans. "Kongzi suwang he Chunqiu de chuantong" 孔子素王和《春秋》的傳統. In *Shengyu lun Lin jing: 2018 Chunqiu xue luntan lunwen ji* 聖域論麟經：2018 春秋學論壇論文集. Foguang daxue, 2018.

Vankeerberghen, Griet. "Choosing Balance: Weighing (Quan) as a Metaphor for Action in Early Chinese Texts." *Early China* 30 (2005–2006): 47–89.

Vogelsang, Kai. "Beyond Confucius: A Socio-historical Reading of the *Lunyu*." *Oriens Extremus* 49 (2010): 29–61.

Waley, Arthur, trans. *The Analects of Confucius.* Random House, 1989.

——. *Three Ways of Thought in Ancient China.* G. Allen and Unwin, 1939.

Wang, Pu. *The Translatability of Revolution: Guo Moruo and Twentieth Century Chinese Culture.* Harvard University Asia Center, 2018.

Wang Fuzhi 王夫之. *Sishu xunyi* 四書訓義. In *Chuanshan quanshu* 船山全書, vol. 7. 16 vols. Ed. *Chuanshan quanshu* bianji huiyuan hui 船山全書編輯委員會. Yuelu shushe, 1988.

Wang Genlin 王根林, Huang Yiyuan 黃益元, and Cao Guangfu 曹光甫, eds. *Han Wei Liuchao biji xiaoshuo daguan* 漢魏六朝筆記小說大觀. Shanghai guji chubanshe, 1999.

Wang Guowei 王國維. "Kongzi zhi meiyu zhuyi" 孔子之美育主義. In *Xiandai Zhongguo meiyu wenxian xuanbian yu daodu 1900–1960* 現代中國美育文獻選編與導讀 1900–1960, 1–13. Ed. Guo Huanling 郭煥玲. Shandong wenyi chubanshe, 2023.

Wang Xiaoming 王小明. *Chunqiu wei yu Han dai sixiang shijie* 春秋緯與漢代思想世界. Ba Shu shushe, 2020.

Wang Yangming 王陽明 [Wang Shouren]. "Moonlight Night: Chanting Poems with Various Disciples at Heavenly Spring Bridge, Two Poems" 月夜二首 與諸生歌於天泉橋. In Wang Shouren, *Wang Yangming quanji* 王陽明全集, 2 vols. Shanghai guji chubanshe, 1992).

Wei Heng 衛恆. "Siti shushi" 四體書勢. In *Quan Jin wen* 全晉文, in *Quan shanggu Sandai Qin Han Sanguo Liuchao wen*. 4 vols. Comp. Yan Kejun, 2: 1629–30. Zhonghua shuju, 1991.

Wen Kang 文康. Ed. Rao Bin 饒彬. Ann. Miu Tianhua 繆天華. *Ernü yingxiong zhuan* 兒女英雄傳. 2 vols. Sanmin shuju, 1999.

Weingarten, Oliver. "Confucius and Pregnant Women: An Investigation Into the Intertexuality of the 'Lunyu.'" *Journal of American Oriental Society* 129, no. 4 (2009): 597–618.

——. "The Figure of Yan Zhuoju 顏涿聚 in Ancient Chinese Literature." *Monumenta Serica: Journal of Oriental Studies* 63, no. 2 (December 2015): 229–61.

——. "Recent Monographs on Confucius and Early Confucianism." *T'oung Pao* 97 (2011): 161–201.

Wilson, Thomas, ed. *On Sacred Grounds: Culture, Society, Politics, and the Formation of the Cult of Confucius*. Harvard University Asia Center, 2002.

Wu Daofang 武道房. "Jingxue shi shiye zhong Zeng Dian zhi zhi de duowei jiedu—jian ping *Lunyu* Xianjin 'Shi zuo' chanshi shi de deshi" 經學史視野中曾點之志的多維解讀——兼評《論語。先進》「侍坐」闡釋史的得失. *Zhongguo zhexue shi* 中國哲學史 (2009): 5–12.

Wu Hsiao-yun 吳曉昀. *Dao yu zheng zhijian—Zhou Qin zhiji de Kongzi lunshu* 道與政之間——周秦之際的孔子論述. Xin wenfeng chuban gongsi, 2022.

Wu Yu 吳虞. *Wu Yu wenlu* 吳虞文錄. Ya dong tushu guan, 1921.

Wu Zhenxun 伍振勳. "Shengren xushi yu shensheng dianfan: *Shiji* Kongzi shijia xilun" 聖人敘事與神聖典範：史記孔子世家析論. *Qinghua xuebao* 清華學報 39, no. 2 (2009): 227–59.

Xia Changpu 夏長樸. "Zi wei zheng yan yong sha—lun Kongzi zhu Shaozheng Mao" 子為政焉用殺——論孔子誅少正卯, 87–124. In Xia Changpu, *Rujia yu ruxue tanjiu* 儒家與儒學探究. Da'an chubanshe, 2014.

Xia Xiaohong 夏曉虹. *Wan Qing wenren funü guan* 晚清文人婦女觀. Beijing daxue chubanshe, 2016.

Xiao Gongquan 蕭公權. *Zhongguo zhengzhi sixiang shi* 中國政治思想史. 2 vols. Lianjing chuban gongsi, 2022.

Xing Yitian 邢義田. *Hua wai zhi yi: Handai Kongzi jian Laozi huaxiang yanjiu* 畫外之意：漢代孔子見老子畫像研究. Sanmin shuju, 2018.

Xu Fuguan 徐復觀. "Yige lishi gushi de xingcheng jiqi yanjin—lun Kongzi zhu Shaozheng Mao" 一個歷史故事的形成及其演進—論孔子誅少正卯. In Xu Fuguan, *Rujia zhengzhi sixiang yu minzhu ziyou renquan* 儒家政治思想與民主自由人權, ed. Xiao Xinyi 蕭欣義. Xuesheng shuju, 2013.

——. *Zhongguo yishu jingshen* 中國藝術精神. Xuesheng shuju, 1984.

Xu Xingwu 徐興無. "Zuowei pifu de xuansheng suwang: chenwei wenxian zhong de Kongzi xingxiang yu sixiang" 作為匹夫的玄聖素王：讖緯文獻中的孔子形象與思想. In *Dongya Lunyu xue: Zhongguo pian* 東亞論語學：中國篇, ed. Huang Chun-chieh [Huang Junjie] 黃俊傑, 139–68. Taida chuban zhongxin, 2009.

Xu Zhongshu 徐中舒. "Lun jiagu wen zhong suojian de ru" 論甲骨文中所見的儒. In Xu Zhongshu, *Xu Zhongshu wencun* 徐中舒文存, 270–82. Jiangsu renmin chubanshe, 2016.

XZ Xunzi jianshi 荀子柬釋. Comp. Liang Qixiong 梁啟雄. Shangwu yinshuguan, 1993.

Yan Yuan 顏元. *Yan Yuan ji* 顏元集. Zhonghua shuju, 1987.

Yang Rubin 楊儒賓. *Rumen nei de Zhuangzi* 儒門內的莊子. Lianjing chuban gongsi, 2016.

——. *Yuan ru: cong Di Yao dao Kongzi* 原儒：從帝堯到孔子. Guoli Qinghua daxue chubanshe, 2020.

Yang Xiong 揚雄. *Exemplary Figures / Fayan* (法言). Trans. Michael Nylan. University of Washington Press, 2013.

——. *Fayan yishu* 法言義疏. Comp. and comm. Wang Rongbao 汪榮寶. Zhonghua shuju, 1987.

Yang Shuda 楊樹達. *Lunyu shuzheng* 論語疏證. Shanghai guji chubanshe, 2007.

Yang Yi 楊義. "*Lunyu* neiwai de shikong kaoyi"《論語》內外的時空考異. In *Dong Ya hanxue yanjiu xuehui shinian ji* 東亞漢學研究學會十年集, ed. Li Jikai 李繼凱, Yang Xiao'an 楊曉安, and Jiang Shujun 江淑君. Shanxi Shifan daxue chuban zongshe, 2020.

Ye Mengde 葉夢得. *Shilin xiansheng chunqiu zhuan* 石林先生春秋傳. In *Tongzhi tang jingjie* 通志堂經解, comp. Nara Singde 納蘭性德. 1673 edition. Harvard-Yenching Library Rare Books.

YM Yuan Mei 袁枚. *Yuan Mei quanji xinbian* 袁枚全集新編. Ed. Wang Yingzhi 王英志. 20 vols. Zhejiang guji chubanshe, 2015.

Youxi zhuren 遊戲主人. *Xiaolin guangji* 笑林廣記. Gu Wu xuan chubanshe, 2021.

Yu Ying-shih 余英時. *Shi yu Zhongguo wenhua* 士與中國文化. Shanghai renmin chubanshe, 2003.

YZCQ Yanzi chunqiu jishi 晏子春秋集釋. Ann. Wu Zeyu 吳則虞. Zhonghua shuju, 1962.

Zeng Guofan 曾國藩. *Zeng Guofan quanji* 曾國藩全集. Hebei renmin chubanshe, 2016.

Zizhi tongjian 資治通鑑. Sima Guang 司馬光 et al. With phonetic glosses by Hu Sanxing 胡三省. Ed. Biaodian *Zizhi tongjian* xiaozu 標點資治通鑑小組. Guji chubanshe, 1956.

Zhang Chengjian 張乘健. "Shenghua de yu mohua de Kong fuzi: Dunhuang 'Kongzi Xiang Tuo xiangwen shu' kaoping" 聖化與魔化的孔夫子：敦煌《孔子項橐相問書》考評. *Wenzhou daxue xuebao* 溫州大學學報 (1990): 44–49.

Zhang Dake 張大可 and Chen Xi 陳曦. *Zhisheng xianshi Kongzi* 至聖先師孔子. Shangwu yinshuguan, 2018.

Zhang Hongsheng 張宏生. *Kongzi de xingxiang jiqi wenxue jingshen* 孔子的形象及其文學精神. Liwen wenhua shiye jigou, 1995.

Zhang Hongxun 張鴻勛. "'Kongzi Xiang Tuo xiangwen shu' chengchuan yanjiu" 《孔子項托相問書》承傳研究. *Minjian wenxue luntan* 民間文學論壇, no. 6 (1986): 35–43.

Zhang Taiyan 章太炎. *Guoxue gailun* 國學概論. Jiangsu renmin chubanshe, 2013.

——. "Lun zhuzi xue" 論諸子學. In *Zhang Taiyan zhenglun xuanji* 章太炎政論選集. Ed. Tang zhijun 湯志鈞. 2 vols. Zhonghua shuju, 1977.

——. "Yuan Ru" 原儒. In *Guogu lunheng* 國故論衡, 151–55. Guangwen shuju, 1977.

——. *Zhang shi congshu: bielu* 章氏叢書：別錄. Shijie shuju, 1958.

Zhanguo ce 戰國策. Comp. Liu Xiang 劉向. Shanghai guji chubanshe, 1978.

Zhao Lu. *Weird Confucius: Unorthodox Representations of Confucius in History.* Bloomsbury, 2024.

Zheng Acai 鄭阿財. "Dunhuang xieben 'Kongzi Beiwen shu' chutan" 敦煌寫本《孔子備問書》初探. *Dunhuang xue* 敦煌學 17 (1991): 99–128.

Zheng Haoyue 鄭浩月. "'Zi jian Nan Zi' an zhong Lu Xun yu Lin Yutang de sixiang fenqi." "子見南子"案中魯迅與林語堂的思想分歧. *Zhongguo xiandai wenxue yanjiu congkan* 中國現代文學研究叢刊, no. 1 (2021): 64–75.

Zhongyong zhangju 中庸章句. In *Dianjiao Sishu zhangju jizhu* 點校四書章句集注, comm. Zhu Xi 朱熹 et al. Zhonghua shuju, 2003.

Zhou Yutong 周予同. *Kongzi, Kong sheng he Zhu Xi* 孔子、孔聖和朱熹. Ed. Zhu Weizheng 朱維錚. Renmin chubanshe, 2012.

Zhouyi zhushu 周易注疏. Comm. Wang Bi 王弼 and Han Kangbo 韓康伯. In *Chongkan Songben Shisan jing zhushu fu jiaokan ji*, ed. Ruan Yuan et al. (1815). Yiwen yinshuguan, 1965.

Zhu Fenghan 朱鳳翰 and Ke Zhonghua 柯中華, eds. *Haihun jiandu chulun* 海昏簡牘初論. Beijing daxue chubanshe, 2020.

Zhu Weizheng 朱維錚. "Lishi de Kongzi he Kongzi de lishi" 歷史的孔子和孔子的歷史. In *Zhu Weizheng, Zouchu zhong shiji—cong wan Ming dao wan Qing de lishi duanxiang* 走出中世紀—從晚明到晚清的歷史斷想. Zhonghe chuban youxian gongsi, 2013.

Zhu Yuanqing 朱淵清 and Liao Mingchun 廖名春. *Shang bo guan cang Zhanguo Chu zhushu yanjiu xubian* 上博館藏戰國楚竹書研究續編. Shanghai shudian chubanshe, 2004.

Zhuzi yulei 朱子語類. Comp. Li Jingde 黎靖德. Ed. Wang Xingxian 王星賢. Zhonghua shuju, 1986.

Zufferey, Nicholas. "On the *Ru* and Confucius." In *The Analects / Confucius: A Norton Critical Edition*, trans. Simon Leys, ed. Michael Nylan, 129–40. Norton, 2014.

——. *To the Origins of Confucianism: The "ru" in Pre-Qin Times and During the Early Han Dynasty*. Peter Lang, 2003.

Zuo Tradition / Zuozhuan: Commentary on the "Spring and Autumn Annals." Trans. Stephen Durrant, Wai-yee Li, and David Schaberg. University of Washington Press, 2016.

ZY Ziyue quanji 子曰全集. Comp. Guo Yi 郭沂. Zhonghua shuju, 2018.

ZZ Zhuangzi jishi 莊子集釋. Ann. Guo Qingfan 郭慶藩. Ed. Wang Xiaoyu 王孝魚. 4 vols. Zhonghua shuju, 1995.

Index

civil service examination, 9, 14, 214–15, 220, 227–28, 231, 275; essays for, 220, 227–28, 231, 273, 275, 324n97

chronology, 12, 90, 113, 117, 145

Confucian aesthetics, 11, 115–16, 230; *see also* music; *Odes*

Confucianism, 2, 4, 7, 10, 14–15, 149, 197, 218, 231, 232

Confucius (Kongzi), ancestry of, 19–23, 28–30; and the *Annals*, 125–31, 132–36; *see also Annals*; appearance of, 19, 22–23, 30–31, 70–73; as author, 97–98, 132–36; birth of, 19–23; and *Changes*, 116–17, *see also Changes*; critics of, 38–39, 90–92, 105–6; *see also Han Feizi*, Hong Xiuquan, *Mozi*, recluses, Xiang Tuo, *Zhuangzi*; death of, 136–41; deportment of, 120–22; descendants of, 141–42; diplomatic aplomb of, 49–54; *see also* law, punishment; disciples of, 4–12, the disciples' appraisal of Confucius, 123–24; *see also* Ran Qiu, Yan Hui, Yan Zhuozhou Zeng Dian, Zeng Shen, Zigong, Zilu, Ziyou, Zixia, and discourse on anomalous things, 40–44, 73–74, 123; early career of, 30–31; on governance, 37–40, 89–90, 107–9, 111–12; in *Han Feizi, see Han Feizi*; hosts of, 62–64, 66; jokes featuring, 197, 219–20; on learning, 122; in Lu Xun's writings, *see* Lu Xun; and Marx, *see* Guo Moruo; in *Master Yan's Annals (Yanzi chunqiu), see Master Yan's Annals*; on uses of the military, 49–54, 76–77, 84–84, 109–11; meeting with Laozi, 31–34; *see also* Laozi; in *Mr. Lü's Annals (Lüshi chunqiu), see Mr. Lü's Annals*; in *Mozi, see Mozi*; and music, 35–37, 64–66, 79–82, 115, 123; not being

employed, 37–40, 60–62, 66–69, 77, 82, 84–85, 87–89, 104–5, 109–11; on the *Odes, see Odes*; parents of, *see* Shuliang He, Zhengzai; policies of, 47–49, 54–60; *see also* Shaozheng Mao; and precocious children, 197–98, 202–12; prescience of, 86–87; sacrifices to, 140–42; as the sage, 3–4, 9, 16, 22, 28–29, 41–42, 65–66, 86–87, 99, 110, 121, 126, 32, 137, 142, 144, 147, 153, 158, 166, 216–17, 273; *see also* sage; self-evaluation of, 89–90, 124; Sima Qian's biography of, *see* Sima Qian; status of, 25–28; teachings of, 119–20; *see also Analects*; tempted by rebels, 45–47, 77–79; titles of, 273, 324n95; and textual traditions, 44, 113–35; trials and tribulations of, 64–66, 69–70, 75–76, 92–102; as uncrowned king, 126, 128, 130, 135, 137, 196; on uses of the past, 112–15; and water, 83–84; and women, 60–62, 144, 198–202; *see also* Nan Zi; in *Zhuangzi, see Zhuangzi*

"Confucius and Xiang Tuo Asked Each Other Questions", 14, 203–12; *see also* Xiang Tuo

"Confucius in Modern China." *See* Lu Xun

Confucius Meets Nan Zi. See Lin Yutang

Confucius temples, 2, 44, 269–71, 274–75; *see also* Guo Moruo

Cui Shu, 19, 28, 36, 68, 69, 76, 78, 84, 97, 133

Cultural Revolution, 2, 14, 234, 236

Daoism, 4, 7–8, 10, 13, 33, 68, 149, 158, 197, 208–11, 218

Liu Bang, 115, 140, 285, 294n7, 302n111, 302n113; *see also* "Ancestral Emperor"

Liu Xiahui (Liu Xiaji), 131–32, 155, 158

Liu Xiang, 33, 39, 67, 87, 200, 245

Lord Ai of Lu, 61, 85, 98, 106–7, 111, 124–26, 129, 131–32, 138, 163, 166–70, 172–73, 181, 286–87

Lord Ding of Lu, 40, 45, 47, 49, 51, 53–56, 67, 130, 247

Lord Huan of Lu, 33, 87

Lord Huan of Qi (Xiaobai), 95

Lord Jing of Qi, 34–40, 49, 50–51, 61, 89, 143, 171

Lord Ling of Wei, 62–63, 66–68, 76–77, 84–86, 107–8, 111, 144, 147, 247

Lord Mu of Qin, 34, 112

Lord of She (Zhuliang), 89–90, 162, 174

Lord Ping of Jin, 34–35

Lord Wen of Jin, 132–34, 192–94; *see also* Chong'er

Lord Zhao of Lu, 34–37, 40–41, 48–49, 107, 143–44

Lu Jia, 52, 149; *New Discourses (Xinyu)*, 52–53, 149

Lu Xun, 15–16, 232–33, 246, 270–83; "Confucius in Modern China," 271–77; "Diary of a Madman," 232–33, 271; "Kong Yji," 278–83

Mao Zedong, 234, 236, 244–45, 271

martial prowess, 21, 29, 110, 191; *see also wu*

"Marx Enters the Temple of Confucius." *See* Guo Moruo

Master Yan's Annals (Yanzi chunqiu). *See* Yan Ying

May Fourth Movement, 233–34

"The Mean" (Zhongyong), 111, 114, 141, 210

Mencius, *Mencius,* 30, 35, 37, 61–63, 69, 73–75, 80, 83, 88, 93, 104, 108, 121, 132, 134–35, 140, 146–47, 49, 153–54, 72, 174–75, 179, 185–87, 191, 196, 210, 211, 214, 217, 226

Meng lineage, 30, 38, 40, 55

Meng Xizi, 20, 28–29, 88

Meng Yizi, 29, 55–56

Mi Zixia, 63, 145, 247–69

Ming dynasty, 15, 44, 130, 164, 209, 214–15, 227; *see also* Neo-Confucianism

Mohists, 38–40, 63, 96, 98, 148–49, 186; *see also Mozi*

mourning, 25, 27–28, 72–73, 122, 139, 140, 145–46, 164–66

Mozi, 20, 39, 78, 98, 122, 148, 151, 154–55, 186, 196, 218, 286; *see also* Mohists

Mr. Lü's Annals (Lüshi chunqiu), 20, 40, 63, 98–99, 103, 119, 145, 170, 176–78, 194,

music, 4–12, 35–37, 49–54, 60–61, 65–66, 79–84, 92, 101–3, 115–19, 122–23, 143, 169, 246–69

Nan Zi, 15, 16, 66–69, 76, 107, 144, 147, 202, 217, 245–69

Nangong Jingshu, 29–31, 86

Nationalist Party (KMT, GMD), 234, 235, 270

Neo-Confucianism, 9, 37, 124, 130, 143, 164, 215, 231

New Life Movement, 234, 271

Northern Expedition, 235, 269

Odes (*Shi, Shijing*), 21, 44, 66, 29, 87, 94, 96–97, 112–19, 134, 138, 142, 175, 185–88, 210, 221

Ousted Lord of Wei (Zhe), 67, 85, 107–8

physiognomy, 30–31, 70–73

proper duty (*yi*), 3, 32, 43, 63, 83, 103, 116, 148, 159, 165, 170–75, 180, 196, 248–49; *see also* righteousness

punishment (*xing*), 50, 54, 57, 105–7, 149, 165–69, 174–75, 179–84, 188–91, 213; *see also* justice, law, litigation

Qian Mu, 19

Qing dynasty, 8, 44, 141, 209, 214, 231, 233, 273

Qu Boyu, 66, 68, 82, 245–69

quan (to weigh alternatives), 79, 145, 285; *see also* adaptability, expediency

Ran Qiu, 4–12, 87–89, 109–10, 128, 180

recluses, 79, 90–92, 131, 148, 163

Record of Rituals (*Liji*), 23–24, 31, 34, 48, 58, 71, 111, 114, 122–25, 136–37, 139, 141, 178, 182–83, 186, 210, 244, 286

rectification of names (*zhengming*), 38, 107–9, 172, 211

remonstrance, 61–62, 95, 120, 156, 160, 162, 173, 190–92

reverence (*jing*), 3, 28–29, 80, 93, 121, 173, 179

rhetoric, 106, 138, 155, 159, 162–63, 176–77, 195–200, 202; dangerous rhetoric, 58, 149, 177; glib rhetoric, 38–39; rhetorical competition, 199, 202; rhetorical missteps, 78; rhetorical prowess, 7, 39, 50, 149, 200; rhetorical sleights of hand, 97, 134, 162, 217; rhetorical training, 119

riddle, 198–200, 202; *see also* "Confucius and Xiang Tuo Asked Each Other Questions"

righteous, righteousness (*yi*), 3, 50, 82, 95, 98, 122, 166, 188, 191; *see also* proper duty

ritual propriety (*li*), 3, 28–29, 63, 73, 86, 122, 179; and diplomacy, 49–54; and governance, 5, 10, 121, 149, 179–84, 241; infractions of, 20, 28, 49, 61–62, 106, 138; and power hierarchy, 171, 173; and pruning the *Odes*, 115; vigilance about, 201–2

ru (traditional scholars and ritual experts), 77, 126, 141, 154–55, 286–88

sage (*shengren*), 2–4, 9, 28–29, 197; anomalous features of, 23, 170–72; and Confucius's disclaimer, 90, 216; and esoteric knowledge, 141, 144, 186; exegetes as, 220; imitation of the, 125–26, 217, 219; three great sages, 218; self-presentation as, 137; and timeliness, 121, 132; with unworthy parents, 22

sage kings. *See* Yao, Shun, Yu

Sayings (*Sayings from the House of Confucius, Kongzi jiayu*), 20, 27, 29, 33, 40, 43, 48, 54, 56, 76, 80, 86–86, 99, 110, 116, 126–28, 172, 182–83

scholar's garb (*rufu*), 285–88

Shang dynasty, 20–22, 24, 41, 73, 113–16, 134, 137, 167, 260; Zhou conquest of Shang, 82, 96, 116, 132, 191

Shang Yang, 167, 288

Shaozheng Mao, 54, 56–58, 149

shi, definitions of, 25–26

Shuliang He (father of Confucius), 19–23

Shun, 65, 112, 127, 156, 161, 252, 260; and abdication, 184–86, 189–90; as regent, 185–86, 190; choice of ministers, 71, 112, 184; compared to Confucius, 9, 153; eyes of, 70–71; and his family, 22, 184–88; and his

Yao, 65, 112 127, 156, 160–61; abdication of, 184–90; anomalous features of, 70, 71; choice of ministers, 71, 169; compared to Confucius, 9, 153

Yu (founder of Xia dynasty), 40–42, 128, 134, 145, 160; anomalous appearance, 70–72; choice of ministers, 71; and Shun's abdication, 184, 190

Yuan Mei, 15, 113, 220, 220–31; "The Qilin Cried Out Against the Injustice It Suffered," 220–29

Yuan Shikai, 15, 233, 275–76

Zen (Chan), 10, 217

Zeng Dian, 4–12, 27, 163, 230

Zeng Guofan, 214

Zeng Shen (Master Zeng), 6, 31, 93, 140

Zhang Hua, 22, 42, 198; *Record of Broad Knowledge of Things (Bowu zhi)*, 22, 42, 198

Zhang Taiyan, 16

Zhao Jianzi, 74, 77–78, 82–86, 256

Zheng Kaofu, 28–29

Zheng Xuan, 24, 137, 220–231

Zhengzai (mother of Confucius), 20–22, 130

Zhòu (last king of Shang), 65, 134, 159, 82, 191, 255, 260

Zhou dynasty, 3, 24, 41, 74, 80–82, 87, 112–16; and the *Annals*, 132–34;

ancestor of, 21; conquest of Shang, 82, 96, 132, 191; decline of, 128–30, 192; in the east, 46–47, 146; funeral rituals of, 136–37; in Confucius's time, 29–33, 38, 84, 112

Zhou Dunyi, 228, 313n71, 314n72

Zhu Xi, 9, 37, 47, 58, 79, 93, 108, 114, 130, 143, 215–7, 220, 225–28

Zhuangzi, *Zhuangzi*, 20, 32–33, 44, 64–70, 79, 92, 96, 99–106, 113, 125, 148, 151, 155–66, 211, 287

Zichan, 42, 59, 70, 71, 122–23

Zigong (Duanmu Ci, Ci), 7, 25, 34, 70–72, 75, 82–83, 87–88, 93–99, 102–9, 117, 119, 123–27, 136–40, 163–67, 171, 173, 178, 181–82, 191, 198–201, 236–43

Zilu (Zhong Yóu, Yóu), 4–12, 33–34, 46–47, 54–56, 59–67, 76–80, 89–108, 111, 127–28, 136, 139, 146–47, 150, 171–72, 178, 206, 217–18, 236–51

Zisi (grandson of Confucius), 141

Zixia (Bu Shang, Shang), 112, 118–19, 129, 135, 140

Ziyou (Yan Yan, Yan), 140, 229–30, 243

Zuo Tradition (Zuozhuan), 20, 29, 35–36, 39, 42, 44, 46, 48, 50, 52–56, 49, 63–64, 68, 76–80, 84–89, 93, 106, 109–10, 126, 131, 133, 138, 149–50, 167, 173, 179, 194; *see also Annals, Gongyang Tradition, Guliang Tradition*

GPSR Authorized Representative: Easy Access System Europe, Mustamäe tee
50, 10621 Tallinn, Estonia, gpsr.requests@easproject.com